The Rhetorical Power
of Popular Culture

I would like to dedicate this revision to the late Bernard L. Brock.
I owe Bernie for teaching me so much about doing rhetorical criticism
and for encouraging me to pursue this project in the first place.
As always, to God be the glory!

The Rhetorical Power of Popular Culture

Considering Mediated Texts

Deanna D. Sellnow
University of Kentucky

Los Angeles | London | New Delhi
Singapore | Washington DC

Los Angeles | London | New Delhi
Singapore | Washington DC

FOR INFORMATION:

SAGE Publications, Inc.
2455 Teller Road
Thousand Oaks, California 91320
E-mail: order@sagepub.com

SAGE Publications Ltd.
1 Oliver's Yard
55 City Road
London EC1Y 1SP
United Kingdom

SAGE Publications India Pvt. Ltd.
B 1/I 1 Mohan Cooperative Industrial Area
Mathura Road, New Delhi 110 044
India

SAGE Publications Asia-Pacific Pte. Ltd.
3 Church Street
#10-04 Samsung Hub
Singapore 049483

Acquisitions Editor: Matthew Byrnie
Assistant Editor: Megan Koraly
Editorial Assistant: Gabrielle Piccininni
Production Editor: Libby Larson
Copy Editor: Pam Schroeder
Typesetter: C&M Digitals (P) Ltd.
Proofreader: Dennis W. Webb
Indexer: Molly Hall
Cover Designer: Candice Harman
Marketing Manager: Liz Thornton
Permissions Editor: Karen Ehrmann

Printed in the United States of America

Library of Congress Cataloging-in-Publication Data

Sellnow, Deanna D.

The rhetorical power of popular culture : considering mediated stexts / Deanna D. Sellnow, University of Kentucky. — Second Edition.

pages cm

ISBN 978-1-4522-2995-9 (pbk. : alk. paper)
ISBN 978-1-4833-1144-9 (web pdf)

1. Popular culture—Study and teaching. 2 Rhetorical criticism. 3. Mass media and public opinion. I. Title.

HM623.S45 2013
302.23—dc23   2013020894

This book is printed on acid-free paper.

13 14 15 16 17 10 9 8 7 6 5 4 3 2 1

Brief Contents

Detailed Contents

CHAPTER 3. A NARRATIVE PERSPECTIVE   49

CHAPTER 4. A DRAMATISTIC PERSPECTIVE   73

CHAPTER 5. A SYMBOLIC CONVERGENCE PERSPECTIVE 97

(Thomas G. Endres, University of Northern Colorado)

CHAPTER 6. A NEO-MARXIST PERSPECTIVE 115

CHAPTER 9. VISUAL PERSPECTIVES

CHAPTER 10. MEDIA-CENTERED PERSPECTIVES

Preface

Writing a book is never an easy task, and writing this book was no exception the first time around. My goal then was to teach readers to think critically about arguments posed in popular culture entertainment media texts using methods of contemporary rhetorical theory and criticism. That remains my goal with this revision; however, doing so this time has been even more daunting. What has been so challenging this time stems from the fact that new media have exploded and dramatically changed the way we interact with entertainment media today. We can now access information in seconds by Googling. We can watch commercials, TV programs, and movies from any decade by visiting social media websites like YouTube. We can share things with friends and family across the globe by texting, Skyping, and Tweeting, as well as posting or chatting on Facebook. We can do so on iPads, smartphones, and laptops.

At the time I wrote the first edition, we might have watched major events like the president's State of the Union Speech or the Super Bowl and recorded them to watch again later. Today, according to a poll published in *USA Today,* we use our smartphones while watching events such as the Super Bowl to text, e-mail, or instant message (26 percent); to post to social networking sites such as Facebook and Twitter (21 percent); to talk to friends and family (20 percent); to check related and unrelated news reports (14 percent); and to re-watch favorite commercials (13 percent) (Carey & Gonzalez, 2013). We have become a global village of multitasking, technology-driven communicators. Even as I write this, I realize that I have no idea what "new media" will exist by the time this edition is published and which of the things I've just mentioned will be out of date. With that caveat in mind, I offer this update to *The Rhetorical Power of Popular Culture: Considering Mediated Texts.*

I remain convinced that mediated popular culture texts, especially those couched in the form of entertainment, are still particularly powerful in influencing our taken-for-granted beliefs and behaviors about how things ought to be or, perhaps, just are, as well as what is normal and abnormal, or desirable and undesirable.

So my goal was and still is to offer a book that anyone—whether a communication major, a college student, or a layperson—can make sense of and then use these theories to examine underlying messages about taken-for-granted beliefs and behaviors couched in mediated popular culture texts. This time, however, I made a deliberate attempt to also acknowledge how new media are changing the way we interact with these texts and the arguments embedded within them.

The next sections highlight what's new to this edition and how previous features have been updated to resonate with readers today.

New to This Edition

- New sample student essays on, for example, *The Help, The Hunger Games, Boys Don't Cry, Weeds,* and *Modern Family.*

- New sample published essays on topics such as video games, YouTube, and reality TV.

- Expanded coverage of the rhetorical theories that ground the rhetorical perspectives in each chapter.

- New media and social media examples integrated throughout the book.

- Expanded coverage of the rhetorical traditions in Chapter 2, visual perspectives in Chapter 9, and media-centered perspectives in Chapter 10.

- New chapter on symbolic convergence theory and fantasy theme analysis contributed by my good friend and colleague, Dr. Thomas G. Endres, from the University of Northern Colorado.

Features Retained and Updated for This Edition

1. *Applying What You've Learned, Questioning Your Ethics, and Challenge Features*

I continue to believe it is crucial to provide readers with opportunities as they read to apply concepts to their own life experiences and the popular culture texts with which they are most familiar. That's why I sprinkle *Applying What You've Learned* questions throughout every chapter. We all retain material better when we can apply it to our own lives. Similarly, I integrate *Questioning Your Ethics* questions throughout the chapters to challenge readers to consider what they'd do regarding the ethics of various practices. Would they engage in such behaviors? If so or if not, why? Finally, at the end of each chapter, I pose a challenge to view a particular mediated text using the rhetorical perspective described in the chapter. In doing so, readers have an opportunity to make each abstract theory concrete by using it to examine a relevant mediated popular culture text before moving on to learn about another perspective.

2. *Appendix. Writing a Popular Culture Rhetorical Essay*

In the appendix, I propose a means by which to prepare a rhetorical analysis essay that could be submitted to a journal for publication as well as an approach for transforming it into a presentation for an academic conference. My goal in doing so is to provide readers with a systematic approach for getting their analyses out of their heads and onto paper in order to share them with larger audiences. Although the approach I describe for writing an essay and then converting it into a presentation is by no means the only way, it is one model for doing so.

3. Contemporary Examples, Extended Examples, Sample Published Essays, and Sample Student Essays

Examples are crucial to succeed in making abstract theoretical concepts accessible to readers. I did not want to write a book that only a niche population could understand. Through a variety of examples from TV (e.g., *Modern Family, Justified, Newsroom, Downton Abbey, Weeds, Girls*), music (e.g., Papa Roach, Eminem, Dixie Chicks, Nine Inch Nails, Taylor Swift, Metallica), films (e.g., *Lord of the Rings, Harry Potter, Life Is Beautiful, The Help, Silver Linings Playbook, The Matrix*), advertisements (e.g., for Red Zone, Pond's, Samuel Adams, Budweiser Beer, MasterCard), and comics or cartoons (e.g., *Dennis the Menace, A Charlie Brown Christmas, The Simpsons, Family Guy*), readers should clearly see the relevance of these theories for understanding how mediated popular culture texts influence us to believe and behave through covert strategies about what we take for granted as normal and desirable.

4. Step-by-Step How to Conduct an Analysis Sections for Each Theory Presented

Here my goal is to assist readers to examine texts of their own choosing via description, interpretation, and evaluation. I believe that, by helping readers walk through the systematic analysis process for each perspective applied directly to texts relevant to them, the way they experience mediated popular culture texts will be forever changed. Although readers might continue to enjoy mediated popular culture texts, my hope is that they will no longer do so without understanding what and how such texts are also proposing arguments about what is normal (and not) and desirable (and not).

5. Glossary of Key Terms

Although many books offer key terms, I believe doing so is crucial in this book because I want readers to be able to deconstruct academic jargon rather than be confounded by it. Thus, I use jargon of the field and deconstruct it by defining it clearly within each chapter and providing a comprehensive glossary of key terms at the end of the book.

I don't pretend to know all the answers. But I do want to share with my readers the strategies I have learned that help me understand what and how mediated popular culture texts communicate and persuade.

Chapter-by-Chapter Revisions

Chapter 1: This chapter continues to focus on defining popular culture and mediated popular culture as well as providing a rationale for studying it. What is new to this edition is the intentional focus on new media and social media and the ways in which they have altered how we interact with mediated popular culture texts today.

Chapter 2: The goal of this chapter is still to ground the analysis of popular culture in the rhetorical tradition and begins with a discussion about the nature of rhetoric and rhetorical criticism. However, this edition also offers an accounting of the evolution of the rhetorical tradition from the classical period (or Golden Age through the Middle Ages) and the Renaissance to the Age of Reason (or Enlightenment) and then into the 20th and 21st centuries. This grounding leads into a description of the neo-Aristotelian approach using President Obama's speech after the Sandy Hook massacre as an extended illustration. I intentionally begin by describing the rhetorical situation, then interpreting the text according to the five canons, and finally evaluating its potential implications on its target audience(s). The chapter concludes by calling attention to a sample published essay and a brand-new student sample focused on Newt Gingrich's concession speech following his loss to Mitt Romney in the 2012 Florida primary election.

Chapter 3: Before getting into an explanation of how to conduct a rhetorical analysis based on a narrative perspective, I spend more time up front in this edition discussing narrative theory and contributions made to it by multiple scholars. Also new to this edition are examples from apps like Foursquare and Navizon, TV programs such as *How I Met Your Mother* and *The Newsroom,* and a brand-new student sample on the award-winning film, *The Help*.

Chapter 4: This chapter, which discusses the dramatistic perspective, now begins with an explanation of Burke's conception of the dramatistic life cycle grounded in consubstantiality and the order-pollution-guilt-purification-redemption processes within it. Then I discuss cluster analysis and the Pentad using contemporary examples, such as *Les Miserables* and *Silver Linings Playbook,* as well as an illustration of how dramatism can focus on feel-good messages (*It's a Wonderful Life*) when a protagonist breaks one of society's rules for living. The chapter closes by calling attention to a new sample published essay that examines the video game Bioshock using Burke's Pentad and a brand-new sample student essay on the HBO TV series *Weeds*.

Chapter 5: Chapter 5 is entirely new for this edition. This chapter, which is focused on symbolic convergence theory and fantasy theme analysis, was written by Dr. Thomas G. Endres from the University of Northern Colorado. Dr. Endres, once a doctoral student of Ernest Bormann, provides a cogent description of the theory and its application using both the TV program *Big Bang Theory* and the popular cult classic film *The Rocky Horror Picture Show* as extended examples. The chapter closes by calling attention to a published essay and a sample student essay examining the TV series *Firefly*.

Chapter 6: I have chosen to refer to this perspective as neo-Marxist in this edition to distinguish it from some of the negative connotations that arise when some readers see the word *Marxist*. I also call attention to the larger genre of critical studies or critical rhetoric that it can fit within. As such, I also discuss the concept of *othering* as it informs critical and cultural studies including neo-Marxist ones. In this edition, I illustrate aspects of neo-Marxist criticism using examples from TV such as *Mike and Molly, Modern Family, New Girl, Cougar Town,* and *Downton Abbey*. The chapter closes by calling attention to a sample published essay on new media's role in contributing to the U.S. hegemony becoming increasingly materialistic and a new student sample essay examining the TV program *Modern Family* from a neo-Marxist perspective.

Chapter 7: This chapter remains focused on multiple feminist perspectives as related to the waves of feminism. I have expanded it, however, to include queer theory as a way to explore how texts privilege heteronormativity. Moreover, I include examples from TV (e.g., *New Girls, Game of Thorns, Girls),* movies (e.g., *The Hunger Games, Boys Don't Cry),* and video games (e.g., Bioshock, Grand Theft Auto*)* to illustrate concepts of feminist perspectives throughout the chapter and end by pointing to published essays on the representations of gay men on TV and a sample student essay on the popular movie *The Hunger Games,* focused on Katniss as the hero from a feminist perspective.

Chapter 8: I am very pleased with the revision of this chapter in that it provides a more focused explanation of the illusion of life perspective and how to use it to examine the role of both musical sound and lyrical content in conveying arguments in music. To do so, I have added a section that distinguishes musical rhetoric from both musical aesthetics and music as communication. I also explain the role of genre in shaping the argument. I include a host of examples throughout the chapter to illustrate aspects of the perspective including, for example, "I Will Survive" first made popular by Gloria Gaynor, "Loser" as performed by Beck, several well-known rock anthems including "Do They Know It's Christmas?" by the Band Aid charity group and its follow-up, "We Are the World," by Live Aid. The chapter ends by pointing to two sample published essays and a sample student essay examining music from Creed.

Chapter 9: This chapter has been expanded to discuss several visual perspectives that can be used to examine visual texts rhetorically. As with the music chapter, I begin by distinguishing visual rhetoric from visual art aesthetics. Then I include a new section about the history and nature of visual communication, as well as a discussion of Gestalt, semiotics, and cognitive theory, before moving into visual pleasure theory as an example of one psychoanalytical cognitive theory approach to examine visual arguments embedded in mediated popular culture texts. I have also taken care to illustrate how the theory has been expanded to include visual images of women, men, race, and multiple sexualities. The sample student essay that closes this chapter illustrates such expanded thinking in its close reading of the film *Boys Don't Cry* to reveal rhetorical strategies inviting viewers to embrace transgendered sexuality as appropriate rather than deviant.

Chapter 10: This chapter remains focused on media-centered perspectives but is expanded to intentionally acknowledge the important role of new media today. I have expanded the theoretical discussion to include media ecology theory and Marshall McLuhan's contributions to our understanding of it even today. To do so, I offer Neil Postman's notion of technopoly to describe the endless ways technology dominates our thinking and behaviors today and include examples from video games to social media to TV programs to digital remixes to illustrate my points. I close by pointing to a sample published essay on reality-based televisual black fatherhood and another on the "you" portrayed in YouTube videos, as well as a sample student essay focused on realism and intimacy conveyed in Harry Potter.

COMPANION SITE FOR STUDENTS

To maximize students' understanding of popular culture and promote critical thinking and active learning, we have provided the following chapter-specific open-access study materials on **www.sagepub.com/sellnow2e**:

- SAGE Journal Articles
- Web Resources
- Key term, mobile-friendly flashcards
- Mobile-friendly web quizzes
- Web exercises

ACKNOWLEDGMENTS

I'd like to thank Matthew Byrnie for pushing me to keep moving forward on this project when time was of the essence, as well as gently prodding me to let go of some of my personal favorite examples in favor of examples that speak to the digital new media age we now all live in. In doing so, he helped make this a much stronger version of a book I was proud of in its first edition. Thanks, Matt! I would like to thank my many colleagues and the students who used the first edition for providing me with such meaningful feedback and suggestions for improvement. You, too, played an important role in making this edition what it is today. I'd like to express the sincerest thanks to everyone who helped make this revision a reality.

I would also like to thank the reviewers for taking the time to really read and critique the first edition:

Mary Elizabeth Bezanson, *University of Minnesota, Morris;* Valerie L. Guyant, *University of Wisconsin—Eau Claire;* Randy Harris, *University of Waterloo;* Agnieszka Kampka, *Warsaw University of Life Sciences;* Steven Listopad, *Jamestown College;* and LaChrystal D. Ricke, *Sam Houston State University.* You pushed me to revisit classical rhetorical theory from Aristotle's *Rhetoric* and *Poetics* to Thonnssen and Baird's *Speech Criticism.* And you pushed me to revisit contemporary rhetorical thinking about, for example, semiotics, media ecology, neo-Marxism, visual pleasure, and heteronormativity. Although I admit I was frustrated at times as I tried to respond to your critiques, doing so ultimately resulted in a revision much more firmly grounded in theory. Thank you all!

Of course I also want to thank my family. First I thank Tim for supporting me in undertaking this revision even as I worked night and day. Second, I thank Debbie and Rick for their ideas and examples of new media to help keep what I say at least somewhat relevant. Thank you to all who guided my hand in writing this book. I am forever grateful for being allowed to serve as the conduit for getting these ideas from the "Ivory Towers of the academy" to its readers.

Reference

Carey, A. R., & Gonzalez, A. (2013, January 25–27). How we'll use our smartphones during Super Bowl 2013. *USA Today,* p. 1A.

Chapter 1

What Is Popular Culture and Why Study It?

T ake a moment or two to jot down a favorite: (1) movie, (2) TV program, (3) song, (4) cartoon, (5) comic strip, and (6) advertisement. Beside each selection, identify in a sentence or two why it is a favorite of yours. The reasons you offer actually demonstrate the influential role each one plays in how you interpret the world around you. Now jot down a favorite of a friend or family member that you don't like at all. What assumptions do you make about their beliefs, attitudes, and values because they like it?

Research has shown that these and other forms of entertainment can both reflect and shape what people believe and how we behave. If you are reading this book, I suspect this statement does not surprise you. What you may not know, however, is how these movies, TV programs, songs, cartoons, comic strips, and advertisements actually do so. The purpose of this book, then, is to equip you with tools to analyze their underlying messages that advocate a particular viewpoint about how we "ought to" and "ought not to" believe and behave. By the time you finish this book, you will be a more critical consumer and able to make educated choices about whether or not to embrace such messages as valid in your own life.

Developing your ability to make educated choices is particularly important when it comes to entertainment media (e.g., movies, TV programs, songs, cartoons, comic strips). Why? Some reasons include satisfying curiosity about the variety of topics and issues explored in them, developing self-awareness about your own norms and values, and increasing understanding about why you believe and behave as you do. Another reason might be because influential messages couched in entertainment media can be used ethically or unethically. Ethics refers to principles about what is right and wrong, moral and immoral, fair and unfair (Johannesen, 1990; Nilsen, 1974; Wallace, 1955). Unlike legal choices that are governed by rules to which we must abide, ethical choices are guided by our values, conscience, and sense of fairness. As such, producers of entertainment media may operate by ethical standards that differ from yours. Developing your ability to discern those underlying ethics-based messages couched in entertainment media affords you the freedom and ability to choose whether or not to be influenced by them.

This chapter lays the groundwork for studying popular culture as rhetoric by, first, defining *popular culture* and *mediated popular culture texts* as they relate to other definitions of culture and texts. Second, the chapter provides a clear rationale for studying popular culture as rhetoric. Third, the chapter presents a systematic approach for examining underlying messages embedded in popular culture texts using an extended example for comparison. By the time you finish the chapter, I hope you will be eager to expand your understanding of and ability to examine the many kinds of popular culture texts that pervade daily life.

WHAT IS POPULAR CULTURE?

To fully understand what popular culture is, it is particularly helpful to begin by explaining what it is not. Let us begin with the concept of *culture* and then move on to the concept of *popular culture*.

Sometimes the word *culture* is defined within an elitist context. That is, one definition of the concept of *cultured* refers to the means by which to improve one's station in life. I must admit I encouraged my children to play in the school orchestra because I believed it was a means of self-improvement for them. After all, musical ability has been positively correlated with intellectual capacity and leadership potential. *Culture* is also often defined within a diversity context (e.g., racial, ethnic, religious, and other demographic associations). For example, Muslim, Jewish, and Christian religions could denote different cultures. Although these demographic characteristics often play roles in determining target audiences of various movies, songs, advertisements, and such, they are insufficient for defining popular culture.

APPLYING WHAT YOU'VE LEARNED . . .

Have you ever gone to an event like a symphony, a play, or some other sophisticated dinner, reception, or social event as a means by which to become more cultured? If so, was it your idea or someone else's? What do you recall from the experience? Do you think it influenced your appreciation for fine and performing arts? Why or why not?

Popular culture, in contrast, is not associated with the elitist definition of becoming cultured to improve oneself nor is it narrowly defined by demographic characteristics of a community or group. Rather, for purposes of this book, popular culture is comprised of the everyday objects, actions, and events that influence people to believe and behave in certain ways. (Essentially, everything we experience in our daily lives could be considered an element of popular culture.) They do so through subtle messages proposing a particular perspective about what is "appropriate" and "inappropriate," "desirable" and "undesirable," "good" and "bad," and so on.

Because this definition of popular culture is so broad, we focus specifically on mediated popular culture in this book. Mediated popular culture can be defined as the everyday objects, actions, and events we experience through a media channel (e.g., movies, TV programs, songs, comic strips, advertisements) that may influence us to believe and behave in certain ways. We encounter mediated popular culture via old media—which includes both print media (e.g., magazines, newspapers, billboards, brochures) and traditional electronic media (e.g., TV, radio)—as well as new media. For purposes of our discussions, new media consist of all forms of digital media (e.g., websites ranging from YouTube, to Facebook, to Twitter, to multiplayer gaming sites) accessed from the Internet and satellite via computers and various handheld devices.

Mediated popular culture pervades our daily lives. In fact, since publishing the first edition of this text, mediated popular culture has become increasingly infused in our lives 24 hours a day and 7 days a week. Check out these five-year comparisons to illustrate my point. Annual sales of smartphones worldwide jumped from 131 million in 2008 to 310 million in 2012 with an estimated 1.1 billion smartphone users worldwide (Parks Associates, 2012). In 2008, Facebook had about 90 million members compared to 938 million in 2012 (Miniwatts Marketing Group, 2012). Twitter had less than 1 million members in 2008 compared to more than 500 million in 2012 (Lunden, 2012). Tablets didn't even exist in 2008. In 2012, 120 million were purchased, which represents a 98 percent increase from the 60 million purchased in 2011 (Gartner, 2012). And the number of downloadable apps increased from about 10,000 by the end of 2008 to more than 700,000 by the end of 2012 (Etherington, 2012; Thurner, 2012).

Thanks to this technology explosion of new media, we can now have access to friends, family, coworkers, information and entertainment sources, as well as advertisements and shopping outlets across the globe nearly anytime and anyplace. Wireless (Wi-Fi) technology provides quick and easy access in homes, schools, libraries, shopping centers, waiting rooms, restaurants, and hotels, as well as in planes, trains, and automobiles.

Although accessibility in some ways liberates us and increases productivity, it can also consume us and decrease productivity even to the point of disrupting our ability to function effectively in occupational and social interactions (Kung, 2012). One such condition that is becoming more prevalent is nomophobia, which refers to a fear of being out of mobile phone contact (D'Agata, 2008). According to recent surveys, 66 percent of us are afraid to be separated from our cell phones, 40 percent would begin to miss our phone in less than an hour without it, and as many as 11 percent would, in fact, rather leave home without pants than without a phone (SecureEnvoy, 2012). Another debilitating condition is Internet Addiction Disorder (IAD), which refers to excessive computer use that interferes with daily life (Byun et al., 2009). This addiction causes the same kinds of changes in the brain as observed in alcoholics and drug addicts and is now being diagnosed in 5 to 10 percent of the population (Jaslow, 2012). With the ever-increasing accessibility to and use of new and old media, understanding what and how they communicate seems even more imperative today than ever before.

Assess Yourself: Are You Addicted to the Internet?

Go to this website to take a 20-question quiz to determine whether you might be considered an Internet addict: http://www.netaddiction.com/index.php?option=com_bfquiz&view=onepage&ca tid=46&Itemid=106

Mediated popular culture texts communicate to and for us regarding what we believe we ought to and ought not to believe and do during every waking moment. To clarify, allow me to use my encounters with mediated popular culture texts before going to work one morning. At 5 A.M., I awoke to my alarm, which is set to a local radio station. Before I even got out of bed, I was influenced by a story I heard about an NYC police officer who purchased boots for a homeless man. A bystander had snapped a picture of the event on her smartphone and posted it on Facebook, which went viral. That story influenced me in several ways. It confirmed my belief that it is desirable and good to help those in need. It also influenced me that I, too, should think about what I ought to do to pay it forward, so-to-speak, in my own community. I decided to go online to make a donation to the local food bank. After making my donation, I checked Facebook to see the photograph for myself. Good people, I surmised, help those in need.

I then went to the kitchen where I poured myself a cup of coffee, picked up the newspaper, and turned the TV to The Weather Channel (TWC). I watch TWC every morning because the "Local on the 8s" segment helps me decide what I ought to wear. I also enjoy the banter that usually goes on among the meteorologists on *Wake Up With Al*. They seem to genuinely enjoy working with each other. As I watch, I think it is both appropriate and desirable to enjoy what you do and to have fun while doing it. The newspaper further reinforced my belief that it is *good* to help those in need and my belief that there are still good people in the world when I read a story about 5,000 blankets, toys, and clothing items that were donated to various shelters across the state this month.

Mediated popular culture messages also shape how I ought not to believe and behave. For instance, my belief that we ought not to be able to purchase assault weapons was reinforced as I read a newspaper story about the senseless massacre at Sandy Hook elementary school in Newton, Connecticut. And when perusing *US Weekly*, my belief that it is bad for women to starve themselves to be thin was reinforced when I saw a picture of country singer LeAnn Rimes's popsicle-stick figure. My opinion that it's wrong to glamorize teen pregnancy on TV was confirmed when I read about *Teen Mom 2* star Jenelle Evans's engagement to boyfriend of two months, Courtland Rogers, and him seeing her as his "meal ticket." As I paged through the magazine, I noticed a picture of Mary Kate Olsen smoking a cigarette and thought, "I wish she wouldn't do that because smoking is bad." And as I looked at the outfits on the "Fashion Police" pages and read the comments accompanying them suggesting which ones looked good and bad, I made a mental note about inappropriate and undesirable attire. These kinds of images and stories influence us by shaping our beliefs and behaviors.

Assess Yourself: Are You Addicted to the Internet?

Identify messages that have been sent to you so far today via media, friends, or observations. What beliefs or behaviors did they reinforce for you about what is "appropriate" or "inappropriate," "desirable" or "undesirable," "good" or "bad," and why?

QUESTIONING YOUR ETHICS . . .

Do you think it is "appropriate" or "inappropriate" to consume alcohol during a business lunch meeting? Consider now the Samuel Adams beer commercials where several businessmen order water until one fellow orders a Samuel Adams beer. At that time, the others quickly change their orders to Samuel Adams beer as well. What is this commercial arguing about whether or not it is OK to consume alcohol during a business lunch meeting? Now go watch this short video online: http://www.youtube.com/watch?v=KZ11PO-vjBk

What messages is it portraying about when and where it is "appropriate" to consume alcohol?

WHAT ARE POPULAR CULTURE TEXTS?

Popular culture communicates to us and for us through signs and artifacts. A sign is simply something that makes you think of something else. For example, when I look at the ring on the third finger of my left hand, I think of what that means in terms of the bond of marriage. I also reminisce about purchasing the ring with my spouse more than 30 years ago. And, I think of the summer when we replaced our first wedding rings with new rings we purchased in a favorite vacation spot (Medora, North Dakota). An artifact is a sign or series of signs that is socially grounded. That is, its meaning is widely shared by some identifiable community or cultural group. The ring I just described can be considered an artifact for the dominant American culture in terms of symbolizing the bond of marriage but not in terms of the personal meanings I described. Those personal meanings are valid signs but only for my spouse and me. When analyzing the communicative potential of popular culture, then, one looks for signs that function as artifacts.

Each of us is a member of (or identifies with) more than one cultural group simultaneously. The various groups with which we identify often share characteristics, beliefs, or value systems. For example, I am a parent, a college professor, a Christian, a pet owner, and a middle-class American, among other things. Each of these groups is distinct, yet I identify myself with each of them. Moreover, some beliefs are held by all of them, and others are not.

Each cultural group is also identifiable because it embraces an ideology. An ideology is a cultural group's perceptions about the way things are and assumptions about the way they ought to be. Thus, an ideology is not a factual description of objects and events but rather a perception shared by members of a particular group. For example, as a pet owner, I embrace a perception that pets are good for families with kids because pets are loving and lovable. This is not a factual statement but rather a perception I share with others who identify with the pet owners cultural group. A factual statement, on the other hand, might merely be that pets are domesticated animals some families with kids choose to own.

Ideologies are formed, reinforced, and sometimes reformed through rhetoric. Rhetoric can be defined simply as messages designed to influence people. In other words, rhetoric is persuasive communication. A rhetorical argument, then, is a persuasive message designed to reinforce or challenge a taken-for-granted belief or behavior about what is "appropriate" or "inappropriate," "desirable" or "undesirable," "good" or "bad."

Rhetorical arguments are conveyed through texts. A text is any set of interrelated signs and artifacts that contribute to a unified message. Texts argue rhetorically as sites of struggle that confirm or disconfirm an ideology held by a cultural group (Brummett, 2011, pp. 77–80). Texts can be, but are not limited to, books and other written materials. A popular culture text, for example, is any set of interrelated written, oral, or visual signs and artifacts focused on everyday objects, actions, and events that contribute to a rhetorical argument. A mediated popular culture text is a subset of the broad range of popular culture texts limited to those conveyed through media channels (e.g., movies, music, TV programs, advertisements, comic strips).

To illustrate how rhetorical arguments are conveyed through mediated popular culture texts, let us focus, for example, on the ideological debate in the United States regarding marriage. Some groups hold firm to the ideology that the right to marry should be limited to heterosexual partners, and other groups believe the right to marry should be available to all committed partners in both heterosexual and homosexual relationships. Consider now how different mediated popular culture texts argue in ways that support or oppose one of these competing ideologies. How might the rhetorical argument differ among TV's *Modern Family, Cougar Town, The New Normal, Big Bang Theory*, and *Awkward* or among the movies *The Birdcage, The Kids Are All Right, I Now Pronounce You Chuck and Larry, The Vow*, and *What to Expect When You're Expecting*?

This book focuses on mediated popular culture texts for a number of reasons. First, we can usually demarcate a beginning and an end to something like a film or a piece of music, at least for analytical purposes. Second, mediated texts—particularly those couched as mere entertainment (e.g., popular music, blockbuster movies, sitcoms)—can be particularly influential because consumers often fail to realize their persuasive potential. Limiting my examples in this way does not in any way mean that these are the only examples of popular culture texts, but rather, they provide a focus for this book.

WHY STUDY POPULAR CULTURE?

Because popular culture consists of everyday objects, actions, and events, people sometimes fail to see the rationale for studying it. Yet the fact that popular culture communicates and persuades in these subtle and covert, or hidden, ways actually points to the need for such study. As noted earlier, ultimately, popular culture persuades by empowering and disempowering certain people and groups by conveying messages about "desirable" and "undesirable," "appropriate" and "inappropriate," "normal" and "abnormal" beliefs and behaviors.

Thus, popular culture is significant because it has the persuasive power to shape beliefs and behaviors. Doing so successfully can have positive or negative implications. For example, according to the standards set by the American Dietetic Association, most female TV actresses are notably underweight. These images and the assumptions they make about what the "ideal" woman *ought to* look like have been shown to influence women's perceptions of their own bodies (Harrison, 2000). To help clarify this point, a study was conducted a few years ago on the remote island of Fiji. Before the introduction of satellite TV, about 3 percent of the island's adolescent girls reported to have dieted. Two years later—after the introduction of satellite TV—that figure rose to 66 percent. Moreover, 15 percent of these girls admitted they had vomited to control their weight (Becker Grinspoon, Klibanski, & Herzog, 1999).

This example illustrates the negative consequences of rhetorical arguments conveyed in mediated popular culture texts. However, the rhetorical arguments made in such texts can also shape beliefs and behaviors in ways that promote positive consequences.

■ **FIGURE 1.1**   Editorial Cartoon

Source: © Tribune Media Services, Inc. All Rights Reserved. Reprinted with permission.

Consider, for example, the growing number of feature films and documentaries focused on understanding and respecting people who live with a disability. In 2010, HBO produced a biopic about the real life of Temple Grandin, an animal science professor who, thanks in part to her unique experiences of living with autism, improved the ethical treatment of animals. *Music Within,* initially released in 2007, tells the true story of what two Vietnam veterans did to help get the Americans With Disabilities Act passed. *Front of the Class,* a 2008 Hallmark Hall of Fame made-for-TV movie, is based on the true story of Brad Cohen, a gifted teacher who also lives with Tourette's syndrome. The American reality TV series *Push Girls,* which debuted on the Sundance Channel in 2012, follows the lives of four paralyzed women and their daily challenges and triumphs. And on the award-winning Showtime TV series *Homeland,* CIA agent Carrie Matheson also lives with bipolar disorder. Films and TV programs like these encourage viewers to realize people who happen to live with a disability are real people who think, feel, and make meaningful contributions to society. In doing so, they challenge an ideology about what is "normal," "desirable," and "appropriate."

Popular culture is also important to study because of its persuasive power to reinforce taken-for-granted beliefs and behaviors. By examining these arguments, we can make informed choices about whether to accept them as normal, desirable, or appropriate. Consider for a moment the dominant American ideology surrounding the notion of *family.* Programs like *Leave It to Beaver* in the 1950s reinforced a taken-for-granted belief that a "normal" family was one where the father worked outside the home and the mother did not. In the 1960s and 1970s, programs like *I Love Lucy* and *The Brady Bunch,* while challenging other taken-for-granted beliefs, continued to reinforce this ideology. Although the 1980s introduced programs like *The Cosby Show,* where the mother who worked outside the home was portrayed as normal, such shows continued to be the exception, not the rule.

Even into the 21st century, the most popular TV shows about families with children depict mothers who do not work outside the home (e.g., *Everybody Loves Raymond* [1996–2005]; *According to Jim* [2001–2007]; *Parenthood* [2010–]) or work part-time while still running the household (e.g., *Malcolm in the Middle* [2000–2006]; *Everybody Hates Chris* [2005–2009]; *The Middle* [2009–]). At the same time, many shows that actually depict men raising children or running the household often focus on their inability to do it well (e.g., *Titus* [2000–2002]; *Arrested Development* [2003–2006]; *Two and a Half Men* [2003–]). In doing so, these shows also reinforce the notion that the "normal" role for men is not raising children or caring for the home.

To further illustrate this point, let's consider the popular TV show *Modern Family.* In it, the family portrayed as "typical" is the Dunphy family. The family consists of a heterosexual couple with three children where the father works outside home and the mother does not. Even though all of the parents in *Modern Family* are at times depicted as inept, most of the male characters are portrayed consistently as not being good at raising children or caring for the home. The one exception is Cam. But he is also portrayed as an effeminate gay man in contrast to the other, "typical" men.

The previous examples point to another reason to study popular culture. Not only do popular culture texts shape and reinforce beliefs and behaviors, they do so both (1) in covert ways and (2) on multiple levels. For example, among other things, *The Brady Bunch* (1969–1974) argued that normal middle-class family homes are always neat and tidy.

Contrast this with *Roseanne* (1988–1997), *Malcolm in the Middle* (2000–2006), or *The Middle* (2009–) and you will see what I mean. *The Brady Bunch* employs Alice as their full-time housekeeper, which argues covertly (among other things) that a neat and tidy home is desirable for normal middle-class families. Moreover, washing clothes, doing dishes, tidying rooms, cleaning house, and mowing the lawn are embedded in the day-to-day routine of each episode. None of the families in the other programs employ a housekeeper, and their homes are rarely depicted as neat and tidy. In fact, when cleaning or tidying up is part of an episode's plot, doing so is often portrayed as a disgusting chore or nuisance rather than a normal part of the family's day-to-day routine. Thus, the different arguments about whether it is normal for middle-class homes to be neat and tidy are conveyed covertly and on multiple levels.

Popular culture is also significant because it is so pervasive. As we have already discussed, popular culture is everywhere. It is in our homes, our communities, our workplaces, and our social clubs. In fact, research conducted by the Nielsen Company (2013) reports the average American home has more TV sets than people, and the average American spends at least 20 percent of their day watching TV in addition to streaming video via social networks. Because it is impossible to avoid popular culture, and it does function rhetorically, becoming educated consumers of it provides us the freedom to choose what and how its messages will influence our beliefs and behaviors.

APPLYING WHAT YOU'VE LEARNED . . .

Identify as many popular culture signs, artifacts, and texts you have encountered in the past 24 hours. Now identify what belief or behavior each one played a role in reinforcing or shaping. Finally, describe at least two meanings being reinforced or shaped in each of them.

CONDUCTING RHETORICAL ANALYSES OF POPULAR CULTURE TEXTS

Examining a popular culture text to effectively reveal covert messages about taken-for-granted beliefs and behaviors is essentially a three-step process of (1) selecting a text and formulating a research question, (2) selecting a rhetorical perspective, and (3) examining the text via description, interpretation, and evaluation.

Step 1: Selecting a Text and Formulating a Research Question

The first step in the process of unpacking the underlying messages in popular culture texts is to select a text and formulate a research question. You can do so in one of two ways. You might start with a text. By that, I mean you might watch a program or see an advertisement that piques your curiosity somehow. You may have a hunch that something more is going on than what the surface message is communicating. For example, maybe you enjoy watching a show like *Parks and Recreation*. On the surface, you like the program because it's funny. It makes you laugh. But maybe you wonder why it's funny. That is, what is it saying about what is normal and abnormal behavior? Who are viewers lead to laugh at and why? This is an example of starting with a text.

On the other hand, you might start with a question. Perhaps you wonder what arguments popular sitcoms like *Parks and Recreation* propose about appropriate and inappropriate behaviors for men and women in society. When viewers laugh at something a character does or does not do, they do so because it reinforces that behavior as inappropriate or undesirable. So you might decide to examine what beliefs and behaviors the program is actually attempting to reinforce about appropriate and inappropriate roles and rules for men and women. This is an example of starting with a question.

It doesn't matter whether you start with a text or with a question. Ultimately, the goal is the same: to form the research question you will seek to answer in your analysis.

APPLYING WHAT YOU'VE LEARNED . . .

Consider a TV program you enjoy watching. Which characters are portrayed as "normal," and which ones are depicted as "different" in some way? Now identify the characteristics and behaviors of each as they serve to reinforce an ideology about how one ought to and ought not to believe or behave if one wants to be perceived by others as "normal."

Step 2: Selecting a Rhetorical Perspective

Once you have identified a text and formulated a research question, you need to select a rhetorical perspective through which to examine it. A rhetorical perspective is simply a lens through which you look to magnify the underlying messages that have to do with the question you are asking. I like to compare a rhetorical perspective to a spotlight that has different colored filters on it. If you put the red filter on, everything on the stage has a certain hue. If you put the blue filter on, everything on the stage looks quite different than it did through the red filter. Because each popular culture text sends multiple messages simultaneously, the rhetorical perspective you select helps bring to the forefront the messages you are trying to understand to answer your particular research question.

In the chapters that follow, we look at nine different rhetorical perspectives and how you use them to systematically analyze texts. This chapter provides a brief overview of the main goals of each perspective. The first perspective, the neo-Aristotelian approach, was actually designed to analyze public speeches based on the philosophies of the Greeks and Romans more than 2,000 years ago. The next five perspectives were developed in the 20th century in response to perceived limitations of the neo-Aristotelian approach. These perspectives are: narrative, dramatistic, symbolic convergence, neo-Marxist, and feminist.

Although each of these perspectives is often used to understand how messages conveyed in music, visuals, and media function rhetorically, none of them spell out the unique ways in which musical form (irrespective of lyrics), or visual images, or media communicate. Thus, an additional chapter is devoted specifically to each of them.

As an overview for what is to come in the remaining chapters, let us discuss briefly how each perspective helps identify underlying messages in a given mediated popular culture text. We do so by applying each of them to the animated Christmas cartoon *A Charlie Brown Christmas*. If you have not seen this animated classic, it might prove helpful to do so before reading the rest of this chapter.

Neo-Aristotelian Perspective. A **neo-Aristotelian perspective** helps us discover persuasive strategies used by orators and their impact on the audience. We do so by reconstructing the context where the speech occurred and audience expectations and then examining the message and its influence according to the five classical canons (a.k.a. categories or rules) of rhetoric. These canons are invention (content and argument development), arrangement (organizational structure), style (language choices, sentence composition, tropes and figures), memory (mnemonic devices), and delivery (controlled use of voice and body). In *A Charlie Brown Christmas,* a critic might examine the speech, "That's What Christmas Is All About Charlie Brown," delivered by Linus. In terms of context, the speech comes toward the end of the program, at a point when Charlie Brown is ready to give up on the commercialism of Christmas. Context is important because the speech serves as a turning point regarding the meaning of Christmas. Considering the canons, the credibility of the speech and of Linus are enhanced when he delivers his speech confidently from memory and verbatim from the Christmas story chapter in the Holy Bible (Luke). As such, a critic might conclude that Linus's speech was effective in communicating an alternative message (from commercialism) regarding "what Christmas is all about."

Narrative Perspective. A **narrative perspective** helps us discover the underlying moral of the story—that is, its argument about how we ought to and ought not to believe or behave. Throughout the text, actions and consequences are offered as good reasons to accept the moral as being valid. In *A Charlie Brown Christmas,* whereas the overt or surface message is the answer Linus provides regarding "what Christmas is really about," the covert or underlying moral might be that everything and everyone is beautiful and ought to be treated with respect. In the end, even Charlie Brown is treated kindly, the tree is treated kindly, and so forth.

Dramatistic Perspective. A **dramatistic perspective** helps us determine the underlying motives offered as justification for breaking various *rules for living*, rules regarding how we ought to or ought not to behave. In *A Charlie Brown Christmas,* Charlie Brown breaks a number of rules. Perhaps most significant is when he is asked to buy a fancy pink aluminum Christmas tree but instead brings back a puny real tree. The other children initially reprimand Charlie Brown because he did not follow the rules of commercialism that tend to be associated with the holiday. In the end, viewers accept that he is justified in breaking these rules of commercialism because he was transcending them and following a higher order. Ultimately, he is accepted as being OK because he broke the rules for a justifiable reason. Therefore, through the dramatistic perspective, viewers learn that it is acceptable to break the rules if one is following a higher calling.

Symbolic Convergence Theory Perspective. A **symbolic convergence theory** (SCT) perspective helps reveal a shared reality a particular cultural group uses to make sense of the world around them. The plotline, characters, scene, and sanctioning agents (forces that legitimize behavior) work together to convey a shared ideology. This shared ideology is called a **rhetorical vision**. Groups arrive at a shared rhetorical vision by putting together shared stories among them. These stories might be righteous, social, or pragmatic. Righteous story lines focus on shared concerns about what is "right" and "wrong," "proper" and "improper," "superior" and "inferior," or "moral" and "immoral." Social story lines focus on shared values about friendship, trust, camaraderie, and being humane. Pragmatic visions focus on getting the job done efficiently, practically, simply, and so on. In *A Charlie Brown Christmas,* the children ultimately act humanely as they encircle the tree, hold hands with one another, and sing "Hark! the Herald Angels Sing." This social story line reinforces a shared reality or rhetorical vision of the importance of friendship, camaraderie, and being humane.

Neo-Marxist Perspective. A neo-Marxist perspective helps reveal who is empowered and who is disempowered in a popular culture text. In the purest sense, it has to do with socioeconomic status. That is, it reveals ways in which the text's underlying messages either support or oppose the ideological assumption that those with more money and material possessions ought to be empowered and those who do not have money ought not to be empowered. The perspective has become broader than that today, though, to include groups associated with race, religion, ethnicity, ability or disability, age, and so on. The neo-Marxist perspective chapter will explore some of these approaches rooted in critical and cultural studies.

In *A Charlie Brown Christmas,* the ultimate message communicated tends to reinforce the status quo that, the more money and stuff you can buy at Christmas, the better. Consider, for example, that Lucy wants real estate; Sally wants her "fair share," preferably in the form of $10 and $20 bills; that Snoopy wins the contest for the best decorated house; and even the real Christmas tree ends up being decorated with lots of stuff before it is perceived as beautiful. From a neo-Marxist perspective, one might conclude that the primary message conveyed in *A Charlie Brown Christmas* reinforces the ideological assumption that the more money and material stuff one has, the better.

Feminist Perspectives. Feminist perspectives focus on what are proposed as "appropriate" and "desirable" as well as "inappropriate" and "undesirable" roles and rules for men and women (including heterosexual, homosexual, bisexual, lesbian, and transgender people). When viewed through a feminist perspective, *A Charlie Brown Christmas* reinforces many negative stereotypes about women. For example, Lucy is aggressive and outspoken. Viewers are led to believe these are behaviors women should not embrace because the other characters don't particularly like Lucy, although they may tolerate her. Snoopy even makes fun of her during the rehearsal. Sally wants lots of money for Christmas. The girl with the naturally curly hair is only worried that someone might hurt her beautiful "naturally curly hair."

The Illusion of Life Perspective. The rhetorical nature of music as communication has interested scholars, particularly in sociology, since the 1960s. In the 1970s and 1980s, the rhetorical nature of music gained momentum in the field of communication as well. Since then, a number of theories have been proposed to help us understand how music communicates to and for individuals and groups. One such theory is the illusion of life. The illusion of life theory focuses specifically on how lyrics and music function together to persuade (e.g., Sellnow & Sellnow, 2001). The ultimate goal is to determine whether the lyrics (cognitive content) and music (emotional content) are congruent or incongruent and how that relationship shapes the argument. For example, the slow and mellow music of a lullaby combined with lyrics about falling asleep peacefully are congruent. Likewise, the upbeat, fast-paced sounds of a school fight song combined with lyrics about going and fighting and winning are congruent. If the lyrics to the lullaby were combined with the music of the school fight song or the lyrics of the fight song were combined with the music of the lullaby, however, they would be incongruent.

Three songs play important roles in *A Charlie Brown Christmas*. The first is the song that the children dance to while rehearsing their Christmas play. The fact that it is not a familiar Christmas tune and that it has no words reinforces the idea that people seem to have forgotten the meaning of Christmas. Essentially, the song is incongruent with the message of the Christmas play, which actually contributes to the argument that the meaning of Christmas seems to have been lost. The second song is "Jingle Bells" as played by Schroeder. The gradual dumbing down of the tune until it is a one-finger melody to which Lucy exclaims "That's it!" also reinforces the lack of substance to Christmas celebrations today. Finally, the program ends with all the children singing "Hark! The Herald Angels Sing" while forming a circle around Charlie Brown's Christmas tree. As such, this final song is congruent—that is, the lyrics and music reinforce each other, as well as the narrative message being argued regarding the true meaning of Christmas.

Visual Perspectives. Since the mid-1980s, concern has been growing steadily about the influential nature of visual rhetoric on individuals and groups. As a result, a number of visual theories and perspectives have emerged. We will describe several of them later in the text. Here, we focus on how visual pleasure theory can inform an analysis of *A Charlie Brown Christmas*. Visual pleasure theory focuses on the messages communicated through visual images (e.g., Mulvey, 1989). More specifically, it focuses on messages of narcissism (i.e., which characters are portrayed as models whom viewers ought to be like and anti-models (whom viewers ought not to be like), fetishism (pleasure derived from looking openly at an object that is in itself satisfying), and voyeurism (the pleasure of looking at someone without them being aware of being looked at).

In *A Charlie Brown Christmas,* Linus constantly carries a blanket around. At the outset, the blanket-carrying boy might be perceived as a spectacle (fetishism) in a negative sense, that is, as an anti-model whom viewers ought not to be like (narcissism). By the end of the program, however, his blanket warms the spindly Christmas tree and turns it into something "beautiful," thereby becoming transformed into a spectacle in a positive sense. Because Linus is portrayed as wise beyond his years, he appears to be the role model viewers ought to be like (narcissism). As for the girls, with regard to fetishism, they ought to wear dresses and ought to be perceived as pretty. Because they are portrayed as shallow and catty, narcissistically the message is only about what girls ought not to be like. Although very little occurs in terms of voyeurism, viewers do see Snoopy make fun of Lucy behind her back and laugh. Hence, the message sent seems to be that it is appropriate to make fun of a girl like Lucy behind her back.

Media-Centered Perspectives. A good number of media-centered theories have been developed over the years. These perspectives were developed primarily to study media effects (causal and correlation effects of watching a particular TV program, viewing an advertisement or series of advertisements, etc.). Elements of them, however, are often used to enhance rhetorical analyses of popular culture texts. We discuss many of them later in the text. Here, we consider how parasocial relationship theory can inform our analyses of *A Charlie Brown Christmas* (e.g., Bryan & Zillman, 1994; Gerbner, Gross, Morgan, & Signorielli, 1994; Horton & Wohl, 1956; Rubin, Perse, & Powell, 1985; Rubin & Perse, 1987). Essentially, a parasocial relationship is a perception by a viewer of "knowing" a character as in a face-to-face relationship. This relationship develops primarily through rhetorical illusions of realism (depicting a version of "everyday life") and intimacy (characters are real people with real feelings, norms, and values).

With regard to realism, although no adults ever supervise the children in *A Charlie Brown Christmas,* viewers are lead to think that is normal. Even when Charlie Brown and Linus get the Christmas tree, they do so alone and at night. In terms of intimacy, although this is an animated program, viewers see the characters as real folks. That is, they say and do things that real kids often say and do (e.g., writing letters to Santa and enjoying seasonal songs like "Jingle Bells"). Moreover, viewers get to know Linus as a deep thinker and Charlie Brown as someone whose heart is in the right place. Viewers want the other kids to like Charlie Brown and to be nice to him. Even in an animated feature like *A Charlie Brown Christmas,* rhetorical strategies of realism and intimacy encourage the development of parasocial relationships.

Step 3. Examining the Text (Describe and Interpret)

Once you have selected a popular culture text, formulated a research question, and decided upon a rhetorical perspective through which to analyze it, you need to systematically examine it for the underlying messages it sends. Doing so involves a three-step process of description, interpretation, and evaluation.

First, you must describe the messages being sent. That is, what taken-for-granted belief, behavior, or social issue does the text address? In *A Charlie Brown Christmas,* you might want to focus on the underlying arguments it is presenting about men and women in society, or about what society ought to value as important, or about racism, among other things. These issues, beliefs, and behaviors are essentially the ways in which the text operates as a site of struggle. That is, the text reinforces or calls into question some taken-for-granted ideology about "the way things are" or "ought to be." The particular focus you take helps determine the rhetorical perspective you will choose. During this step, then, you describe what the text seems to be saying about the issue, belief, or behavior.

Second, you interpret how the messages are being conveyed by applying the tools of a particular rhetorical perspective. In this step, you consider who are portrayed as normal, desirable, and appropriate and who are not. Then you explain what they look like, what they do and say, how they are treated by others, and so on as each contributes to the argument portrayed regarding the issue you identified as a site of struggle. Here, you essentially make a case for your argument with evidence from the text.

Step 4: Evaluating Potential Implications of the Text

Finally, you must evaluate the significance of the argument you make about the text's messages. You do so by considering the various audiences who might view it and how it might influence them to believe and behave as a result. What impact might it have on individuals and groups? Consider the adolescent girls from Fiji mentioned earlier. The evaluation component of the visual images they received about how women ought to look (visual pleasure theory) appeared to have affected their eating habits to the point of a significant increase in disordered eating behaviors.

Some people argue that exposing children to repeated violence on TV makes it appear normal and may, in fact, increase violent behaviors in them. Based on a narrative perspective of *A Charlie Brown Christmas,* we might speculate that people ought to engage in more acts of kindness and charity during the holidays than mere consumerism. From a dramatistic perspective, we might argue that people ought to have more empathy for those who choose to celebrate the season in different ways. From an SCT theory perspective, we might argue that people ought to treat each other humanely. From a neo-Marxist perspective, we might conclude that parents become aware of the persuasive messages about consumerism their children are exposed to in programs like this one. From a feminist perspective, we might raise the issue that children need to see programs that portray girls in positive ways to counter the messages in programs that portray them only as shallow, self-centered, and sassy. And from an illusion of life perspective, we might argue that children ought to be exposed to Christmas music that reinforces a sense of charity and goodwill rather than just meaningless music that offers only emotional messages comprised of musical dance sounds. From a visual pleasure perspective, we might argue that children's programs ought to offer positive messages of narcissism for girls as well as boys. Finally, from a parasocial relationship perspective, we might point out potential implications of children's programs that portray no adult characters, particularly when children are depicted walking on city sidewalks alone at night.

This cursory look at how one examines the messages embedded in popular culture texts is intended to give you a sense of the big picture. The remaining chapters will offer more in-depth explanations of each one and how it works.

SAMPLE STUDENT ESSAY

What follows is a student essay that offers a cursory analysis of the critically acclaimed Stephen Sondheim musical *Into the Woods*. Although the paper is not perfect (if there even is such a thing), Carol Mikkelson offers a nice example of how one text, in this case *Into the Woods*, often conveys underlying arguments regarding how we ought to believe or behave. Her analysis reveals arguments being made from narrative, dramatistic, neo-Marxist, and feminist perspectives. Notice that Carol begins by piquing the reader's curiosity about what fairy tales "teach" us. She then offers a rationale for examining the musical she selected for analysis. These are important introductory elements in any popular culture criticism.

As you read, consider what Carol offers as (1) the moral of the story from a narrative perspective, (2) justification for breaking society's rules for living from a dramatistic perspective, (3) a rationale for who ought to be empowered and why from a neo-Marxist perspective, and (4) the appropriate roles and rules for men and women from a feminist perspective. Based on the evidence she draws from the text to support her arguments, do you agree or disagree and why?

Into the Woods

Carol Mikkelson

Fairy tales become a part of life's "education" beginning at a very young age. People are exposed to fairy tales in almost every culture. In addition to "Cinderella," some version of which can be found in many cultures, are "Goldilocks and the Three Bears," "Little Red Riding Hood," "Sleeping Beauty," "Jack and the Beanstalk," and "Snow White," which are probably among the most common. These stories provide entertainment for children and parents alike as the stories are told, embellished, and retold. Indeed, Bruno Bettelheim (1976), author of *Uses of Enchantment*, explains that the experience of literature through the use of fairy tales is important in enriching a child's cultural heritage (p. 4).

(Continued)

(Continued)

Many of these stories have found their way onto the stage in the form of ballet, opera, and musical theatre. In the process, lessons are being taught and learned by both children and adults. Western society, especially, has a fascination with the "happily-ever-after" ending and is often disappointed when modern stories don't come to such a resolution. Because traditional male/female roles are reinforced in those fairy tales, they have become recognizable symbols of expected and approved behavior for the idealized man and woman or prince and princess. The female is portrayed as the beauty, and anything beautiful surely cannot be bad. To be beautiful and well-dressed must certainly mean life is good. By contrast, anything or anyone that is ugly must therefore be evil or at least bad and therefore should and sometimes must be destroyed. Beauty is good and ugly is evil. In addition, the male is always "in charge," and the female is always subservient to the male. She may "allow" him to be victorious but never lets him know it. It is only relatively recently that these traditional roles have begun to change. Modern versions of these tales "tweak" the stories just a bit, but many of the old characteristics remain.

Stephen Sondheim and James Lapine have written an immensely popular newer musical version of four such fairy tales, three of which are familiar to most Americans. *Into the Woods* opened on Broadway in 1987 to critical acclaim and lasting appeal to popular culture (Artsedge, 2002). To justify such a statement, it is important to step back and analyze this work from the perspective of four rhetorical theories: narrative, dramatistic, Marxist, and feminist. It is these "lenses" that will sharpen the focus of the critical viewer. Before those views are explored as they pertain to this work, however, it is important to elucidate the background of the authors and the work itself.

Stephen Sondheim has been a writer/composer of merit since he began working in the theatre in 1957 with *West Side Story*. His success continued with such shows as *Gypsy* (1959), *A Funny Thing Happened on the Way to the Forum* (1962), and *Company* (1970) (Anonymous, 2002). He worked for many years with the famous Hal Prince and then began working with James Lapine on *Sunday in the Park With George* (1984), for which they received a Pulitzer Prize in 1984 (Sondheim, cover). Numerous other shows complete his continuing list of credits. "Stephen Sondheim's work can be taken as a metaphor for something bigger than musical theatre" (Artsedge, 2002). In an interview with Edwin H. Newman, Sondheim himself does not claim he set out to educate his audiences with this musical, although he does say, "All art is a form of education." It is this "metaphor," however, that becomes apparent in *Into the Woods*.

Although Sondheim contests the assertion by drama critics of his frequent use of metaphor in his texts, there can be no doubt of his use of metaphor in *Into the Woods*. The woods actually become the metaphor for the age-old quest for knowledge and experience. As drama critic Ash DeLorenzo (1988) insists, "Those who expect just one message from Sondheim are expecting too little" (p. 112). Indeed, the text portrays the three stages of pubescence to adolescence in the characters from Red Riding Hood to Jack and then to Cinderella, who gain their knowledge by going "into the woods." Red Riding Hood begins the trek in Act I when she sings:

Into the woods,

It's time to go,

I hate to leave,

I have to, though.

[And]

Into the woods,

And who can tell,

What's waiting on the journey?

(Sondheim & Lapine, 1987, p. 9)

Drama critic Gerald Weales (1988) explains the show as a "standard maturation play in which preoccupation with self gives way to sharing" (p. 19). Life's experiences are often daunting at best, and it is within the woods, where knowledge and those experiences are found, that so many of the darker moments of the text occur.

The story of this musical revolves around four fairy tales that are interwoven: "Cinderella," "Jack and the Beanstalk, "Little Red Riding Hood," and "The Baker and His Wife," which also includes a bit of "Rapunzel" and her mother, the Witch. Typical of Sondheim, the presentation is much like an operetta in that most lines are sung and few are spoken. The stories, which initially are overlapped in the telling, soon become blended into each other, using slapstick humor and witty lyrics to frequently poke fun at society. The music often has odd syncopations and is frequently in varying styles such as "rap." Actually, the rap allows for greater portions of exposition to be shared with the audience, which wouldn't have the patience to listen to it had it been spoken. A prime, although shortened, example can be found in Act I when the Witch explains:

He said, "All right,"

But it wasn't, quite,

'Cause I caught him in the autumn

In my garden one night!

(Sondheim & Lapine, 1987, p. 12)

Act I concludes the way most audience members expect the stories to end: "and happy ever after" (p. 78)! Act II, however, is another story that brings upheaval. Having it all, it turns out, isn't so easy or so much fun. Because it is much darker, we move out of the arena of "light" children's theatre and into that "metaphor" for which Sondheim is known. In this case, it is the woods where some of the characters' wishes are fulfilled.

It would seem that every character has all one could wish for, but such is not the case. Each one wishes for something more. What they wanted so badly in Act I isn't quite what they expected. Then, a new character the audience doesn't actually see, the Giant's Wife, makes her presence known. In her process of looking for Jack, who had stolen from her and caused the death of her husband, she destroys homes, gardens, etc., and more people die: Jack's mother, the Baker's Wife, the narrator, Red Riding Hood's Granny, Rapunzel, and the giant herself. All of a sudden, life drastically changes, and people must work together. Now sadder and wiser, the Witch directly admonishes the audience to be

Careful the things you say,

Children will listen.

Careful the things you do,

Children will see.

And learn. (Sondheim & Lapine, 1987, p. 136)

The characters plan to live and work together one day at a time, being careful, and not necessarily "happily ever after" because life really isn't

(Continued)

(Continued)

like that. The argument of this paper is that it is Act II that speaks more to popular culture and makes the musical itself interventionist to a society willing to listen.

In 1988, *Into the Woods* received nine Tony Award nominations resulting in three awards and a Grammy Award for Original Cast Album (Sondheim, cover). It was also "named best musical by both the Drama Desk and the New York Drama Critics Circle" (Artsedge, 2002). It is interesting to note that two of the Tony awards were for Best Book and Best Score, which are the subjects for this discussion (Sondheim, cover). The show continues to be presented by community and high school theatre groups throughout the country. Although its message is not one of total escapism, its appeal to popular culture continues nonetheless. This musical, this text, is already enjoyable, but for a critical viewer, it becomes even more so. The music itself is "catchy," but it is the award-winning book that provides the foundation for the following analysis.

Because so much of this text has characteristics of the four criticisms already previewed, any thorough analysis of *Into the Woods* needs to contain elements of each. It is important to begin with the narrative criticism to establish the genre of this text. In *Rhetoric in Popular Culture,* Brummett (1994) states: "The characteristics of stories and dramas underlie all symbolic behavior. All texts of popular culture can be viewed in this way, by placing them within a genre" (p. 132). The genre of this text is a dramatic story that contains a moral: Be careful what you wish for. Beginning with the music in the Prologue, each character "wishes" for many things. Cinderella wishes to go to the festival, Jack wishes his cow would give milk, the Baker and his wife wish they had a child, and Jack's

mother wishes for a lot of things (Sondheim, p. 4). Those don't seem to be too much to ask for. We almost expect life to turn out like those fairy tales.

We often "wish" our life was like a fairy tale: "If only. . ." Act I ends predictably, but it is Act II that supports the moral as valid. No one is happy. Cinderella has married the Prince, Jack and his mother are rich, the Baker and his wife have a child, and the Witch is beautiful once again, but no one is happy. Each one wants more. By the end of the act, when seven lives have been lost, each of the characters has reassessed his or her life.

It is the darker side of Act II that has dissatisfied some critics, but Sondheim dismisses "criticisms of the second act, maintaining that audiences do not like to be surprised when watching musicals" (Artsedge, 2002). Although such a statement may be considered as harsh, it could also be argued that audiences do not like to think when attending musical theatre. Indeed, the first act fulfills all expectations of the genre, but the second act tends to catch the audience off guard. Remember society's preference for the "happily ever after" ending. The second act and its ending actually hold up a mirror through which we may see ourselves, painful though it may be.

Secondly, this text can be viewed from a Marxist perspective simply because of all the allusions to happiness being equated with economic status, which, as a result, play right into the standards of capitalism. "Marxism is an approach that is concerned with ideology, with class, and with the distribution of power in society" (Brummett, 1994, p. 111). It is that economic base that guides a culture. While Act I of *Into the Woods* begins as a prime example of the subtle lessons taught and reinforced in fairy tales, namely, that beauty, wealth, and position equal happiness, it is Act II that provides the true message: "Things" gained through conquest may not be what is best. The text appears to begin with a blatant preferred message reinforcing the desire for beauty, youth, and wealth; however, by Act II, the message becomes oppositional, subverted as the audience is told point blank: "Careful what you wish for" (Sondheim, p. 136).

From Cinderella's first line in Act I, "I wish . . ." to the very last line of Act II, also "I wish," the audience sees and hears each character continually fixated on wanting more. These drives follow the characters as they do in most fairy tales and are presented in obvious economic metaphors: Cinderella needs to be married to the handsome, wealthy Prince to be happy, Jack and his mother need gold to be happy, the Witch needs youth and beauty to be happy, the Princes need beautiful, desirable women to be happy, Red Riding Hood needs to satisfy her appetite to be happy. The implication is that those with beauty, youth, and wealth are logically the ones who are empowered, and everyone should strive to be just like them. Those who are disempowered, like Cinderella and Jack and his mother, seek the empowerment that wealth will guarantee. Act I shows the gullible in the audience that "things" enable one to live happily ever after, but Act II slaps reality back into place.

Almost immediately in Act II, the characters are shown to be "wishing" for more or different things. The "things" or "positions" sure to give each one the kind of power they had wanted so desperately now don't quite "cut it." Cinderella is bored and wishes to sponsor a festival. The Baker's Wife wishes they had more room. Prince Charming, also bored, "dallies" with a variety of ladies, including the Baker's Wife, who is deluded by thinking he is worth it. Add a giant to the scene and life becomes a struggle, but it is exciting once again. By the end of the show, seven characters die and the Marxist lesson slaps the remaining characters in the face: Be careful what you wish for; you may get it.

Although it might appear to be a stretch, there is also validity in examining this text in terms of dramatistic criticism. Burke explains that, when people try to explain their reasons for their actions, they often do so by basing them on what he calls a "Pentad" of five terms: act, agent, agency, scene, and purpose. The audience of *Into the Woods* is presented with such justifications by the characters as they try to rationalize why so many people are dying. Whose "fault" is it? The act is plural because several people have been killed, although not all by the Giant's Wife. The primary agent is the Giant's Wife; the agency is her strength, the scene is the woods, and the purpose is to avenge her husband's death. She exhibits no guilt, but the characters do as they blame each other for being the reason that the giant is killing so many. They each attempt to resolve their guilt through victimage by pointing the finger of blame at everyone but themselves. Because the use of victimage has become so commonplace in today's popular culture, the tendency might be to dismiss this text as merely adding to the list; however, it is the Witch, oddly enough, who sets everyone straight. She shows them that none of them is blameless:

Told a little lie,

Stole a little gold,

Broke a little vow,

Did you?

(Continued)

(Continued)

Had to get your Prince,

Had to get your cow,

Have to get your wish,

Doesn't matter how—

Anyway, it doesn't matter now (script, p. 120) [And]

No, of course what really matters

Is the blame,

Someone you can blame (Sondheim & Lapine, 1987, p. 12)

The audience members should feel some discomfort if they see a tendency in themselves to behave similarly and transfer any of this chiding to themselves, but they probably won't. Remember, it is the tendency of modern society to use victimage when resolving guilt and blame others.

Finally, *Into the Woods* can be viewed from a feminist perspective. Examining the text from a feminist perspective allows one to understand what are "appropriate" and "inappropriate" roles and rules for women and men. As long as fairy tales have been told, male and female roles have been stereotypically fixed, and children have been raised accordingly. Girls are emotional; they cry and are sweet but are weak and need a male to help them. Males, on the other hand, are not to be emotional and should never cry but always be strong and able to solve whatever difficulty manifests itself. Such characteristics place unfair expectations on both genders in that the lines are so definite. Thankfully, present society now more often encourages females to be strong and males to show emotion but not too much for either one, of course. The characters in this text attempt to fit the new, more liberal view of present-day society; however, traces of the traditional masculine hegemony still shine through.

In Act I, the male/female roles exhibit traditional fairy tale characteristics. Cinderella is on her hands and knees in the kitchen, wishing to "go to the festival" to meet Prince Charming, of course. Rapunzel is stranded in her tower, waiting for someone to rescue her. The Baker's Wife assists her husband in their business but wishes for a child. Even the Witch needs help to become young and beautiful again, but when she does, her magical powers vanish. These women are allowed to show strength but only so much. Each "pulls back" in the face of preexisting male dominance, even though each male is weaker by comparison. Only Red Riding Hood becomes a stronger female, but her strength, by implication, is seen as a negative because she is "too strong." After all, she wears the skin of the wolf and carries a knife. Logic might dictate that, if the female characters are presented traditionally, with only modest enhancement, such would be true for the males, but such is not the case.

Although most of the principal male characters are attractive to the eye, each one displays a weakness. Poor Jack is dull witted and has his "head in a sack," according to his mother (Sondheim, p. 15). True, he is tall and strong, but he has a really light grasp of reality. Because they display almost identical characteristics, the Princes can be characterized together. Each is tall, handsome, and physically fit; however, that is where their "perfection" ends. Also not very bright, each one is incredibly egotistical and only lives for the moment without concern for anyone but himself. As Cinderella's Prince says, "I was raised to be charming, not sincere" (p. 127). The Baker is not very brave, but tries to be by asserting himself. By the end of the musical, he is the only male character who realizes his weaknesses and his wife's strengths, although this happens primarily after her death. Most fairy tales show the male as strong, handsome, fearless, and victorious. The authors of this text have attempted to reflect the change in society's attitude toward the hierarchy of traditional gender roles, yet they have merely reinforced it.

The females are allowed to show strength but not too much. The males fit the traditional fairy tale image of their characters; although they all display obvious weakness, they still maintain a position of power. The females continue to be seen as subservient to the males. In the end, the truly strong females who are still alive, the Witch and Red Riding Hood, are not "rewarded" with some kind of relationship. It is worth noting that other strong, independent females, like the Baker's Wife, the Giant's Wife, Jack's mother, and Granny, are dead. Perhaps their strength was too much for them? It is doubtful that Sondheim or Lapine intended such debate.

Why, then, should anyone debate this text? What does any of this matter? Because this text is a reflection of popular culture, it matters. Brummett (1994) defines popular culture as "systems or artifacts that most people share and that most people know about" (p. 21). Of course, this text isn't widely known by American culture, but the fairy tales are, and the new twist of their presentation reflects this popular culture, thus becoming of interest. Because of their upbringing, which often involves the telling of fairy tales, Americans generally love stories and enjoy seeing and hearing the old ones retold. Act I, therefore, satisfies that desire. The audience usually laughs at the clever lyrics and can spot the obvious lessons in the moral of the story. Truth be told, there are usually some serious lessons taught in fairy tales, even if it is in reference to what not to do: Stay out of other people's homes. Don't take what doesn't belong to you. Don't be greedy. Don't trust strangers. Don't try to be something you are not. Be careful what you wish for. These kinds of lessons are not hard to find, and audiences don't mind using them indexically as a base for lessons to the young.

When the authors throw in something else, however, the audience becomes impatient, even dissatisfied. Audiences want fairy tales to be happy and end happily ever after. Anything else is regarded as too "grown up" and more within the realm of adults, not children, who are to be protected. At a certain age, however, children need more than the seemingly light "fluff" of fairy tales. Michiko Kakutani, Sondheim biographer, explains that Sondheim and Lapine have created "a vehicle by which to examine some of their own preoccupations: the hold of time past over time present, the responsibilities of adulthood, the necessity of forming connections, the tensions between individual and community" (1988). Children need to know that life isn't a fairy tale. A text such as *Into the Woods* may therefore challenge parents to do some deeper explaining to children.

(Continued)

(Continued)

Some parents can handle those deeper lessons, but many can't. Consider the ethics of some of the characters; a few are not very admirable. Jack steals from the Giant. Red Riding Hood and her Granny kill the Wolf. Cinderella misrepresents herself as a Princess. Cinderella's Prince "fools around." The Baker's Father abandons his family. The Baker's Wife "fools around" with Cinderella's Prince. The Witch keeps Rapunzel in a tower and falsely tells her she is her mother. If a person stops to think about it, these are some pretty disreputable people. Of course, each has a plausible excuse. Yet these particular fairy tales are among the favorites of audiences. With giants and spells, are the stories realistic? No. Even children know these are only stories, but these stories continue to be a part of popular culture in the telling and retelling of them through the ages. If they are so popular and so accepted, can this particular text, especially Act II, be interventionist and serve as a learning tool for audiences? Perhaps, but only if audiences are alert and attentive to the messages.

"Be careful what you wish for" is the most obvious message, but consider the ethics of the characters. Then, consider the excuses each makes for his or her part in all the deaths. Notice who has power and who doesn't. Finally, examine how males and females are portrayed. Maybe this text is more realistic than first thought. With all these aspects to contemplate, the message becomes darker and heavier, and the alert audience member squirms. Unfortunately, the majority of audience members aren't going to notice all these angles. Only an analysis such as this paper can then be interventionist.

Now this paper isn't going to have more than extremely limited readership. The only way audiences are going to sit up and take notice of the broader implications is by telling them personally. Will it make a difference? Slowly but surely, like the tortoise and the hare. Fairy tales will continue to be told, acted out, sung about, written about, and illustrated in books. Children of all ages will delight in their part of all of it. It is to be hoped, however, that each popular culture of the age will tweak those stories just a bit to make audiences more aware of the broader implications of each.

References

Anonymous. (2002). *Stephen Sondheim: A biography.* Retrieved May 24, 2004, from http://www .nodanw.com/biographies/sondheim.htm

Artsedge. (2002). *Celebrating Sondheim.* Retrieved May 24, 2004, from http://www.artsedge.kennedy center.org/exploring/mt/sondheim/works/intothewoods.html

Bettelheim, B. (1976). *Uses of enchantment: The meaning and importance of fairy tales.* New York: Alfred A. Knopf.

Brummett, B. (1994). *Rhetoric in popular culture.* New York: St. Martin's Press.

DeLorenzo, A. (1988, February). Dark and deep: Sondheim's witty fairy tale about trying to have it all. *Vogue, 178,* 112, & 116.

Kakutani, M. (1988). *Theatre; beyond happily ever after.* Retrieved May 24, 2004, from http://vvww.sjsondheim.com/sondheim-happily.html

Sondheim, S., & Lapine, J. (1987). *Into the woods.* New York: Theatre Communications Group.

Sondheim, S., & Lapine, J. (1988). A conversation with Edwin H. Newman. Public television video of *Into the Woods.*

Weales, G. (1988, January 15). Stage tales and dragons: *Into the Woods* and *Nixon in China. Commonweal,* 18–19.

Summary

In this chapter, we defined popular culture, discussed why popular culture is important to study, and described very briefly how one goes about doing so. Popular culture is pervasive, and its arguments about how we ought to and ought not to believe and behave are often covert. By learning to examine these underlying messages embedded beneath the surface, we can become educated consumers with the ability to choose whether or not to agree with them. Moreover, as we learn to see these underlying messages, we can begin to educate others to understand them as well. Ultimately, we can manage the persuasive impact of such messages because we will no longer be unaware consumers of them.

Challenge

Now that you have a sense of what popular culture texts are and how they communicate, I challenge you to apply what you have learned to a TV program or commercial. Because it is often easier for beginning critics to see the underlying messages in texts from earlier decades, I encourage you to select an episode from a 1950s, 1960s, or 1970s TV sitcom (e.g., *Leave It to Beaver*, *I Love Lucy*, *That Girl*, *The Mary Tyler Moore Show*, *The Brady Bunch*, *Gilligan's Island*). Then answer the following questions:

If a speech is delivered during the program, what is it communicating via a neo-Aristotelian perspective? Be sure to consider context and audience expectations as well as the five classical canons of rhetoric. What implications might such a message have on viewers?

What is the program communicating via a narrative perspective? Be sure to provide some examples as good reasons to support the moral you identify. What implications might such a message have on viewers?

What is the program communicating via a dramatistic perspective? Be sure to identify what rule for living is being broken and then what is offered to justify breaking it. What implications might such a message have on viewers?

What is the program communicating via an SCT perspective? Be sure to identify evidence from the plotline, characters, scenes, and rationales for behavior to support the shared reality communicated in it. What implications might the message have on viewers?

What is the program communicating via a neo-Marxist perspective? Be sure to identify the people who are portrayed as being empowered and disempowered and why. What things happen to reinforce that such empowerment and disempowerment is "normal" or "how it ought to be?" What implications might such a message have on viewers?

What is the program communicating via a feminist perspective? What are identified as "appropriate" and "inappropriate," "desirable" and "undesirable," "normal" and "abnormal" roles and rules for men and women? What implications might such a message have on viewers?

If music is used, from an illusion of life perspective, are the lyrics and music congruent or incongruent, and how does that affect the message? What implications might such a message have on viewers?

What is the program communicating via a visual pleasure theory perspective? Consider narcissism, fetishism, and voyeurism as you seek to find an answer. What implications might such a message have on viewers?

What is the program communicating via a parasocial relationship theory perspective? Consider how realism and intimacy enhance the message being communicated. What implications might such a message have on viewers?

References

Becker, A. E., Grinspoon, S. K., Klibanski, A., & Herzog, D. B. (1999). Current concepts: Eating disorders. *The New England Journal of Medicine, 340,* 1092–1098.

Brummett, B. (2011). *Rhetoric in popular culture* (3rd ed.). Thousand Oaks, CA: Sage.

Bryan, J., & Zillman, D. (Eds.). (1994). *Media effects: Advances in theory and research*. Hillsdale, NJ: Lawrence Erlbaum.

Byun, S., Ruffini, C., Mills, J. E., Douglas, A. C., Niang, M., Stepchenkova, S., Lee, S. K., . . . Blanton, M. (2009). Internet addiction: Metasynthesis of 1996–2006 quantitative research. *CyberPsychology & Behavior, 12*(2), 203–207. DOI: 10.1089/cpb.2008.0102.

D'Agata, C. (2008, April 3). Nomophobia: Fear of being without your cell phone. *CBS News.* Retrieved March 22, 2013, from http://web.archive.org/web/20080412042610/http://www.wsbt.com/news/health/17263604.html

Etherington, D. (2012, September 12). iOS app store boasts 700K apps, 90% downloaded every month. *TechCrunch*. Retrieved March 22, 2013, from http://techcrunch.com/2012/09/12/ios-app-store-boasts-700k-apps-90-downloaded-every-month/

Gartner, C. P. (2012). Forecast: Media tablets by operating system, worldwide, 2010-2016, 1Q12 update. *Gartner, Inc.* Retrieved March 22, 2013, from https://www.gartner.com/login/loginInitAction.do?method = initialize&resume = /idp/resumeSAML20/idp/SSO.ping&spentity = gartnersp

Gerbner, G., Gross, L., Morgan, M., & Signorielli, N. (1994). Growing up with TV: The cultivation perspective. In J. Bryan & D. Zillman (Eds.). *Media effects: Advances in theory and research* (pp. 17–41). Hillsdale, NJ: Lawrence Erlbaum.

Harrison, K. (2000). The body electric: Thin-ideal media and eating disorders in adolescents. *Journal of Communication, 50,* 119–143.

Horton, D., & Wohl, R. R. (1956). Mass communication and para-social interaction: Observations on intimacy at a distance. *Psychiatry, 19,* 215–229.

Jaslow, R. (2012, January 12). Internet addiction changes brain similar to cocaine: Study. *CBS News.* Retrieved March 22, 2013, from http://www.cbsnews.com/8301-504763_162-57357895-10391704/internet-addiction-changes-brain-similar-to-cocaine-study/

Johannesen, R. (1990). *Ethics in human communication* (3rd ed.). Prospect Heights, IL: Waveland Press.

Kung, V. (2012, March 7). Rise of "nomophobia": More people fear loss of mobile contact. *CNN Cable News Network*. Retrieved on March 22, 2013, from http://www.cnn.com/2012/03/06/tech/mobile/nomophobia-mobile-addiction

Lunden, I. (2012). Analyst: Twitter passed 500M users in June 2012, 140M of them in US; Jakarta "biggest tweeting" city. *TechCrunch*. Retrieved March 22, 2013, from http://techcrunch.com/2012/07/30/analyst-twitter-passed-500m-users-in-june-2012–140m-of-them-in-us-jakarta-biggest-tweeting-city/

Miniwatts Marketing Group. (2012). *Facebook users in the world: Facebook usage and Facebook growth statistics*. Retrieved March 22, 2013, from http://www.internetworldstats.com/facebook.htm

Mulvey, L. (1989). *Visual and other pleasures*. Bloomington, IN: University of Indiana Press.

Nielsen Company. (2013). The Nielsen March 2013 cross-platform report: Free to move between screens. *The Nielsen Company*. Retrieved from http://www.nielsen.com/us/en/reports/2013/the-nielsen-march-2013-cross-platform-report--free-to-move-to-betwe.html

Nilsen, T. (1974). *Ethics of speech communication* (2nd ed.). Indianapolis, IN: Bobbs-Merrill.

Parks Associates. (2012). *Mobile services: Global outlook*. Parks Associates, 1998–2012. Retrieved March 22, 2013, from http://www.parksassociates.com/report/mobile-services—global-outlook

Rubin, A. M., Perse, E. M., & Powell, R. A. (1985). Loneliness, parasocial interaction, and local TV news viewing. *Human Communication Research, 12,* 155–180.

Rubin, A. M., & Perse, E. M. (1987). Audience activity and soap opera involvement: A uses and effects investigation. *Human Communication Research, 14,* 246–268.

SecureEnvoy. (2012, February 16). *66% of the population suffer from nomophobia the fear of being with out their phone*. SecureEnvoy. Retrieved December 23, 2012, from http://www.securenvoy.com/blog/2012/02/16/66-of-the-population-suffer-from-nomophobia-the-fear-of-being-without-their-phone/

Sellnow, D., & Sellnow, T. (2001). The "illusion of life" rhetorical perspective: An integrated approach to the study of music as communication. *Critical Studies in Media Communication, 18,* 395–415.

Thurner, R. (2012, March 29). The latest app download statistics: A breakdown by country of the most popular app download statistics to help make the business case [Web log post]. Retrieved on December 21, 2012, from http://www.smartinsights.com/mobile-marketing/app-marketing/app-download-statistics/

Wallace, K. (1955). An ethical base of communication. *The Speech Teacher, 4,* 1–9.

Student Study Site

Visit the Student Study Site at www.sagepub.com/sellnow2e to read interesting SAGE journal articles, view mobile-friendly key term flashcards, take chapter-specific online web quizzes to test your knowledge, and more!

Chapter 2

Expanding the Rhetorical Tradition

I n Chapter 1, we discussed definitions of *culture, popular culture,* and *popular culture texts,* as well as *mediated popular culture* and *mediated popular culture texts* as they are used in this book. We also explained why popular culture is important and how to examine popular culture texts through a process of describing, interpreting, and evaluating. This chapter focuses on rhetoric and its evolution over the years. We begin with a discussion of the nature and definitions of rhetoric and rhetorical criticism. We then explore the roots of the rhetorical tradition, as well as how and why rhetoric evolved to include popular culture texts as rhetorical texts. Finally, we describe the first rhetorical criticism method created to distinguish the analysis of speeches from literary criticism and offer sample essays using this neo-Aristotelian approach.

THE NATURE OF RHETORIC AND RHETORICAL CRITICISM

Many of the most common uses of the word *rhetoric* have negative connotations. Sometimes, for example, speeches by politicians are criticized as being "nothing but a bunch of rhetoric," inferring that they (1) lack any meaningful substance, (2) are filled with lies offered merely to placate the public, or (3) use metaphors and figures of speech as a means by which to avoid addressing the issues. These uses of the word *rhetoric* are not what we are talking about in this book. Rather, as defined in Chapter 1, rhetoric has to do with the ways in which signs influence people. That is, rhetoric is persuasive communication. This definition represents an historical evolution of our understanding of the nature of communication in general and persuasion in particular. In other words, what counts as rhetoric (i.e., persuasive communication) is much broader than was once the case. Let's look now at each of the elements of rhetoric in more detail.

APPLYING WHAT YOU'VE LEARNED . . .

Identify a time when you dismissed a speech by a public official as "meaningless rhetoric." What did he or she say or do that lead you to that conclusion?

First, rhetoric is accomplished through signs. As defined in Chapter 1, a *sign* in rhetorical terms is something that makes you think of something else. More specifically, because every sight, sound, touch, taste, and smell has the potential to prompt us to think about something else, everything has the potential to be a sign. This distinction is important because some of the earlier definitions of rhetoric were limited only to words. Scholars would study, for example, the transcripts of speeches and how words were used to influence audiences. The contemporary definition of rhetoric we use in this book certainly acknowledges the persuasive potential of words but not at the exclusion of others kinds of signs.

Signs can influence us in a number of ways. Sometimes we think of something else because the sign resembles something else. For example, when actors play the role of a real person—as Morgan Freeman did in portraying Nelson Mandela in the film *Invictus,* as Meryl Streep did in portraying Julia Child in *Julie and Julia* and Margaret Thatcher in *Iron Lady,* and as Daniel Day-Lewis did in portraying Abraham Lincoln and Sally Field in portraying Mary Todd Lincoln in *Lincoln*—their success or failure rests with their ability to resemble the person in as many ways as possible. Likewise, the success or failure of comic strips such as *Dilbert* or *Dennis the Menace* often rests on the characters' resembling our perceptions of real-life coworkers, employers, kids, parents, and neighbors. In these cases, we say the sign functions iconically. In other words, it functions as an icon, which is a symbol of the thing (in this case, the person) it represents.

QUESTIONING YOUR ETHICS . . .

Sometimes celebrities achieve success because they make themselves look like or act like someone else. Consider, for example, Elvis impersonators or Madonna, who got her start by resembling Marilyn Monroe. Do you think this strategy is ethical? Why or why not?

Sometimes a sign leads us to think of something else because we associate the sign with another thing. For example, some people have a difficult time thinking of Madonna as a mother and an author of children's books because they associate her so strongly with a sexual pop diva. Conversely, some argue that actor Anthony Perkins had a difficult time securing movie roles after starring in *Psycho* because he was so believable as psycho killer Norman Bates that viewers could not disassociate him from that character. Some argue that Sylvester Stallone (Rocky) suffered a similar plight. Interestingly, upon learning that I lived in Fargo, many people often associated me with the stereotypes portrayed in the film *Fargo*. They expected my sentences to be filled with "yeah sure" and "ya betcha," and sometimes even asked me what it was like to live on a "tundra." In fact, the concierge at a hotel where I stayed in Paris even asked me if I had seen "the film by the brothers Coen" after seeing my home address on my driver's license. In these cases, we say the sign functions indexically, that is, associated with something else.

APPLYING WHAT YOU'VE LEARNED . . .

Identify a popular musician you know who has either successfully or unsuccessfully crossed over from one genre to another. What role do you think his or her indexical association played in the result?

Sometimes a sign leads members of an identifiable group to think of something else merely by conventional agreement. Signs that function in this way operate symbolically. In other words, a group comes to mutually agree on the meaning of the sign by custom or habit. Slang often functions in this way. Consider the word *wicked*, which dictionaries define as evil and mean but that can mean quite the opposite in some cultural groups (Rader, 2007–2013). Computer and Internet jargon are also examples of signs that function symbolically. Their meaning is often arrived at by conventional agreement among users. Many product brands function symbolically using visual images or musical sounds (e.g., visuals such as Nike's swoosh and Apple's apple and musical jingles such as McDonald's and Coca-Cola's). Colors can also operate symbolically when meaning is attached to them arbitrarily by conventional agreement among group members (e.g., blue is for boys, and pink is for girls). Interestingly, the way in which signs function symbolically often results in miscommunication across cultures as such definitions typically do not always translate. This is particularly true with nonverbal body language (e.g., gestures, eye contact). For example, the hand symbol used in the United States for "OK" has an obscene sexual meaning in some European countries, means "worthless" in France, is a symbol for money in Japan, and stands for "I'll kill you" in Tunisia (Axtell, 1998).

So, signs can make us think of something else iconically, indexically, or symbolically. When they do so, they have the potential to influence us to believe and behave in certain ways. Recall from Chapter 1 that, when we study rhetoric—in this case, popular culture texts as rhetoric—we are concerned with signs that function as artifacts (i.e., a sign or series of signs that is socially grounded). In other words, the meaning of signs as artifacts is widely shared by some identifiable cultural group. Hence, an artifact worthy of rhetorical analysis is one that offers many signs contributing to a unified message or argument about the way things ought to or ought not to be. For example, although the song "Can't Help Falling in Love" by Elvis Presley functions as a sign for me personally because I associate it with my wedding day, it doesn't function as an artifact in this way. It might function as an artifact (with a meaning that is shared by an identifiable group), however, in terms of its message of believing in unrequited love or soul mates. In this way, the song as an artifact could serve as a popular culture text worthy of rhetorical analysis.

Second, rhetoric implies attitude or behavior change. In other words, we must do something with the signs we encounter. What we do might be mental (i.e., reinforcing or altering an attitude, belief, or value) or physical (i.e., continuing to behave in a certain way or changing behavior). In other words, we ask, what do the signs mean, and how does that meaning influence my ideology about "the way things are" or "the way things ought to be." For example, a biology professor recently told me that students are "learning" more about DNA from television programs like *CSI* than in her classroom lectures, regardless of whether the information on *CSI* is, in fact, accurate. For her students, the signs in the mediated popular culture text (*CSI*) are communicating as artifacts to influence them what to believe about DNA. Reality TV programs like *Jersey Shore*, *Little People*, and *Big World*, which are presented as unscripted stories of ordinary people going about their daily lives, are another example of mediated popular culture texts offering an ideology about "the way things are." When it debuted in 2006, the academy-award winning documentary *An Inconvenient Truth* attempted to influence viewers about "the way things are" with regard to global warming. The message it conveyed spurred a great deal controversy at the time, but today, it is credited by many for raising international awareness about global warming and is actually shown in many school science classes. Multiple award-winning American singer–songwriter, Taylor Swift's autobiographically based songs attempt to influence listeners about "the way things are and ought to be" regarding relationships. And makeover programs like *What Not to Wear* and *The Biggest Loser* attempt to influence viewers about "the way things both ought to and can be" regarding self-image.

The goal of this book is to provide you with tools you need to examine the signs offered as artifacts in popular culture texts that might influence your ideology about "the way things are" or "the way things ought to be." This analytical process is referred to as *rhetorical criticism*. Note that rhetorical criticism is not merely the process of pointing out all the flaws in a popular culture text, which we might assume if we think of the common use of the word *criticism*. Rather, rhetorical criticism is the systematic analysis of an argument about "what things are" or "the way things ought to be" conveyed in a text through signs as artifacts. Recall that our focus in this book is on mediated popular culture texts (i.e., a subset of the broad range of popular culture texts limited to media such as movies, music, television programs, etc.). Hence, we are concerned with how mediated popular culture texts function rhetorically. To do so, we must draw on what is known about rhetorical criticism and its roots in the rhetorical tradition.

EVOLUTION OF THE RHETORICAL TRADITION

Rhetoric has a long and rich history throughout the world (Sloane, 2001). The roots of rhetoric in Western civilizations (including the United States) can be traced to the fifth century B.C.E. in the ancient city–states of Greece. Thus, we begin our historical accounting there.

Classical Period

The classical period, also known as the Golden Age, began in the fifth century B.C.E. and lasted until the Middle Ages (Sloane, 2001). The bulk of rhetorical study and practice took place in Greece and Rome, and Athens was the focal point for advancing democracy and liberal arts through rhetoric. The earliest philosophers defined rhetoric as *peithō technē logōn*, which means the art of persuasive speaking (p. 94).

This emphasis on public speaking (a.k.a. oratory, public address) arose from a felt need for effective civic engagement. To clarify, because Greece was a practicing democracy, citizens needed to engage in self-governance for it to persist and flourish. Self-governance decision making was limited, however, to free, adult, native-born, property-owning males. These male citizens were required to participate in public forums in order to conduct business, debate issues, make public decisions, as well as gain and maintain power. Doing so required them to address large groups of people at once. Because written discourse could not be mass-produced and distributed (the printing press had not yet been invented), the means by which to exchange such information was through public speeches. Hence, competent public speaking skills were crucial for both individuals and the government to survive and thrive (Golden, Berquist, Coleman, & Sproule, 2011).

Because public speaking skills were in high demand, a market for public speaking teachers arose. A group of professional public speaking experts known as Sophists emerged to meet the demand. Sophists would travel from place to place and teach public speaking skills to wealthy Greek men for a fee. Teaching public speaking skills to citizens so they could engage effectively in public forums was a laudable goal and, quite frankly, continues to be a primary reason for including public speaking courses in general education programs today. However, many classical rhetoricians of the day agreed with Plato, who took issue with what the Sophists were doing.

Plato articulated reasons for rebuking the Sophists in his two seminal works, *Gorgias* and *Phaedrus*. First, he argued that the Sophists claimed to be experts but were not. Second, and somewhat more disconcerting, he contended that what the Sophists actually taught was to persuade regardless of the subject matter topic, the truth of their claims, the substance of their content, or the logic of their reasoning. In other words, Plato claimed they taught structure and delivery techniques without attention to substance. Frankly, some argue that many public speaking teachers today continue to practice such sophistry. For Plato, however, to do so was to deceive the public and would ultimately lead to flawed decision making and destructive consequences. Plato and his colleagues believed orators were morally obligated to "know the truth and understand logical reasoning and human psychology" and then to lead people to understand the truth through public speeches (Sloane, 2001, p. 98). Because Sophists did not educate themselves first about the subject matter and use that as the rationale for engaging in public speaking, Plato argued they were teaching people to manipulate others through "flattery and deceit" (p. 98).

Plato offered a thorough critique of sophistry and its flaws; however, his student Aristotle actually provided the grounding for rhetoric that still guides our understanding of public speaking today. In his famous treatise, *Rhetoric* (trans. 1954), he defines *rhetoric* as the power of "observing in any given case [on almost any subject] the available means of persuasion," that is, examining the ways in which texts (i.e., public speeches) influence people (Solmsen, 1954, p. 24). In Books 1 and 2, he explains how effective speakers develop content, which was later termed *invention*. He describes the means of developing persuasive content as nonartistic proofs (support appeals not invented by the speaker) and artistic proofs (rhetorical appeals invented by the speaker). The three forms of artistic proofs are ethos (perceived speaker credibility and character), pathos (emotions stirred in the audience by the speaker), and logos (logical arguments based on evidence and reasoning).

Much later (during the first century B.C.E.), a great Roman orator, philosopher, and politician named Cicero and his contemporary Quintilian extended Aristotle's teachings on rhetoric to develop a theory of speaking based on five canons (or rules). Some of the most significant works include *De Inventione (On Invention), Rhetorica ad Herennium (On the Theory of Public Speaking)* and *Institutio oratoria (The Education of the Orator)*. These rhetorical canons, which will be described in detail later, are invention (audience-centered goal, content, and argument development), arrangement (organizational structure), style (language choice, sentence composition, tropes, and figures), memory (mnemonic devices), and delivery (controlled use of voice and body).

These principles first articulated by Plato and Aristotle, which were then developed further by Cicero, Quintilian, and other Roman orators, still inform public speaking today. Many centuries have passed between then and now, so it seems prudent to provide at least a snapshot chronology of contributions made to the rhetorical tradition along the way.

Middle Ages

The major contributions to rhetorical study during the Middle Ages focused on three new genres: poetics, letter writing, and preaching (Sloane, 2001, pp. 474–478). Poetics focused intentionally on elements of written discourse. We can thank rhetoricians like Horace (*Ars poetica*) for conceptualizing features of literary style and decorum, using existing literary sources as support material, and legitimizing translation as an element of invention. We can also thank Middle Age rhetoricians for creating a standardized format for composing a five-part letter (i.e., salutation, establishing good will, narration, petition, and conclusion). And we can thank preachers like Saint Augustine for his treatise *De doctrina christiana*, which is considered to be the first Christian rhetoric text. Because a primary goal of Christian rhetoric was to interpret the Bible for parishioners, Augustine reorganized the canons into two parts: the "means of discovery" (invention) including signs and symbols beyond language and the "means of setting forth that which is understood" (arrangement, style, delivery) (p. 472). This goal to interpret and inform marks an important digression from the classical rhetoricians who claimed the goal of rhetoric was to persuade.

Renaissance

We have Humanists of the Renaissance to thank for their contributions to our understanding of audience analysis and adaptation. These Humanists were not only outstanding and devoted scholars of classical rhetoric but also practical-minded men. As practical-minded men, they believed scholarship was most valuable when it could be shared with many people. So they made it their goal to disseminate academic scholarship to a wider public (Sloane, 2001, p. 680). Thus, they would tailor a treatise for different audiences by writing and publishing it in several different forms (e.g., a textbook, an academic essay, an annotated folio, and various vernacular translations). Today, audience analysis and adaptation remains a central component of effective rhetoric.

18th and 19th Century

The 18th century is often referred to as the Age of Reason or the Age of Enlightenment. This was an era of cultural reformation on many fronts. For example, people challenged traditions, religious doctrines, and political practices. Both the French and American Revolutions serve as cases in point. Immanuel Kant (1784) described enlightenment as freedom to use one's own intelligence to interpret the world and to make decisions. Consequently, rhetoric in the 18th and 19th centuries was transformed in ways that accounted for individual freedom to think and speak for oneself based on logic, reasoning, and scientific discovery.

Enlightenment and reformation for rhetoricians took the form of reestablishing and building on concepts of logic and reasoning as fundamental, the emergence of female voices, and formalizing the processes of constructive rhetorical criticism. For example, Richard Whately (1855) expanded rhetorical logos to include the notions of presumption and burden of proof. To clarify, every argument has two sides. The position that reinforces the status quo enjoys the position of presumption, meaning its position is presumed to be correct until proven incorrect. The burden of proof (i.e., to prove the status quo position to be false) to design and deliver a compelling argument rests with the opposing position.

Enlightenment and reformation also marked a turning point for women who were beginning to demand a place in the public sphere for their voices to be heard. One of the most noted is Mary Wollstonecraft (1787, 1790, 1792), a schoolteacher who wrote essays about self-improvement and female empowerment as well as an elocutionary textbook on the art of public speaking. Her philosophies served as the foundation for 19th-century women's suffragists like Susan B. Anthony and Elizabeth Cady Stanton to ultimately lead the movement championing equal rights for women, including women's right to vote in the United States.

And reformation brought with it more refined thinking and development of sophisticated processes for systematically critiquing rhetoric, which today we refer to as *rhetorical criticism*. George Campbell (1776) and his colleagues, for example, were keenly interested in understanding how people think and began to realize that people may be influenced by things other than formal essays and speeches (i.e., perhaps even by everyday objects, actions, and events that may include words as well as other signs and symbols). Hugh Blair (1783) and his colleagues introduced the idea of aesthetic taste or preference as an important way people communicate, judge the rhetoric of others, and are influenced to believe or behave. In sum, rhetoric was conceived as a rational art with unlimited applications using a variety of symbols. And freethinking humans, they argued, were obligated to thoughtfully critique the rhetorical arguments they perceive in order to make educated decisions about them.

Modern Rhetoric

Modern 20th-century rhetoric emerged from 19th-century developments in linguistics, philosophy, and literary theory. And rhetorical scholars who studied both writing and speaking in U.S. colleges and universities had their "home" in English departments. By 1914, however, speech teachers had become increasingly frustrated about the diminishing status of speech in English departments and actually withdrew from the National Council of Teachers of English to form the National Association of Academic Teachers of Public Speaking, which eventually became the National Communication Association. As a result, research and teaching in rhetoric occurs in both Departments of English and Communication still today (e.g., Palmer, 1965; Thonssen & Baird, 1948).

To distinguish the differences between rhetorical analyses of public speeches from that of the written word, Herbert A. Wichelns (1925) wrote his pivotal treatise titled, "The Literary Criticism of Oratory." In it, he explained that "literary critics unite in the attempt to interpret the permanent value of the works they examine," whereas rhetorical critics of public speeches are "not concerned with permanence, nor yet with beauty," but with the speech's "effect [on] a specific audience" and "the analysis and appreciation of the orator's method of imparting his [sic] ideas to his [sic] hearers" (pp. 208–209).

Thus, the neo-Aristotelian method was created. As originally conceived, the method was intended to examine the effect of a public speech on a specific audience. Three edited volumes of *A History and Criticism of American Public Address* serve as strong evidence for the valuable role this neo-Aristotelian approach played in examining the impact of public speeches on audiences for 30 years (Brigance, 1943; Nichols, 1955). As we discuss later in the chapter, rhetorical critics continue to use the neo-Aristotelian approach to examine speeches; however, its scope extends beyond just public speeches to also include a variety of other texts including mediated popular culture texts.

THE NEO-ARISTOTELIAN APPROACH TO RHETORICAL CRITICISM

As the name implies, the neo-Aristotelian (new-Aristotle) approach draws from the foundations of rhetoric as conceptualized by Aristotle and further developed by Cicero and his contemporaries (as well as from a number of 20th-century rhetoricians). For these reasons, this approach is also sometimes called *neo-classical* or *traditional*. We start with this perspective because it is essentially the first formalized method developed for examining rhetorical criticism of public speeches as distinct from literary criticism of written documents.

This brief summary of how to conduct a neo-Aristotelian rhetorical criticism is based on a more comprehensive explanation provided by Thonssen and Baird (1948) and Thonssen, Baird, and Braden (1970). Essentially, you begin by describing the rhetorical situation, which includes the speaker, occasion, audience, exigence, and constraints (Bitzer, 1968). Second, you interpret the rhetorical text according to the five classical canons: (1) invention, (2) arrangement, (3) style, (4) memory, and (5) delivery. Finally, you evaluate the apparent impact of the message on the audience to whom it was delivered.

Step 1: Describing the Rhetorical Situation

Your goal in describing the rhetorical situation is to ground your analysis in the reasons the speech was given, including by whom and for whom. One way to do so is by formulating and then answering a series of questions addressing each element of the rhetorical situation. Realize as you do, however, that these elements are not necessarily mutually exclusive. Nevertheless, they do provide a starting point for developing your rhetorical criticism.

(1) Who is speaking (literally, as in a public speech; or figuratively, as in a newspaper editorial, song, advertisement, etc.) and what are their credentials for doing so? When answering this question, be sure to address what makes the speaker credible regarding the specific topic, particular audience, and occasion. For example, as U.S. commander and chief, President Barak Obama was both appropriate and credible for the rhetorical situation when he gave his speech, "These Tragedies Must End," at the Sandy Hook Vigil paying tribute to lives lost in the school shooting at Newtown, Connecticut, on December 14, 2012.

(2) Where (location) and when (timing) does the speech take place? What might be important to note about the location of the event? Did the speech occur at a business conference in a hotel conference room, as a keynote speech in a large auditorium, as an after-dinner speech in a ballroom, as a sports team pep talk in an outdoor stadium or ball field? In addition to location, consider timing. The Greek term for the rhetorical impact of the timing of an event is kairos. What might be important to note about when the speech was given, including recent events surrounding it? For example, did the speech occur on the site of a tragic event such as the World Trade Center in New York City (where) on the anniversary of the 9/11 terrorist attacks (when) or on the New Jersey shoreline (where) shortly after Superstorm Sandy (when)? Regarding the Sandy Hook Vigil speech, what might be important to note about the location and timing of the president's speech in the school auditorium on December 16th and why?

(3) To whom is the speech being given? What are the demographic characteristics of the audience members and their expectations regarding the purpose of the speech? Can they act as change agents in some way and, if so, how? A group comprised mostly of underemployed, uninsured Americans, for example, is likely to bring different expectations about universal health care to a speech by presidential hopefuls than is a group made up of corporate executives.

In its purest form, the neo-Aristotelian approach is concerned about the impact of the speech on the specific audience to whom it is given. Today, however, critics often consider the multiple audiences who might also experience the speech as broadcast in real time on

TV or over the radio or Internet, as well as after-the-fact in rebroadcasts or on websites. The nature of audience is becoming increasingly more complex, and many critics employing a neo-Aristotelian critique consider that in their analyses. For example, the specific audience for Martin Luther King, Jr.'s (MLK's) "I have a Dream Speech" on August 28, 1963, consisted of 200,000 people at a political rally in Washington, D.C. More than 50 years later, we might consider audiences viewing it today in K–12 and university classrooms as part of MLK Day events.

In terms of the Sandy Hook speech, who was Obama's audience? Was it the grieving parents and community members in the auditorium at the actual vigil in Newtown, and if so, what might be important for the analysis? Was Obama's audience larger than the people attending the event? Did it include people observing it from a distance via electronic or digital media? If so, who are those multiple audiences, and what might be important to consider about them with regard to the speech? Does the audience include people viewing it months or years later? If so, who are those audiences and what might be important to consider about them regarding the speech?

(4) Why is the speech being given? The reason might be to pay tribute to or celebrate someone, something, or some event. Other reasons might be to introduce, welcome, thank, nominate, commemorate, explain, convince, or incite action. Regarding persuasive speeches, Bitzer (1968) introduced the notion of exigence as a means for exploring the answer to this question. **Exigence** is the reason the speech needs to be given. To clarify, exigency refers to an urgent need or problem that exists in the world. Exigency becomes rhetorical exigence when persuading others (1) to agree that a problem exists, (2) to agree that a particular course of action must be taken, or (3) to actually take action. For example, the shooting at Sandy Hook elementary school points to a problem of violence in the United States that can be addressed by human action that requires persuasion. Immediately following the event, a plethora of persuasive messages advocating different courses of action appeared in the form of public speeches, newspaper and TV news editorials, and others.

(5) What are the constraints? Constraints are the potential obstacles (e.g., people, objects, events, circumstances) that limit decisions and actions. What potential obstacles must be overcome to achieve positive change regarding the problem and proposed action steps? For a speaker advocating gun control in a speech responding to the events at Sandy Hook, for example, the National Rifle Association (NRA) would be a constraint. Additional constraints might be in the speaker him- or herself. In other words, what constraints about the speaker's perceived character and credibility regarding the particular issue and with the specific audience might need to be overcome? If, for instance, Joanna Cole, author of *The Magic School Bus* children's books, were to speak about the Sandy Hook shooting, it might enhance her perceived credibility if she were to also explain that she is a Newtown resident.

Step 2: Interpreting the Text According to the Five Canons

Your goal in the second step is to examine the actual speech text according to each of the five canons. These are invention, arrangement, style, memory, and delivery.

Phase 1: Invention. In the **invention** phase, focus on the speaker's content—that is, his or her major ideas and lines of argument—by considering two things. First, what does the speaker use as inartistic proofs (e.g., facts, statistics, and personal examples found in books, journal articles, and research reports or taken from interviews with credible sources to support claims)? Here, you will evaluate the information and sources of information to determine validity, reliability, bias or stance, among other things.

Second, what does the speaker use as artistic proofs (logos, ethos, pathos). In terms of logos, critique the arguments proposed by examining the claims made, the evidence provided to support each claim, and the warrants—or reasoning—used to connect the evidence to the claim. Is the reasoning solid, or does it have flaws? For example, does the speaker employ reasoning fallacies (e.g., hasty generalization, false cause, ad hominem, red herring)? Stephen E. Toulmin's (1958, 2003) *The Uses of Argument* books are good sources for more comprehensive explanations of logos and argumentation. In terms of ethos, extend what you discovered regarding the initial credibility the speaker conveyed at the outset of the speech to discuss specific rhetorical strategies employed during the actual speech to enhance perceived credibility (derived credibility). Also, assess the speaker's perceived credibility by the time she or he has finished the speech (terminal credibility). In terms of pathos, examine appeals to both negative emotions (e.g., fear, sorrow, grief, guilt, shame, anger) and positive emotions (e.g., joy, pride, hope, compassion) and the degree to which they serve to compel the audience to agree with the speaker's argument.

In the Sandy Hook speech, for example, Obama develops content with logos by inserting quotes from the Bible, specific examples and quotations from school staff as they reassured and protected the children, and references to similar shootings (Tucson, Aurora, Oak Creek, Columbine, Virginia Tech) as he reasons that we are obligated to do something to stop the senseless acts of violence. By naming every person who died and the school staff who acted heroically, he enhances ethos in terms of displaying positive character in knowing and acknowledging them by name. Perhaps most masterful is his use of pathos—appeals to negative emotions of anger, sorrow, and grief about the senseless shooting and loss of innocent loved ones followed by appeals to positive emotions of hope and courage to do something to reduce the potential for additional crimes of violence such as these.

QUESTIONING YOUR ETHICS . . .

In the Sandy Hook speech, President Obama quotes the Bible, offers prayers on behalf of the nation, and references God's love and grace several times. Explain why doing so might have strengthened or weakened his perceived ethos among (1) audience members at the event and (2) audiences observing it via electronic or digital streaming. As a result, would you say his choice to do so was an ethical one? Explain.

Phase 2: Arrangement. In the arrangement phase, focus on the organizational structure of the speaker's message and its effect on the audience. Determine the organizational pattern (e.g., chronological, spatial, comparative advantages, problem/solution) of the message and how the speaker arranged his or her main points, and speculate as to the value (or lack thereof) of choosing that order. For example, did Obama begin with the least controversial topic and build to the most controversial? Did he begin by seeking common ground with his audience? What appear to be the implications of the order he chose on the audience?

Phase 3: Style. With regard to the style phase, focus on the speaker's language choices and sentence structure. What kinds of words did the speaker use, and what effect did they seem to have on the audience? Ultimately, seek to determine the degree to which the speaker's language style contributes to the goal of influencing the audience to agree with his or her main argument. In Obama's speech, for example, you might discuss his choice of using numerous emotionally charged words throughout to describe the shooting (e.g., indescribable violence, unconscionable evil), the victims (e.g., beautiful children, our children), and the heroes (e.g., remarkable adults, inspiring, courageous).

Phase 4: Memory. The memory phase has to do with specific things that make the message positively memorable days, weeks, and even years later. Whereas "Greek and Latin students were once required to memorize . . . whole orations," doing so is no longer the case (Sloane, 2001, p. 113). Today, memory focuses more specifically on **mnemonic devices**, strategies employed to translate information into a form that aids retention. So critics might focus on a variety of strategies employed in any of the canons that make the speech particularly memorable in a positive way. These mnemonics might come in the form of compelling appeals developed in the speech content (e.g., appeals to give money to feed starving children for the cost of a cup of coffee per day). Or they might come in the form of creative organizational and style strategies (e.g., Martin Luther King, Jr.'s use of repetition in his "I Have a Dream" speech in a way that also served to organize his main points). Or they may come in the form of presentational aids that convey ideas using a nonlinguistic symbol system (e.g., visual images of starving children the viewer could help save). And a particularly expressive and dynamic delivery style can also serve as an effective mnemonic device.

APPLYING WHAT YOU'VE LEARNED . . .

Consider a famous comedian like George Carlin, Chris Rock, or Dane Cook, who are known for talking about controversial subjects and interjecting profanity throughout their presentations. How might their style and delivery choices affect different audiences and why? Would you say the speeches are positively memorable? Ethical? Explain.

Phase 5: Delivery. In the delivery phase, focus on the speaker's actual presentation with regard to use of voice and body. In terms of voice, is the speaker understandable, conversational, and engaging? What impact does each seem to have on the success of his or her message reaching and influencing the audience? In terms of body, do the speaker's attire, eye contact, facial expression, gestures, and movement contribute to or detract from the impact of his or her intended goal? How and why?

> **APPLYING WHAT YOU'VE LEARNED . . .**
>
> Access a recording of President Obama's Sandy Hook Vigil speech at this website: http://www
> .huffingtonpost.com/2012/12/16/obama-speaks-at-sandy-hoo_n_2312869.html?view=screen
>   Watch the speech and make notes about his delivery style in terms of use of voice (understandable,
> conversational, expressive) and use of body (poised, confident, expressive). Do you think his delivery
> was effective for the audience there that day? Why or why not? Do you think his delivery was
> effective for viewers accessing it through electronic or digital media? Why or why not?

Step 3: Evaluating the Overall Effect and Implications

After examining the speech according to each canon in isolation, the critic must judge the overall effect of the message. Did the speaker seem to achieve his or her goal? What were the immediate and long-term responses by the audience(s)? Essentially, your goal here is to answer the question: So what? In terms of immediate impact, Obama seemed to achieve his goal at Sandy Hook, judged by respectful silence throughout the speech and applause afterward. The number of viewings online and posts on Twitter might suggest its immediate and perhaps long-term impact on broader audiences, as well. As for answering the "so what" question, one speech usually cannot cause major effects. However, you might be able to suggest a link to positive changes, lack of changes, or negative changes related to an issue or problem it addresses. For Obama, did any reforms occur in, for instance, gun control restrictions, mental health care accessibility, school safety regulations, or violent video game distribution or regulations?

NEW (CONTEMPORARY AND POSTMODERN) RHETORICAL APPROACHES

The neo-Aristotelian approach enjoyed its position as the rhetorical criticism method of choice until the 1960s. Beginning in the 1960s, however, a need for additional approaches became apparent. To clarify, although people have been and continue to be influenced via a plethora of signs, symbols, artifacts, and texts including but not limited to musical sounds and visual arts to everyday objects, actions, and experiences, traditional theorists limited the definition of rhetoric to traditional texts. In the 1960s, scholars began to realize this fact and take it seriously.

Since the neo-Aristotelian approach was originally designed to examine public speeches, it was (and is) in some ways inadequate for examining nontraditional texts. As originally conceived, the neo-Aristotelian approach was based on the assumption that humans engage in persuasion via rational and reasoned discourse. Although certainly true, theorists began to appreciate the fact that human beings also can be moved as a result of nonrational appeals and began to devise new methods for doing so, methods that would answer questions about how, for instance, stories, art, music, and visual images function rhetorically.

Scholars began to realize that new approaches were required for studying the unique ways in which various media themselves function rhetorically. Marshall McLuhan's (1967) bestseller *The Medium Is the Massage: An Inventory of Effects* articulated this idea most cogently. The 1960s technology explosion and its rhetorical significance have continued to explode exponentially since then. For example, although TV was invented much earlier, it became a mainstay in most middle-class homes across the United States by the 1960s. This marked a dramatic shift in terms of access to entertainment media. However, if one wanted to watch a particular TV program, we had to arrange our schedules accordingly in order to do so. The 1980s marked another accessibility turning point because we could videotape programs to watch in our homes at our convenience. Today, we can stream programs off the Internet to watch anytime and anyplace. Technology changes now also make it possible to access music and movies nearly anytime and anyplace. Not only that, new technology also makes it possible to share favorite images, videos, and music with others instantly by posting them on social networking sites like Facebook and Twitter or in texts or e-mail messages.

Although a neo-Aristotelian approach remains useful, the technology explosion that began in the 1960s and that continues to explode exponentially today requires additional rhetorical methods. Consequently, many contemporary rhetorical approaches have been and continue to be created for examining the influential nature of contemporary rhetorical forms, including mediated popular culture texts. Several of these contemporary rhetorical approaches are described in detail in subsequent chapters.

SAMPLE PUBLISHED ESSAY

Read the article by Martin Carcasson and James Arnt Aune titled "Klansman on the Court: Justice Hugo Black's 1937 Radio Address to the Nation" that appeared in the *Quarterly Journal of Speech*. In it, the authors examine the nationwide radio address Justice Black gave in response to charges that he was once a member of the Ku Klux Klan. The analysis applies a neo-Aristotelian perspective to detail how Black was able to appeal successfully to multiple audiences simultaneously through his rhetorical choices of invention, arrangement, style, delivery, and memory. Ultimately, his choices resulted in redirecting the opinions of "two audiences (the press and ordinary Americans) and avoid[ing] mobilizing another (the Klan)" (p. 166). As you read the essay, consider how the authors dissect the radio address using the five canons of a neo-Aristotelian approach to make their case for how and why he was successful in addressing these competing audiences in one speech.

SAMPLE STUDENT ESSAY

This paper, titled "Newt Gingrich and the Florida Republican Primary: A Neo-Aristotelian Analysis," was written by Matthew Pavelek for a class project. He used a neo-Aristotelian approach to examine Newt Gingrich's concession speech following his loss to Mitt Romney in the 2012 Florida primary election. Consider how Matt illustrated the effect of Gingrich's speech based on aspects of the rhetorical situation and rhetorical canons. Regardless of your political affiliation or opinion of Gingrich, do you agree with Matt's analysis and evaluation from a neo-Aristotelian perspective? Why or why not? What could other people who choose to run for office learn from Gingrich's speech and Matt's analysis of it?

Newt Gingrich and the Florida Republican Primary:

A Neo-Aristotelian Analysis

Matthew Pavelek

Presidential election years are filled with opportunities to examine the good, the bad, and the ugly when it comes to the rhetoric of public address. And 2012 was no exception. Campaign speeches abounded as candidates attempted to convince Americans that they were the best person for the job. The artifact under examination in this essay is the concession speech Newt Gingrich delivered following his loss to Mitt Romney in the 2012 Florida primary election (Gingrich, 2012). This public speech is certainly rhetorical, as it was obviously Mr. Gingrich's goal to persuade the audience that, despite this setback, his bid for the U.S. presidency was still alive and well. Moreover, his speech serves as an example of "many signs contributing to a unified message or argument about the way things ought to or ought not to be" (Sellnow, 2010, p. 5).

Gingrich's ultimate goal was to influence behavior change, in this case, to persuade Republican primary voters to cast their votes for him. However, this speech also represents a larger goal; that is, to influence a national power shift that would result in significant implications for public policy. If successful, Gingrich could eventually be running against President Barack Obama for president of the United States.

What specific rhetorical strategies did Gingrich employ to persuade supporters that the Florida result was merely a minor setback, to continue to support his candidacy, and ultimately, to cast their vote for him? Was he successful? If so, what strategies might others take note of in order to emulate them should they find themselves in a similar situation? And if not, what might others seek not to emulate as strategies in concession speeches? These kinds of questions can perhaps be answered by examining Gingrich's speech through a neo-Aristotelian lens. The following paragraphs first describe the rhetorical situation and then interpret Gingrich's message according to the five canons of rhetoric. Finally, I offer a concluding evaluation and implications for Gingrich and others who find themselves faced with the need to give a concession speech in the middle of a race that has yet to be decided.

The Rhetorical Situation

To conduct a Neo-Aristotelian analysis, one must begin by describing the rhetorical situation.

(Continued)

(Continued)

Doing so provides a context for understanding the reason the speech needed to be given. The rhetorical situation consists of the speaker, occasion, audience, exigence, and constraints.

Newt Gingrich served as Georgia's U.S. representative from 1979 to 1999, as House Minority Whip from 1989 to 1995, and as Speaker of the U.S. House of Representatives from 1995 to 1999. His long record of political service enhanced his credibility to run for the Republican Party nomination in the first place and to speak to his supporters in Florida for this speech. In addition to his impressive political career, Gingrich's ability to win primary elections in other states as well as the nearly 500,000 votes he collected in the state of Florida buttress his credibility—especially in this speech in Florida.

The location is simultaneously significant and insignificant. The speech was delivered at Gingrich campaign headquarters in Florida on the night of the election immediately following the news that Gingrich had lost the state to rival Republican Massachusetts Governor Mitt Romney. For the physical audience, Florida voters who supported him, the location is especially significant. However, Gingrich's real message was targeted at voters in upcoming primary election states since he had already lost Florida. However, if Gingrich were ultimately to win the nomination, the Florida voters' support would again become important. So, Gingrich needed to consider his Florida audience in multiple ways as well as voters in upcoming state primaries.

Sellnow (2010) defines exigence as the reason the speech needs to be given. For Gingrich and his supporters, exigence is tied to responding effectively to the defeat in this crucial state.

If there was to be any hope of a Gingrich victory, he must simultaneously console Florida voters in ways that would retain their support should he win the Republican bid as well as win undecided voters in other states who had not yet cast their votes.

The demographic characteristics of Gingrich's audience are challenging to define, which also offers the most significant constraints on his message. Indeed, Gingrich's primary audience, whether in the physical audience hearing this speech or in other areas of the country, were undecided voters. He would most likely garner the votes of hard-core Republicans and not hard-core Democrats regardless of the speech. Thus, his primary target audience was made up of those voters that had not yet decided which candidate they would support. This constraint forced him to be deliberately vague when it came to specific policy decisions so as not to alienate undecided voters. For example, he insisted that voters have the chance to "nominate a conservative who knows what he's doing, who has done it before, and who has the courage and determination to get it done..." He never clearly defined what "it" was that he planned to get done.

Interpretation: The Canons

With the rhetorical situation in mind, it becomes prudent to examine more specifically the strategies Gingrich employed in his speech to achieve his outcome. In doing so, critics can determine what rhetorical strategies other candidates may want to both employ and avoid to be successful in terms of both short-term and long-term outcomes.

Invention: In terms of content, Gingrich opened his speech blaming the "elite" media for his setback. He challenged mass media outlets and the way his campaign had been covered by political pundits, most notably referring to the "elite" media. "We did this in part for the elite media, because, you know, the same people who said I was dead in June and July and said I was gone after Iowa..." By classifying the mainstream media as "elite," Gingrich subtly unified himself with his audience and supporters by blaming them for the outcome, projecting an us-versus-them argument and insinuating that they were disconnected from average Americans.

Gingrich went on to offer numerous inartistic proofs to bolster his argument including the fact that his campaign was ahead in the Gallup poll nationally by 12 or 13 points at the time of the speech. He also offered several artistic proofs to support his position. First, he appealed to the audience logically by stating that it "is now clear that this will be a two-person race between the conservative leader, Newt Gingrich, and the Massachusetts moderate. And the voters of Florida really made that clear." Second, Gingrich emphasized his own ethos as a speaker by reminding the audience of his political qualifications. "The reason I'm comfortable telling you all this is I have been studying what America needs to do, since the fall of 1958, when my dad was stationed in Europe in the army. I have been working at what we need to do, as congressman, speaker of the House, and in the private sector."

Third, Gingrich made several emotional appeals to the audience. Most notably by sharing an anecdote about President Lincoln and the first national cemetery that had little to do with the occasion, save perhaps to proffer a slight amount of name association between Lincoln and Gingrich, it did thrust the audience's "power" to the fore. "And we're going to have people power

defeat money power in the next six months," Gingrich promised. He also appealed to emotions by trying to persuade the audience that this election was the most important in their lifetime. He insisted that any outcome resulting in Barack Obama's reelection would be disastrous. He also argued that action must be taken in the form of voting for him, but he took it a step further when he urged his audience to begin to use their social networks and influence to persuade others to vote for him, as well.

Arrangement: This speech was arranged largely by focusing on the theme and positive and negative future outcomes. Gingrich began his speech with the standard pleasantries of thanking those folks who worked so hard, demonstrating a keen awareness of the occasion as he thanked the more than a half-million Floridians who voted for him. He also addressed his own ethos as a speaker while catering to the audience and its collective vanity concerning its own significance by stating that he thought "Florida did something very important, coming on top of South Carolina." Indeed, Gingrich's speech took a hard turn into selling the notion of continued prosecution of a vigorous and lively campaign that would ultimately culminate with him earning the Republican Party's nomination to run in the general election. Next, Mr. Gingrich addressed the audience members holding up signs that read "46 More States to Go." This simple message was a carefully integrated facet of the persuasion as it implied that the race had just begun and its nascent stage carried the additional future boon of 46 future victories in state primary elections. Gingrich bolstered this point by promising that not only would he "win," but he would "be in Tampa as the nominee in August."

(Continued)

(Continued)

Once again Gingrich incorporated the audience by acknowledging the considerable financial advantage the Romney campaign enjoyed over his own campaign. Apparently Romney had been able to generate five times the amount of campaign funding as Gingrich, but these odds were nothing compared to what people can do. In closing, Gingrich again demonstrated a keen awareness of the occasion by giving the audience a job to do. He tasked them with basically using their own personal connections and influence to persuade other voters to vote for him. He very cleverly attached a pseudo-civic duty to the task by insisting that "this is America."

"If you will reach out across the country, if you will use Facebook and YouTube and Twitter and phone calls and even visits, if you will tell all of your friends in the other 46 states that there is a chance to nominate a conservative who knows what he's doing, who has done it before, and who has the courage and determination to get it done, I promise you that if I become your president, I pledge to you my life, my fortune, and my sacred honor. This is about America."

Style: Gingrich adopted a very aggressive style in attacking both Mitt Romney and Barack Obama, insisting that this was the most important election in his and the audience's lifetimes. He said, for example, "If Barack Obama gets reelected, it will be a disaster for the United States of America. Make no bones about it. If he can have a record this bad, unemployment this bad, deficits this bad, policies this bad, gasoline prices this high, and still get reelected, you can't imagine how radical he'll be in his second term." In contrast, Gingrich insisted that he was committed to unleashing "the spirit of the American people." He argued that his leadership and policies would fundamentally get "America back on the right track."

Memory: Gingrich employed several methods to make his message memorable. First, he repeatedly addressed the audience and what they were able to accomplish. Next, he mentioned his family and their contributions to his campaign as a way of making himself seem more similar to those average Americans in his potential voter population. Finally, he addressed key issues that affect people daily in his vision for the future, a word he repeats five times in this sentence: "It's a future of jobs, it's a future of lower gasoline prices, it's a future of a balanced budget, it's a future of a smaller Washington, it's a future of more power back home to you and your family and your neighborhood. This is a future we ask you to join us in imposing on the establishment in Washington and imposing it on both parties."

Delivery: Gingrich is a dynamic and charismatic speaker. His passion for what he feels is right and his desperation after losing such an important primary election served to reinforce his delivery. He is articulate and well-spoken. He also speaks in a very conversational style that relates to the audience, especially those audience members who already support him. But, he was careful to address key issues and challenge his opponents by providing examples to support his argument and augment his own credibility as a speaker. He was effective at pausing to emphasize key points and also effectively engages the audience and their contributions to the occasion. However, his aggressive tone and indifference to the actual results of the Florida election may have alienated some moderate conservative voters.

Evaluation and Implications

Ultimately, Gingrich lost the Republican Party nomination to Mitt Romney. In that sense, this speech failed to achieve the outcome Gingrich desired. If it was effective in consoling and even energizing the Florida supporters in his audience, it did not persuade the remaining primary voters across the country to vote for him. Conversely, it may have had the opposite effect since Mitt Romney and the Republican Party ultimately lost the general election to Barack Obama. If his attempts to persuade voters throughout the primary campaign that Romney would not be the best choice for president were successful with undecided voters, it is possible his rhetoric ultimately played a role in galvanizing them to vote for Obama when the alternative ended up being Romney rather than Gingrich.

In fact, some experts have argued that Gingrich's speech damaged Romney's general election campaign considerably. In describing Florida as the "bloodiest stop" in the Republican primary, *New York Times* editorialist David Firestone (2012) argued that Gingrich proved he was a man who would do virtually anything to earn even minor support among voters, regardless of the absurdity of his claims. Moreover, Gingrich's tactics forced Romney to reciprocate with a more aggressive campaign, alienating voters who had grown weary of the mudslinging rhetoric. He writes:

> But Florida cost Mr. Romney some standing as well. He was relentlessly negative in the final days of the campaign, frustrating many voters who wanted to hear an upbeat message. Exit polls showed that he tacked further to the right on issues such as immigration than most Floridians, and his claim that he would get millions of illegal immigrants to "self-deport" may have cost him the endorsement of Jeb Bush, as well as the backing of many other moderate Republicans and independents. (para. 5)

Ultimately there is an important lesson to be learned from Gingrich's speech. Focusing purely on beating a rival candidate and delivering heated arguments to rooms full of supporters largely removes the undecided voting public from the equation. By focusing on why he was still going to win the presidential election and refusing to actually acknowledge his loss in Florida, Gingrich forced Romney to take a more aggressive position simply to beat Gingrich. The undecided voters Romney may have alienated as a result may have seriously damaged Romney's ability to campaign successfully against Barack Obama in the general election.

In sum, elected officials exist in a representative democracy to serve the will of the people who elect them. Campaigns that focus exclusively on making rival candidates look bad to win votes ultimately may do so at the expense of focusing on the important issues people actually care about. Moreover, when this mudslinging approach occurs during a primary campaign, it could ultimately convince frustrated undecided voters to support the other party during the general election. Candidates and future political hopefuls should learn from Gingrich's mistakes and focus their campaigns on their positions regarding pertinent issues and why they deserve the public's support, not on why the other candidate does not deserve it.

(Continued)

(Continued)

References

Firestone, D. (2012, January 31). The cost of a bloody Florida battle. *The New York Times.* Retrieved from http://takingnote.blogs.nytimes.com/2012/01/31/the-cost-of-a-bloody-florida-battle/

Gingrich, N. (February, 2012). *Concession speech following the Florida Republican primary presidential election.* Presented at Gingrich Florida campaign headquarters, Orlando, Florida. Retrieved from http://www.ibtimes.com/newt-gingrich-florida-concession-speech-2012-full-text-video-403754

Sellnow, D. D. (2010). *The rhetorical power of popular culture: Considering mediated texts.* Thousand Oaks, CA: Sage.

Summary

In this chapter, we focused on rhetoric—on how and why its meaning has evolved over the years. *Rhetoric* consists of the signs as artifacts used to influence people to agree with a particular perception about how to believe and behave. *Rhetorical criticism* is the analysis and evaluation of those messages. The roots of the rhetorical tradition date back more than 2,000 years and evolved to include the study of popular culture texts in the 1960s. The *neo-Aristotelian* approach was originally conceived as a means for examining public speeches as distinct from literary criticism. Although the neo-Aristotelian approach remains a viable method for rhetorical criticism today, it is no longer the only or even the primary method for examining the many kinds of rhetorical texts that may influence us today.

Challenge

Select one of the following speeches, or choose another one that was delivered by a fairly well-known politician, activist, or celebrity in recent years. You might look to the appendices of some basic public speaking textbooks for ideas. Analyze the speech using the neo-Aristotelian approach.

- Steve Carell's acceptance speech for Favorite TV Comedy Actor at the January 6, 2010, People's Choice Awards
- Clint Eastwood's speech at the 2012 Republican National Convention
- Michael Moore's acceptance speech for Best Documentary at the 75th Academy Awards ceremony in 2003
- Condolezza Rice's 2012 Commencement Address at Southern Methodist University

- President Obama's 2013 State of the Union address.
- Al Gore's acceptance speech for Best Documentary at the 80th Academy Awards ceremony in 2008.

1. First, describe the rhetorical situation—including the speaker, occasion, audience, exigence, and constraints. Speculate about the target audience for the original presentation as well as the multiple audiences who may also be exposed to its message and, thus, be impacted by it.

2. Then, interpret the speech using the five canons (invention, arrangement, style, memory, delivery) of the neo-Aristotelian approach.

3. Finally, evaluate the speech based on its apparent effect on the audiences you described earlier. Was the speaker successful? Based on your analysis, why or why not? Ultimately, offer implications for other speakers who may try to influence these audiences. How does your analysis contribute to our understanding and evaluation of the speech topic as well as our understanding of and ability to present such messages more effectively?

References

Aristotle. (1954). *Rhetoric.* (W. R. Roberts, Trans.). New York: Modern Library.

Axtell, R. E. (1998). *Gestures: The dos and taboos of body language around the world.* Hoboken, NJ: John Wiley and Sons.

Bitzer, L. F. (1968). The rhetorical situation. *Philosophy and Rhetoric, 1*(1), 1–14.

Blair, H. (1783). *Lectures on rhetoric and belles lettres.* London: Oxford University Press.

Brigance, W. N. (Ed.). (1943). *A history and criticism of American public address* (Vols. I and II). New York: McGraw-Hill.

Campbell, G. (1776). *The philosophy of rhetoric (Landmarks in rhetoric and public address).* Carbondale, IL; Southern Illinois University Press. (L. Bitzer, Ed, 1969)

Carcasson, M., & Aune, J. A. (2003). Klansman on the court: Justice Hugo Black's 1937 radio address to the nation. *Quarterly Journal of Speech, 89*(2), 154–170.

Golden, J. L., Berquist, G. F., Coleman, W. E., & Sproule, J. M. (2011). *The rhetoric of Western thought: From the Mediterranean world to the global setting* (10th ed.). Dubuque, IA: Kendall-Hunt.

Kant, I. (1784, September 30). *An answer to the question: What is enlightenment?* Prussia: Konigsberg.

McLuhan, M. (1967). *The medium is the massage: An inventory of effects* (with Quentin Fiore). Berkeley, CA: Gingko.

Nichols, M. H. (Ed.). (1955). *A history and criticism of American public address* (Vol. III). New York: Longman.

Palmer, D. J. (1965). *The rise of English studies: An account of the study of English language and literature from its origins to the making of the Oxford English school.* London: Oxford University Press.

Rader, W. (1996–2013). *The online slang dictionary.* Retrieved on March 22, 2013, from http://onlineslangdictionary.com/

Solmsen, F. (Ed.). (1954). *The rhetoric and the poetics of Aristotle.* New York: The Modern Library.

Sloane, T. O. (2001). *Encyclopedia of rhetoric.* New York: Oxford University Press.

Thonssen, L., & Baird, C. (1948). *Speech criticism.* New York: Ronald.

Thonssen, L., Baird, C., & Braden, W. W. (1970). *Speech criticism* (2nd ed.). New York: Ronald.

Toulmin, S. E. (1958). *The uses of argument.* New York: Cambridge University Press.

Toulmin, S. E. (2003). *The uses of argument* (2nd ed.). New York: Cambridge University Press.

Whately, R. (1855). *Elements of rhetoric.* Boston: James Munroe.

Wichelns, H. A. (1925). The literary criticism of oratory. In A. M. Drummond (Ed.), *Studies in rhetoric and public speaking in honor of James Albert Winans* (pp. 181–216). New York: Century.

Wollstonecraft, M. (1787). *Thoughts on the education of daughters: With reflections on female conduct, in the more important duties of life.* London: Joseph Johnson.

Wollstonecraft, M. (1790). *A vindication of the rights of men, in a letter to the right honourable Edmund Burke.* London: Joseph Johnson.

Wollstonecraft, M. (1792). *A vindication of the rights of woman with strictures on moral and political subjects.* London: Joseph Johnson.

Student Study Site

Visit the Student Study Site at www.sagepub.com/sellnow2e to read interesting SAGE journal articles, view mobile-friendly key term flashcards, take chapter-specific online web quizzes to test your knowledge, and more!

Chapter 3

A Narrative Perspective

The narrative perspective as a rhetorical method for examining ideological arguments conveyed through storytelling is often attributed to Walter R. Fisher (1984, 1987), professor emeritus of communication at the University of Southern California. In actuality, Fisher is only one of many rhetoricians whose work contributes to our understanding of narrative (e.g., Booth, 1961, 1983, 1988; Burke, 1957; Chatman, 1978; 1990; Lucaites & Condit, 1985; Lucaites, Condit, & Farrell, 1985; Martin, 1986; Mitchell, 1981; Mumby, 1993; Newton, 1995; Ricoeur, 1984-1988; Riessman, 1993; Rowland, 1987; Warnick, 1987). Moreover, Artistotle (1954) actually conceptualized the basic structure of narrative as characters, rising action, complication, climax, and resolution more than 2,000 years ago in the *Poetics*. That said, the narrative approach was one of the first methods to be formalized and offered as an alternative to traditional neo-Aristotelian rhetorical criticism, and Fisher played an important role in that process (Black, 1978).

Rather than examining texts as logical arguments supported with evidence and reasoning using the five canons, the narrative perspective identifies arguments proposed as morals through storytelling, complete with characters, plot, and actions. A moral as used in narrative criticism, then, refers to the value-laden ideological argument a story proposes directly or indirectly (as well as intentionally or unintentionally) about how we ought to or ought not to believe or behave. This "ideological rhetorical force" is essentially what makes stories rhetorical (Chatman, 1990, p. 198).

Narratives do not occur just in novels, storybooks, TV programs, and films. As professor emeritus of English Language and Literature at the University of Chicago, Wayne Booth (1988) explains, narratives are in "every presentation of time-ordered or time-related experience" including but not limited to visual images and objects, musical ballets and symphonies, as well as everyday events and activities "like birth, copulation, death, plowing and planting, getting and spending" (p. 14). In other words, human beings contantly "experience and comprehend life as a series of ongoing narratives, as conflicts, characters, beginnings, middles, and ends" (Fisher, 1987, p. 24).

A narrative perspective is valuable for studying popular culture texts because it proposes a systematic means by which to analyze how they function as narrative stories and what underlying ideological messages are being conveyed in them. Simply put, critics seek to discover what underlying "moral of the story" is being argued and the "good reasons" offered to support that ideological perspective as valid (Fisher, 1984, pp. 7–9). Narrative criticism serves to unpack the sender's attempt to impose his or her worldview (albeit intentionally or unintentionally) on the audience (Booth, 1983). In essence, narrative propositions often argue indirectly about the kind of person a story is asking us to identify with and, thus, become (White, 1984, p. 15). A narrative analysis affords us the ability to make a conscious choice about whether or not we want to or should want to, in fact, be that kind of person.

NARRATION

Narration, the "symbolic actions—words and/or deeds—that have sequence and meaning for those who live, create, or interpret them," is at the heart of the narrative perspective (Fisher, 1987, p. 58). This concept of what can be considered rhetorical or persuasive represents a shift from the rational-world paradigm, which undergirds the neo-Aristotelian approach. A paradigm is simply a conceptual framework for understanding the world around us. The rational-world paradigm, then, is a framework that assumes people are rational beings who make decisions based on logical arguments, evidence, and reasoning (pp. 59–62). Conversely, the narrative paradigm is a conceptual framework that places narration and storytelling at the core of all human communication.

NARRATIVE RATIONALITY

Although narratives are all around us and come in a variety of forms, not all narratives are equally good. People evaluate these narratives by applying the standards of narrative rationality to them. Narrative rationality is our assessment of the value-laden ideological argument(s) proposed. In other words, we evaluate "good reasons" (i.e., value-laden warrants) offered to persuade us to believe and accept the "moral" (i.e., ideological argument) about how to believe and behave (Fisher, 1995, p. 176). The two standards of narrative rationality we apply to stories are coherence (a.k.a. probability) and fidelity.

Coherence

Coherence is essentially the degree to which the story hangs together. In other words, how plausible does the story seem? To come to a decision, we may evaluate structural, character, and material coherence. Does the sequence of events flow, or are pieces of the story line missing? Are the characters believable? Do they act consistently? Is this story consistent with similar stories we have encountered on a similar theme? Stories hang together when we are persuaded to believe that important details haven't been left out, that the characters seem authentic, that the facts haven't been altered, and that multiple possible interpretations have been accounted for.

The HBO series *The Newsroom* builds its coherence argument as consistent with other stories by focusing on actual events that have been in the news (e.g., Gulf oil spill, Iraq war, Japanese nuclear crisis), modeling itself after what viewers believe a typical newsroom looks like from watching any number of network and cable news programs, and portraying characters to look and act like we believe of a typical news cast and crew. In fact, some critics even suggest the program is modeled after MSNBC's *Morning Joe,* including two of the main characters (Will McAvoy modeled after Joe Scarborough and MacKenzie after Mika Brzezinski).

Coherence can also be argued in science fiction stories, fantasies, and cartoons that viewers realize are not true as long as structural, character, and material coherence are portrayed as plausible. In the film *The Matrix,* for example, viewers come to accept the ideological argument as reasonable in part because it is coherent. Regarding structural coherence, there are no holes in the sequence of events. Viewers are not left to piece together bits of the story that got left on the cutting room floor, so to speak. And character coherence is achieved as viewers are led to relate to the characters as consistent with preconceived notions of how "good guys" and "bad guys" look and act.

Most challenging to achieve in science fiction films, however, is material coherence. When *The Matrix* was first released in 1999, some criticized the plot as too far-fetched. Today, however, it is regarded as one of the best science fiction films of all time (Heritage, 2010) and was placed on *National Film Registry* for preservation in 2012. The argument seems plausible today when we consider the fact that computer technology is becoming increasingly intelligent. Not only do we have instant access to information over the Internet from our computers, but smartphones and apps can also tell us anything we want to know and more. Apps like Foursquare, for example, tell us where other users in our social network are located at any given time. Apps like Navizon tell us how to get where we want to go from wherever we may be. And apps like GPS-R not only track where we are going but tell us when we are near a place to accomplish a task on our to-do lists (e.g., drop off library book, pick up milk, or as the TV commercial goes, stop at Jared's to get that diamond watch for our partner).

Fidelity

Fidelity is the degree to which the values offered in a story ring true with what we regard as truthful and humane. In other words, the story strikes a responsive chord. A story has fidelity when it provides good reasons to accept its moral (i.e., ideological argument). These good reasons emerge from the values embedded in the message, the relevance of those values to the decisions made, the consequences that result from adhering to or defying those values, and the degree to which those values conform to the worldview and values of the audience.

Some of the questions we might ask to determine the logic of the good reasons proposed include the following: (1) What are the implicit and explicit values espoused in the narrative? (2) Do the values confirm or oppose our personal set of values? (3) Are the values relevant and appropriate to the decision(s) made? (4) What consequence(s) result from adhering to these values? (5) Are the values a legitimate basis for appropriate human conduct (even if they are not part of our personal values system)? Finally, Fisher (1987) argues that most people uphold the values of "truth, the good, beauty, health, wisdom, courage, temperance, justice, harmony, order, communion, friendship, and oneness with the Cosmos" (pp. 187–188). So, we judge fidelity based on the degree to which a story's good reasons are portrayed as relevant and appropriate to both the decision(s) made and the resulting consequences, as well as the degree to which they ring true with our personal values and what we perceive as ideal values by which to live.

Why conduct a narrative analysis of popular culture texts? Well, for one reason, each of us can't experience all of life firsthand, so we learn from the stories told by others about how we ought to believe and behave. Popular culture texts help us make sense of the people, places, and events we may encounter in our lives (Riessman, 1993). We draw our conclusions about how to believe and behave based on the consequences of the actions employed by the characters. The positive or negative outcomes lead to the value-laden argument proposed in the story. Some stories and their moral arguments may not be grounded in the kinds of values we want to embody. For example, many people find the film *Ferris Bueller's Day Off* to be pretty funny (myself included). From a narrative perspective, however, it sends messages that skipping school, as well as deceiving parents and defying authority figures such as teachers and principals, are not only acceptable but also appropriate and even desirable. This ideological argument proposed in *Ferris Bueller's Day Off* has been retold again and again in movies and on TV programs since it was first released in 1986. Hence, narrative analyses may also highlight these kinds of paradoxes, affording us the skills to be conscious consumers of their persuasive, value-laden arguments (Farrell, 1985; Johannesen, 1983).

APPLYING WHAT YOU'VE LEARNED . . .

Go to this website and view the award-winning Budweiser commercial about Hank: http://www
.youtube.com/watch?v=XWbO-oq6ZPw

Examine the ideological moral argument proposed in it using the concepts of narrative rationality (coherence and fidelity). How does it meet the standards of structural, material, and character coherence? Does it ring true in terms of fidelity? Explain.

CONDUCTING A NARRATIVE ANALYSIS ━━━━━━━━━━

The narrative perspective is a useful tool for studying mediated popular culture texts like television programs and commercials, movies, comic strips, songs, and music videos. This approach can also reveal stories being told visually in print advertisements, magazine photographs, and even the visual images within television programs, music videos, and movies (Jhally, 1995). The following paragraphs explain how to conduct a narrative criticism of popular culture texts by (1) selecting an appropriate text, (2) examining it using the tools of the narrative perspective, and (3) evaluating its conclusions and potential implications.

Step 1: Selecting an Appropriate Text

Appropriate texts that can be analyzed from a narrative perspective must fulfill four requirements. They must (1) offer at least two events, (2) be organized by time, (3) depict a relationship between earlier and later events, and (4) present a unified subject (story).

First, the text must offer at least two events to be considered a narrative. These events can be active or stative. An active event expresses action of some sort. For example, in the print advertisement for Red Zone Body Spray (see Figure 3.1), the active event is a Friday-night date at a party or dance club. The individuals appear to be dancing or at least partying. A stative event is an expression of a state or condition. Again, in the advertisement, the people appear to be having fun and enjoying themselves. In other words, their state or condition is happy or joyful. So, this advertisement meets the first requirement because it offers at least two events: action (partying) and state or condition (happy or joyful).

Second, these events must be organized by time. That is, the text must offer a sequence of events. The events might be arranged chronologically, or they might offer flashbacks and flash-forwards, but they are somehow related temporally to each other. Again, the advertisement in Figure 3.1 meets this requirement because the caption superimposed over the characters says "Sometimes Friday night doesn't get started until Saturday morning." As such, the reader understands the story is arranged by time, that is, Friday night and Saturday morning.

Third, there must be some element of causation or some sense of relationship between early and later events in the story. *Causation* may depict how some early event causes a later event. Sometimes, however, the earlier event is not depicted as causing the later event but, rather, is depicted as having been necessary for the later event to occur. In the advertisement, Red Zone is implied as necessary for the fun Friday night that might not really get started until Saturday morning.

Fourth, the text must present its story as a unified subject. As such, the story has a beginning and an end that makes sense. The setting, the characters, and their actions must be connected in ways that together tell the story. In the advertisement, the setting (party event), the characters ("good looking" young adults), and their actions (having fun with each other) are all related as they lead viewers to believe that the ending (that their real fun might not even get started until Saturday morning) makes sense. Obviously, viewers who might want to find themselves in a similar situation would be wise to use Red Zone so as not to ruin their chances because of body odor. Now, if the setting was unappealing (like

■ **FIGURE 3.1**   Red Zone Ad

sitting through a college classroom lecture), or the characters didn't seem to go together (perhaps, for example, a young adult dancing with someone old enough to be a grandparent), or their actions implied that one or both were not enjoying themselves, the story would fail to meet this requirement of presenting itself as a unified subject.

APPLYING WHAT YOU'VE LEARNED . . .

Consider an advertisement that you find compelling. Examine it based on these four requirements. How would you study it from a narrative perspective and why?

Step 2: Examining the Text (Describe and Interpret)

You may recall from Chapter 1 that we examine a popular culture text via description, interpretation, and evaluation. When conducting your analysis from a narrative perspective, you use the elements of storytelling to examine the text via these three dimensions. You begin by describing the setting, characters, narrator, events, causal relations, temporal relations, and intended audience. You then interpret them in terms of the moral of the story (i.e., value-laden ideological argument) and evaluate it as it might influence various audiences to whom it is directed.

Describing the Setting. In terms of the setting, you simply describe where the action takes place. In the advertisement for Red Zone, the setting is at a party or a dance club. Sometimes there is more than one setting. If the Red Zone advertisement was a split screen also showing, for example, a scene from what may be one of the character's apartments, you would note that, as well. You examine the setting for coherence and fidelity to determine whether to accept the ultimate argument as valid.

Describing the Characters. In terms of *characters*, you describe their physical and mental traits, whether their physical or dispositional traits change over the course of the story, the actions they engage in, and whether their traits or actions are predictable (i.e., what we would expect based on preconceived social norms). Flat characters are predictable in that they look and act in ways that do not deviate from preconceived status-quo norms and expectations. Round characters are unpredictable in that their looks and actions don't fit preconceived social norms of the culture. In the Red Zone advertisement, the physical traits of the characters are these: a Caucasian male and female who appear to be middle-class based on their attire and in their early 20s. Both are slender as well as able-bodied. Both appear to be dancing. Both are wearing T-shirts and jeans; however, the woman's midriff shows. As this is only one snapshot, so to speak, there is no message communicated with regard to change over time. He is looking at her, and she is looking down. Because the characters seem to fit preconceived social norms of the dominant American culture (predictable), we would describe them as *flat* according to a narrative perspective. If, on the other hand, the characters appeared to be from very different socioeconomic groups, generations, ability or disability, and so on, they might be described as unpredictable (not what we'd expect based on the social norms of the dominant American culture) and, thus, *round.*

APPLYING WHAT YOU'VE LEARNED . . .

Consider a favorite movie or television program. Who are the main characters? Describe the physical and mental traits of each of them. Are the traits predictable? Which of the characters seem to be portrayed as ones viewers ought to admire or aspire to be like or not? Why?

Describing the Narrator. The story is sometimes communicated directly to the audience. In these cases, the audience witnesses the actions without added commentary. At other times, however, a narrator mediates the events and, as such, offers an interpretation of the events and characters for the audience as the audience observes them. The narrator may communicate orally or visually. In the Red Zone advertisement, the narrator communicates visually via the message placed directly on top of the picture: "Sometimes Friday night doesn't get started until Saturday morning." Essentially, the narrator tends to clarify what the audience might imply from a potentially ambiguous story.

Describing the Events. In terms of *events,* you look for both major events that cannot be left out of the story without destroying its meaning and minor events that are not necessarily crucial to the story but add breadth and depth to it. Recall that you will consider both active events (expressing action) and stative events (expressing a state or condition). In the Red Zone advertisement, the major event is having a good time (stative event) at a Friday night party (active event) and the minor event is the added connotation that having a good time on Friday night is nothing compared to the real party that won't start until Saturday morning. In this case, the major event being told is blatant, whereas the minor event is implied.

Describing Causal Relations. In terms of causal relations, you look for cause-and-effect relationships and whether the effects are caused by human action, by accident, or by forces of nature. Which causes and effects seem to dominate the story and how? In the Red Zone advertisement, a great time Friday night is nothing compared to the party that might not begin until Saturday morning. Moreover, wearing Red Zone contributes to the potential for the Saturday-morning party to occur.

APPLYING WHAT YOU'VE LEARNED . . .

Consider once again the television program or movie you identified earlier. What major and minor events help tell the story? What cause-and-effect relationships can you identify? How do these events and causal relationships lead to believing certain behaviors are normal or not, appropriate or not, desirable or not?

Describing Temporal Relations. In terms of *temporal relations,* you look at whether the order of events is *syntagmatic* (that is, one thing leads naturally to another) or *paradigmatic* (that is, flashbacks and flash-forwards are used). The movie *Pulp Fiction* is a fine example of a paradigmatic story told with flashbacks and flash-forwards. Other films that use flashbacks include *The Usual Subjects, The Bourne Trilogy, The Notebook,* and *Memento.* The popular TV program *How I Met Your Mother* is another good example. In addition, you might consider whether the story is being told in past, present, or future tense. Finally, you might consider the speed at which various parts of the story are told. That is, how much detail is provided about one event compared to other events? The Red Zone advertisement is syntagmatic and told in future tense. Viewers are shown a picture of the Friday-night event and led to believe what will probably occur as a result. And, wearing Red Zone helps make it all possible.

Describing the Intended Audience. Refer to our discussion of the rhetorical situation in Chapter 2 (sender, occasion, audience, exigence, constraints) to make an educated guess as to the target audience, that is, the group of people the sender is attempting to persuade (albeit intentionally or unintentionally) (Verderber, Verdeber, & Sellnow, 2014, pp. 416–417). Describe the intended target audience and the attitudes toward the subject and values they might bring with them to the occasion. Then juxtapose these assumptions with the attitudes and values that are presumed. The Red Zone advertisement came from *Maxim,* a magazine targeted to young men aged 18 to 30. The young, heterosexual, middle-class, able-bodied white couple in the advertisement assumes viewers will be males who embody or want to embody these same traits.

Interpreting the Moral Conveyed. Next, you interpret what these elements mean. You start by determining what moral is being conveyed, that is, what is the story trying to convince us about how we ought to or ought not to believe or behave. Then point out which elements seem to be most important in terms of contributing to the ultimate value-laden argument and why. In other words, you show how they provide good reasons for accepting the moral as legitimate.

Some examples of morals include "good triumphs over evil," "there's a silver lining inside every cloud," "perseverance will pay off in the end," "it is important to look nice," "teachers are out of touch with reality," "college students abuse alcohol," "politicians are corrupt," "violence is appropriate," "unmarried young adults engage in casual sex," and "feminists are bitches."

A moral of the Red Zone advertisement appears to be related to the notion that "unmarried young adults engage in casual sex" and, perhaps, even that Red Zone can help make it happen. Granted, the viewer is not offered a clear definition of what is meant by "Saturday morning," however, the characters (young, able-bodied, middle-class, white heterosexuals who are dancing and partying so that their bodies are touching and they are enjoying it), the ambiguity of the message conveyed by the narrator, the event (Friday-night party), the causal suggestion (good Friday-night date leads to the real party that won't start until Saturday morning), the temporal relations (Friday-night partying is clear, and Saturday morning is suggested), and the intended audience (young heterosexual men aged 18 to 30) suggests that this is a moral being communicated.

APPLYING WHAT YOU'VE LEARNED . . .

Consider again the television program or movie you identified. Based on the characters who are portrayed as well as the positive and negative consequences each experiences from their actions, what might be the moral—the ideological rhetorical force—of the story about how viewers are led to believe or behave in our daily lives?

Step 3: Evaluating Potential Implications of the Text

Finally, you evaluate the text as it might influence the various audiences to whom it is directed. In other words, what are the potential implications for individuals and groups who decide the ideological argument conveyed as a value-laden moral is valid? What might they believe, or how might they behave as a result? Who might be affected by these beliefs or behaviors and how? Your goal here is to reveal what argument the narrative is proposing about how we should live our lives. Is that good or bad? Why? Ultimately, you answer the question "So what?" based on what, how, and why we might choose to believe and behave if we accept the moral as valid. Obviously, no one advertisement, film, television program, comic strip, or song can be causally linked to behaviors by individuals or groups of individuals; however, a proliferation of texts that espouse similar messages can eventually penetrate the beliefs and behaviors of individuals and groups. This bombardment of similar messages across texts targeted to a particular group, which can have a cumulative persuasive effect on receivers, is known as the cultivation effect (Gerbner, 1969; Gerbner, Gross, Morgan, & Signorielli, 1994).

That said, let us speculate about some of the potential implications of the Red Zone advertisement on what or how people might believe or behave, particularly if a similar message is communicated across texts targeted to them. If the young male reader of *Maxim* accepts the moral that "unmarried young adults engage in casual sex" as valid, then some potential implications might include perhaps believing that young women who date him, and others like him, and stay out until the wee hours of the night are open to or even expect to have casual sex if they have a good time. Conversely, young women who party with him and others like him, have fun, and are not interested in casual sex are not the norm. Certainly, these ideas about appropriate behavior can influence how unmarried young men and women interact when partying. In fact, some young adults today do believe in what are referred to as "friends with benefits" and "hooking up." Taken to extremes, it could lead to an increase in sexually transmitted diseases, unwanted pregnancies, and so on. Likewise, older adults might presume that these kinds of behaviors are typical for young, unmarried adults today. Negative stereotypes of the youth culture may falsely cloud their opinions about young people they meet, they work with, or even their own children.

APPLYING WHAT YOU'VE LEARNED . . .

Consider the moral you identified from the television program or movie you picked earlier. What might be some "so what?" implications based on the audiences to whom it is primarily targeted?

QUESTIONING YOUR ETHICS . . .

If the messages in some music speak to and for youth and if the morals conveyed are negative, should such music be banned? Censored? If not, what should be done? Based on what you've learned here about the narrative paradigm, what constitutes a negative message, and who gets to decide that? What is your role as a critical consumer of such messages and why?

So the narrative perspective reveals how popular culture texts function rhetorically by proposing value-laden ideological arguments about how to believe or behave. They do so through the storytelling narrative paradigm. Critics evaluate the value-laden ideological arguments through the elements of coherence and fidelity offered as good reasons to accept the moral as valid. Examining texts in this way affords us the ability to make conscious choices about the values we choose to believe, accept, and abide by personally and about the values others may hold that differ from our own.

SAMPLE PUBLISHED ESSAYS

(1) Read the article titled, "Technology and Mythic Narrative: *The Matrix* as Technological Hero-Quest," by Scott R. Stroud (2001) that appeared in the Fall 2001 issue of *The Western Journal of Communication*. In it, Stroud uses the narrative perspective to examine the character Neo as a technological hero. He argues that the narrative theme is that of "solitary enlightenment" and the moral is that alienated heroes may necessarily destroy "disillusioned" human beings in the name of the greater goal of saving humanity.

As you read the paper, identify the good reasons set forth for accepting the moral as valid. Notice the major events Stroud describes as *separation, initiation,* and *return*. Also pay particular attention to the two distinct audiences identified by Stroud as the *alienated* and the *hackers* and how the good reasons are offered in ways that allow each group to identify with Neo as a hero or model figure. Finally, consider the potential implications set forth for alienated individuals who fear their value is being replaced by technology as well as for the hacker individuals who are masters of technology but also recognize corporate abuse of technology as detrimental to democratic society. Why is the notion of *solitary enlightenment* disturbing in this case? As Stroud writes, this separation theme is most troubling because "the hero with whom the modern audience identifies" is an individual who does not see himself or herself as part of society, but somehow above it and "is also the individual who may destroy the community [in the name of enlightenment] in order to save it" (p. 439).

(2) Read the article titled, "Decades away or *The Day After Tomorrow?*: Rhetoric, Film and the Global Warming Debate," by Ron Von Burg (2012) that appeared in the March 2012 issue of *Critical Studies in Media Communication*. In it, Von Burg explores the narrative espoused in it about the truth of climate change, how scientists attempted to use it to educate the general public, and the consequences that resulted in doing so. Essentially, Von Berg argues that, although the underlying argument has merit, the sensationalized plot went too far in terms of material coherence for scientific credibility. Still the film demonstrates that "nontraditional forms of argument in public controversies challenge the norms . . . [in ways that reveal] . . . new sites of critical intervention" (pp. 19–22). As you read the article, consider the elements of narrative rationality and analysis discussed in this chapter. Do you agree with Von Burg's assessment? Explain.

SAMPLE STUDENT ESSAY

Alfred Cotton wrote the following essay as part of a class project. His, paper, "Good Story and Problematic Morality: A Narrative Analysis of *The Help*," examines the critically acclaimed motion picture using a narrative approach to reveal several troubling issues related to the ideological moral being proposed in it. As you read the essay, consider what we have discussed in this chapter in terms of how the characters, plot, and action are portrayed as good reasons to accept the argument or moral as valid. How does this text operate as a site of struggle in terms of reinforcing or opposing taken-for-granted beliefs and behaviors? Finally, consider the implications Alfred discusses if, in fact, viewers are persuaded to agree with ideological rhetoric undergirding the story. Do you agree with Alfred? Why or why not?

Good Narrative and Problematic Morality: A Systematic Narrative Analysis of *The Help*

Alfred J. Cotton, III

The Help was one of the top-grossing and critically acclaimed movies of 2011 (White & Bennett, 2011). The movie garnered Academy Award nominations for best actress, best picture, and two for best supporting actress. Moreover, Octavia Spencer won Best Supporting Actress for her portrayal of Minny. What made this film about racial tension and oppression of black female domestic workers in the 1960s Jim Crowe South resonate so well with filmgoers and critics alike? Moreover, what ideological arguments does it propose, and what might be potential implications of these messages on viewers? This essay examines elements of the film from a narrative perspective in an attempt to answer these very questions.

NARRATIVE ANALYSIS/CRITICISM

Narrative analysis is a method of inquiry wherein the researcher understands human communication as functioning at its most potent when there is a clear narrative with obvious characters, setting, and themes (Fisher, 1984, 1985, 1989). The narrative critic examines how these aspects of a story contribute to persuasive arguments being conveyed (Rowland, 1989, 2009).

Characteristics of narrative were introduced in Aristotle's *Poetics*. He emphasized a set of rules to describe an "ideal narrative" as follows:

- A story needs a plot with a beginning, middle, and end.

- The highest level of tension (i.e., climax) should coincide with the actual middle of the narrative.
- The story should be about a hero/protagonist who represents someone "important" in the polis.
- The tension in the narrative comes from a conflict, which is condensed in the character of the antagonist.
- The narrative should arouse feelings of pity and fear in the spectator as they identify with the hero and, by working together through the conflict with the hero, eventually get a feeling of "catharsis" (a mental/psychic kind of "cleansing" or an obtaining of a "new understanding"). The entire narrative's aim is the bringing about catharsis in the spectator. (Else, 1967)

Each of these aspects of an "ideal narrative" is explored in this analysis of *The Help*.

During the 20th century, narrative criticism as a rhetorical method was heavily influenced by Walter R. Fisher (1984). He introduced the "Narrative Paradigm" to communication theory. Fisher argued that all communication is a form of narrative storytelling. Narration is comprised of symbolic actions, words, and/or deeds that have sequence and meaning for those who live, create, or interpret them. Among his fundamental suppositions are: (1) people are essentially storytellers, (2) we make decisions on the basis of good reasons, history, biography, culture, and character, (3) narrative rationality is determined by the probability and fidelity of our stories, and

(4) the world is a set of stories from which we constantly re-create, our lives.

Robert C. Rowland (1987, 1989, 2009) further developed the narrative perspective and provides the systematic approach used for this analysis. More specifically, I begin by identifying the form of the narrative, followed by an examination of its function. Finally, I link the form and function to understand how the narrative works to convey its argument for a particular audience.

FORM IDENTIFICATION

The Help tells the story of black female domestic workers living in Jackson, Mississippi, in the early 1960s. The film is told from the perspective of Skeeter, a young white woman from Jackson's upper class. Viewers watch as Skeeter begins her journey toward becoming a successful writer and journalist. She gets a job at a local newspaper and is assigned to write a cleaning advice column for women. After a few interactions with some of the black domestic workers in town, she decides to write a story about the experiences of the maids themselves.

Skeeter focuses on two women: Aibeleen and Minny. Aibeleen works for the Leefolt family. The movie opens with Aibeleen telling Skeeter her story about how she knew she was going to be a maid even though she dreamed of doing "something more" with her life. She tells Skeeter this is all she's done, "I've done raised 17 kids in my life. Looking after white babies—that's what I do." Aibeleen is portrayed as a woman that genuinely cares about the children she raises. In fact, when her employer, Elizabeth Leefolt, walks into the room, viewers notice that Aibeleen cares

more about the youngest child, Fanny Leefolt, than Fanny's own mother does. Abileen earns 94 cents an hour[1] and works 48 hours a week. Aibeleen is calm, compliant, and causes no trouble. In contrast, her best friend Minny is framed as a deviant in the context of this oppressive occupation. For example, she is shown using her employers' bathroom without permission and talking back to her employers.

Minny's employer, Hilly Holbrook, is the story's primary antagonist. She represents Jim Crow "old South" values. She's a member of the White Citizens' Council and utters phrases like, "they have different diseases than we do" in response to why she wouldn't use a bathroom she thought Aibeleen possibly used. Hilly Holbrook is the archetypal antagonist. Her role is to cause conflict for the story's heroes. Being Minny's employer, she is framed as a powerful figure within the narrative. This is exemplified when Hilly decides to fire Minny for refusing to use the maids' bathroom (which is located off the property) during a tornado.

Rowland (2009) notes if the power difference between the protagonist and the antagonist is too great, the narrative will not be as interesting for the viewers. Hilly Holbrook is situated as having more power than the domestic workers. Her position as a white woman at the top of the social ladder not only makes her more dominant than Aibeleen and Minny, but she holds power over Skeeter, as

---

[1]This is quite less than the $1.25 minimum wage of 1963 ("History of Federal Minimum Wage Rates Under the Fair Labor Standards Act, 1938–2009," U.S. Dept. of Labor, http://www.dol.gov/whd/minwage/chart.htm).

(Continued)

(Continued)

well. This power situation allows the narrative to function as a site for a cooperative alliance among Skeeter, Aibeleen, and Minny. Because she is white, Skeeter is situated in a position higher than the maids. Thus, it is only through her help that Aibeleen and Minny can achieve their goals of fair representation in the workforce. This power struggle is the heart of the narrative. Hilly Holbrook, as the primary antagonist, becomes the strongest obstacle in Aibeleen and Minny's path toward social justice and freedom from oppression in the workforce.

That the narrative is located in Jackson, Mississsippi, is important in understanding the themes and underlying arguments proposed in the film. Jackson, Mississippi, was one of the most contentious sites of struggle during the fight for civil rights in the 1960s (Dittmer, 1995). The real-life Jackson was the location for sit-ins, read-ins, and numerous civil rights marches, as well as the town where Medgar Evers (receiving a brief mention in the film) was murdered. The real-life Jackson was also the site of many black-helmed organizations that aimed at improving the lot of blacks in the United States. One such notable organization was the Council of Federated Organizations (COFO), an umbrella coalition of civil rights organizations (Andrews, 1997). Among the activities undertaken by the COFO were: the organization of Freedom Vote—an initiative aimed at symbolically demonstrating the power of black voters in 1964 state and national elections; a movement "to unseat the all-White Mississippi delegation to the Democratic Party's 1964 National Convention in Atlantic City" (p. 804); and the formation of several influential civil rights organizations under its jurisdiction such as the Mississippi Freedom Democratic Party, the Student Nonviolent Coordinating Committee, and the Congress of Racial Equality, among others.

The Jackson depicted in *The Help* was not much like the real Jackson during the 1960s. The Jackson in the film represents a site where black women working as domestics did have labor issues but, for the most part, got along with their white employers as long as they kept in line. The Jackson in the film was a site where blacks had little agency with which they could mobilize for their own justice and equality. As such, filmmakers depicted Jackson as a town where black domestic workers had to rely on white allies for any semblance of upward mobility.

Two primary moral messages are posited in the story. First, the narrative attempts to claim that racial progress can only be made through blacks and whites working together. This reiterates a number of common themes in Hollywood's interpretation of race issues. We can look to movies like *Cry Freedom* where the primary issue in the film was racial equality but the narrative was seen through the eyes of a white protagonist. This is not to say that white people cannot or did not have a significant role in helping bring about some racial parity. The problem rests in the fact that this film attempts to tell the audience that the only way these domestic workers could have any voice or agency in changing their lot was through a white interventionist. In truth, however, blacks were implicit in structuring their own ideas of racial equality. There were a number of black-led organizations and movements in Jackson and throughout Jim Crow South where African-Americans were able to make their voices heard without help or handouts from whites.

Second, the film frames the three woman protagonists, Aibeleen, Skeeter, and Minny, as united by their womanhood. Because three women serve as the protagonists of the movie, viewer attention is drawn to the fact these women share a bond as women. This moral argues that "you're black, I'm white, but we're both united as women under the same patriarchy." As bell hooks (1989) argued:

> When liberal whites fail to understand how they can and/or do embody white supremacist values and beliefs even though they may not embrace racism as prejudice or domination (especially domination that involves coercive control), they cannot recognize the ways their actions support and affirm the very structure of racist domination and oppression that they wish to see eradicated. (p. 113)

Thus, Skeeter essentially embodies the injustice she seeks to eradicate for Aibeleen, Minny, and the other domestic workers. Skeeter is not a woman oppressed under patriarchy in the same manner as the maids about whom she writes. Skeeter fails to acknowledge her privileged position in Jackson and, in doing so, invites the audience to ignore it, as well.

FUNCTIONAL ANALYSIS

The second step in Rowland's (2009) systematic perspective on narrative analysis involves answering the following four questions: 1) "Does the narrative energize the audience?" 2) "Does the narrative create a sense of identifications between the characters or the narrator and the audience?" 3) "Does the narrative transport the audience to a place or time different from contemporary life?" 4) "Does the narrative tap into basic values or needs of the audience?" (p. 129). These questions get at the two basic functions of narrative, the epistemic and the persuasive. The epistemological properties of a narrative are grounded in its ability to satisfy a coherent truth (Fisher, 1984), that is, specifically, its narrative probability. The persuasive function is fulfilled by directly addressing these four questions.

Narrative Probability

Mink (1978) argued that narrative is the primary cognitive method through which humans understand the world. This is reiterated when Fisher (1984) argues that the guiding metaphor of human understanding is *homo narrans*, or humans as storytelling animals. Human beings like stories and stories provide a way of "recounting or accounting for human choice and action" (Fisher, 1984, p. 6). Fisher (1985) elaborates:

> Narrative probability refers to formal features of a story conceived as a discrete sequence of thought and/or action in life or literature (any recorded or written form of discourse); i.e., it concerns the question of whether or not a story coheres or "hangs together," whether or not the story is free of contradictions. (p. 349)

When a story "hangs together," an audience views it as probable. When a narrative is probable, an

(Continued)

(Continued)

audience concludes that the narrative makes sense. This is exemplified when (1) stories consist of a traditional narrative with a beginning, middle, and end, (2) the events in the story seem as if they could actually occur, and (3) none of the events in the story make any others seem improbable. This probability is present in *The Help*.

The narrative of *The Help* "hangs together." The narrative arc is present as the film opens with portraying Aibeleen in her role as a maid, taking care of the Leefolt child. Considering the story is set in the 1960s southern United States, it seems probable that Aibeleen would work for the Leefolt family and, in Aibeleen's words, do "all the cooking, cleaning, washing, ironing, and grocery shopping." The middle of the film is concerned with Skeeter's production of the book on the working conditions of the domestic workers in Jackson. These events are presented rationally as a "guide to belief and action" (Fisher, 1985, p. 355). They represent a guide insofar as the descriptions of what the maids go through at the hands of their employers.

One major turning point near the middle of the film is where the death of Medgar Evers represents a call to action for other maids to also tell Skeeter their stories. The film represents Skeeter's book as a guide through which the maids can enact some agency for themselves and have a voice. The tension resolves with Skeeter finding out she got a job for a renowned publisher in New York. Reluctantly, Skeeter accepts the position after telling Aibeleen and Minny how she can't leave them in Jackson without her. They persuade her to go saying she has nothing left to keep her in Jackson. The very next scene shows Hilly Holbrook telling Elizabeth Leefolt to fire Aibeleen for a false theft accusation.

The events in the film flow rationally. That is, the events all occur as if they could actually happen in real life. The setting of Jackson, Mississippi, is important in grounding the film not only in a realistic place but a real place. The audience, even without an extensive knowledge of Jim Crow South or Jackson's civil rights era history, can see Mississippi as a probable place where events involving tense race relations would occur. These elements of both the plot and the setting provide a rational grounding from which the audience can create an understanding of not only the film's narrative but also 1960s racial issues in reality.

Narrative Fidelity

Narrative fidelity has to do with whether the story can energize an audience or keep its attention (Rowland, 2009). Rowland argues that pop culture is "chock full" of narrative; it is the reason why so much of popular culture is narrative movies and television shows. *The Help* grabs and keeps its audience's attention in two primary ways. First, the film uses women as the protagonists and antagonists in the film. Seventy-four percent of the audience for *The Help* was women (McClintock, 2011). Considering the success many 2011 films like *Bridesmades*, for example, that used a primary female cast of the main characters, *The Help* would likely succeed in leading female audiences to subscribe to the morals presented in it. Second, the film uses a white protagonist to tackle issues of racial injustice in the 1960s. Considering the history of the Jim Crow South, it would be hard to make a film where white characters were seen as the sympathetic characters in a movie set during that time period. However, *The Help* accomplishes this by using Skeeter as emblematic of a positive white voice ahead of her time regarding opinions about race and equality. This portrait of Skeeter leads directly into the answer to the second question.

The second question asks, "Does the narrative create a sense of identification between characters and the audience?" Skeeter is the archetypal liberal white woman. She is progressive on ideas about women in the workforce, about women and their relationships to men, and, most importantly, on issues regarding race. One could argue that Skeeter is a prototype of 1990s, 2000s, and 2010s feminism. Unlike the other white women in the film, Skeeter does not define herself by whether she will be married. Though she does date one man briefly during the film, that relationship is not a priority for her, especially when it comes into conflict with her work. This is even a point of contention between Skeeter and her mother and between her and Hilly Holbrook. Both her mother and Hilly suggest that Skeeter is going to end up an old maid (or that she's a lesbian) because she cares more about being a successful writer than finding a husband.

As a writer, Skeeter is the only white woman in the film in Jackson to have a job. She idolizes her future publisher in New York, Elaine Stein, because she is the head of a publishing company. The second scene in the film is in fact a shot of Skeeter walking into a newsroom applying for a job. She is aggressive and assertive about her desire to make it as a successful writer.

Finally, Skeeter is more progressive than any other white female character in the film with regard to her opinions about race. Skeeter is portrayed as the propelling force behind the maids'

efforts to improve themselves by telling their story about their experiences as domestics. Skeeter has few friends, and all of them are maids. These three qualities make her a model for identification for modern white female audiences. Most white females viewing this film would identify more closely with Skeeter than any of the other characters. This is one of the most powerfully persuasive functions of a narrative (Fisher, 1984), creating in the audience's mind an idea that they are just like the character they see on screen.

The third question asks the critic to determine whether the narrative functions "transport the audience to a place or time different from contemporary life." This process functions to "break down barriers to understanding" (Rowland, 2009, p. 122). Jackson, Mississippi, in the 1960s is not like Jackson, Mississippi, today. Quite unlike Jackson then, black women today are not restricted to working primarily as domestic workers. Black women during the early 20th century continuing up through the 1960s were "the main and almost exclusive servant caste" (Glenn, 1992, p. 8). As a result of Skeeter's positioning in the narrative, the audience can assume the film is intended for white, female, American audiences who are led to identify with Skeeter and, thus, come to understand, even without prior knowledge, the struggles experienced by black women who could only find work as domestics up through the 1960s.

The final question asks the critic whether the narrative addresses the values and needs of the audience. To be persuasive in this context, a narrative must create a strong emotional reaction. Rowland (2009) argues that this occurs in the context of a character or set of characters. The relationship among Skeeter, Aibeleen, and Minny hits directly at this emotional appeal. Throughout

(Continued)

(Continued)

the film, Skeeter laughs and cries with Aibeleen and Minny as she experiences their pain and their stories as if they were her own. They act as a group, not as individuals, playing up the idea of their womanly bond. Aibeleen often refers to the book Skeeter is writing as "our stories," or she says things like, "I'm a writer" and refers to the book as something she wrote. This bond represents something the audience wants. The audience does not want to see a rift between black and white characters in this setting. The audience wants the black and white characters to get along similarly to how black people and white people get along in 2011. Not only do they want to see the good black characters and the good white characters become friends, but they also want to see the bad white characters get what's coming to them. This need is fulfilled when Hilly Holbrook eats a pie that Minny defecated in. In a sense, this character gets her just dessert.

The answer to each of these four questions is "yes." This functional interpretation of the narrative shows how the story operates to reinforce the argument of the movie. By making the appropriate characters likeable, the appropriate characters unlikeable, and certain characters dependent on others, the narrative can reinforce the two dominant themes listed above: that women are united through their experiences as women and that only with the help of white allies can blacks, particularly black women, achieve any racial progress.

LINKING FORM AND FUNCTION

The final step is to draw conclusions about the effectiveness of the narrative based on the form and function described above. Rowland

(2009) argues this step involves asking three questions: 1) "Are the formal elements and the plot compelling?" 2) "Does the narrative effectively fulfill narrative functions?" 3) "Is the narrative credible for a particular audience?" (p. 129).

The first question regarding compellingness is linked directly to an assessment of those formal elements of character, setting, plot, and theme. With regard to character, protagonists should be appealing and antagonists should be revolting (Rowland, 2009). This is the case in *The Help*. The protagonists (Skeeter, Minny, and Aibeleen) are characters with many redeeming qualities and few, if any, flaws. The only negative behavior comes in the form of rebellion against oppression aimed at the antagonist. To clarify, after Hilly Holbrook fires Minny for using her bathroom, Minny returns to Hilly's home with a pie to say she's sorry. Hilly thinks Minny is simply returning to ask for her job back, but actually, Minny has altered the pie as a form of payback. After taking more insults from Hilly, Minny tells Hilly, "Eat my shit." This phrase is a literal allusion to what Minny baked into the pie. This example of negative behavior occurs within the context of consistent abuse from the main antagonist, Hilly Holbrook.

An interesting plot and setting are also required to make the story compelling. Even though the movie is about race during one of the most tumultuous periods of American history, the plot often integrates comedy as relief. One example is when the character Celia Foote is introduced. Celia Foote is a social outcast among the white upper-class women in Jackson based on the fact she married one of Hilly Holbrook's old boyfriends. Not only is Celia a social outcast, but she also is a terrible cook. She enlists Minny's services, not as a cook or a maid, but as a cooking teacher. Hilarity ensues when Minny tries to teach Celia how to cook fried chicken and other foods without burning them. The fact that the setting, with regard to both time and place, is quite realistic allows the audience the potential to feel as if they are learning about the 1960s Jim Crow South through the film.

The second question refers to the degree to which the four functions of narrative were fulfilled. In sum, each of the four functions is fulfilled in the narrative of *The Help*. First, using a white protagonist and a primarily female cast grabs the audience's attention. Second, the (intended) audience can identify with Skeeter because she is framed as a modern and progressive woman in a backwards-thinking town. Third, the setting is different from the audience's personal life with regard to both time and place but grounded in realism. Finally, the story taps into the needs and values of a 21st-century audience with progressive views on race because it reinforces the idea that black women and white women are no different from one another.

The final question to be answered is whether the narrative is credible for a particular audience. Rowland (2009) argues that credibility should not be confused with truth. Credibility is the degree to which a story is likely to be accepted by a particular audience. Because the intended audience is white American women, one can argue that they would find this narrative credible. Even the antagonist makes the story more credible because people can imagine Hilly Holbrook as an actual person.

By answering these questions based on both the narrative form and the narrative function, it can be argued that *The Help* functions as a coherent narrative. Specifically, the narrative functions to teach viewers lessons about being open-minded and egalitarian when it comes to issues of race. The primary function is the idea that black women and white women share a common bond.

CONCLUSIONS AND IMPLICATIONS

The story told in *The Help* is a quality narrative. Even though *The Help* holds up as a good narrative, the morals proposed are potentially damaging for three primary reasons.

First, the narrative painted this way presents an inaccurate view of the reality of Jim Crow South, especially in early 1960s Mississippi. The message in the film does not truly discuss the brutal conditions under which black women lived and worked during that time. Ignored in this film are, for example, the sexual harassment, rape, frequent wage garnishing, and lack of job security for black domestic workers.

Second, framing this story from the perspective of a white protagonist normalizes the idea that only through white intervention were black women able to achieve any success in improving their place in southern society. This film ignores the work and struggle of organizations like the Domestic Workers Union, the National Negro Congress, the Council of Federated Organizations, and the National Domestic Workers Union among others. These African-American and African-American woman-led organizations, rallied, protested, and marched, often putting their lives and safety at risk, working to secure for

(Continued)

(Continued)

black women fair wages, appropriate working conditions, and job security (Andrews, 1997; McDuffie, 2008). The film paints black women as voiceless and without agency. Aibeleen and Minny can only have a voice or make something change for themselves through a college-educated, maid-raised, upper-class, white woman's words. In addition, black men's role in helping to improve things for black women is utterly ignored in the film. The only black male directly related to any of the protagonists in the film is Minny's husband—an abuser who beats her for losing her job and forces their daughter to drop out of school to become a domestic worker.

Third, this film paints women as a united monolithic category where race and class are invisible. This framing creates a world where black and white women are equally oppressed under patriarchy, which was far from the case. On the surface, the interaction between white upper-class Skeeter, and black working-class (underclass) Aibeleen and Minny seems like it positively reinforces the notion that people working together in spite of differences can be an impetus to social change. This criticism is not to say that there is no place for white allies or that there were no positive white influences in the civil rights movement. This film overlooks the intersectionality of gender, race, and social class as compounding oppressions or as Louise Thompson (1936) put it, "Over the whole land, Negro women meet this triple exploitation—as workers, as women, and as Negroes. They constituted, therefore, the most exploited group in America." Again, it is not the argument here that white men and women could not be sympathizers of the plight of African-Americans. The argument here is that this film normalizes an exaggerated significance of whites' help in initiating racial

progress and ignores the actual efforts made by and struggles of blacks. These inaccurate constructions also contribute to perpetuating a climate where black women earn 60 cents for every dollar earned by white men or where one quarter of black women live below the poverty line or where black women have an unemployment rate double the national average and 60 percent higher than white women (American Association of University Women, 2012).

The Help is a good film. The movie has narrative rationality, it has consistent temporal progression, and it teaches a moral to which its audience can adhere. The fact that this film is a good narrative, however, is also what makes its problematic discourse on race even more damaging. The negative, offensive, and oppressive messages presented in the film are only exacerbated when a narrative is well produced and cogent enough to allow viewers to identify with the characters, underlying themes, and moral arguments.

References

American Association of University Women. (2012). *The simple truth about the gender pay gap.* Washington, DC. Linda D. Hallman.

Andrews, K. T. (1997). The impacts of social movements on the political process: The civil rights movement and black electoral politics in Mississippi. *American Sociological Review*, 800–819.

Dittmer, J. (1995). *Local people: The struggle for civil rights in Mississippi.* Urbana, IL: University of Illinois Press.

Else, G. F. (1967). *Aristotle: Poetics.* Forgotten Books.

Fisher, W. R. (1984). Narration as a human communication paradigm: The case of public moral argument. *Communication Monographs, 51*(1), 1–22.

Fisher, W. R. (1985). The narrative paradigm: An elaboration. *Communication Monographs, 52,* 347–367.

Fisher, W. R. (1989). Clarifying the narrative paradigm. *Communication Monographs, 56*(1), 55–58.

Glenn, E. N. (1992). From servitude to service work: Historical continuities in the racial division of paid reproductive labor. *Signs, 18*(1), 1–43.

hooks, b. (1989). *Talking back: Thinking feminist, thinking black.* Cambridge, MA: South End Press.

McClintock, P. (2011). "The Help" audience: Just who exactly is going to see it? *The Hollywood Reporter.* Retrieved from http://www.hollywoodreporter.com/

McDuffie, E. S. (2008). Esther V. Cooper's "The Negro woman domestic worker in relation to trade unionism": Black left feminism and the popular front. *American Communist History, 7*(2), 203–209.

Mink, L. O. (1978). Narrative form as a cognitive instrument. In R. H. Canary and H. Kozicki (eds.), *The writing of history: Literary form and historical understanding* (pp. 129–149). Madison: University of Wisconsin Press.

Rowland, R. C. (1987). Narrative: Mode of discourse or paradigm? *Communication Monographs, 54*(3), 264–275.

Rowland, R. C. (1989). On limiting the narrative paradigm: Three case studies. *Communication Monographs, 56*(1), 39–54.

Rowland, R. C. (2009). The narrative perspective. In J. Kuypers (Ed.), *Rhetorical Criticism: Perspective in Action* (pp. 117–142). Lanham, MD: Lexington Books.

Thompson, L. (1936). Toward a brighter future. *The Woman Today, 14*(30).

White, M., & Bennett, A. (2011, August 22). "The Help" rises to no. 1 with $20 million in sales. *Bloomberg,* Retrieved: http://www.bloomberg.com/news/2011-08-21/-the-help-rises-to-no-1-at-box-office-with-20-5-million-in-ticket-sales.html

Summary

This chapter outlined the guidelines by which to conduct a narrative analysis. More specifically, we talked about the general concepts of *narrative rationality* (coherence and fidelity) that ground the narrative perspective as rhetorical. We discussed reasons for conducting a narrative analysis in that the stories told in various texts can reinforce or call into question our value-laden reasons for believing and behaving in certain ways. As such, they also frame our understanding about why others might believe or behave in different ways.

We then detailed the process by which to select a text to examine via the narrative perspective based on four requirements. Essentially, they must: (1) offer at least two events, (2) be organized by time, (3) depict causation or necessary relationship between earlier and later events, and (4) present a unified subject.

From there, we discussed how to conduct a narrative analysis. First, you describe the setting, characters, narrator, events, causal relationships, temporal relationships, and target audience(s). Then, you interpret each of these elements as they function together as good reasons for accepting the ideological value-laden moral argument proposed as valid. Finally, you evaluate the story in terms of potential implications regarding how it may influence audiences to believe and behave.

Challenge

Watch the 1997 Academy-award winning movie *Life Is Beautiful* directed by Roberto Benigni. The film is essentially a love story, but it is set in Italy during and throughout World War II. As such, it violates our expectations of a love story by placing it in this tragic setting. Moreover, the overarching moral conveyed is more than "love conquers all." Rather, it speaks to universal audiences with its argument that "a persistent will to succeed can overcome adversity." As the setting, obstacles, and events grow ever more bleak, the protagonist refuses to succumb to the pressures of hopelessness and giving up. Examine the film using the criteria set forth in this chapter to understand the good reasons offered throughout the film that serve to support the moral as valid. Finally, evaluate the ideological argument by answering the "so what?" question in terms of potential implications it may have on various audiences.

References

Aristotle. (1954). *Poetics* (I. Bywater, Trans.). New York: Modern Library.

Black, E. (1978). *Rhetorical criticism: A study in method.* Madison: University of Wisconsin Press.

Booth, W. C. (1961). *The rhetoric of fiction.* Chicago: University of Chicago Press.

Booth, W. C. (1983). *The rhetoric of fiction* (2nd ed.). Chicago: University of Chicago Press.

Booth, W. C. (1988). *The company we keep: An ethics of fiction.* Berkeley, CA: University of California Press.

Burke, K. (1957). *The philosophy of literary form* (Rev. ed.). New York: Vintage.

Chatman, S. (1978). *Story and discourse: Narrative structure in fiction and film.* Ithaca, NY: Cornell University Press.

Chatman, S. (1990). *Coming to terms: The rhetoric of narrative in fiction and film.* Ithaca, NY: Cornell University Press.

Farrell, T. B. (1985). Narrative in natural discourse: On conversation and rhetoric. *Journal of Communication, 35,* pp. 109–127.

Fisher, W. R. (1984). Narration as a human communication paradigm: The case of public moral argument. *Communication Monographs, 51,* 1–22.

Fisher, W. R. (1987). *Human communication as narration: Toward a philosophy of reason, value, and action.* Columbia: University of South Carolina Press.

Fisher, W. R. (1995). Narration, knowledge and the possibility of wisdom. In W. R. Fisher & F. Goodman (Eds.). *Rethinking knowledge: Reflections across the disciplines* (pp. 169–192). New York: State University of New York Press.

Gerbner, G. (1969). Toward "cultural indicators:" The analysis of mass mediated message systems. *AV Communication Review, 17,* 137–148.

Gerbner, G., Gross, L., Morgan, M., & Signorielli, N. (1994). Growing up with television: The cultivation perspective. In J. Bryant and D. Zillman (Eds.). *Media effects: Advances in theory and research* (pp. 17–41). Hillsdale, NJ: Lawrence Erlbaum.

Jhally, S. (1995). *Dreamworlds II: Desire/sex/power in music videos* [video recording]. Northampton, MA: Media Education Foundation.

Johannesen, R. L. (1983). *Ethics in human communication* (2nd ed.). Prospect Heights, IL: Waveland.

Heritage, S. (2010, October 21). The Matrix: No. 13 best sci-fi and fantasy film of all time. *The Guardian,* Retrieved March 23, 2012, from http://www.guardian.co.uk/film/2010/oct/21/matrix-wachowskis-science-fiction

Lucaites, L., & Condit, C. M. (1985). Re-constructing narrative theory: A functional perspective. *Journal of Communication, 35,* 90–108.

Lucaites, L., Condit, C. M., & Farrell, T. B. (1985). Narrative in natural discourse: On conversation and rhetoric. *Journal of Communication, 35,* 109–127.

Martin, W. (1986). *Recent theories of narrative.* Ithaca, NY: Cornell University Press.

Mitchell, W. J. T. (Ed.). (1981). *Narrative.* Chicago: Chicago University Press.

Mumby, D. K. (Ed.). (1993). *Narrative and social control.* Newbury Park, CA: Sage.

Newton, A. Z. (1995). *Narrative ethics.* Cambridge, MA: Harvard University Press.

Ricoeur, P. (1984–1988). *Time and narrative* (Vols. 1–3, K. McLaughlin & D. Pellauer, Trans.). Chicago: University of Chicago Press.

Riessman, C. K. (1993). *Narrative analysis.* Newbury Park, CA: Sage.

Rowland, R. C. (1987). Narrative: Mode of discourse or paradigm? *Communication Monographs, 54,* 264–275.

Stroud, S. R. (2001, Fall). Technology and mythic narrative: *The Matrix* as technological hero-quest. *The Western Journal of Communication, 65*(4), 416–441.

Verderber, K. S., Verderber, R. F., & Sellnow, D. D. (2014). *Communicate!* (14th ed.). Boston, MA: Cengage Wadsworth.

Von Burg, R. (2012, March). Decades away or *The Day After Tomorrow?*: Rhetoric, film and the global warming debate. *Critical Studies in Media Communication, 29*(1), 7–26.

Warnick, B. (1987). The narrative paradigm: Another story. *Quarterly Journal of Speech, 73,* 172–182.

White, J. B. (1984). *When words lose their meaning: Constitutions and reconstitutions of language, character, and community.* Chicago: University of Chicago Press.

Student Study Site

Visit the Student Study Site at **www.sagepub.com/sellnow2e** to read interesting SAGE journal articles, view mobile-friendly key term flashcards, take chapter-specific online web quizzes to test your knowledge, and more!

Chapter 4

A Dramatistic Perspective

T he dramatistic perspective as a method of rhetorical criticism is most commonly attributed to literary theorist, philosopher, and rhetorician, Kenneth Burke (1897–1993), who published eight major books as well as numerous essays, letters, and articles on the subject. As is the case with Fisher and the narrative perspective, however, Burke is only one of many scholars across disciplines whose work contributes to our understanding of the life-as-drama metaphor that grounds dramaturgical analyses. Among them are Erving Goffman (1959), Victor Turner (1974), Bruce Gronbeck (1980), and Friedrich Nietzsche (1873). Interestingly Burke, who held professorial positions at prestigious universities such as Harvard and Princeton, never earned a college degree (although he attended both the Ohio State University and Columbia University). Still, his work is some of the most respected in the field and continues to inform dramatistic rhetorical analyses across disciplines today.

Dramatism is the label Burke (1965) gives to the study of human motivation by viewing events as dramas (p. 274). A dramatistic perspective differs from a narrative one (which focuses on how we make sense of the world through stories) by focusing on how we do so through dramas. Moreover, a dramatistic perspective is grounded in "theories of *action* rather than theories of *knowledge*" (Burke, 1968, p. 446). In fact, Burke (1966) rejected all theories that reduced human behavior to mere motion. The fundamental difference between a thing and a person, he argued, is that "one merely *moves* whereas the other *acts*" (p. 53). In other words, humans have the unique ability to choose to act. Thus, whereas both the narrative and dramatistic perspectives are focused on sense making about an ideology, a dramatistic perspective is more keenly interested in discovering underlying motives that incite human action.

The critic's ultimate goal is to understand what motivates people to behave in certain ways and the motives we use to justify our actions, particularly when those actions conflict with society's behavioral norms. Popular culture texts viewed through a dramatistic lens function as "equipment for living" by attempting to justify when and how it might be acceptable to break what Burke (1973) describes as society's "rules for living" (pp. 293–304) and, consequently, what we say and do to restore a sense of order. Three conceptual frameworks guide our discussion of dramatism: the dramatistic life cycle, cluster analysis, and the pentad.

THE DRAMATISTIC LIFE CYCLE

According to Burke (1969b), innate in the human condition is our desire to identify with others and with society. Burke calls this process of identification among people who share similar attitudes, values, ideas, experiences, goods, properties, and things consubstantiality (pp. 20–24). The opposite of consubstantiality is *division*. Because we want to feel identification, division produces guilt. Guilt is any feeling of tension within a person such as anxiety, angst, disgust, or embarrassment. We communicate to purge our guilt. Communication motivated by a desire to purge guilt and restore order is the essence of Burke's life as drama metaphor. This life cycle consists of order, pollution, guilt, purification, and redemption.

Order exists when people follow what Burke (1973) calls "rules for living" (pp. 293–304). These rules reinforce the cultural norms and behaviors of the accepted hierarchies of social order in a given society. Burke (1968) describes these rules as value-laden "moralistic" . . . "thou shalts" and "thou shalt nots" (p. 450). He (1984a) further claims that members of a society actively participate in maintaining our place in the hierarchy and accept our "role with relation to it" (p. 5). Pollution occurs when an individual rejects the social order (p. 21). Pollution may come in the form of rejecting our position in the hierarchy or rejecting the hierarchy altogether.

When individuals reject the hierarchy, we do not heed the thou-shalt and thou-shalt-not rules of the social order. Burke calls such violations sins. Sins can result from personal transgressions as well as from impossible demands placed on us by the social order. Whether we violate these rules intentionally or unintentionally, we experience guilt. When we feel guilt, we also feel the need for purification from it.

Purification is the absolution of guilt. We may be absolved from guilt through victimage (blaming someone or something else), mortification (punishing oneself), or transcendence (following a "higher calling"). Purification from guilt leads to redemption.

Redemption is a temporary rebirth into the social order of society. Burke (1984b) equates redemption with "the satisfying of a debtor by the paying of a ransom" (p. 292). He describes redemption as temporary because sin and guilt are eternal. The dramatistic life cycle process begins anew with each new and inevitable violation of the social order.

This ongoing dramatistic life cycle is represented across all popular culture text genres (e.g., comedy, romance, action, Western, horror, science fiction). For example, it appears in cartoons like *The Simpsons* and *Family Guy* where both Homer and Peter perpetually mess up and are then forgiven by Marge and Lois. It occurs in feel-good romance dramas like *The Vow* where Paige fails to heed the thou-shalt rule of loving her husband and is absolved from guilt because the memory loss causing it is not her fault. It shows up in comedies like *The Hangover* where Phil, Stu, and Alan are absolved from guilt about getting so drunk they forget the events of the evening because they couldn't help it; they were having a bachelor party. And it appears in action adventures and science-fiction plots like *The Hunger Games* where Katniss breaks the rules of the game to fight to kill in order to win. She does so over and over throughout the book and film and is both purified and redeemed because she is following a higher calling.

CLUSTER ANALYSIS

The dramatistic perspective maintains that language and other symbols ground our perception of reality and, thus, our motives for acting in certain ways. They do so by functioning as terministic screens, which are essentially verbal and nonverbal symbols that represent a particular worldview. These symbols act as filters that reflect and shape reality and motivate our behaviors. Burke (1965) coined the term *terministic screen* to account for the fact that words communicate more than what their denotative meanings suggest. People use terministic screens sometimes as enablers (granting permission for thinking or doing certain things) and sometimes as deterrents (preventing us from thinking or doing certain things). For example, in the dominant American culture, taking the life of another human being is generally not acceptable. That is, killing another human being is murder (deterrent) and it's wrong. However, if the killing occurs as a consequence of being given the death sentence (enabler) or when fighting in a war (enabler) or in self-defense (enabler), killing may be justified.

Moreover, terministic screens can be grouped together as they represent a particular worldview. Clusters are groups of associated symbols that suggest what goes with what, and agons are groups of symbols that reveal points of conflict by reinforcing opposites, that is, what versus what (Burke, 1973). We identify groups of clusters and agons based on frequency (how often they appear) and intensity (how forcefully they are portrayed). Analyzing groups of associated terministic screens as clusters and agons reveals insight into what social order worldview a text is perpetuating.

Cluster and agon themes that reinforce what is considered to be good, right, or desirable in a social order can be labeled God terms, and those that reinforce a perception of what is bad, wrong, or undesirable can be labeled devil terms (Weaver, 1985). When we speak of a thief as a "dirty rotten crook," for example, thief is a devil term (regarded as bad and wrong). If we describe the thief as a "homeless orphan trying to do what it takes for her and her siblings to survive on the streets of Chicago," thief might be portrayed more as a God term. This dialectic is essentially what Jean Valjean struggled with in *Les Miserables*. He went to prison for stealing a piece of bread to feed his sister's child. From then on, he struggled with the dialectical nature of human behavior as inherently good or bad depending on context and motive. The ways in which word clusters are ultimately completed is referred to as teleology. If, for example, a television program opens with a theft occurring at a convenience store, we want to know what eventually happens to the thief. When we find out, the symbol has been completed (teleology). In the *Les Miserables* example, teleology is illustrated by Jean Valjean's lifetime achievement in, among other things, raising Cosette, saving Marius's life, and "going home" to heaven.

APPLYING WHAT YOU'VE LEARNED . . .

Consider a time when you felt suspense watching a program because you were wondering how something would eventually be resolved. What would you describe as the terministic screens, clusters and agons, God and devil terms, and teleology?

THE PENTAD

Burke (1969a) offers the Pentad as a macrostructural framework for analyzing life as a drama represented in texts. Recall that dramatism rests on the supposition that we have an innate human need to identify with one another and society. Persuasion occurs when viewers of a drama can identify with the actors, their actions, and their motives. When perceived norms (a.k.a. rules for living) are violated, justifiable motives for those actions must be offered. Critics who examine texts from a dramatistic perspective do so by (1) describing the five elements of the drama (i.e., act, agent[s], agency, scene, and purpose), (2) determining the dominant element, and (3) revealing the motive offered as justification.

The Five Elements

The act refers to the rule-breaking behavior. In the example of the thief, the rule-breaking behavior is stealing. The agent(s) refers to the character(s) engaged in the rule-breaking act. In the thief example, in one case, the thief is a crook, and in the other, it is a homeless orphan girl. The agency refers to the tools, means, and techniques employed to accomplish the act. To continue with the thief analogy, the tools might include a weapon, a getaway car, and a mask, as well as a description of the approach used to avoid being caught. For the orphan, the tools might be her hands and picking pockets. The scene refers to the location and situation where the act takes place. The scene could be at a bank in a large city, a gas station along an interstate highway, or on sidewalks and in alleys in an inner city. The purpose refers to the explanation offered as to why the agent(s) engaged in the rule-breaking behavior. The purpose for the thief might be to get rich, to get back at society, or in the case of the orphan, to survive. Purpose is not the same as motive. Whereas purpose merely addresses why the agent(s) broke a rule, motive goes beyond purpose to argue what makes the rule-breaking behavior justifiable.

■ **TABLE 4.1** The Pentadic Ratios

Act-agent	Agent-act	Scene-act	Purpose-act
Act-agency	Agent-agency	Scene-agent	Purpose-agent
Act-scene	Agent-scene	Scene-agency	Purpose-agency
Act-purpose	Agent-purpose	Scene-purpose	Purpose-scene

The Ratios

To determine the motive, the critic creates pairings or ratios among the elements to reveal the dominant one in the drama (see Table 4.1). For each ratio, the critic determines whether or not the first term determines the second. The set of pairings that garners the most yes answers suggests what that motivating force might be. Recall our earlier discussion of the dramatistic life cycle. The motive is offered as justification for the behavior and, consequently, absolution from guilt.

The Motive

The critic's ultimate goal is to determine the motive(s) used to justify the rule-breaking behavior(s). In other words, when someone behaves in ways that do not adhere to the rules of the social order, they are charged as guilty and dissociated with as different from the rest of society. Burke (1969a, 1969b) calls this notion of alienation from others based on perceived difference mystery. To be redeemed and rejoin society, the guilty party labeled as different must be absolved of guilt. Absolution can be justified via transcendence, mortification, or victimage.

Transcendence

Recall that *transcendence* as motivation for breaking society's rules for living occurs when guilty actions are justified because the agent is following a higher calling. Popular culture texts where the actors break a social rule for the sake of love are examples of justification via transcendence. Most people are familiar with the film *It's a Wonderful Life*. Throughout the film, George Bailey (played by James Stewart) breaks society's rules by following a higher calling. As a young boy, for example, he jumps into a rushing river on purpose to save his brother's life and later disobeys his boss to save the lives of the people with diphtheria. As a young man, he foregoes his dreams of going to college and traveling around the world when it is "his turn to do so" to save the town by remaining in Bedford Falls to run the Building and Loan. And, as a husband and father, he almost commits suicide so his family can live by cashing in on his life insurance policy.

Mortification

Guilt is absolved through *mortification* when the agent confesses guilt and is punished for it in order to be purified and redeemed. This form of absolution is most readily apparent in Catholicism. When a person sins, he or she must confess to the sin and then perform some form of penance to be absolved from it. The United States criminal justice system is also based on this concept. When offenders break the law, they are sentenced to pay a fine, serve jail time, or in some other way repay their debt to society. In terms of popular culture texts, the award-winning film *Silver Linings Playbook* offers mortification as a justifiable motive for guilt absolution. When Pat nearly kills the history teacher he catches engaged in sexual relations with wife Nikki, he is sentenced to 8 months in a mental health institution and to abide by a restraining order to stay away from Nikki afterward. And when singer and songwriter Beck sings "I'm a loser baby, so why don't you kill me?" or Weezer sings "I'm sorry for what I did" and "I ain't never coming back; I'm sorry, I'm sorry, I'm sorry," they are also seeking absolution from guilt through mortification.

Victimage

Victimage is an attempt to absolve guilt for rule-breaking behaviors by blaming someone or something else. Hence, the agent is no longer at fault because someone or something else is to blame. This form of justification is sometimes also known as scapegoating. Justification motives offered on the award-winning TV program *Justified* almost always come in the form of victimage. Whether it is something a "good guy" does or a "bad guy" does, someone or something else is almost always to blame. Essentially, the argument posited is that they had no other choice.

APPLYING WHAT YOU'VE LEARNED . . .

Consider a time in your life when you justified doing something that you knew was wrong. What was your reason for doing it anyway? Would you consider your motive an example of transcendence, mortification, or victimage and why?

QUESTIONING YOUR ETHICS . . .

Some scholars contend that justification for rule-breaking behavior through victimage (that is, blaming it on someone or something else) is pervasive in society today. Do you agree with the scholars? Provide examples to support your opinion. If they are right, what might be some implications of this motive pervading society?

When victimage is offered as the motive for justifying behavior and absolving guilt, the rule breaker is also characterized as a *comic fool* or a *tragic hero*. When the guilty party is absolved of guilt because someone or something else is to blame and the error is portrayed as inevitable or as a common human failing, they are accepted back into society as a comic fool. The person may be embarrassed but is also forgiven because he or she "really couldn't help it." For example, when Dennis the Menace enters the house with muddy shoes and his mom does not punish him because "boys will be boys," the text is treating Dennis as a comic fool whose guilt is absolved through victimage. Many of the rule-breaking actions Homer does on *The Simpsons* and Peter does on *Family Guy* are also absolved in this way.

The comic fool label may apply to humorous events as in the two examples provided here; however, a comic fool can also exist in serious ones. Hence, a comic fool is not necessarily linked to comedy as one might at first assume. Consider, for example, the fairly well-known Dixie Chicks song, "Goodbye Earl." The rule-breaking behavior in this song is murder; however, Mary Anne and Wanda are absolved of their sin for murder because it was portrayed as inevitable. The song argues that they had exhausted all other possibilities first, including a restraining order. Earl, in fact, managed to put Wanda in intensive care while he was under that restraining order. The listener is lead to believe that the next time Earl gets near Wanda, he will kill her. Hence, Mary Anne and Wanda poison Earl's food, dump the body in the lake, never get caught, and lose no sleep at night. Earl ultimately becomes a missing person statistic who "wasn't really missed at all." Wanda and Mary Anne were never punished for breaking a rule for living (murder) because it was actually Earl's fault for being abusive (victimage). Furthermore, because the murder was portrayed as inevitable, they were absolved through victimage as comic fools.

"Goodbye Earl" Lyrics

Mary Anne and Wanda were the best of friends

All through their high school days

Both members of the 4H club

Both active in the FFA

After graduation, Mary Anne went out lookin'

For a bright new world

Wanda looked all around this town

And all she found was Earl

Well, it wasn't two weeks

After she got married that

Wanda started gettin' abused

She put on dark glasses and long-sleeved blouses

And makeup to cover a bruise

Well, she finally got the nerve to file for divorce

She let the law take it from there

But Earl walked right through that restraining order

And put her in intensive care

Right away, Mary Anne flew in from Atlanta

On a red-eye midnight flight

She held Wanda's hand as they

Worked out a plan
And it didn't take long to decide

That Earl had to die
Goodbye, Earl
Those black-eyed peas
They tasted all right to me, Earl
You're feeling weak
Why don't you lay down
And sleep, Earl
Ain't it dark
Wrapped up in that tarp, Earl

The cops came to bring Earl in
They searched the house
High and low
Then they tipped their hats
And said, "Thank you, ladies
If you hear from him, let us know"

Well, the weeks went by and
Spring turned to summer
And summer faded into fall
And it turns out he was a missing person
Who nobody missed at all

So the girls bought some land
And a roadside stand
Out on Highway 109
They sell Tennessee ham
And strawberry jam
And they don't
Lose any sleep at night 'cause

Earl had to die
Goodbye, Earl

We need a break

Let's go out to the lake, Earl

We'll pack a lunch

And stuff you in the trunk, Earl

Well, is that all right

Good, let's go for a ride

Earl, hey

When the rule-breaking action is portrayed as someone or something else's fault, but the rhetor must be punished in order to reenter society, she or he is treated as a tragic hero. Similar to the comic fool, the person's actions are portrayed as inevitable or perhaps as a character flaw; however, in this case, the actions cannot be dismissed. If, in "Goodbye Earl," Mary Anne and Wanda had been tried and convicted for murdering Earl, they would have been tragic heroes rather than comic fools. In other words, a tragic hero does not have to do with being a good guy as it often implies. It merely means the action is justified via victimage and the person committing the action must be punished in some way.

So why might one conduct a dramatistic analysis? Essentially, doing so helps us understand why we hold certain opinions about when, where, and why it might be justifiable to break society's rules for living. To clarify, let us continue with the murder example portrayed in "Goodbye Earl." The song argues that murder might, in some cases, be justifiable, such as in domestic abuse cases where nothing else succeeds in protecting the victim. Of course, this notion is certainly debatable. But the fact that it is debatable at all provides a reason for examining the messages conveyed in texts through a dramatistic perspective. Let us take it a step further. Consider capital punishment. Is that murder? Is it ever OK to put someone to death for a crime he or she committed? What if the person had raped or murdered scores of children? These are the kinds of questions the dramatistic perspective encourages us to grapple with, that is, what are portrayed as justifiable motives for breaking society's rules for living? How might such messages in popular culture texts influence our opinions by reinforcing them or, perhaps, challenging them?

QUESTIONING YOUR ETHICS . . .

Redemption through victimage by a comic fool suggests that someone or something else is to blame and that the person who did wrong should not be punished for committing the rule-breaking act. When might redemption through victimage by a comic fool be troubling and why?

CONDUCTING A DRAMATISTIC ANALYSIS

The dramatistic perspective can be used to analyze any mediated popular culture text. It is particularly useful to understand what is being argued about appropriate and inappropriate rules for living in the status quo and justifiable motives for breaking them. The following paragraphs describe how to conduct a dramatistic criticism first by selecting an artifact and examining it using the tools of the Pentad and then by offering sample essays using it. One is a published essay on the popular video game Bioshock and the other is a sample student paper on the popular TV program *Weeds*.

Step 1: Selecting an Appropriate Text

Virtually any mediated popular culture artifact can serve as a text for analysis via the dramatistic perspective. In addition to considering the rhetorical situation (i.e., sender, occasion, audience, exigence, constraints) that you do when selecting any text and perspective, as you select a text for a dramatistic analysis, also consider what rule-breaking behavior seems to be occurring in it. Sometimes, the action is quite obvious as in "Goodbye Earl." Other times, you may only have a hunch that something does not seem right, but you cannot really put your finger on it. A former student, for example, selected the song, "It Wasn't Me," by Shaggy. At the surface, the song seemed to be about cheating on your partner by having sexual intercourse with the neighbor "on the bathroom floor." She sensed there was more to it, though, and ultimately argued that the rule-breaking behavior being justified throughout the song was that lying to your partner is OK (justifiable motive) if you can get away with it.

APPLYING WHAT YOU'VE LEARNED . . .

Select a mediated popular culture text where someone appears to be breaking society's taken-for-granted rules for living. What rule is being broken? Explain.

Step 2: Examining the Text (Describe and Interpret)

Recall that every rhetorical criticism is examined via description, interpretation, and evaluation. When conducting your analysis from a dramatistic perspective, you can begin by describing the drama according to the five elements of the Pentad (act, agent, agency, scene, and purpose).

First, describe the act, which is the rule-breaking behavior that takes place in the text. In "Goodbye Earl," the act is the murder. You usually provide as much detail about the act as the text allows you to do.

Second, identify the agent or agents. These are the main characters that participate in the act. When you describe the agents, you also may include a description of their characteristics. In "Goodbye Earl," the agents are Mary Anne and Wanda. You might describe them as "good" kids who participated in 4H and FFA as best friends through high school who are still best friends today as Mary Anne jumped the "red-eye midnight flight" to get home to help her best friend Wanda.

The agency has to do with the tools, means, and techniques used to accomplish the act. In "Goodbye Earl," the tools are the poison they put in the black-eyed peas Earl ate for dinner, the tarp they used to wrap the body, and the trunk of the car they drove to dispose of the body in the lake.

The scene is the location and situation where the act takes place. This might also include a description of the physical conditions, historical causes, and social or cultural influences. The scene in "Goodbye Earl" is Wanda's home. The women plan the murder there, the murder takes place there, and the police absolve the women there. This is also where Earl abused Wanda so badly that she ended up in intensive care. Hence, Wanda's home is a terministic screen that was ultimately completed as teleology. Her home was where Earl beat her up, and it was also ultimately where Earl "had to die" and did die.

The purpose is the fifth element of the Pentad. The purpose helps determine the motive, but it is not synonymous with motive. The purpose explains why the agent or agents engaged in the rule-breaking behavior. In the case of "Goodbye Earl," the women killed Earl so he would no longer be able to abuse or possibly even kill Wanda. The motive is a larger explanation, an explanation that is not specific only to the situation described in the text but also to us as we seek to clarify our rules for behavior as "equipment for living" (Burke, 1973, pp. 293–304). These larger motives are discovered as we apply the motives for absolution of guilt: transcendence, mortification, and victimage.

Once you have named the terms according to the Pentad, you must interpret what seems to be featured as the main point of the drama. Recall that you do so by charting ratios, which lead to understanding the motive. In other words, what seem to be offered as justifiable reasons for the behavior? In "Goodbye Earl," you might argue that the explanation is purpose driven. The act is justified because these upstanding women had exhausted all possibilities, which essentially left them no alternatives: "Earl had to die."

Step 3: Evaluating Potential Implications of the Text

Finally, you evaluate the text. What value is there in conducting a dramatistic analysis of this text? What are the potential implications of this message on various audiences? In "Goodbye Earl," you might talk about issues like domestic abuse and the failure of the legal system to protect victims. You might talk about the ethical questions involved with taking the law into one's own hands. You might conclude by considering how this message might be used to justify similar actions as unavoidable even before exhausting other avenues. As always, it is the critic's responsibility to speculate about how this message might influence our opinions about when, where, and why it might be "appropriate" to break society's taken-for-granted "rules for living" (Burke, 1973, p. 304).

APPLYING WHAT YOU'VE LEARNED . . .

Consider once again the song, television episode, comic strip, or advertisement you selected earlier. Examine it using the Pentad. Finally, what is offered as justification for redemption (motive)? What might be the implications for society if we accept this motive as valid justification for breaking the rules for believing or behaving?

SAMPLE PUBLISHED ESSAY

Read Bourgonjon, Rutton, Soetaert, and Valcke's article titled, "From Counter-Strike to Counter-Statement: Using Burke's Pentad as a Tool for Analysing Video Games," published in 2011 in *Digital Creativity.* The article focuses on the motives offered in the video game Bioshock as justification for harvesting (i.e., killing) or rescuing (i.e., keeping alive) Little Sisters (i.e., little girls) either by extracting all of the powerful substance from them known as ADAM needed to fight off villains (thereby killing them) or by extracting only a tiny amount (thereby allowing them to live). As you read, consider what the authors conclude regarding the ambiguous mismatch between the representational and procedural levels of the game as experienced by those who actually play it. Based on this analysis, do you think video game producers ought to consider and account multiperspectivism and potential ambiguities among gamers who will ultimately interact with their product? Why or why not?

SAMPLE STUDENT ESSAY

Renee Kaufmann wrote this essay as part of a class project. Her paper, "Love and Greed: It's All About the *Weeds,*" examines how Nancy Botwin's guilt about breaking society's rules (and, frankly, laws) for living (selling marijuana) is absolved through transcendence and victimage over the course of the first season. She discovered that justifications of transcendence and victimage early on focused on motives to be a good and loving mother and providing for her children. The justifications were gradually replaced with victimage motives about personal greed and thrill seeking without regard for the children by season's end. Ultimately, Kaufmann argues that Nancy neglects her children as she becomes more and more concerned about greed and thrill seeking. Do you think motives about loving and providing for family are justifiable reasons for breaking society's rules for living? Do you think the motives of greed and thrill seeking portrayed in *Weeds* reflect society today? Do you think TV programs like *Weeds* and the justifications for rule-breaking behavior they propose may serve to shape society's worldview? Explain.

Love and Greed: It Is All About the Weeds

Renee Kaufmann

When you have a child, he or she becomes the first priority, and everything else takes second place. C.S. Lewis (1996) echoes this belief, stating, "You can't get second things by putting them first; you can get second things only by putting first things first" (p. 14). A plethora of TV shows (e.g., *Supernanny, Modern Family, A Baby Story*), books (e.g., *What to Expect in The First Year, Parenting With Love and Logic*), and movies (e.g., *What to Expect When You're Expecting, Parenthood, Parent Trap*) suggest that, at least idealistically, the dominant

American culture values parents who demonstrate love for their children. Norms of our social order include an expectation that "good" parents who love their children will do whatever is necessary to provide for them (e.g., Douglas, 2003; Simpson, 1997). Parents who put children "second" as C.S. Lewis suggests do not enjoy the honor of being labeled as "good" parents at all.

Watching TV has become a routine habit in most households across the United States today. In fact, surveys suggest that people spend at least 30 percent of their waking hours watching TV, and what they view about parenting and family life does influence them (e.g., Bandura, 1977; Dail & Way, 1985; Douglas, 2003; Ex, Janssens & Korzilius, 2002). According to Douglas (2003), domestic (a.k.a. family) comedies confirm and perpetuate taken-for-granted perceptions about the family experience. Thus, this essay explores underlying messages about parenting and family life being conveyed on the popular TV domestic comedy *Weeds,* which debuted on Showtime in 2005.

Parenting, the Media, and Social Cognitive Theory

Media scholars have long suggested that TV influences the way individuals perceive their lives should and should not be lived. Social cognitive theory suggests that individuals are motivated to model the behaviors of TV characters whose actions produce positive outcomes and avoid modeling behaviors that have depicted negative consequences (Bandura, 2011). This is not to say that TV will cause certain behaviors such as violence or sexual promiscuity; however, it does provide the tools for enacting them (Bandura, 2011).

The transformation of family structures on TV has changed over the past 30 years. In today's shows that portray families, viewers see an array of family units, for example, single parent (e.g., *Suburgatory*), children who misbehave (e.g., *Modern Family*), and parents who are absent or deceased (e.g., *Weeds*). Simpson (1997), for example, explains that there is an "underrepresentation of many cultural groups; stereotypical portrayals of gender roles; depictions of young children as needing little care and supervision; and the depiction of parents as solving family problems quickly, easily, and in isolation from any support system" (p. 1).

This is a strict contrast to domestic shows like *The Dick Van Dyke Show, The Brady Bunch, Family Ties,* and *Cosby* where parents are present, children behave for the most part, and the father is the authority figure of the family.

Today's TV shows that portray the "typical American family" in a comedic way are referred to as domestic comedies. According to Leibman (2012), the term originated in 1974 by Horace Newcomb who provided the phrase as a "useful means of distinguishing between situation comedy, and the more broad-based, comedy" (p.1). Domestic comedies are a part of today's popular culture and "a common vehicle for the transport of family culture" (Douglas & Olson, 1995, p. 326).

Weeds

TV programs like *Weeds* bring a new perspective to the family dynamic portrayed on domestic

(Continued)

(Continued)

comedies. Because of the show's premise (widowed mother trying to maintain a certain lifestyle for her sons), tough conversations around death and how to maintain that lifestyle for the children's sake surface. The show's main character, Nancy Botwin, decides to do so in a somewhat controversial way, which is the foundation for her rule-breaking behavior. This paper employs a dramatistic perspective to examine the underlying arguments proposed in *Weeds* that serve to justify Nancy's rule-breaking behavior—selling illegal drugs.

Season one introduces viewers to main character, Nancy Botwin, a recently widowed mother living in an upper-class gated community in California. Viewers quickly learn that Nancy's profession is as the community's marijuana dealer. She claims to do it because she will do whatever is necessary to provide for her children so they can maintain the lifestyle they enjoyed before their father (Nancy's husband) died.

In this first episode, viewers are also introduced to Nancy's sons, Silas and Shane; Nancy's drug suppliers, Heylia and her family; a nosey and rude housewife named Celia; and the city councilman, Doug, and his drug dealing son, Josh. The format of the *Weeds* plot follows Nancy as she stumbles through the drug dealing game, becomes more and more involved in illegal activities, and attempts to deal with the consequences of doing so (IMDb, 2012).

According to *TV Guide* (2012), *Weeds* was one of the top 20 most popular shows for 2011. The 10 episodes brought in over a half million viewers each week. Examining how a popular show like *Weeds* justifies the rule-breaking behavior of a mother selling drugs to community members may shed light on what might also be suggested as an acceptable motive for doing so in suburbia today.

Dramatistic Perspective

Burke (1945) believes there is an innate need in each of us to identify with one another (Sellnow, 2010). Moreover, when we fail to heed social norms, we become alienated and feel guilty. Thus, we seek motives to justify breaking the rules so we can be redeemed and rejoin the social order. This analysis is grounded in Burke's (1945) dramatistic perspective as the theoretical framework to determine what motives Nancy uses as justification to absolve guilt about breaking the rules, actually the law, by selling illegal drugs. Burke's five elements—act, purpose, agency, agents, and purpose—work together to reveal the motivation behind the rule-breaking act (Foss, 2009). According to Sellnow (2010), "persuasion occurs when viewers of a drama can identify with the actor, their actions, and the motives offered for their actions" (p. 52).

A dramatistic perspective posits when "someone behaves in ways that are usually considered inappropriate, they are essentially charged as guilty in the minds of others" (Sellnow, 2010, p. 63). In order for guilt to be absolved, justification must occur. Guilt may be absolved in one of three ways: transcendence, victimage, or mortification. Sellnow (2010) explains that conducting a dramatistic analysis "helps us understand why we hold certain opinions about when, where, and why it might be justifiable to break society's rules for living" (p. 56). The purpose of this analysis is to examine Nancy

Botwin's rule-breaking behavior on the TV show *Weeds* to provide a better understanding of what might be deemed acceptable motives for parents (i.e., mothers) to break society rules in these ways. By describing the show according to the elements of Burke's Pentad, examining the rule-breaking behaviors enacted by main character, Nancy Botwin, as well as the motives posited as justification for doing so, we can speculate as to the implications such messages might mean for viewers as they may reflect and shape beliefs and behaviors.

METHOD

This analysis employed a textual rhetorical analysis using Burke's Pentad. A rhetorical analysis using the Pentad provides deeper insight into the process of justification and the reasoning provided for accepting the motives as valid (Neuendorf, 2002). The following section describes analytical procedure followed for selecting a text, creating categories, and coding.

The Text. The text consisted of the 10 episodes from the first season of *Weeds*. The episodes were gathered using Netflix. Each episode was 30 minutes long, thus the analysis is based on five hours of viewership. The examination focused only on Nancy Botwin's rule-breaking behavior for three reasons. First, Nancy is the main character of the show, and her actions drive the plot. Second, Nancy is a widowed mother who undertakes the role of pot dealer to make enough money to maintain her family's current lifestyle and so she can be around the house instead away from the kids at a job, thus

the premise of the show. Third, many characters in the show enact rule-breaking behaviors; however, those characters' behaviors are beyond the scope of this project.

The Categories. Nancy's rule-breaking behaviors were coded as they represented one of the three categories for absolving guilt proposed by Burke (1945): transcendence, victimage, or mortification.

Transcendence. According to Sellnow (2010), transcendence refers to "a higher calling." Each time Nancy absolved her guilt for the love of her children was coded as transcendence.

Victimage. This refers to "blaming someone or something else" to justify rule-breaking behavior (Sellnow, 2010, p. 54). Each time Nancy blamed someone or something else as justification for selling marijuana was coded as victimage. Whenever a justification was coded as victimage, it was also noted as either comic fool ("she couldn't really help it") or tragic hero ("someone or something else's fault, but the rhetor must be punished to reenter into society" (Sellnow, 2010, p. 55).

Mortification. This is when a person "confesses guilt and asks for forgiveness" (Sellnow, 2010, p. 53). Whenever Nancy made a public confession (e.g., to her children or others) or a private confession (e.g., to herself), it was coded as mortification.

Coding Process. The pilot episode of the first season was viewed to create guidelines for coding Nancy's rule-breaking behavior. The principal investigator viewed the first season's pilot episode and created a list of rules (a.k.a. social norms) being broken by Nancy Botwin. Based on that list, the rule-breaking behavior,

(Continued)

(Continued)

selling marijuana, was recorded and a description of how the act was justified. Using a table similar to Sellnow and Brown (2004), the rule-breaking behavior was coded by episode with the show's justification for the act (i.e., transcendence, victimage, or mortification). Each of the 10 episodes was then examined and coded in the same way. If a new drug or a new rule-breaking behavior (other than drug dealing) surfaced during the season, it was noted but not coded.

ANALYSIS

In the first episode, "You Can't Miss the Bear," Nancy's initial rule-breaking act is selling marijuana (a.k.a. pot) to her fellow community members. Interestingly, as the show closes, the viewer sees flash-forwards of other rules that would be broken by Nancy (e.g., adultery, lying) in upcoming episodes. The first episode spares no time creating Nancy's (agent) reason for selling drugs as a means for financial survival (purpose). Nancy's neighbors are quick to gossip about her financial issues, revealing tidbits about the family's lack of money due to her husband's sudden death and the new kitchen remodel (agency). Since Agrestic is a small gated community (scene), everyone is involved in each other's business. Nancy works very hard to keep her new profession quiet from her children and her neighbors in several ways. She travels to the other side of town to her supplier's house, only works with select adult clients (through referral), and never deals out of her house.

The main elements from this episode are agent and purpose. Nancy's (agent) reason for contacting a supplier and working as a drug dealer within her community is to earn enough money to support her children and maintain the lifestyle they had before her husband died (purpose). She is continually trying to keep normalcy within her sons' lives, as well as her own by securing her financial situation. Since the character is a widowed mother and her purpose for dealing drugs is for her children, viewers are led to absolve her rule-breaking behavior guilt about being a drug dealer via transcendence (i.e., doing it out of love for and to provide for her children).

Nancy Botwin is engaged in the rule-breaking behavior of selling marijuana throughout the first season of *Weeds*. While the first episodes (specifically 1–7) justify this rule-breaking behavior with a motive of love for children and a desire to provide for them, this shifts dramatically by Episode 8, "The Punishment Light," when the motive is replaced with personal greed and thrill seeking. In fact, this alternative motive leads Nancy to neglect her children as she focuses more on herself. Minor shifts toward this different motive begin to appear as early as Episode 4; however, it becomes glaringly evident by Episode 8 when Nancy sleeps with a rival drug dealer in order to continue selling drugs.

To clarify, her motive for selling weed is no longer for the love of her children and a desire to provide for them. In fact, Nancy often leaves the boys either to be looked after by the housekeeper or by the uncle (who is high most of the time). Nancy realizes at the end of Episode 8 that her motives for selling drugs are no longer about providing for her kids but about her own personal greed and thrill seeking. Nancy realizes her motives have shifted when she screams at herself, *"What the f**k are you doing!?,"* after driving home from confronting and having sex with a rival drug dealer (Episode 8).

This is one of the only times, however, that viewers see Nancy question her behavior, choices, and motives. Nancy has clearly changed from being a mom who "distributes illegal items" to a "drug dealer" (Episode 7 & 8). The season ends with Nancy juggling the idea of joining forces with another drug dealer and growing their own weed to make even more money (Episode 10). She has also entered into a new relationship with a father from Shane's karate class. By the end of the episode, she ends up at his house and sleeps with him. The next morning she stumbles across his DEA jacket and realizes that she has brought a completely new batch of issues into her life. The season ends leaving audience members wondering what she will do next and how the introduction of this new character will impact her illegal profession. The focus of the show is clearly no longer on the children. Viewers are now more consumed with what Nancy will do than with how she will help Shane and Silas cope with their father's death and lead "normal" lives.

Over the course of the first season (10 episodes) of *Weeds,* Nancy's guilt was absolved two ways: first, through transcendence and victimage (tragic hero), and second, with victimage (comic fool) as outlined in Table 1. Essentially, her motives for selling marijuana in the early episodes were focused on doing whatever it took to be a "good" mother that loves and provides for her children. Those motives gradually shifted, however, to ultimately be replaced with those of personal greed and thrill seeking without regard for how doing so might affect the children. In fact, the children were often left to fend for themselves as Nancy sought fulfillment through engaging in more and more illicit behaviors.

■ **TABLE 1:**   Rule Broken and Justification Per Episode

1	**"You Can't Miss the Bear"** (Transcendence) Nancy sells pot to support her family. She knows it is wrong but does it because she loves her sons and wants them to have a sense of normalcy.
2	**"Free Goat"** (Victimage–tragic hero) Nancy sells pot and sons are left alone quite a bit because she is out dealing. Oldest son snaps at her and says she's never around; she replies it is because she is trying to be a good mom for them (refers to doing it all along now).
3	**"Good Sh*t Lollipop"** (Victimage–tragic hero) Nancy sells pot constantly, reinforcing the idea that this is for her children.
4	**"Fashion of the Christ"** (Victimage–tragic hero) Nancy sells pot, reinforcing the idea that this is for her children.

(Continued)

(Continued)

5	"Lude Awakening" (Transcendence) Nancy almost leaves the business but decides to stay a drug dealer because she needs to pay the bills so her family can stay in their house. Note: This is where the shift starts. Nancy's kids are off doing their own things (e.g., Shane writes a rap about killing another student, and Silas is skipping school). She starts to drift away from being involved in her children's lives.
6	"Dead in the Nethers" (Victimage–tragic hero) Begins the process for opening sham bakery to sell marijuana. Nancy is still doing what she has to do to support her family. But, children are still left on their own.
7	"Higher Education" (Victimage–comic fool) Nancy sells pot on school grounds (at a college) and tries to get out of trouble when she gets caught by coercing the cop.
8	"The Punishment Light" This episode is where Nancy's justification for what she does completely shifts. It is no longer because of someone's fault (victimage–tragic hero) or because she wants the best for her kids (transcendence). It is because Nancy cannot help herself. She is already too far in to the drug dealing game and now she is doing it for her financial gain/greed. (Victimage–comic fool. (Victimage–comic fool) Nancy sleeps with a rival drug dealer to earn territory for more clients. Note: Nancy's priorities have shifted. Her first things (i.e., children) are now coming second.
9	"The Punishment Lighter" (Victimage–comic fool) Nancy opens a sham bakery to sell Costco baked goods as a cover-up for her dealing. She employs people to work for her. Nancy's business is growing, showing her investment in the drug business. Children are unattended to and getting in trouble at school.
1	"The Godmother" (Victimage–comic fool) Nancy decides to start her own business of growing weeds. In Nancy's mind, she is no longer a dealer … She is now a grower and supplier. She tells her youngest son what she is doing but tells both sons it is wrong and she cannot stop because she wants to maintain the family lifestyle.

DISCUSSION

The purpose of this analysis was to examine the motives provided in *Weeds* to justify Nancy Botwin's breaking of society's rules for living (i.e., selling marijuana). In doing so, we might better understand what the program is arguing about acceptable reasons for parents (particularly mothers) who break society rules in this way.

Nancy Botwin's initial motive for selling pot was to earn money to support her family. Justifications for her actions revolved around transcendence (i.e., she was doing so out of love for and a desire to provide for her children no matter what) and victimage (i.e., she had to do it [not her fault] since her husband suddenly died and she had no other means of income to maintain the lifestyle).

The show perpetuates Nancy's motive as an act of trying to be a good mother and provide for her sons because she loves them. In the season opener, Nancy discloses the reason she sells drugs was because the money was great, she was able to be home most of the time with her children, and she only has a high school education—logically this is the best-paying job she can get with her level of education and work experience.

In the first episode of *Weeds*, the viewer is not made aware of any other attempts by Nancy to earn money in an honest way (e.g., working a 40-hours-a-week job). The show immediately places her in the role of drug dealer and excusing the behavior using transcendence and victimage. Purpose and agent serve as two important elements of Burke's Pentad. If the purpose was something different, the audience might not excuse the fact that a mom is selling drugs. This rings true especially with the agent of being a recently widowed mom. Because no one would ever believe a well-to-do mother who lives in a gated community would sell drugs, this makes it easier for the audience to digest. This character breaks the stay-at-home mom stereotype, but it is not liberating or model behavior for women viewers.

The story carefully reminds the audience several times that Nancy has lost her husband suddenly; her actions as a drug dealer are justified not only because she loves her children but also because she lost her husband. The story frames her behavior as not her fault. The newly widowed parent is not able to support her children by herself. This plot acts as an enabler for Nancy's actions.

The audience does not question Nancy's choice in profession; instead, she gains their sympathy. As the show's plot is revealed, nothing seems to go right for Nancy and everything around her seems to be falling apart (e.g. her youngest son being bullied while her oldest son is having sex with his girlfriend in Nancy's house [Episode 2]). Because of these reasons, the viewer is able to forgive Nancy and even cheer for her even though the law would clearly not do the same. What does it mean when viewers cheer on a mom who sells drugs? Is it because she is doing it in a wealthy gated community and only to adults? Is it because she is trying to maintain her family's way of life since her husband died? More importantly, what are the implications of a show like *Weeds* that excuses illegal activities for the sake of financial survival and the love of one's children?

The transcendence justification is gradually eroded and replaced with victimage as the season progresses. However, even the victimage justification shifts from a focus on family to a focus on herself. Although justification is still based on victimage, Nancy now acts as a comic fool (she can't help herself) and her common human failing is personal greed rather than family provider. She chooses to use her time to focus on selling drugs and be around drug-related people. She often leaves Silas to take care of his younger troubled brother, Shane. Silas leaves home because he does not want to be responsible for taking care of Shane. Shane is left home alone a lot and begins spends time talking to a manifestation of his dead father because no one in his life is around to support him. By season's end, Nancy

(Continued)

(Continued)

has clearly chosen weed and personal greed over her children.

CONCLUSION AND IMPLICATIONS

Weeds attempts to defy what most shows amplify when it comes to stereotyping drug dealers—the initial motivation for Nancy's actions are opposite of most dealers, which is monetary gain and personal greed. In Nancy's case, she sells marijuana out of her love for her children and a desire to provide for them after her husband's passing. This justification based on transcendence (higher calling of love) and victimage (her husband died and she is not qualified to get a job that would allow the family to maintain its lifestyle) holds steady for several episodes but gradually shifts to victimage as a comic fool (Nancy's personal greed and thrill seeking from engaging in illicit behavior beginning with selling weed and leading to additional forms of illicit behavior). Not only do viewers see Nancy's justification shift but also the consequences doing so has for her and her family, as well.

Based on this analysis, what is troubling about the show's message is that it is OK to engage in illegal activities such as selling drugs if you are doing it for someone you love (transcendence) and have no other options (victimage). By the season's end, viewers see that personal greed and thrill seeking (rather than love for children and a desire to provide for them) are not acceptable motives for illicit behavior, reinforced by the negative consequences Nancy and her family experience. This shift actually reinforces the original justification as acceptable.

Overall, the show's argument about acceptable motives for breaking society's rules for living should not be taken lightly. Research based on Bandura's (1977) social cognitive learning theory suggests that viewers can be influenced to accept such behavior as justifiable under similar circumstances. However, Nancy's actions on *Weeds* are not just breaking a social norm; she is breaking the law. Viewers who are influenced to agree that Nancy's behavior is justifiable for motives of transcendence and victimage and who decide to model it in their own lives could find themselves in jail or worse even though they were following a higher calling and had no other means by which to provide for the children they love. Perhaps there is a line that should not be crossed even when doing whatever is necessary to provide for our children. Perhaps "putting first things first" as C.S. Lewis (1996, p. 14) suggests should not be taken to the extreme of participating in illicit and illegal activities when it comes to providing for our children. In fact, maybe doing so in the long run isn't really out of love at all. Behaviors like Nancy's should not be confused with being appropriate just because her motive is love. In the end, is she really putting first things first?

References

Bandura, A. (1977). *Social learning theory*. New York: General Learning.

Bandura, A. (2011). A social cognitive perspective on positive psychology. *Revista de Psicologia Social, 26*, 7–20.

Burke, K. (1945). *Grammar of motives*. London, England: Prentice-Hall.

Dail, P. W., & Way, W. L. (1985). What do parents observe about parenting from prime time television. *Family Relations, 34*(4), 491–499.

Douglas, W. (2003). Television families: Is something wrong in suburbia?. Mahwah, NJ: Lawrence Erlbaum.

Douglas, W., & Olson, B. M. (1995). Beyond family structure: The family in domestic comedy. *Journal of Broadcasting & Electronic Media, 39*(2), 236.

Ex, C. T. G. M., Janssens, J. M. A. M., & Korzilius, H. P. L. M. (2002). Young females' images of motherhood in relation to television viewing. *Journal of Communication, 52*, 955–971.

Foss, S. K. (2009). *Rhetorical criticism: Exploration and practice* (4th ed.). Long Grove, IL: Waveland. ISBN: 1-57766-586-4 or 978-1-57766-586-1.

IMDb. (2012). *Weeds.* Retrieved from http://www.imdb.com/title/tt0439100/

Leibman, N. (2012). Comedy, domestic setting. *The Museum of Broadcasts Communications.* Retrieved from http://www.museum.tv/eotv section.php?entrycode=comedydomes

Lewis, C. S. (1996). *Readings for meditation and reflection.* W. Hooper (Ed.). San Francisco, CA: Harper.

Neuendorf, K. (2002). *The content analysis guidebook.* Thousand Oaks, CA: Sage.

Nordyke, K. (2007). Weeds on a roll for fourth season. *Rutgers.* Retrieved from http://www.reuters.com/article/2007/11/04/television-weeds-dc-idUSN0420878220071104

Sellnow, D., & Brown, A. (2004). A rhetorical analysis of oppositional youth music of the new millennium. *North Dakota Journal of Speech & Theatre, 17*, 19–36.

Sellnow, D. (2010). *The rhetorical power of popular culture: Considering mediated texts.* Washington, DC: Sage.

Simpson, A. (1997). *The role of mass media in parenting education.* Boston: Centre for Health Communication, Harvard School of Public Health.

TV Guide. (2012). TV guide most popular shows. Retrieved from http://www.tvguide.com/top-tv-shows

Summary

This chapter outlined the guidelines by which to conduct a dramatistic analysis. We began by introducing the major tenets of the theory as described by Burke. Essentially, the dramatistic perspective focuses on the analysis of human motivation by viewing texts as dramas. More specifically, we explained the dramatistic life cycle of human experience and how it is represented in popular culture texts. Then we focused on language and terministic screens as they cluster around themes reflecting and shaping a particular worldview and described the elements of the Pentad as a macrostructural framework for examining texts from a dramatistic perspective. We illustrated how doing so leads the critic to determine how guilt is absolved, which reveals one of three possible motives: transcendence, mortification, and victimage. Finally, sample essays that employ the dramatistic perspective were offered as examples to help clarify why the analysis of texts from this perspective actually function as "equipment for living" (Burke, 1973, pp. 293–304). In summary, the dramatistic perspective sheds light on human motivation. Why do we follow certain rules for living as normal and desirable and, moreover, what do our perceptions about the justifiable motives for breaking such rules tell us about ourselves and our society?

Challenge

(1) Watch the movie, *Seven Pounds* (2008), starring Will Smith and Rosario Dawson, both of whom won awards for their performances in it. The movie is about Tim Thomas's (Will Smith) attempts to absolve his guilt about killing seven innocent people in a car crash because he was texting. The plot revolves around Thomas as he seeks redemption by donating his organs to repay the debt he believes he owes to society. Consider the dramatistic life cycle and Pentad as you watch. What motives are offered to justify Thomas's rule-breaking behavior? In what ways are his actions justified through victimage? Mortification? Transcendence? What is ultimately argued as a justifiable motive for suicide? Do you agree? Explain. What implications might this have for viewers who may be feeling guilty over similar actions?

(2) Watch the movie, *28 Days* (2000), starring Sandra Bullock. The movie is about Gwen Cummings (Sandra Bullock), a successful New York journalist who loves to party. Consider how her guilt is eventually absolved after she essentially ruins her sister's (Elizabeth Perkins) wedding and ends up with a DUI and 28 days in rehabilitation. Consider the Pentad as you watch. What is the purpose for Gwen Cummings's rule-breaking behaviors? What do we learn to be the ultimate motive? How is guilt absolved? What are some terministic screens used in the movie, and how are the symbols completed (teleology)? Consider each character in her life drama and how each is completed (teleology). How do these characters as teleology impact the ultimate message about what is necessary for absolution? What impact might the dramatistic messages of this film have on various audiences and why?

(3) Watch the movie, *Se7en* (1995), starring Brad Pitt, Kevin Spacey, and Morgan Freeman. The movie is about serial killer John Doe (Kevin Spacey), who justifies his horrific crimes as absolution for the world's ignorance and tolerance of the Seven Deadly Sins (gluttony, greed, sloth, envy, wrath, pride, and lust). Doe claims to be following a higher calling (transcendence) as he kills "sinners" who deserve to be punished for their transgressions (victimage). The final scene leaves viewers with a paradox regarding what we ought to consider justifiable motives for rule-breaking behavior. Consider the arguments for absolution of guilt conveyed by each of these main characters (Somerset, Mills, and Doe) in the film's final scene. Do the choices made by any character leave the viewer feeling satisfied? Why or why not? What do you think the goal of the movie was: to lead viewers to see one of these methods of absolution as more justifiable than the others or merely to make viewers think about the paradoxes we live with each day? What implications might these paradoxes about absolution have on various audiences and why?

References

Bourgonjon, J., Rutton, K., Soetaert, R., & Valcke, M. (2011). From counter-strike to counter-statement: Using Burke's pentad as a tool for analysing video games. *Digital Creativity, 22*(2), 91–102.

Burke, K. (1965). *Permanence and change: An anatomy of purpose.* Indianapolis, IN: Bobbs-Merrill.

Burke, K. (1966). *Language as symbolic action: Essays on life, literature, and method.* Berkeley: University of California Press.

Burke, K. (1968). Dramatism. In D. I Sills (Ed.), *International encyclopedia of the social sciences* (Vol. 7). New York: Macmillan.

Burke, K. (1969a). *A grammar of motives.* Berkeley: University of California Press.

Burke, K. (1969b). *A rhetoric of motives.* Berkeley: University of California Press.

Burke, K. (1973). *The philosophy of literary form* (3rd ed.). Berkeley: University of California Press.

Burke, K. (1984a). *Attitudes toward history.* Berkeley: University of California Press.

Burke, K. (1984b). *Language as symbolic action: Essays on life, literature, and method.* Berkeley: University of California Press.

Goffman, E. (1959). *The presentation of self in everyday life.* New York: Anchor.

Gronbeck, B. E. (1980). Dramaturgical theory and criticism: The state of the art (or science?). *Western Journal of Speech Communication, 44,* 315–330.

Kaufmann, R. (2012). Love and greed: It is all about the *Weeds.* Unpublished manuscript, University of Kentucky.

Nietzsche, F. (1873). On truth and lying in an extra-moral sense. In S. L. Gillman, C. Blaire, D. J. Parent (Eds. and Trans.), *Friedrich Nietzsche on rhetoric and language* (pp. 246–257). New York: Oxford.

Turner, V. (1974). *Dramas, fields, and metaphors: Symbolic action in human society.* Ithaca, NY: Cornell University Press.

Weaver, R. (1985). *The ethics of rhetoric.* Davis, CA: Hermagoras. (Originally published 1953)

Student Study Site

Visit the Student Study Site at www.sagepub.com/sellnow2e to read interesting SAGE journal articles, view mobile-friendly key term flashcards, take chapter-specific online web quizzes to test your knowledge, and more!

Chapter 5

A Symbolic Convergence Perspective

Thomas G. Endres,
University of Northern Colorado

T he world can be a confusing and intimidating place. As Fisher and Burke have demonstrated, narratives and dramas come at us from all sides, often creating an information or entertainment overload. As the theme song to the sitcom *Cheers* used to tout, "Sometimes you want to go where everybody knows your name." Whether or not they know our name, we tend to feel more comfortable when we are with like-minded people who accept or reject the same story lines that we do. That is the driving force behind Ernest Bormann's (1972, 1973, 1982, 1983, 1985) work. Bormann (1972) developed symbolic convergence theory (SCT) to tap into and interpret the dramatizing messages which "catch on and chain out" through small groups, in the mass media, and within the public sphere (p. 398). They are the shared narratives, crafted in organized and artistic ways, which create a sense of us and them within a community.

Bormann's work was inspired by the work of psychoanalyst Robert Bales (1950), who developed a measurement system called the Interaction Process Analysis for studying small group behavior. Bales listened to small group dialogue and coded comments according to his schema. Each of his categories had two sides (e.g., *friendly* or *unfriendly* comments, *asking for* or *giving* information). One category that originally gave him trouble was *shows tension*. The flip side might seem to be *shows tension release*, but Bales realized that behaviors that at the surface appeared to be relieving tension, such as giggling, were sometimes actually tension producing. He needed to identify what we do in groups that is the opposite of showing tension. Eventually, Bales figured it out. In order to reduce tension, we tell stories! He used the word *dramatizes* (similar to the way Burke defined it, including the Freudian overtones) to refer to tension-releasing narratives, which he called "group fantasizing" (Bales, 1970, p. 396). Bales, however, only cared that a story was told, not what the story was about. Bormann took it from there and developed a method for interpreting the stories themselves and how they create a rhetorical community of shared believers. Anybody who is, or has met, a Trekkie, a ComicCon devotee, or an ardent *Twilight* fan, has encountered just such a rhetorical community.

APPLYING WHAT YOU'VE LEARNED . . .

How many popular media rhetorical communities, like Trekkies, can you identify? Do you belong to any? What are some of the common characteristics you find among such fan groups? What characteristics might be unique to a particular fan group? Keep those distinctions in mind, and consider them in light of the following terminology.

Many scholars refer to SCT as *fantasy theme analysis*. SCT is actually the larger theoretical notion that like-minded individuals accept, reject, or are neutral to certain symbolic narratives and that those symbols converge to create a common consciousness. Fantasy theme analysis (FTA) is the tool or methodology rhetoricians use to identify, understand, and interpret those converged symbols. If SCT were a larger genre, like carpentry, then FTA would be the hammer and saw that helps make it happen. Thus, in order to understand a community's symbolic convergence, to gain insight into their meanings, motives, and emotions, one must first know the terminology of FTA. (The terms can be found in many seminal SCT articles and books, including Bormann, 1972, 1982, 1985; Bormann, Cragan, & Shields, 2001; Cragan & Shields, 1981, 1995).

FANTASY THEME ANALYSIS

Let's start with a fantasy theme itself. This is a basic unit of communication, like a joke, analogy, metaphor, wordplay, pun, double entendre, figure of speech, anecdote—or perhaps a reference to an imaginary or non-present person—that, when shared with others, constitutes the base of social reality. In other words, it's more than just information. If you look out the window and say, "It's another hot day out there," well, this is not the stuff of drama. However, if you add that it's so hot you could bake cookies on the dashboard of your car, maybe you would get a reaction. If others laugh at the thought, or add comments about how wonderful it would be to have fresh-baked, warm cookies waiting on your dashboard after a long day at school, you could say that the fantasy chained out and was bought into by others. So it begins with a message, often pertaining to a here-and-now problem, which attempts to ease the tension by referring to something or someone out in the there and then. If the mind-set of others is in sync with yours (e.g., they, too, are sick of the hot weather), then you have the basis for symbolic convergence.

The more people who buy into and add to the narrative, the further the fantasy chains out and takes root.

APPLYING WHAT YOU'VE LEARNED . . .

Have you seen the movie *Jaws?* There is a scene where the main characters sit around a table in the boat and share stories of how they obtained their various scars. The three men continually try to outdo each other and add story upon story as their symbols converge. The fantasy chain ends when one character reveals that he was aboard the *U.S.S. Indianapolis,* a wrecked ship whose crew was mostly eaten alive by sharks. Why do you think the fantasies chained out between them, and why do think the *Indianapolis* story caused them to end so abruptly?

Popular culture is, of course, filled to the brim with fantasy themes. Every slogan, catchphrase, punch line, and cliffhanger is intended to catch you up in the narrative. To help clarify the notion of fantasy theme, and all its attendant characteristics, let's consider the popular sitcom *The Big Bang Theory*. A primary characteristic of many narratives are the dramatis personae, or characters who populate the drama. Most characters are protagonists, or heroes. In the case of *The Big Bang Theory*, that would include the nerdy university scientist main characters: the antisocial genius Sheldon Cooper, his roommate Leonard Hofstadter, their friends and colleagues Howard Wolowitz and Rajesh Koothrapalli, and Sheldon and Leonard's aspiring-actress neighbor Penny (who, for some reason, has yet to be given a last name). More recent seasons have added additional female protagonists, including Sheldon's girlfriend Amy Farrah Fowler and Howard's new wife Bernadette Rostenkowski. Generally, story lines include an antagonist, or villain, who attempts to thwart the progress of our heroes. *The Big Bang Theory* offers a few adversaries, such as rival scientist Barry Kripke, university president Siebert, or *Star Trek: The Next Generation's* Wil Wheaton appearing as a sometimes mean-spirited version of himself. In addition to heroes and villains, narratives are often accompanied by a cast of supporting players, such as Sheldon's mom, Penny's dad, Raj's parents, or Stuart, who owns the local comic book shop.

Characters are regularly involved in a plotline, which provides the action of the narrative; for example, Penny and Leonard's on-again-off-again relationship or Sheldon's ongoing quest to prove string theory. Those plotlines can be augmented by the scene, or the setting or social backdrop where the dramatizing stories take place. That could be a locale as specific as Sheldon and Leonard's apartment or the university cafeteria, or the more general cultural milieu, such as a society where jocks still pick on the nerds. Finally, fantasy themes can be identified by the sanctioning agent, which is the legitimizing force that guides the narrative. "Sometimes, a higher power such as God, or Justice, or Democracy serves as the sanctioning agent" (Cragan & Shields, 1995, p. 41). In *Big Bang*, different characters have different "forces" that legitimize or help rationalize or explain their behavior. For Sheldon, it is the quest for scientific truth (and a hoped-for Nobel Prize), while for Leonard it is more the dream of a stable, intimate relationship with Penny.

RHETORICAL VISIONS, MASTER ANALOGUES, AND LIFE CYCLES

When you put together the characters, plotline, scene, and sanctioning agent, you generally have a complete story or at least one shareable way of interpreting the story. This unified "putting together of things" is what Bormann and colleagues call a rhetorical vision. Cragan and Shields (1995) define it as a "composite drama that catches up large groups of people into a common symbolic reality" (p. 41). Sometimes adherents to a particular rhetorical vision can be named as a collective. Trekkies is the obvious example. Justin Bieber fans call themselves Beliebers, while Lady Gaga affectionately calls her fans Little Monsters. Hard-core *Twilight* fans are called Twihards, and Harry Potter fans are called Potterheads. While some have suggested that fans of *The Big Bang Theory* be called Bangers, the label hasn't caught on. Still, the fan base does indeed share a rhetorical vision. All of these labels simply refer to a rhetorical community of people who, even though they might not live in the same geographic vicinity, share a common reality based on their mutual heroes, villains, and story lines.

> ### QUESTIONING YOUR ETHICS . . .
>
> The function of a rhetorical vision is to bond individuals together based upon their shared beliefs. Generally, as in the case of popular culture fan groups, the result is positive. You might not like Justin Bieber or Lady Gaga, but the fact that other people do is basically harmless. Is there a dark side to this? Can you think of any instances where rhetorical communities are based on a shared hatred rather than a shared attraction? That use derogatory or spiteful language as their fantasy themes? For example, are the Internet memes and "funny" pictures that encourage individuals to shoot Justin Bieber simply harmless humor, or is there a risk of creating a rhetorical community that could prove to be dangerous?

According to SCT, rhetorical visions tend to adhere to one of three types of deep structure frameworks called master analogues. In reality, there could be as many rhetorical visions within a community as there are individuals because each person will have his or her own unique take on the fantasy themes. At some point, you need to look not at what divides the community but rather what core values and orientations they have in common. It seems that people tend to be drawn to one of three primary orientations: *righteous*, *social*, or *pragmatic*.

A rhetorical vision that reflects a righteous master analogue "stresses the correct way of doing things with its concerns about right and wrong, proper and improper, superior and inferior, moral and immoral, and just and unjust" (Cragan & Shields, 1995, p. 42). Story lines that emphasize God and country, for example, tend to be popular with those predisposed to the righteous master analogue. Other individuals are drawn to social master analogues; storylines focusing on friendship, trust, camaraderie, brotherhood or sisterhood, and being humane. Finally, some individuals find most appealing the pragmatic master analogue, which values "expediency, utility, efficiency, parsimony, simplicity, practicality, cost effectiveness, and whatever it takes to get the job done" (p. 42). This is why some people are drawn to law-and-order shows on TV, where the bad guys get punished; while others are drawn to social dating shows like *The Bachelor* or *The Bachelorette*; and still others are attracted to cooking and home improvement shows that cut to the chase. These discrete orientations are often at war with each other in a given community, and one eventually prevails. Though *Big Bang* has elements of righteousness and pragmatism, especially in the ongoing debates about religion versus science, the underpinning master analogue is primarily social as it looks at the friendships and star-crossed romances within this unique group of people from Pasadena.

APPLYING WHAT YOU'VE LEARNED . . .

Not everyone may consider politics to be popular culture but, especially during an election year, there is not much that dominates the TV screens more than political ads and analyses by pundits. Think about the last major election. What candidate did you prefer? When you think about his or her messages, which of the three master analogues—righteous, social, pragmatic—do you think most underpinned their platform? What examples back this up? Are you predisposed to those types of master analogue messages? Can you think of other examples, such as why you choose the music that you listen to, that exemplifies that predisposition?

Regardless of the underlying master analogue, all rhetorical visions tend to exist in one of five stages of a rhetorical vision life cycle. Just as a human being develops from birth through death, so too do most shared realities. The first stage, consciousness creating, is where a rhetorical vision is initially formed. This is an exciting concept when you realize it refers to the creation of a shared symbolic reality that did not previously exist. When a meme first explodes in popularity on the Internet, when everybody cheers at the selection of a new company motto, when a funny story is told at a family reunion for the first time—this is the birth of group consciousness. The fantasy theme(s) at the heart of the vision must be sufficiently novel to catch up and chain out within a group of people. The second stage is consciousness raising, which is where those who already share an existing vision attempt to attract and indoctrinate newcomers. Examples might include attracting people to a new religion or spiritual belief or instructing new hires on corporate culture. Bormann (1983) says the new messages must "get the potential converts to break loose of their emotional attachments" to any previous rhetorical visions they might have (p. 78). You need to convert enough of the newcomers to achieve critical mass within the intended audience. Once both old and new members of a rhetorical community share a vision, it is occasionally necessary to retell the fantasies to keep everyone from losing sight of their shared story line. This third phase of the life cycle is called consciousness sustaining. Anyone who has ever renewed their marriage vows or watched their favorite movie for the 100th time is hoping to revitalize the narrative that they already know via consciousness sustaining. This process rewards those who have been faithful to the story line and allows transgressors to rejoin the fold.

But rhetorical visions cannot necessarily live forever. In the realm of popular culture, we see heroes shine and eventually fade away. Fans of comedians like Dane Cook, Brian Regan, and Josh Blue may have only a vague recollection of their predecessors such as Richard Pryor and George Carlin and may not recall at all early comics such as Milton Berle, Pat Paulsen, and Steve Allen. This is because many rhetorical visions enter the fourth stage, known as decline. Here the novelty dims; the shared stories lose their power and dim in the face of better alternatives. If it dims enough, a rhetorical vision may reach terminus, or the end of the life-cycle process. Occasionally, the vision simply loses enough adherents that it fades out of public consciousness. Other times, a rhetorical vision may end abruptly. This typically happens when an inflexible drama implodes upon itself. Comedian Michael Richards, who played the wacky neighbor Cosmo Kramer in the hit sitcom *Seinfeld* fell immediately from grace in the eyes of his fans when he went into a racist tirade during one of his 2006 stand-up acts. Rather than back off, he dug in his heels and continued to taunt two African-Americans who heckled him. Thanks to cell phone videos and YouTube, Richards announced his resignation from stand-up comedy in 2007.

CONDUCTING A SYMBOLIC CONVERGENCE ANALYSIS

Step 1. Selecting an Appropriate Text

Most popular culture texts are amenable to an SCT-perspective FTA. The best are those that have obvious dramatic characteristics, such as a plotline with characters. It is most relevant when the goal is to identify the shared reality of those who buy into certain texts. Better yet are those texts that have an explicit or implied us versus them. This allows the critic to examine the messages that differentiate the in-group from the out-group and whether or not the dramas are sufficiently compelling to attract and maintain converts.

After considering the rhetorical situation (i.e., sender, occasion, audience, exigence, constraints), three criteria can help determine if a text is worthy of SCT FTA. Though it is not necessary to identify any or all of the criteria, they do provide a useful guideline for determining the appropriateness of a text. The first is shared group consciousness; is there proof of a rhetorical community and audience buy-in? There are a lot of stories out there that fall flat and do not get any followers. Those are probably not worth analyzing. Identifying this can be as simple as watching for any type of emotional reaction from participants (e.g., the story makes them happy, sad, fearful) to looking at larger empirical data such as the existence of fan sites and media sales. Any visit to *The Big Bang Theory's* Facebook page, with more than 22 million Likes, gives ample evidence that a shared group consciousness exists.

Closely related to those latter examples, the second criterion is the rhetorical vision reality link, where there is evidence of the senses which provides authentication for the vision. One can validate *Big Bang's* popularity by referencing, among other things, DVD sales, syndication episodes, and Nielsen ratings. Closer to home, you could also look to see if adherents to the vision differ from others in certain ways. If members of your social group refuse to go out with you on Thursday nights because there is a new *Big Bang* episode airing, you can be certain there is a link between reality and the vision it represents.

Finally, and perhaps most important, is the criterion of fantasy theme artistry, which speaks to the rhetorical skill and communication competence of the storyteller. Sometimes a drama gains adherence simply because it is so well told. Cragan and Shields (1995) fine-tune this even more, distinguishing between different standards of artistry (p. 48). They first look at absolute standards, which confirm that the story is obviously well crafted compared to general societal expectations for quality. For example, is *Big Bang* well written, appropriately paced, and legitimately funny? Second is the comparative standard, which looks at the quality of story compared to other stories competing for the same audience. How does *Big Bang* fare in comparison to similar sitcoms on network or cable television? Last is the closeness-of-fit standard, which asks how well an individual theme works within the larger rhetorical vision. *Big Bang* will only work if the writers and cast can maintain the clever banter among nerdy intellectuals and the world around them. If the show were to deviate into, say, political or economic territories, it might not be so well received.

QUESTIONING YOUR ETHICS . . .

What are the implications of fantasy theme artistry? Essentially, this implies that the power of persuasion belongs to the person who can tell the best story. Can a well-told story short-circuit our logic and reason? Knowing the power of story, what are our own responsibilities as storytellers? Consider much of today's advertising. What can we do as consumers of messages in order to appreciate the quality of a good narrative without necessarily being sucked mindlessly into its appeal?

Step 2. Examining the Text (Describe and Interpret)

In his original 1972 article, Bormann proposed a series of questions that a rhetorical critic might ask when conducting an FTA to describe the symbolic convergence of a given community. What follows is a partial list of the many questions he provides:

> Who are the dramatis personae? Who are the heroes and villains? How concrete and detailed are the characterizations? Motives attributed? How are members of the rhetorical community characterized? For what are the insiders praised, the outsiders or enemies castigated? What values are inherent in the praiseworthy characters? Where are the dramas set? Is the setting given supernatural sanction? What are the typical scenarios? What lifestyles are exemplified as praiseworthy? What meanings are inherent in the dramas? Where does the insider fit into the great chain of being? How does the movement fit into the scheme of history? What emotional evocations dominate the dramas? How does the fantasy work to attract the unconverted? How does it generate a sense of community and cohesion from the insider? How capable is the drama to arouse and interpret emotions? (pp. 401–402)

Essentially, the description phase of the rhetorical analysis is to identify as many of the fantasy theme characteristics (e.g., dramatis personae, plotline, scene, sanctioning agent) as you can. Focus on those that best meet the criteria of shared group consciousness, rhetorical vision reality link, and fantasy theme artistry. If it isn't shared, if there's nothing to back it up, or if it lacks artistry, don't include it in the description.

In addition to these characteristics, there are two additional concepts that give proof to a shared symbolic reality. The first is called a fantasy type, which is "a stock scenario repeated again and again by the same characters or by similar characters" (Bormann, 1985, p. 7). Many times we see the same types of fantasy themes crop up multiple times, and the best way to refer to them is through some larger, overarching descriptor. For example, *The Big Bang Theory* is an example of a situation comedy, or *sitcom*. We know that other shows like *Modern Family*, *The Cosby Show*, or *Seinfeld* also fall under that general heading. The fantasy type of sitcom helps us to differentiate those kinds of stock television formats with others such as *dramas, reality shows,* or *documentaries.* Or we could have a more specific, yet still overarching, fantasy type such as *sexual tension in sitcoms.* Leonard's on-again, off-again relationship with Penny in *Big Bang* is similar to: Sam and Diane (or Sam and Rebecca) from *Cheers*, Tony and Angela from *Who's the Boss?,* Ross and Rachel from *Friends*, and Jim and Pam from *The Office*. While the names of the characters may change, the stock scenario does not.

The second thing to look for is evidence of a symbolic cue, or "cryptic allusions to common symbolic ground" (Bormann, 1985, p. 6). This is a concise and generally not self-explanatory reference, like an inside joke or motto, which only those who know the story line will understand. For example, in *Big Bang*, whenever Sheldon plays a practical joke or tricks someone with an ironic or sarcastic statement, he says, "Bazinga"—his version of saying, "Ha, ha, I got you with that one." The word *bazinga* is then a symbolic cue for the reality shared by *Big Bang* fans. Similarly, whenever Sheldon is sick, he insists that someone sing to him the "Soft Kitty" song his mother sang to him as a child. His roommates and neighbors all know the words: "Soft Kitty, warm kitty, little ball of fur. Happy kitty, sleepy kitty, purr, purr, purr." Members of the viewing audience, this chapter's author included, may sing "Soft Kitty" to one another when they are not feeling well; it's a symbolic cue referencing their shared rhetorical community.

What is important to remember is that both fantasy types and symbolic cues can only be understood if the individual has first shared in the original fantasy theme. Talking about sexual tension in sitcoms to someone who has never watched television (a rare person indeed) would make no sense. And shouting "bazinga" after playing a prank on someone or singing "Soft Kitty" to a sick friend who has never heard of *The Big Bang Theory* will only leave him or her confused.

APPLYING WHAT YOU'VE LEARNED . . .

"Ohhh Myyyyy." "Come on down!" "Oh my God, they've killed Kenny!" "Danger, Will Robinson!" "Holy crap." "Is that your final answer?" "Live long and prosper." "You rang?" "Suit up!" Do you recognize any of these popular culture catch phrases? Are these symbolic cues or inside jokes referencing some larger story line that only insiders will recognize? In what ways can insiders integrate those phrases into their own interaction with others? What examples can you add?

As the critic moves toward interpretation, the ultimate job is to pull all the pieces together to identify and label any rhetorical visions that have emerged from the analysis. Though not mandated, it is helpful to try and identify the master analogue of the rhetorical vision, or the conflicts between competing rhetorical visions, as well as what phase of the life cycle the rhetorical vision represents. Collectively, this gives the fullest sense of who comprises the rhetorical community and what narratives they accept or reject.

Step 3. Evaluating Potential Implications of the Text

In a SCT evaluation, you want to address the value found in identifying the rhetorical vision of community. What does the interpretation tell us about the community? About their meanings, their motives, and their emotions? On a larger scale, what does it tell us about the power of storytelling? About which dramas can catch up and convert a potential audience? And which dramas will push them away?

In looking at the implications, consider the impact of a shared social reality within a community. For starters, a shared rhetorical vision—especially one from the consciousness creating stage—creates a collective identity and ego for a group. It helps them to bond and feel unified. Some groups even develop a founding fantasy: a narrative tale about their inception. Many a brochure, website, docudrama, or even a group of friends, start their saga with some type of "It all began when . . ." fantasy theme. Interestingly, those founding stories don't even have to be true as long as the followers share them. Having that common beginning allows both participants, and the critic who is studying them, to better understand the collective's goals and their possible directions for the future.

In our study of human communication, we often ask the question, "What is it that separates human beings from other animals?" The easy answer seems to be message exchange, though the world is filled with evidence of animals communicating: bees dance, dolphins chatter, and apes learn sign language. The one thing animals cannot do, however, is tell stories in the there and then about their future. If I tell my Pomeranian, Topper, that he will get special food tomorrow, he will not be awake all night anxiously awaiting the meal. Only human beings have the capacity to envision a common future together, and SCT and FTA give us a way to unpack and assess the impact of those forward-looking narratives.

Finally, in some cases, the analysis can be used to identify hidden agendas, or ulterior motives of alleged adherents within the vision. If you listen to a group of professors talk about their mission and note that their statements are filled with words like *pedagogy, objectives, education,* and *learning,* the person who is talking about "paycheck" and "retirement" is going to stand out as not buying into the shared reality. The same goes for a fellow student in a group project who does not chime in on cues such as "quality," "teamwork," or "distribution of workload," and instead talks about "getting it over with." Listening closely to the fantasy themes people share can tell you a lot.

SAMPLE ANALYSIS

Endres (2008) analyzed the cult classic *The Rocky Horror Picture Show* and argued that two distinct rhetorical visions, each with its own master analogue, were at play. The film centers on two main protagonists, the virginal and naive fiancés Brad and Janet, whose car breaks down in front of a castle—the scene—inhabited by the flamboyantly transvestite scientist Dr. Frank-N-Furter and his servants, siblings Riff Raff and Magenta (all three, incidentally, are aliens from the planet Transsexual Transylvania). The plotline thickens as we discover they have arrived on the night Frank gives life to his new muscle-bound creation and boy toy, Rocky. What ensues is a raunchy farce about forbidden pleasures and sins of the flesh. The entire cast is lured under Frank's spell until Riff Raff and Magenta declare that Frank has gone too far.

Endres labeled one rhetorical vision the *Vision of Righteous Decadence*. At first, the label seems paradoxical. The concept is borrowed from the liner notes of the *Rocky Horror* movie novel, which speak of the "defiantly decadent morality" of the 1970s. Looked at through the lens of adherents to the vision, Frank's decadent fantasy themes and behaviors (e.g., prancing in lingerie, murder, tricking both Brad and Janet into having sex) is considered righteous and correct behavior in his castle. Bormann says fantasies "clearly divide the sympathetic, good people (we) from the unsympathetic or evil people (they)" (1985, p.12). In Frank's eyes, characters who use pleasure as their sanctioning agent and sex as their plotline are the "we" of the righteous master analogue, and anyone who stands in his way are the unsympathetic "they." For most of the movie, righteous decadence prevails, with characters—especially Janet—seduced by Frank's vision. In the infamous floor show scene, where main characters are shuffled onto a stage wearing corsets and fishnet stockings, Janet sings:

> I feel released. Bad times deceased. My confidence has increased. Reality is here. The game has been disbanded. My mind has been expanded. It's a gas that Frankie has landed. His lust is so sincere.

At this point, a competing rhetorical vision enters the picture, which Endres labels the *Vision of Pragmatic Justice*. Foreshadowed early in the film in a scene outside a church, where a sign reads "Be Just and Fear Not," the pragmatic master analogue provides a simple message: "Do the right thing or suffer the consequences" (p. 214). The movie is subtlety infused with such fantasy themes. As most moviegoers see *Rocky Horror* in an interactive venue, with participants yelling at the movie screen, many of these moments go unnoticed. During the scene where the car breaks down in a rainstorm, while audience members recreate the storm with squirt guns and newspapers over their heads, most do not hear what is playing on the car radio. It is Richard Nixon delivering his actual resignation speech following Watergate, proclaiming, "I must put the interests of America first," clearly an example of someone who broke the rules and is now paying for his actions. A similar fantasy theme is enacted when Rocky is brought to life. Rather than reveling at his birth, Rocky begins his life by singing a song titled "The Sword of Damocles." This is based on the legend of King Dionysius, a wealthy tyrant who was envied by many. Dionysius trades places with his friend Damocles until Damocles looks up and notices a razor-sharp sword suspended above his head by a thin thread. The lesson for Damocles, and for Rocky, is that pleasure and riches are often an illusion. There is always danger, and to partake of the spoils often means risking death.

All of these warnings eventually culminate in the floor show scene where Riff Raff and Magenta enter and tell Frank, "Your mission is a failure. Your lifestyle's too extreme." They kill Frank and Rocky with a laser gun, leaving Brad and Janet crawling on the ground as they return, castle and all, to their revered home planet. Endres concludes that, while many believe *The Rocky Horror Picture Show* condones decadence, it is in reality a fairly conservative morality play whose rhetorical message is that those who attempt a life of pure hedonism will face retribution. "Rocky Horror is a temporary escape from normalcy and traditional definitions of morality. For one hundred minutes, audiences can join Frank and share in the vision of righteous decadence. However, whether it be on the big screen surrounded by costumed congregants or on the small screen surrounded by one's furniture, the outcome remains the same: Pragmatic Justice prevails" (p. 218).

SAMPLE PUBLISHED ESSAY

Read the article titled "The Gospel According to Wyatt: Failed Religious Dramas in *Easy Rider*" written by Thomas Endres and published in the conference proceedings of the 2007 Hawaii International Conference on Arts & Humanities. The essay examines religious imagery—particularly Roman Catholic imagery—that are infused throughout the 1969 movie *Easy Rider*. Hailed as a classic counterculture road narrative, most audience members and critics fail to recognize or identify the numerous religious symbols. Endres argues that a key element is missing in the religious fantasy themes; they are not tied to a religious sanctioning agent. For example, Wyatt and Billy (Peter Fonda and Dennis Hopper) enter a brothel and watch a scantily clad woman dance on a table. The background music is a modified version of the Latin chant *Kyrie Eleison* (Lord Have Mercy). In another scene, set in a New Orleans cemetery, a young girl reads aloud the Apostles Creed, the Hail Mary, the Glory Be, and the Our Father. However, her words are overshadowed by the fact that the main characters (Wyatt, Billy, and two prostitutes) are in the midst of a darkly psychedelic acid trip. Endres concludes that, when the protagonists are motivated by illicit means and ends, no amount of religious symbolism is going to convince anyone that something sacred is taking place.

SAMPLE STUDENT ESSAY

Tying together the genres of science fiction, Westerns, and road narratives, Natalie Stevens uses FTA to identify rhetorical visions in the TV series *Firefly*. What follows is a condensed version of the original paper, "Protest, Freedom, and Transformation in Space: *Firefly* as Road Narrative," which was written for a graduate-level course in popular culture. The focus on road narrative was purposeful, as Natalie submitted the full paper for consideration at 2012 conference of the Society for the Interdisciplinary Study of Social Imagery, whose theme was "The Image of the Road." The full paper was accepted, presented, and published in the conference proceedings. In the paper, she argues that the series *Firefly* (and the movie *Serenity*, which continued the story line) evoked three rhetorical visions—protest, freedom, and transformation—most particularly through the words and actions of the spaceship's captain, Malcom "Mal" Reynolds. Led by this space hero and cowboy who takes to the sky rather than the road, the crew and company of Firefly struggle against and gain freedom from the totalitarian government that pursues them and manage to grow and improve themselves in the process. As you read the paper, consider the elements of SCT FTA we've discussed in this chapter. Do you agree with her analysis, conclusions, and implications? Would you add or modify anything? Explain.

Protest, Freedom, and Transformation in Space: *Firefly* as Road Narrative

Natalie Stevens

In September 2002, the television show *Firefly* debuted on television screens. In time, the show developed a large cult following. Due to a growing fan base, the feature film *Serenity* was produced in 2005 to continue the story line established on television. The action of *Firefly* takes place in the year 2517, after the earth "was used up." Various planets and moons were terraformed for human use. Some places in this universe have glossy futuristic technologies; other places resemble the dusty 19th-century American Southwest, reminiscent of the setting in a classic Western. The universal government, known as the Alliance, is a totalitarian regime that rules all of the planets but focuses on the core planets and neglects the outer planets (the frontier).

Firefly follows the adventures of nine people traveling on a Firefly-class spacecraft, named Serenity, into the far reaches of space. The crew consists of a captain (Malcolm Reynolds), a first mate (Zoe), a pilot (Wash), a mechanic (Kaylee), and a mercenary (Jayne). The crew makes money from crime such as smuggling jobs and transporting illegal cargo. The ship also takes passengers as a way to make an income. Inara is a companion (a high-end prostitute), who travels to meet with clients and serves as the ship's ambassador. Shepherd Book is a preacher with a mysterious past. Simon Tam is a doctor on the run with his sister, River, a fugitive who was tested upon in a government lab.

The show's creator Joss Whedon created the show as a Space Western, mixing science fiction (SF) and Western genres. Whedon said that part of his inspiration came from the original *Star Wars* trilogy, stating, "I wanted to tell the boring stories about Han Solo smuggling when he wasn't involved with the Rebellion" (Whedon, 2005 p. 10). Captain Mal's persona is referred to as a Han Solo-like hero. Another of Whedon's inspirations is the 1939 film, *Stagecoach*, about a group of diverse settlers traveling out to the frontier and overcoming obstacles in the process. *Firefly* "incorporates allusion to many attributes of the Western as it develops its motifs, but it always comes back to the foundation of *Stagecoach*, the model that gives it its shape and its direction" (Erisman, 2006 p. 257).

Many have written about the genres of Western and science fiction being similar including themes of exploring new frontiers and the philosophical direction regarding heroes and villains. Another concept that is related to both Westerns and science fiction is the road. "The road genre contains frequent use of myths and symbols of the American West or the frontier, such as references to cowboys, hostile Indians, pioneers, gunslingers, shoot-outs, wagon trains, and so on" (Ireland, 2003 p. 475). In *Firefly*, the action takes place in the sky, instead of the land or the highway, but basic road ethics and elements are visible in *Firefly*.

Firefly shares the rhetorical visions of mobility of the road genre; this paper will reveal this using FTA. This form of rhetorical criticism was developed by Ernest Bormann in the early 1970s to examine how stories shared by a group is "a way to examine messages" (1972, p. 396). Common themes of road narratives create rhetorical visions, a composite drama "which catch up large groups of people in a symbolic reality" (Bormann, 1972, p. 398). The poignant connection and sprit that people have to the road, as seen in popular culture, is part of the *Firefly* narrative. This paper will look at the road rhetorical visions of protest, freedom, and transformation in *Firefly*, focusing primarily on the captain of the ship Malcolm Reynolds and his motives for mobility and a nomadic lifestyle.

VISION OF PROTEST

Stories of the road often take place in opposition to the dominant culture. From the mid-century Beats in *On the Road*, to the 1960s counterculture of *Easy Rider*, to the hedonistic lifestyle of 1980s rock bands on tour, the road is a place for outsiders that rebel against cultural norms. "People leave home to change the scene, to overcome being defined by custom, tradition, and circumstances back home, and at least for a while—to construct an alternative way of living. Time on the road creates opportunities to question the existing social order and explore values that run counter to what is the dominant culture" (Primeau, 1996, p. 33). The heroes of the road genre are "rebels who defy the prohibitions that immobilize others" (Mills, 2006, p.22).

Mobility as a form of protest and defiance is important in *Firefly* and most significantly to the ship's captain, Mal Reynolds. Mal is a veteran from the losing side (the Independents or Browncoats) of the War of Independence, where the Alliance took control of the universe. Mal names his ship Serenity after the battle of Serenity Valley, where the Independents lost the war, as a constant reminder of his loss and the

reason to keep moving away from Alliance control. His character is compared to heroes of the Western genre, who gravitate toward the frontier as they were scarred by their war experience as Confederate soldiers in the Civil War (Canavan, 2011, p.182).

The journey and the "sky" is one thing that Mal can have power over. The theme song to the series has the line, "You can't take the sky from me." In the episode, *Out of Gas*, there is a flashback to when Mal first purchases Serenity. He says, "No matter how long the arm of the Alliance might get, we'll just get ourselves a little further." Mal is a rebel. Bledsoe makes a distinction between rebellion and revolution in regards to Mal, "Revolution seeks change; rebellion seeks separation" (2007, p.152). Mal still wears his Browncoat, a uniform of those who fought the Alliance, proudly. He defies the Alliance with relish; he accomplishes this by stealing their goods, harboring fugitives, disseminating classified information, and doing his best to make the Alliance government look incompetent.

The vision of protest is viewed through the avoidance of the dominant culture of the Alliance and the outright defiance of their laws and culture. A great portion of Mal's rebellion and protest is mobility to the outer reaches of space, where the Alliance power is limited. Making the ship and the sky his home in this permanent state of constant movement flies in the face of the Alliance's ideal of the colonization of space. "Instead of violently defying the Alliance's control, Reynolds and his crew 'choose' a nomadic life in the black of deep space, a transient life in constant motion" (Hill, 2009, p. 491).

(Continued)

(Continued)

VISION OF FREEDOM

The Road genre also portrays travel and mobility as an expression of freedom. "Some road heroes saw the highway not as renewal but the sheer frenzy of escapism" (Primeau, 1996 p. 27). Travelers do not have to play strictly by society's rules when moving across a sparsely populated highway. In *Firefly*, the concept of freedom can be seen in the discussions and plotlines about the rejection of civilization and creating a free society on the spaceship Serenity. Mal "values his freedom above all other traits" (Erisman, 2006 p.257). This is also characteristic of his journey and need for mobility. "Mal embraces travel and motion as a means toward both physical and psychological freedom" (Hill, 2009 p. 491).

This nomadic lifestyle is counter to the civilization of utopia/dystopia created by the Alliance that is focused on the control of people and environments. The need for freedom and rejection of the Alliance pushes Serenity and Mal deeper into space. "Freedom . . . is under constant threat, pushed further and further out towards the periphery" (Canavan, 2011 p. 184). Mal and the crew reject notions of a civilized culture as a protest to the dominant culture, as he would rather live on the border. Civilizing is also a topic that many of those writing and analyzing *Firefly* address. "Firefly is about those who live at the mercy of those in power in the galaxy, outsiders living on the margins, or who are left out entirely, of civilization and 'progress'" (Hill, 2009 p.489).

VISION OF TRANSFORMATION

The power of the road, in part, is due to its ability to be a catalyst for personal change, growth, and redefinition. "The road presents a way to experience life, affect others, and change ourselves" (Mills, 2006, p.22). "The theme of transformation of identity or rebirth . . . crops up often in the road genre" (Ireland, 2003, p. 475). *Firefly* creator Joss Whedon spoke about the show and the powerful personal aspects of travel on the DVD commentary for the first episode of the series, *Serenity*, "You take people, you put them on a journey, you give them peril, you find out who they really are." The interpersonal aspects of the series are what give it more depth. *Firefly*, on the surface, may be just about the action of science fiction and Westerns, but it is more in tune with the road genre as it is more about interpersonal interactions and things that happen along the way as agents of change. "Explosions may be a visually attractive part of getting there, but it's the small, seemingly inconsequential moments, the ephemera of daily conversation, that are the worthier part, and *Firefly* is really more a show about small moments than it is a show about train jobs and space ships" (Battis, 2008, para. 36).

Part of Mal's growth is through the Simon and River story line. In the beginning of the series, Mal reluctantly takes up the case of Simon and River as a way to protest against the Alliance and as a business opportunity. At first, he does not want them on the ship at all. Mal tells Simon, that "you've heaped a world of trouble on me and mine" and he says that he will drop them off the on the next stop. He does not. Somewhere on the journey he begins to genuinely care about them and they are part of his quasi-family on Serenity. He confronts Jayne for selling River and Simon out, in the episode "Ariel," by saying, "You turn on any of my crew, you turn on me." They have become part of his crew/family. If it were not for River and Simon, Mal "might never have opened himself up to a cause greater than himself" (Swendson, 2007, p.124).

During the series, Mal in many ways grows up. His path "is marked by his gradual maturing from the inherently adolescent impulse that led to his rebellion to the adult sense of responsibility" (Bledsoe, 2007, p. 152). This change is also a product of his hero's journey. "Our heroes have taken on their mission, faced death, and returned as new men" (Swendson, 2007, p.124).

CONCLUSION

Firefly is a television series that resonates with many people. The collective visions of protest, freedom, and transformation are topics that connect deeply with the human experience and *Firefly* taps into these topics in interesting ways. Science fiction, Westerns, and the road genre have overlapping themes that also touch a need, highlighting the desire for mobility, exploring new places, and discovering ourselves in new environments.

Further research can be done on the science fiction, Western, and road genres to discover additional places where these genres intersect with one another. This phenomenon can be observed in other television shows and movies such as *Star Wars*, *Star Trek*, *Battlestar Galactica*, and *Doctor Who*.

An approach to the road should not be defined by automobile travel or literal pavement; it can take place by foot, on a horse, on a train, or in a spaceship. It does not matter how you get there but what you express and learn about yourself along the way.

References

Battis, J. (2008, Winter). Captain Tightpants: Firefly and the science fiction cannon. *Slayage, 7*(1), 1–38 pars. Retrieved from http://slayageonline.com/essays/slayage25/Battis.htm

Bledsoe, A. (2007). Captain Reynolds grows up. In J. Espenson (Ed.), *Serenity found: More unauthorized essays on Joss Whedon's Firefly universe* (Kindle ed., pp. 150–166).

Bormann, E. G. (1972, Winter). Fantasy and rhetorical vision: the rhetorical criticism of social reality. *The Quarterly Journal of Speech, 58*(4), 396–407.

Canavan, G. (2011, Fall). Fighting a war you've already lost: Zombies and zombis in Firefly/Serenity and Dollhouse. *Science Fiction Film and Television, 4*(2), 173–203.

Erisman, F. (2006, Summer). Stagecoach in space: The legacy of Firefly. *Extrapolation, 47*(2), 249–258.

Hill, M. B. (2009, Fall). "I am a leaf on the wind": Cultural trauma and mobility in Joss Whedon's Firefly. *Extrapolation, 50*(3), 484–511.

Ireland, B. (2003, December). American highways: Recurring images and themes of the Road Genre. *The Journal of American Culture, 26*(4), 474–484.

Mills, K. (2006). *The road story and the rebel: Moving through film, fiction, and television.* Carbondale: Southern Illinois Press.

Primeau, R. (1996). *Romance of the road: The literature of the American highway.* Bowling Green, OH: Bowling Green State University Popular Press.

Swendson, S. (2007). A tale of two heroes. In J. Espenson (Ed.), *Serenity found: More unauthorized essays on Joss Whedon's Firefly universe* (Kindle ed., pp. 108–125).

Whedon, J. (2005). *Serenity: The official visual companion.* London: Titan.

Summary

This chapter outlined the guidelines by which to conduct an analysis of popular culture artifacts using SCT and its methodological tool, FTA, to identify the shared symbolic reality of a rhetorical community. We discussed how people shared stories, or converge their symbols, in order to make sense of the confusing and chaotic world. They share imaginative units of communication called fantasy themes, generally stories about characters acting within a plotline and scene who are motivated by sanctioning agents. Those themes combine to create rhetorical visions, which can be interpreted in terms of their master analogue (righteous, social, or pragmatic) and life-cycle stage. We discussed questions a critic can ask while conducting a fantasy theme analysis and added the additional suggestions of looking for fantasy types (stock scenarios) and symbolic cues (such as inside jokes) that stem from the original fantasy theme. We concluded that FTA is well suited for analyzing mediated messages, especially those with a we and they orientation, as it helps us identify both the shared realities and the hidden agendas of those who accept or reject certain messages. Finally, we shared two sample essays looking at the rhetorical visions found in the movie *The Rocky Horror Picture Show* and the television series *Firefly*.

Challenge

Watch any version of the movie *12 Angry Men*. Choices include the classic 1957 black-and-white version starring Henry Fonda and Lee J. Cobb, the updated 1997 color version starring Jack Lemmon and George C. Scott, or the 2007 Russian version (with English subtitles) titled simply *12*. Each tells the story of a jury at odds with one another. Battling stereotypes and hidden prejudices, one man uses his storytelling ability to change his fellow jurors' minds. Examine the movie using the following SCT questions.

1. Describe the group's makeup. What are the here-and-now tensions they are trying to overcome?

2. Identify any elements of the dramas: heroes, villains, plotlines, scenes, sanctioning agents.

3. Which dramas symbolically explode and chain out amongst the jury? Which do not? Explain why.

4. Do any stories reveal group member's motives? Emotions? Hidden agendas?

5. What rhetorical visions emerge? Does any master analogue (i.e., righteous, social, or pragmatic) dominate the arguments?

6. What are the implications about the power of narratives in a small group setting?

References

Bales, R. F. (1950). *Interaction process analysis.* Reading, MA: Addison-Wesley.

Bales, R. (1970). *Personality and interpersonal behavior.* New York: Holt, Rinehart.

Bormann, E. G. (1972). Fantasy and rhetorical vision: The rhetorical criticism of social reality. *Quarterly Journal of Speech, 58,* 396–407.

Bormann, E. G. (1973). The Eagleton affair: A fantasy theme analysis. *Quarterly Journal of Speech, 59,* 143–159.

Bormann, E. G. (1982). Fantasy and rhetorical vision: Ten years later. *Quarterly Journal of Speech, 68,* 288–305.

Bormann, E. G. (1983). The symbolic convergence theory of communication and the creation, raising, and sustaining of public consciousness. In J. I. Sisco (Ed.), *The Jensen lectures: Contemporary communication studies* (pp. 71–90). Tampa: University of South Florida.

Bormann, E. G. (1985). *The force of fantasy: Restoring the American dream.* Carbondale: Southern Illinois University Press.

Bormann, E. G., Cragan, J. F., & Shields, D. C. (2001). Three decades of developing, grounding, and using symbolic convergence theory. In W. D. Gudykunst (Ed.), *Communication yearbook 25* (pp. 271–313). Mahwah, NJ: Erlbaum and the International Communication Association.

Cragan, J. F., & Shields, D. C. (1981). *Applied communication research: A dramatistic approach.* Prospect Heights, IL: Waveland.

Cragan, J. F., & Shields, D. C. (1995). *Symbolic theories in applied communication research: Bormann, Burke and Fisher.* Cresskill, NJ: Hampton.

Endres, T. G. (2008). "Be Just and Fear Not": Warring visions of righteous decadence and pragmatic justice in *Rocky Horror.* In J. A. Weinstock (Ed.), *Reading Rocky Horror: The Rocky Horror Picture Show and popular culture* (pp. 207–220). New York: Palgrave Macmillan.

Student Study Site

Chapter 6

A Neo-Marxist Perspective

A neo-Marxist perspective helps expose how material conditions and economic practices shape dominant ideology regarding taken-for-granted assumptions about who "ought to be" and "ought not to be" empowered. In this chapter, we focus specifically on how popular culture texts reinforce or reject status quo power structures regarding socioeconomic status and materialism as *normal* and *common sense*. In other words, we examine ways in which popular culture texts function rhetorically to simultaneously empower and disempower people and groups based on materialism and economic practices.

Sometimes people misinterpret the intent of the neo-Marxist perspective based on the negative connotations (e.g., communism) the term can bring to mind. For this very reason, communication scholars continue to debate whether or not to label it as such and why we label it *neo*-Marxist throughout this book. Regardless of the label, however, the assumptions guiding this perspective's development were, in fact, first proposed by 19th-century German philosopher Karl Marx (1978), who argued "the ideas of the ruling class are in every epoch the ruling ideas" (p. 172).

Although the perspective is named after Karl Marx and is grounded in notions of egalitarianism posited by him and Friedrich Engels, its historical evolution as a rhetorical perspective can be attributed to a number of other key scholars. Among them are Antonio Gramsci (1971), Louis Althusser (1971), Theodor Adorno (1973, 1984), Jürgen Habermas (1979, 1984, 1987), Stuart Hall (1973, 1980, 1982, 1997a), Michel Foucault (1980), Hannah Arendt, Dana Cloud (1994), John Fiske (1987, 1989, 1992), Lawrence Grossberg, James Jasinski, and Dennis Mumby.

The neo-Marxist perspective can be conceptualized within a larger genre of communication theory referred to by some as critical studies and others as *critical rhetoric*. Critical rhetoric is an orientation that encompasses a number of perspectives that examine how texts "create and sustain the social practices which control the dominated" (McKerrow, 1989, p. 92). In short, the underlying goal shared across critical rhetoric perspectives is emancipation from oppression by revealing the ways in which discourse, albeit intentionally or unintentionally, helps create or maintain social and political oppression (Jasinski, 2001, p. 117).

These critical rhetoric perspectives may focus on oppression and empowerment based on race (e.g., critical or cultural studies such as Afrocentrism, Eastern rhetoric, visual rhetoric, Whiteness studies), sex, gender, and sexual orientation (e.g., feminist perspectives, feminine style and gynocriticism, invitational rhetoric, queer theory, visual pleasure), as well as materialism and economic practices (e.g., neoliberalism, neo-Marxism). For example, the caption for the Dove advertisement (see Figure 6.1) below reads: "Visibly more beautiful skin from the most unexpected of places—your shower." In terms of critical rhetoric, the messages it sends about race and empowerment matter whether the creators of the advertisement did so intentionally or unintentionally. Critics who argue that the ad is racist because the before image shows a black woman, the transition image shows a Latina woman, and the after image shows a blonde, white woman are actually basing their conclusion on an examination rooted in what we refer to as critical rhetoric.

Key concepts that cut across these unique but related perspectives are (1) ideology and hegemony (including power, empowerment, freedom, and oppression) and (2) texts as sites

■ **FIGURE 6.1**   Dove Advertisement

of struggle. Although these concepts may function within underlying arguments of narrative, dramatistic, or symbolic convergence analyses, they are particularly fundamental to critical rhetoric perspectives. Thus, we discuss them in some detail here as they relate specifically to a neo-Marxist approach. We will also revisit each of them in the chapters that follow.

IDEOLOGY AND HEGEMONY

Recall that *ideology* is a cultural group's perceptions about the way things are and their assumptions about the way things ought to be based on taken-for-granted norms and values. A neo-Marxist critic defines ideology more specifically as "a false set of ideas perpetuated by dominant political force[s]" regarding materialism and consumerism (Littlejohn & Foss, 2008, p. 331). An Italian Marxist philosopher by the name of Antonio Gramsci (1891–1937) further developed this conception of ideology to clarify how even those who are subordinated by the dominant ideology tend to willingly accept it as *common sense* (Gramsci, trans. 1971). Hence, even oppressed groups essentially participate in their own oppression! Gramsci coined the term *hegemony* to account for all the everyday practices, events, and texts that are interpreted subtly as natural (by both those in power and those oppressed) to promote the interests of the empowered group. Simply put, hegemony is the privileging of a dominant group's ideology over that of other groups.

In the United States, the dominant cultural group may be defined in terms of socioeconomic status, race, gender, and ability. When the norms, practices, and values of the dominant cultural group are privileged and taken for granted as normal and desirable, all other groups and their norms, practices, and values are simultaneously disempowered and oppressed. The consequence of hegemony that may be played out in linguistic, psychic, social, and cultural beliefs and behaviors is known as *othering* (Hall, 1997b, p. 238). Othering is the devaluing consequence of hegemony that perceives those not in the empowered group as different from and as *them*. A goal of critical rhetoric is to free othered people and groups from oppression by unpacking how the norms, practices, and values of the dominant group are oppressing them and then making space for multiple voices to be heard and valued. Hegemony in the United States can be illustrated, for example, in the following statements:

- Wealthy people are more empowered than poor people.

- Caucasians are more empowered than other races.

- Native-born Americans are more empowered than immigrants.

- Men are more empowered than women.

- Heterosexual people are more empowered than homosexual, bisexual, or transsexual people.

- Able-bodied people are more empowered than people living with disabilities.

Hegemony, then, supports the interests of those in power, and it also privileges the interpretations of artifacts, objects, events, and practices that maintain the existing power structure as normal. Messages that challenge the status quo in terms of power are perceived as abnormal, undesirable, or even wrong. Moreover, as Foucault (1980) claimed, this power or knowledge ideology permeates every "crack" and "joint" of a social system and serves as the dynamic force that actually holds it together (p. 119).

QUESTIONING YOUR ETHICS . . .

What thoughts come to your mind when you pass a homeless person on the sidewalk? Your responses shed light on the degree to which you adhere to the hegemony in the United States.

MATERIALISM AND ECONOMIC METAPHORS

Neo-Marxist theory is grounded in a philosophy of materialism. Classical Marxist theory suggested that the economic base (e.g., who owns what, who controls what) determined all ideas, rules, laws, norms, customs, and social practices. Today, neo-Marxists conceive of materialism much more broadly to include any and all of our daily life experiences (Fiske, 1989). In other words, neo-Marxist materialism today posits that all ideas, rules, laws, norms, customs, and social practices of a given society come to be based on real, concrete, observable objects, conditions, and practices related to material possessions and wealth.

Moreover, materialism is influenced by discourse. Dana Cloud (1994), a professor of Communication at the University of Texas in Austin, argues that neo-Marxist critics ought to examine mediated popular culture texts as they intersect with lived experiences and economic interests. In other words, popular culture texts are contained within and constrained by hegemony, so critics ought to examine them as they reflect as well as perpetuate hegemony.

Classical Marxist critics also examined how hegemony was being perpetuated through economic metaphors. Economic metaphors were conceived at the time as limited to objects, events, and practices that reinforce the notion that power ought to belong to the wealthy. As the definition of materialism expanded, so did the definition of what constitutes an economic metaphor. Today, neo-Marxist theorists use the term economic metaphor to include anything (e.g., images, language, objects, events, practices) that signifies (sheds light on) something about the culture's ideas, norms, values, and practices regarding wealth and empowerment.

APPLYING WHAT YOU'VE LEARNED . . .

Compare the *Zits* comic strip to *The Family Circus*. What does each one suggest about what is normal and common sense? How might each one influence viewers with regard to hegemony in the United States today?

SITES OF STRUGGLE

One of the most fruitful channels through which hegemony is disseminated is the mass media. This is due, in part, to the fact that "the class which has the means of material production at its disposal has control at the same time over the means of mental production . . . [and] the ideas of those who lack the means of mental production are subject to it" (Curran, Gurevitch, & Woollacott, 1982, p. 22). In other words, one way empowered groups maintain their power is through the messages they repeatedly send in mediated popular culture texts. And "people's material social experience constantly reminds them of the disadvantages of subordination" (Fiske, 1992, p. 291). Hence, people continually struggle with the congruity and incongruity between what they see and hear in popular culture texts and their actual life experiences. When these popular culture texts reinforce or call into question taken-for-granted beliefs about what is normal regarding empowerment, they operate as sites of struggle. When the struggle is rooted in materialism, the text is arguing from a neo-Marxist critical perspective.

Neo-Marxist critics examine popular culture texts as sites of struggle via preferred or oppositional hegemonic arguments regarding materialism. Critical theorists, including neo-Marxist critics, call the ideological arguments about empowerment couched beneath the surface of texts **readings**. These readings are proposed through interpellation (Althusser, 1971). **Interpellation** occurs when a text leads us to identify with certain roles or **subject positions**. One way popular culture texts do so is by portraying characters as **models** who look and act in ways portrayed as normal, attractive, and desirable as well as **anti-models** who look and act in ways portrayed as abnormal, unattractive, and undesirable.

A **preferred reading** reinforces the status quo ideology about empowerment by proposing taken-for-granted assumptions as common sense. Consider, for example, the numerous TV programs that depict a "good-looking" Caucasian heterosexual married couple and their children living in a "nice home" with "nice things," wearing "nice clothes" and driving "nice vehicles" while living in a "nice neighborhood." Viewers typically perceive them as normal and don't think twice about them as representative of a normal family. Perceiving them as representative of a "typical American family" is common sense. Viewers perceive them as model subjects to emulate in their own lives in order to be judged as normal and desirable, as well.

Sometimes the preferred reading is blatant as in the aforementioned example. Other times, however, the ideological argument about empowerment is couched within what seems to be—at least at the surface—an oppositional argument. Critical rhetoric, including a neo-Marxist perspective, labels these kinds of messages **occluded, preferred readings**. Consider, for example, a program like *Mike and Molly*. This show appears to propose an alternative worldview about empowerment. Compared to other popular sitcoms like, for instance, *Modern Family, 30 Rock, Cougar Town,* and *New Girl,* Mike and Molly—the main characters—do not live in what the status quo would call a "nice home" or appear to own lots of "nice things." Not only that, both are portrayed as overweight (having met at Overeaters Anonymous). On the surface, the program might seem to be operating as a text that challenges the hegemony of the status quo. However, few viewers conclude that looking like or living like Mike and Molly is desirable, and many ultimately disassociate with them (e.g., "at least I'm not THAT fat"). You may even recall the controversial postings on the

Marie Claire website about whether a show featuring an overweight couple as attractive and normal is appropriate. In this sense, *Mike and Molly* ultimately supports hegemony as an occluded, preferred reading.

APPLYING WHAT YOU'VE LEARNED . . .

Consider a favorite TV program. Why do you enjoy it? Does it seem to support hegemony in one of these ways? Why or why not?

Many mediated popular culture texts offer preferred readings that reinforce hegemony. Sometimes, however, a mediated popular culture text will challenge the status quo argument about who ought to and ought not to be empowered and why. Critics label these texts as oppositional readings. They are oppositional because they challenge the dominant ideology with regard to taken-for-granted beliefs about empowerment.

There are actually two types of oppositional readings: *subversions* and *inflections*. A subverted oppositional reading is a text whose messages reject hegemony outright. For example, in the classic film, *Dances With Wolves,* Kevin Costner's character ultimately rejects the values of the dominant American culture to embrace the values of the Sioux culture instead. In recent years, a number of feature films and documentaries have been produced that reject hegemony outright with regard to othering people living with disabilities. For example, *Temple Grandin* tells the story of how the work of an animal science professor living with autism improved the ethical treatment of animals. *Music Within* tells the story of how two Vietnam veterans living with disabilities worked to get the Americans With Disabilities Act passed. And *Front of the Class* tells the story of a gifted teacher who happens to also live with Tourette's syndrome.

In terms of neo-Marxism, subverted oppositional readings reject materialism and consumerism. The premise of the Oxygen Network TV program *Pretty Wicked* attempts to reject materialism by focusing instead on demonstrating one's inner beauty. The award-winning TV soap opera *Muvhango* attempts to portray success in the form of simple people reflecting township and Sowetan life in South Africa.

APPLYING WHAT YOU'VE LEARNED . . .

Read the stories of the two families described on this website: http://www.verdant.net/families .htm

Which family are you lead to identify with as a model and an anti-model and why? In terms of neo-Marxism, what kinds of readings are portrayed in each of them regarding materialism and consumerism?

An inflected oppositional reading is one where the messages represent a mere bending of hegemony to suit one's own needs rather than an outright rejection of it. One might argue, for example, that the popular 1980s TV sitcom *The Cosby Show* offered an inflected oppositional reading in terms of race. The Huxtables were of high socioeconomic status (he was a medical doctor and she was an attorney), and they lived in a "nice home," had lots of "nice things," and were the parents of "normal, middle-class kids" (i.e., no one was addicted to drugs, no one was homosexual, no one was "fat" or "ugly," and so on). It was inflected because portraying the empowered and affluent parents as a doctor and a lawyer would have suggested a preferred reading, but portraying these parents as black was oppositional to the hegemony of the time that tended to define empowered people narrowly as white.

Mediated popular culture texts that offer subverted oppositional messages are fairly easy to spot. Why? Because messages that challenge forthrightly our taken-for-granted beliefs about empowerment and disempowerment force us to struggle with the possibility that the dominant worldview is at best limited and at worst wrong. Because such texts challenge hegemony squarely, however, they often fail to gain broad appeal by general audiences (Sellnow & Sellnow, 2001). Consequently, relatively few TV programs or mainstream feature films present subverted oppositional messages as doing so would likely result in less profit (Littlejohn & Foss, 2008, p. 261). The Academy-award winning film *Good Will Hunting,* however, is one example. Will, a mere custodian (disempowered group) at MIT, is more brilliant than even some of the professors. Had Will accepted the million-dollar academic research position he was offered, we might argue that the film posed an inflected oppositional reading, much like *The Cosby Show* did. Ultimately, however, viewers were drawn to identify with and root for Will in his quest for happiness over material wealth or status and may have even cheered for him when he turned down the position and followed his heart. In this sense, the film argued a subverted oppositional message.

Over the years, the music industry has offered perhaps as many messages that oppose hegemony as messages that reinforce it, and oppositional messages are becoming increasingly prominent in popular music (Sellnow & Brown, 2004). This may be due at least in part to the fact that gatekeepers (mainstream recording labels and radio stations) have less control over the industry than they once did. Thanks to the Internet, our ability to break free from gatekeepers is not limited only to the music industry. Today, anyone can record and post music, videos, and other popular culture texts to a variety of websites, and anyone can access them. One implication of this phenomenon is the growing prevalence of what scholars have labeled *intertextuality*. Intertextuality refers to the blending of texts in ways that make it difficult if not impossible to separate them from prior texts, context, and any other utterances that surround them (e.g., Barthes, 1981; Culler, 1981; Jasinski, 1997). Consider, for example, the complex nature of an argument conveyed in a song like "I Will Survive," first performed by Gloria Gaynor and later performed by Cake. Or think about message meaning when videos and music are digitally remixed. Undoubtedly, the full impact of these changes has yet to be realized and is a fertile field of study among rhetoricians today.

To illustrate the music industry's offering of numerous examples of oppositional neo-Marxist texts, consider the lyrics to Beatle's 1960s classic "Can't Buy Me Love." Certainly, these lyrics offer a subverted oppositional challenge to hegemony:

Can't buy me love, love
Can't buy me love

I'll buy you a diamond ring, my friend, if it makes you feel all right
I'll get you anything, my friend, if it makes you feel all right

'Cause I don't care too much for money; money can't buy me love
I'll give you all I got to give if you say you love me too

I may not have a lot to give, but what I got, I'll give to you
I don't care too much for money; money can't buy me love

Can't buy me love, everybody tells me so
Can't buy me love, no no no, no

Say you don't need no diamond ring, and I'll be satisfied
Tell me that you want the kind of thing that money just can't buy
I don't care too much for money; money can't buy me love

Subverted oppositional messages can be found in music throughout the decades since then. Consider, for example, Garth Brooks's 1990s country hit "Friends in Low Places" as he sings about ruining his ex-lover's "black tie affair" by showing up "in boots." He argues that it's "OK . . . 'Cause I've got friends in low places," which surely beats "that ivory tower that you're livin' in." And, more recently in "Lost in Hollywood," System of a Down sings about the "phoney people" in Hollywood who are nothing more than "maggots" who take you, remake you, tell you you're on the top, then get disgusted with you and turn away. They end with their oppositional message about selling out to Hollywood when they sing, "You should have never trusted Hollywood. You should have never gone to Hollywood." And in "Welcome to Heartbreak," Kanye West sings:

My friend showed me pictures of his kids
And all I could show him was pictures of my cribs.
He said his daughter got a brand-new report card
And all I got was a brand-new sports car . . .
Dad cracked a joke; all the kids laugh
But I couldn't hear 'em all the way in first class.
Chased the good life my life long.
Looked back on my life, and my life gone.
Where did I go wrong? . . .
Welcome to heartbreak.

The music industry is certainly one manufacturer of popular culture where arguments that challenge hegemony thrive alongside those that reinforce it.

We can also find examples in movies and on TV. The popular PBS TV series *Downton Abbey* serves as an excellent example of a mediated popular culture text positing ideological arguments rooted in neo-Marxism. At the surface, viewers might be called to identify with Lord and Lady Grantham and their daughters who seem to have it all regarding materialism (e.g., money, power, status, servants, "nice stuff"). They seem to be more empowered than the valet (Mr. Bates), the butler (Mr. Carson), or the head housekeeper (Mrs. Hughes). Similarly, Mr. Bates, Mr. Carson, and Mrs. Hughes seem to be more empowered than the other housemaids, the cooks, or the footmen. Levels of hierarchy and power are clearly distinguished at the outset.

As the stories unfold, however, viewers are invited to see some aspects of the aristocracy as disempowering. For example, Mary, Ethel, and Sybil are supposed to marry an "appropriate" person of position and rank rather than for love. In this sense, viewers might be led instead to identify with the love story of Mr. John Bates and Anna or to root for Sybil to pursue her romantic relationship with Tom Branson (the chauffeur turned journalist). When Lord Grantham is denied his request to fight in the war, he talks of feeling worthless. In this sense, viewers might see him as disempowered compared to Matthew Crowley and even servant footmen, Thomas Barrow and Alfred Nugent, who did fight in the war. When Matthew Crowley became a paralyzed veteran, however, he became othered and disempowered until he miraculously regained his ability to walk. These are a few of the ways competing stories conveyed in *Downton Abbey* operate as sites of struggle from a neo-Marxist perspective.

APPLYING WHAT YOU'VE LEARNED . . .

Consider a TV program or movie that seems to oppose hegemony. Based on what you've read here, does it actually do so, or does it really reinforce hegemony in an occluded way or perhaps oppose it in only an inflected way? Why?

CONDUCTING NEO-MARXIST ANALYSIS

As with the other perspectives detailed in this text, many mediated popular culture texts can be conducive to a neo-Marxist analysis. A neo-Marxist perspective is useful because it calls our attention to the subtle ways in which hegemony is embedded in popular culture texts that, at the surface, do not seem to be sending messages about privileging the elite at all. As such, neo-Marxist analyses empower us to be more critical consumers about the ways hegemonic materialism is reproduced and reinforced in mediated texts. The following paragraphs explain how you might go about conducting a neo-Marxist criticism of mediated popular culture texts by first selecting an appropriate artifact to analyze as a text and then examining it using the tools of the neo-Marxist perspective.

Step 1: Selecting an Appropriate Text

In addition to considering elements of the rhetorical situation (e.g., rhetor, audience, occasion, exigence, constraints), you might choose to focus on a text that reinforces the status quo overtly, reinforces the status quo in an occluded (hidden) way, or challenges the status quo in a subverted or inflected way. Consider, for instance, the comic strip in Figure 6.2. Underneath the humor lies a message that reinforces hegemony. That is, the ability to buy material goods makes people happy. Moreover, if credit card debt and juggling balances provide spending money for more material goods, then by all means, charge it. If readers of this comic strip do so, thinking credit card debt is normal even if it isn't desirable, and "everybody juggles bills" whether we want to or not, then you can argue that this comic strip essentially perpetuates hegemony.

■ **FIGURE 6.2**   Comic Strip

Source: Used by permission of John Forgetta and Creators Syndicate, Inc.

APPLYING WHAT YOU'VE LEARNED . . .

Consider any of the MasterCard advertisements today. Consider how they perpetuate hegemony by arguing that owning and using a MasterCard is empowering, or "priceless?"

Step 2: Examining the Text (Describe and Interpret)

As with any popular culture analysis, you examine the artifact though description, interpretation, and evaluation. When you describe the messages via a neo-Marxist perspective, you begin by identifying *subject positions,* that is, economic metaphors embodied in the characters presented as *models* whom receivers are encouraged to want to be like and *anti-models* whom viewers are encouraged to not want to be like. Sometimes the characters are identified explicitly as in a television program or movie, and other times, the receiver must conceptualize the model and anti-model characters as in many advertisements and songs.

TV sitcoms targeted toward adolescents such as *Saved by the Bell* in the 1990s, *Hannah Montana* in the 2000s, and *Austin and Ally* today provide very clear subject positions. On *Saved by the Bell,* young male viewers are led to want to be like Zach or Slater and definitely not like Screech. Young female viewers are more likely to want to be like Kelly than either of the other female characters. On *Hannah Montana,* young viewers are led to want to be like Miley Ray Stewart, Hannah Montana, Lilly, or Oliver but probably not like Jackson or Rico. And on *Austin and Ally,* viewers are invited to be like Austin or Ally but probably not like Trish or Dez.

You can also determine models and anti-models by considering who is portrayed as us and who is portrayed as them. In the MasterCard advertisements, viewers are led to want to be like those who have the "priceless" buying power that owning the credit card provides. Hence, us is anyone who owns a MasterCard, and them is anyone who does not own one.

Once you have identified and described the model and anti-model characters, you interpret the text according to other economic metaphors offered and the value attached to them. You can do so by examining the characters' possessions, their positions (status), and the interactions among them. Consider what is being emphasized as positive about *us* (or the characters we are led to identify with as models) and negative about *them* (or the characters we are led to see as anti-models)? Likewise, consider what is being deemphasized that may be negative about us and positive about them.

Look at the MasterCard advertisement in Figure 6.3 as an example. The characters are the MasterCard owner, server, coworker, dad, plumber, dog walker, accountant, and crossing guard. Readers are led to see the MasterCard owner as the model (us) and all the others as anti-models (them). Why? Because the power to pay for everyone else's meal is emphasized

■ **FIGURE 6.3**   MasterCard Ad

as positive (priceless), and the disempowerment of not being able to say "it's on me" is emphasized as negative. Even the slogan, "There are some things money can't buy. For everything else there's MasterCard," presumes most things can be bought. Moreover, one negative thing about MasterCard owners that is deemphasized—actually, not mentioned at all—is the fact that credit card debt will accrue exponentially after paying for all these lunches. The positive power the credit card provides us with, combined with the negative disempowerment not owning the card provides them, ultimately reinforces hegemony. That is, those who have money are empowered, even if the "money" is in the form of a plastic façade of debt, and those who do not have the money are disempowered.

Step 3: Evaluating Potential Implications of the Text

Finally, you evaluate the message offered in the text in terms of the potential implications it may have on individuals and on society. The implications of the MasterCard advertisement are that it creates a sense that buying things on credit is just as good as paying for them outright. In fact, it is normal and even desirable to do so in order to be perceived as empowered. These sorts of beliefs and behaviors could lead to frivolous spending, credit card abuse, and a lifetime of trying to pay off the expenditures with interest, which could even lead to a ruined credit rating or bankruptcy.

APPLYING WHAT YOU'VE LEARNED . . .

Identify a popular television sitcom or series. Analyze it according to a neo-Marxist perspective. Does it reinforce or oppose hegemony? Do you think the neo-Marxist messages it sends contribute to its success? Why or why not?

SAMPLE PUBLISHED ESSAY

Read the article titled, "The Crisis of Public Values in the Age of the New Media," written by Henry A. Giroux and published in volume 28 of *Critical Studies in Media Communication* (2011). The article argues that the prevailing hegemony of the United States is becoming increasingly materialistic and selfish. As a result, the gap between the rich and the poor continues to widen, and public values are being eroded and critical thinking and civil discourse are being replaced with spectacles of entertainment and "a winner-take-all consumer mentality" (p. 13). Although he acknowledges concerns that new electronic media may "undermine institutions and make critical thought and democratic speech difficult," he also points to the potential of new media to be a vehicle for "enhancing public discourse by making power visible" (pp. 20, 24). As you read, consider how he frames new media as a site of struggle that can reinforce neo-Marxist ideology of selfish consumerism or oppose it by serving as "a tool for democratic empowerment" (p. 23). After reading the article, where do you stand in the debate and why?

SAMPLE STUDENT ESSAYS

Anne Marie Vaughn wrote the following essay titled, "Unplugged: A neo-Marxist Analysis of the Dunphy Clan From *Modern Family*" for a class project. In it, she examines the episode, "Unplugged," to demonstrate what is argued about the need for iPads, TVs, video games, cell phones, and Internet access as normal and desirable in middle-class American households. Ultimately, she argues that "modern" families are not just diverse and nontraditional in makeup but also must be "plugged in" to new media to function successfully and happily in our modern world. As you read the essay, compare her examples to your own life. Do you agree? Why or why not?

Unplugged: A Neo-Marxist Analysis of the Dunphy Clan From *Modern Family*

Anne Marie Vaughn

Since its debut in 2009, ABC's multi-Emmy-winning sitcom *Modern Family* has become one of the highest-rated and most critically acclaimed comedies on television. In fact, it earned the honor of Outstanding Comedy Series in 2010, 2011, and 2012 (Boster, 2012). The show is often praised for its portrayal of diverse and formerly nontraditional family units, notably a gay male couple with an adopted Vietnamese daughter and the family patriarch with his Hispanic trophy wife and her son. A third family completes the triad of the *Modern Family* structure. This family, the Dunphy Clan, is comprised of Phil and Claire Dunphy and their three adolescent children (Haley, Alex, and Luke). Although each member displays distinguishing personality quirks, the family most closely mimics the hegemonic ideology of what constitutes a "typical American family."

Numerous studies report that Americans are becoming increasingly selfish, materialistic, and greedy. Judt (2010), for example, claims that "the materialistic and selfish quality of contemporary life" is widening disparities of the rich and poor.

An article in the *Chicago Tribune* reported that 15 million Americans are unemployed, several million are underemployed, and an alarming 45 million live in poverty (MCT News, 2009). And "corporate abuse and greed" are leading to an identity shift from people as "citizens" to people as "consumers" (Hedges, 2009, p. 117). What might mediated popular culture texts, in this case the TV show, *Modern Family*, be arguing about materialism and power?

Examining *Modern Family's* Dunphy Clan from a neo-Marxist perspective is appropriate because the Dunphys are likely to be perceived as the model characters representing a typical American family. They appear to be upper middle class. Claire is a homemaker, and Phil is a real estate agent whose business is suffering because of the nation's economy. Nevertheless, they own several cars, a large and well-furnished house in a nameless California suburb, go on family vacations across the continental United States and Hawaii, and own many personal electronic gadgets.

As a self-referential "mockumentary"-style sitcom, technology is inherently built into every

(Continued)

(Continued)

episode. The show's writers embrace technology and immerse their characters in a "digital fun-house" of iPads, cellphones, and YouTube videos (Feiler, 2011). I argue that the plethora of technology embedded throughout the show reinforces hegemony regarding empowerment based on wealth and material possessions.

NEO-MARXIST PERSPECTIVE

A neo-Marxist perspective examines how "material conditions and economic practices shape the dominate ideology about who *ought to be* and *ought not to be* empowered" (Sellnow, 2010, p. 71). In the United States, the dominant cultural group is defined in large part in terms of socioeconomic status. In other words, those who possess great wealth have more power than those who do not. Materialism is at the root of the neo-Marxist perspective. The critic's role is to uncover underlying arguments conveyed in texts as they reinforce or challenge the ideology that wealthier people who possess more material goods should be empowered. This argument is sometimes conveyed overtly but is constantly played out in covert arguments offered as normal and common sense.

Critics conducting a neo-Marxist analysis do so by examining the roles of the characters portrayed as models (those viewers are invited to be like) and anti-models (those portrayed as something other than normal, attractive, or desirable). Then the critic examines the economic metaphors played out by the models and anti-models to determine what hegemonic argument is being proposed regarding materialism and empowerment. This essay examines one episode of *Modern Family* in terms of the messages it sends to viewers regarding the role of technological gadgets and material

possessions as normal and desirable in typical modern American families. Doing so will lead to conclusions about how it may reflect as well as shape hegemony in the United States today.

ANALYSIS

This analysis examines the episode "Unplugged," which originally aired on October 20, 2012, as Episode 5 of the show's second season. The Dunphy parents, frustrated by their family's poor communication and their children's reliance on technology, announce a one-week ban on all things electronic. The prospect of spending an entire week without the use of cell phones, Internet access, and other electronic media distresses and angers the children. During one exchange, Alex, the brainy daughter, argues that she has "a huge science paper due" so she needs to use her computer to access the Internet. Claire responds that the family's set of encyclopedias and the public library are both options. Referring to the public library, Alex's older sister Haley replies, "I thought that was a bathroom for homeless people." This comment, while sure to elicit laughter, sets the tone of the episode's argument that *normal* middle-class families have access to and use new media and modern technology regularly.

The children go on to complain about being prevented from playing games and chatting with friends online and then ask their father if the ban also pertains to him using technology for the week. Phil replies, "I am completely on board with your mother's horse and buggy to yesteryear. For the next week I may as well be Amish. Jebediah Dunphy." Here the Amish are jokingly used as a metaphor equating the "primitive" life with lack of access to and use of technology and the Internet. The scene ends with Phil promising a prize for the person who remains "unplugged" the longest. Alex wants a computer if she wins, and Haley wants a car. Phil agrees to both. When Haley eventually wins, however, Phil claims to have been bluffing. The fact that the prizes are not ultimately rewarded does not detract from the neo-Marxist argument proposed. That is, viewers were not led to believe the promise of a computer or new car as a prize for complying with a one-week lifestyle change was unreasonable. Yet, for most viewers watching the show, such promises are probably unreasonable and even beyond the realm of possibility in their own lives.

Phil, who is characterized as having arrested development and being extremely eager to be perceived as a "cool" dad, usually speaks with his children using a lighthearted tone. Therefore, although he claims to agree with his wife while they make this authoritative announcement, his tone conveys his attitude about the absurdity of Claire's demands. Throughout this short scene, which is less than two minutes long, the children and Phil express either verbally or nonverbally that the prospect of a week without technology will be arduous, unproductive, and absurd. Claire, the only sincere proponent of the technology ban, is made out to be the anti-model when, for example, Phil likens her request to the "primitive" ways of the Amish and jokes that she used to study with "a chisel and a piece of stone." She is portrayed as the out-of-touch anti-model who does not embrace technology and all that it can offer providing information, fun, and convenience in daily life. Conversely, Haley, Alex, Luke, and Phil are portrayed as the model characters that value technology for doing productive things like homework, socially engaging things like communicating with friends, and positively stimulating activities like playing games.

Although the overt plotline of this episode centers around access to and use of technology, underlying messages about access to these material possessions at all as *normal* in typical American families are threaded throughout the subtext. Claire bans the use of "cell phones, texting, IM-ing, video chatting and video gaming, and anything on the Internet." The children and Phil perceive these technologies positively as they represent freedom, convenience, as well as communication and engagement opportunities. Although Claire's purpose for the ban—improving interpersonal interactions among the family members—is an ideal value in American hegemony, linking it to a technology ban makes it negative. To the rest of the family, making room for more healthy face-to-face communication at the cost of a technology ban is not worth the pain and suffering price.

CONCLUSION AND IMPLICATIONS

The comedic plots about family life presented in 30-minute episodes on *Modern Family* use humorous anecdotes and situations to propose arguments about how *normal* modern American families behave and what they value. Although the overarching premise of the show may be to broaden our perspective about the structure of *normal* modern American families, a closer look at the episode "Unplugged" reveals that additional messages about wealth and materialism are also being communicated. When the Dunphy children complain about a one-week ban on electronics, their lines make the audience laugh—but they also send occluded messages reinforcing hegemony that normal children will be both

(Continued)

(Continued)

unhappy and unproductive if deprived of technology use and Internet access. Suggesting that low-tech options are absurd and outdated further reinforces this argument.

What, then, is the audience of *Modern Family* learning about normal and desirable beliefs and behaviors? Judging from this episode alone, happiness and productivity are contingent upon access to electronic products, technology, and access to the Internet. And normal families can offer prizes like new computers and cars for winning in a week-long family competition. Audiences can see that the Dunphy family owns a nice home and multiple cars, as well as computers, iPads, televisions, video games, and personal cell phones for each family member. Depicting them as typical in middle-class families suggests to viewers they *ought to* own all of them, as well.

From a rhetorical perspective, this casual display of material wealth as commonplace and its necessity for happiness and productivity could influence viewers to purchase items they cannot really afford. If left unchecked, doing so could result in unmanageable credit card debt and more. When audiences are invited to identify with the overt messages about accepting multiple family structures and diversity offered in *Modern Family,* they might also be influenced to try to imitate these other behaviors related to owning technology as a sign of wealth and empowerment. Unfortunately, the relationship between materialistic possessions and happiness is featured just as prominently as the acceptance of diverse family structures. Thus, "modern" does not just refer to diverse and nontraditional families but also to what those families must own and how they must behave in order to successfully function in contemporary society.

The preferred neo-Marxist reading couched within oppositional readings regarding race and sexuality may, in fact, contribute to the growing sense of materialistic entitlement that pervades the dominant hegemony of the United States today. If authors such as Hedges (2009) and Judt (2010) are right that Americans are becoming increasingly selfish, materialistic, and greedy at the expense of democratic values, arguments portraying wealth and material possessions as taken for granted and commonplace in middle-class American homes such as these in *Modern Family* actually may be perpetuating it.

References

Boster, M. (2012, September 23). Emmy winners and nominations 2012. *Los Angeles Times.* Retrieved from http://www.latimes.com/entertainment/envelope/emmys/la-et-st-emmy-nominations-2012-list-20120718,0,521498.htmlstory

Feiler, B. (2011, January 21). What *Modern Family* says about modern families. *The New York Times.* Retrieved from http://www.nytimes.com/2011/01/23/fashion/23THISLIFE.html?pagewanted=all

Hedges, C. (2009). *Empire of illusion.* Toronto: Knopf, Canada.

Judt, T. (2010). *Ill fares the land.* New York: Penguin Books.

MCT News. (2009, November 2). 3.6 million older Americans living in poverty. *Chicago Tribune.* Retrieved from http://www.chicagotribune.com/business/yourmoney/sns-2009110208 04mctnewsservbc-pfp-graymatters-nd52,0,3069729,print.story

Sellnow, D. (2010). *The rhetorical power of popular culture: Considering mediated texts.* Thousand Oaks, CA: Sage.

Jennifer Burnside wrote the following essay as a final class paper. Her paper, *"Sex and the City:* What Popular Culture Teaches Us About 'Normal,'" illustrates how the TV program perpetuates hegemony. That is, those who have material possessions and wealth are "rightly" empowered and those who do not are "rightly" disempowered. She argues that the cultivation effects of showing obsessive consumerism as a "fashion mecca" may result in viewers who become overly materialistic as a means to finding success and happiness. She points out that viewers, particularly women and teenage girls as target audiences, are particularly vulnerable to its messages. As you read, consider the specifics she offers as economic metaphors and subject positions to support her argument. Do you agree? Why or why not?

Sex and the City: *What Popular Culture Tells Us About "Normal"*

Jennifer Burnside

INTRODUCTION

Recently, I was listening to Minnesota Public Radio, and one of the hosts was reading an excerpt from the book by David Sedaris, *Dress Your Family in Corduroy and Denim.* One part stood out to me: The neighbors didn't have a television, and so they didn't know that they were weird. They didn't know when every family ate dinner (sometimes they didn't sit down together until 8:00 P.M.) or what to put on the table when they did. The idea that they didn't know how strange they were because they hadn't seen "normal" on television seemed to be revolutionary. Do we learn "normal" from watching television, and what is it that we are learning? HBO's recently retired and now in syndication comedy, *Sex and the City,* certainly teaches its viewers something about normal. As a show that has been hailed for presenting women with role models that embrace single life and their friendships, is this all women see when they watch?

Bill Carter of *The New York Times* wrote that *Sex and the City* is "a show that has become a phenomenon, the most popular comedy in the history of cable television" (2003, p. E1). The show is set in

New York City, primarily Manhattan, and centers on articles written by the primary character, Carrie Bradshaw. Carrie and her friends, Miranda Hobbes, Charlotte York, and Samantha Jones, are looking for love, dealing with being single, and trying to answer all of the questions women have while balancing careers in stilettos and couture.

Indeed, it is popular, and women are watching. "On HBO, which has 28 million subscribers, the sixth and final season of 'Sex and the City' attracted 12.4 million viewers each week" (Salamon, 2004, p. E1). In fact, 12.4 million viewers tuned in to peek into the lives of Carrie, Charlotte, Miranda, and Samantha and, more than likely, entered into conversations about what they saw. However, is what they say and discussed necessarily what they learned?

Adult women and men aren't the only ones who have bought into this pop culture phenomenon. In the same article by Julie Salamon that is quoted above, a 14-year-old girl is quoted as saying that *Sex and the City* is "'one of her favorite shows. . . . HBO makes it special, because the show can be raunchy. . . . The language and sex aren't the most important part, but they add to it.'" *Sex and the City* is obviously in many homes

(Continued)

(Continued)

and is having an effect on a wide range of viewers. The success of the show doesn't end with the viewers either. According to HBO.com, the show has won over 47 awards since 1999, including Screen Actors' Guild awards, Golden Globes, and Emmy awards. "In the six years since Carrie first strode through Manhattan in a tutu and tank top, all smarts, sass and—thanks to a passing bus—street-water-splattered vulnerability, the show has won five Emmys and eight Golden Globes—including the best-comedy-actress statue Parker picked up on Jan. 25 (her fourth)" (Schneider, 2004, p. 88). You cannot ignore the impact that *Sex and the City* has had on society.

Its popularity and influence contribute to making *Sex and the City* an excellent text for analysis. However, I'd like to stray from the usual perspective that many people broach when discussing the pop culture phenomenon: feminism. Whether or not *Sex and the City* shows the empowerment of women or embraces the feminist movement is of less consequence in this analysis than what the women of the show need in order to be empowered and be *normal:* material goods. One cannot discuss *Sex and the City* without paying homage to it as a fashion Mecca. There isn't an article written about the show that doesn't, to some degree, discuss the impact that the show has had on the fashion world and thus on society. Therefore, it is important to discuss the materialistic impact that the show has had and is having on society, primarily women. To this end, *Sex and the City* will be analyzed from the Marxist perspective and informed media-centered criticism.

RHETORICAL PERSPECTIVE

The Marxist perspective, as it will be used to examine a popular culture text, is the critical lens that examines who is and is not valuable and why, as well as what it is that empowers the valuable. According to Brummett (1994), "This philosophy holds that ideas, rules, laws, customs, social arrangements—in short, everything belonging to the world of ideas or concepts—grows from material conditions and practices" (p. 112). Through this lens, critics are able to analyze either the reinforcement of or opposition of hegemony. David Craig expands on this by writing, "According to the Marxist view, it is not just that the media 'reflect' any or every facet of social life, which is obvious, but that the work done by a social group to create the means of its livelihood, and the social relations it enters into through this productive activity, are the main forces that go to shape the media in which people create images of the world as they experience it and of themselves in it" (Bigsby, 1976, p. 130). In other words, even though the media is partially a reflection of society, it is through what a person experiences through the media that he or she develops an idea of self and value in society.

Examination of the media, primarily television and specifically *Sex and the City,* is valuable "because ideas of who has power and who does not have power stem from, take shape in, and are worked out in just such 'little,' everyday experiences. It is these two concerns—materialism, and the way material affects power—that together form the core of Marxist analysis" (Brummett, 1994, p. 113). The "core of Marxist analysis" when studying television can be benefited by also examining media-centered criticism, which lends itself perfectly to studying the effectiveness of television as a breeding ground for perpetuation of hegemony. Three primary components of media-centered criticism—commodification, realism, and intimacy—make it possible for the preferred hegemony to thrive. "A commodity is a good, something that is bought and sold, something with intrinsic value that can be traded economically. There are several reasons why television in the United States today has a logic that includes commodification. The first and most obvious reason is that television broadcasting is a commercial enterprise and is constantly selling commodities to the public" (p. 140). It is this constant selling of goods, no matter what they might be, that promotes the value of material goods and thus perpetuates the hegemony.

Adding to the effectiveness of television as a tool to promote the preferred hegemony are realism and intimacy. "Americans think that pictures cannot lie. So what we see on television, we assume to be real" (p. 141). It is this assumption of reality that helps viewers to buy into the preferred hegemony that they witness on television. What makes *Sex and the City* an ideal text for study is not only the use of commodification and realism, but also the added manipulation of intimacy. Intimacy attempts to offer something more personal to the viewer, something that will create attachment and thus draw an audience member into the show and into the messages being sent. Media-centered criticism makes it possible to see how audiences are drawn in to witness the reality of what is being sold.

Utilizing the Marxist perspective makes it possible to examine the impact of *Sex and the City* on the preferred hegemony. Casting aside all issues of feminism and female empowerment, this analysis will focus on how *Sex and the City* maintains the preferred hegemony in terms of why the primary characters are of value—materialism. This analysis will present the ways in which *Sex and the City* maintains the status quo and promotes the preferred

hegemony that value is equated with material goods.

ANALYSIS

"Consumer cultures are characterized by widespread personal consumption rather than socially conscious and useful investment in the public sphere. The focus is on private expenditure and leisure pursuits.?.?.?. Advertising is held by many critics to be a primary instrument of those who own the means of production in generating consumer lust and consumer cultures and distracting people from social and public matters" (Berger, 2000, p. 142). What makes HBO different from network television broadcasting is the lack of paid commercial programming before, during, and after a broadcast. What makes HBO, specifically *Sex and the City,* a remarkable tool for perpetuating consumer culture is the amount of "generation of consumer lust" within the program. If you log on to the *Sex and the City* page of the HBO website, you can find a photo album of the characters' fashion trends and descriptions of what and, most important, who they are wearing. "Carrie supplements her raw foods meal with an after-dinner slice in an elegant beaded dress by Alberta Ferretti and a vintage satin cape purchased at La Reina. She wears a diamond and emerald 'Wendy' necklace by Sol Rafael. The necklace is 18 carat gold; the diamonds total ten carats" (www.hbo.com/city). This example of commodification without a commercial to interrupt the viewing illustrates how *Sex and the City* creates consumer lust. In addition, "... people who work for fashion companies told me they had successfully placed products, like handbags, on the show, and hoped to do more in the future" (Horyn, 2000,

(Continued)

(Continued)

p. 9.1). It is this product placement that allows the show to advertise without the annoyance of actual commercials.

In Episode 2, Carrie says, "Suddenly, I felt like I was wearing patchouli in a room full of Chanel" (www.hbo.com/city/episode/season1/episode2.shtml). This line within the programming promotes the value of one designer, thus perpetuating a consumer culture. "Perched on Jimmy Choos and wrapped in Gucci, sipping pink cosmopolitans with an assortment of handsome suitors, the women are witty, glamorous, independent and sexually liberated—in short, who wouldn't want to be them?" (Orenstein, 2003, p. A.19). The problem with this statement is that these women are dependent—on the products that they are surrounded with. There is virtually no mention of Sarah Jessica Parker (the actress who portrays Carrie) and *Sex and the City* that doesn't provide a description of something that is possessed or worn. Orenstein continues, "...the heroines of *Sex and the City* are vapid, materialistic and hysterical...their lives are flattened backdrops for their dates, and their dates, like their shoes, are accessories."

According to "All Consuming Passion: Waking Up From the American Dream" found in *Ads, Fads, and Consumer Culture*, the "93 percent of teenage girls who report store-hopping as their favorite activity" (2000, p. 42). This sad fact is not refuted by *Sex and the City*. We rarely see any of the four primary characters of the show at work, and yet viewers often see them shopping and always see them looking fabulous. "The most scandalously unrealistic aspect of the show is that Carrie Bradshaw (Sarah Jessica Parker) manages to stock her closet with thousands of dollars worth of designer clothes each month on a journalist's salary without ever coming home to

voice-mail messages from creditors informing her that her Bergdorf Goodman bill is 206 days past due" (Bellafonte, 2003, p. 9.1).

Viewers buy into all of this commodification for two reasons: They have developed a relationship with the primary characters (intimacy), and they assume that they are witnessing truth (realism). Intimacy is created in the first episode of *Sex and the City*. Carrie talks directly to the camera at times and given peeks into the characters' lives that create a pseudo relationship. "It's like the riddle of the Sphinx...why are there so many great unmarried women, and no great unmarried men" (www.hbo.com/city/episode/season1/episode1.shtml). When Carrie says this line (among many others) directly to the audience, we feel that we are talking with a friend and thus buy into the images that we see. We listen to the women's conversations, and we see them in some of their most vulnerable situations. Viewers, as a direct result of the intimacy created, develop a relationship with the characters that skews their sense of what is real.

Is the reality set forth on *Sex and the City* real? The answer is absolutely not. However, it looks real, and because we feel bonded to the characters, we attach realism to it and "assume it to be real." I must admit, I wanted a pair of Manolo Blahniks desperately after witnessing her obsession with them for years. Audiences witness an empowered woman, one who wears and discusses particular types of shoes repeatedly, and they try to replicate the aura of the character. I wanted Manolo Blahniks because I wanted to be fabulous, like Carrie. However, the predominant hegemony doesn't support being fabulous on your own—you must purchase fabulous. Even though the show clearly shows "...in one episode Carrie discovers that she has only $957 in savings—but $40,000 in designer shoes in her closet" (Orenstein, 2003, p. A.19), audiences don't care. They find it perfectly acceptable that in the next season she "marries herself" and registers only at Manolo Blahnik. What does this teach our society about "normal"?

Conclusions and Implications

Sex and the City perpetuates the dominant hegemony: Those who are empowered are those who have material possessions and continue to buy them. Many may hail the show as an awesome opportunity for an independent female role model. However, what the show is teaching as "normal" to its predominantly female viewers is that empowerment does not come from within, but comes from what you wear.

Sex and the City, through commodification, realism, and intimacy, perpetuates a preferred reading of Marxist hegemony through its continued cultivation of a consumer culture. What is most disturbing is that the women being influenced are not only adults who can balance what they see with what they experience. Surprisingly, viewers are as young as age 14 and, as quoted earlier, credit the show with being their favorite. These younger viewers are far more easily influenced than their older counterparts and may not be able to decipher what is realism as opposed to what is reality.

Older women who watch the show may buy into the consumer culture messages for a different reason. Many single women ages 25–40 may be preoccupied with the idea of independence and sexual freedom and, therefore, subconsciously support the consumer cultural truths they are witnessing. In addition, male viewers may view the women that are depicted in the series as ideal and may try to subject this reality onto real women.

The popularity of *Sex and the City* spans different cultures, age groups, and sexes. Therefore, the powerful messages that it sends have a very broad audience. Furthermore, having retired the series on HBO, executives have sold the show to TBS, which boasts many more viewers as a basic cable channel. This means that not only will the show continue to perpetuate a consumer culture, but also commercials will be added to further the commodification. What HBO viewers are seeing as "normal" will now be seen by even wider and younger audiences. Will anybody be able to escape the influence of *Sex and the City*? Perhaps only David Sedaris and his neighbors who dress in denim and corduroy and don't know they are weird.

References

Bellafante, G. (2003, August 17). Poor little rich girls, throbbing to shop. *The New York Times*, p. 9.1.

Berger, A. (2000). *Ads, fads, and consumer culture*. Lanham, MD: Rowman & Littlefield.

Bigsby, C. W. E. (Ed.). (1976). *Approaches to popular culture*. Bowling Green, OH: Bowling Green University Popular Press.

Brummett, B. (1994). *Rhetoric in popular culture*. New York: St. Martin's Press.

Carter, B. (2003, July 30). Baryshnikov is cast as heartthrob for "Sex and the City" finale. *The New York Times*, p. E1.

Horyn, C. (2000, June 4). How hip? Undressing those trendy "city girls." *The New York Times*, p. 9.1.

Orenstein, C. (2003, September 5). What Carrie could learn from Mary. *The New York Times*, p. A19.

Salamon, J. (2004, June 9). Will "Sex and the City" without the sex have much appeal? *The New York Times*, p. E1.

Schneider, K. S. (2004, March 1). Mom & the city: After six years as the life of the party, Sarah Jessica Parker trades the Manolos and men of Sex and the City for playdates in the park with baby James Wilkie. *People Weekly*, 88.

Summary

A neo-Marxist perspective exposes material conditions and economic practices that shape the dominant ideology about who "ought to be" and "ought not to be" empowered. This privileging of one ideology as the norm is known as hegemony. Popular culture texts can reinforce hegemony through blatant or occluded readings, or they can challenge hegemony through inflected or subverted readings. Examining mediated popular culture texts through a neo-Marxist lens is particularly important because they can reflect and shape our assumptions about materialism and empowerment.

When examining texts from a neo-Marxist perspective, we begin by discovering the subject positions. That is, who are the characters that viewers or receivers are led to identify with as models (us) and to not identify with as anti-models (them). We then interpret the text according to economic metaphors offered and the value attached to them by examining the characters, their possessions, their positions (status), their actions and consequences, and the interactions among them. Finally, we evaluate the possible implications of such messages on various target audiences. Because the dominant American ideology is rooted so firmly in socioeconomic status, materialist possessions, wealth, and consumerism, the underlying messages about empowerment and disempowerment that a neo-Marxist perspective reveals is crucial to transforming and maintaining the democratic values we espouse.

Challenge

Because television programming is so strongly market driven, most of it tends to reproduce hegemony. Select any popular television program today that has broad audience appeal (e.g., *The Big Bang Theory*, *Downton Abbey*, *Modern Family*, *New Girl*, *Game of Thrones*, *Justified,* or *Breaking Bad*). Examine the program using a neo-Marxist perspective, and answer the following questions:

1. Before examining the program, do you think it is likely to reinforce or oppose hegemony regarding materialistic possessions and wealth and why?

2. Identify the primary subject positions, that is, the characters that are portrayed as the models and the anti-models. Who are viewers led to want to be like and not be like and why?

3. What are some examples of economic metaphors offered and the value attached to them? Consider what is being emphasized as positive about us (or the characters we are led to identify with as models) and negative about them (or the characters we are led to see as anti-models)? Likewise, consider what is being deemphasized that may be negative about us and positive about them?

4. What are some potential implications of these kinds of messages on the various target audiences who watch the program? On society as a whole?

References

Adorno, T. (1973). *The jargon of authenticity* (K. Tarnowski & F. Will, Trans.). Evanston, IL: Northwestern University Press.

Adorno, T. (1984). *Aesthetic theory* (G. Adorno & R. Tiedman, Eds., C. Lenhardt, Trans.). London: Routledge and Kegan Paul.

Althusser, L. (1971). Ideology and ideological state apparatuses (notes toward an investigation). In L. Althusser, *Lenin and philosophy and other essays* (B. Brewster, Trans.). New York: Monthly Review Press.

Barthes, R. (1981). Theory of the text. In R. Young (Ed.), *Untying the text: A post-structuralist reader* (pp. 31–47). London: Routledge and Kegan Paul.

Cloud, D. (1994). The materiality of discourse as oxymoron: A challenge to critical rhetoric. *Western Journal of Communication, 58,* 141–163.

Culler, J. (1981). Presupposition and intertextuality. In J. Culler, *The pursuit of signs; Semiotics, literature, deconstruction* (pp. 110–131). Ithaca, NY: Cornell University Press.

Curran, J., Burevitch, M., & Woollacott, J. (1982). The study of the media: Theoretical approaches. In M. Gurevitch, T. Bennett, J. Curran, & J. Woollacott (Eds.), *Culture, society and the media* (pp. 6–25). London: Methuen.

Fiske, J. (1987). *Television culture.* New York: Methuen.

Fiske, J. (1989). *Understanding popular culture.* Winchester, MA: Unwin Hyman.

Fiske, J. (1992). British cultural studies and television. In R. C. Allen (Ed.). *Channels of discourse, reassembled: Television and contemporary criticism* (pp. 284–326). New York: Routledge.

Foucault, M. (1980). *Power/knowledge: Selected interviews and other writings, 1972–1977.* New York: Random House.

Giroux, H. A. (2011). The crisis of public values in the age of the new media. *Critical Studies in Media Communication, 28*(1), 8–29.

Gramsci, A. (1971). *Selections from the prison notebooks* (Q. Hoare & G. Nowell Smith, Trans.). New York: Internaltional.

Habermas, J. (1979). *Communication and the evolution of society.* (T. McCarthy, Trans.). Boston: Beacon.

Habermas, J. (1984). *The theory of communicative action, volume I: Reason and the rationalization of society.* (T. McCarthy, Trans.). Boston: Beacon.

Habermas, J. (1987). *The theory of communicative action, volume II: Lifeworld and system: A critique of functionalist reason* (T. McCarthy, Trans.). Boston: Beacon.

Hall, S. (1973). *Encoding and decoding in the television discourse.* Birmingham, AL: University of Birmingham Press.

Hall, S. (1980). Cultural studies: Two paradigms. *Media, Culture and Society, 2,* 57–72.

Hall, S. (1982). The rediscovery of "ideology": Return of the repressed in media studies. In M. Gurevitch, T. Bennett, J. Curran, & J. Woolacott (Eds.), *Culture, society and the media.* London: Methuen.

Hall, S. (Ed.). (1997a). *Representation: Cultural representations and signifying practices.* Thousand Oaks, CA: Sage.

Hall, S. (1997b). The spectacle of the "other." In S. Hall (Ed.). *Representations: Cultural representation and signifying practices* (pp. 225–279). Thousand Oaks, CA: Sage.

Jasinski, J. (1997). Instrumentalism, contextualism, and interpretation in rhetorical criticism. In A. G. Gross & W. M. Keith (Eds.), *Rhetorical hermeneutics: Invention and interpretation in the age of science* (pp. 195–224). Albany: State University of New York Press.

Jasinski, J. (2001). *Sourcebook on rhetoric: Key concepts in contemporary rhetorical studies.* Thousand Oaks, CA: Sage.

Littlejohn, S., & Foss, K. (2008). *Theories of human communication* (9th ed.). Belmont, CA: Thomson Wadsworth.

Marx, K. (1978). The German ideology. In R. C. Tucker (Ed.), *The Marx-Engels reader.* New York: W. W. Norton.

McKerrow, R. E. (1989). Critical rhetoric: Theory and praxis. *Communication Monographs, 56,* 91–111.

Sellnow, D., & Brown, A. (2004). A rhetorical analysis of oppositional youth music of the new millennium. *North Dakota Journal of Speech and Theatre, 1,* 19–36.

Sellnow D., & Sellnow, T. (2001). The "illusion of life" rhetorical perspective: An integrated approach to the study of music as communication. *Critical Studies in Media Communication, 18,* 395–415.

Student Study Site

Visit the Student Study Site at www.sagepub.com/sellnow2e to read interesting SAGE journal articles, view mobile-friendly key term flashcards, take chapter-specific online web quizzes to test your knowledge, and more!

Chapter 7

Feminist Perspectives

Feminist perspectives focus on the taken-for-granted as "normal" roles and rules for men and women in society. Like the neo-Marxist perspective, feminist perspectives are grounded in critical rhetoric, which suggests that a dominant ideology controls what people take for granted as commonsense beliefs, values, and behaviors. In this case, however, the focus is on oppression based on sex, gender, and sexual orientation. More specifically, we seek answers to questions about how the dominant ideology privileges men and a masculine perspective over women and a feminine perspective. We also seek answers to questions about how the dominant ideology privileges heterosexuality. And we seek answers to questions about how the dominant ideology empowers stereotypical gender styles and oppresses, for example, males who do not look or act masculine "enough" and females who do not look or act feminine "enough."

Before continuing, let's clarify the meaning of some key terms. Just as the Marxist label is sometimes misinterpreted, so are the meanings of the terms *feminist* and *feminist perspectives* sometimes misunderstood. Feminist perspectives do not claim that men oppress women. Rather, the *hegemony* (dominant ideology)—which is reinforced and reproduced by both women and men—simultaneously empowers men and oppresses women as well as both men and women who do not behave in stereotypically gender appropriate ways. It follows, then, that a feminist is anyone (male or female) whose beliefs and actions challenge hegemony by respecting and valuing women as well as respecting and valuing both men and women who embrace and enact multiple gender styles and sexualities.

APPLYING WHAT YOU'VE LEARNED . . .

Based on your observations and what you've learned here, who from the following list would you consider to be and not to be a feminist and why?

- Jon Stewart (*The Daily Show*)
- Phil McGraw (*Dr. Phil*)
- Ellen DeGeneres (*Ellen*)
- Joan Rivers (*The View*)
- Chris Brown (rapper)
- Michele Bachmann (Senator)
- Charlie Harper (*Two and a Half Men*)
- Katniss (*The Hunger Games*)
- Tyrion Lanister (*Game of Thrones*)
- Jessica "Jess" Day (*New Girl*)

HEGEMONY

Feminist critics, like neo-Marxist critics, use *hegemony* to describe the ideology that simultaneously empowers the elite and disempowers all others. Whereas neo-Marxist critics focus on materialism, however, feminist perspectives focus on the ways in which hegemony empowers men, a masculine perspective, gender stereotypes, and heterosexuality. Three important concepts to unpack with regard to feminist perspectives are *patriarchy, masculine hegemony,* and *heteronormativity*.

Scholars originally articulated the concept of patriarchy to illustrate power inequities among women and men in industrialized societies. Essentially, patriarchy describes the structuring of society around family units where a male is the authority figure and is responsible for the welfare of his family members and the community. Popular culture critics who examine the way in which TV sitcoms perpetuate structures of conventional families comprised of a male authority figure and submissive female figures, for instance, are examining them within the framework of patriarchy.

Masculine hegemony is a term that originated in the field of men's studies and masculinity theory. Masculine hegemony is more specific than hegemony in that it describes gender and power inequities in ways that account for multiple masculinities and how hegemonic structures oppress all forms other than heterosexual masculinity (Connell, 1987). In contrast to sex, which is defined as the biological traits of women and men, gender is defined as the socioculturally constructed traits of masculinity and femininity. French feminist philosopher Simone de Beauvoir (1949) captured the essence of gender when she argued that a woman is not born a woman, but becomes one. It follows, then, that a man is not born a man with regard to gender either but also becomes one. Popular culture critics who examine the ways in which mediated texts negatively stereotype men with feminine traits and women with masculine traits, for example, are operating within the framework of masculine hegemony as it oppresses people and groups based on gender.

Literary critic, social theorist, queer theorist, and professor of English Literature at Yale University Michael Warner (1993) is credited with popularizing the notion of heteronormativity. In essence, heteronormativity refers to the privileging of heterosexuality and an alignment among biological sex, sexuality, gender identity, and gender roles (Lovaas & Jenkins, 2007). Heteronormativity promotes a "sex hierarchy" ideology suggesting there is such a thing as "good sex" and "bad sex" and, in doing so, stigmatizes gay people as morally deviant and "bad" (Rubin, 1993). Othering in this way oppresses lesbian, gay, bisexual, and transgender people and groups. Popular culture critics who examine mediated texts to expose how they (1) promote heteronormativity, (2) negatively stereotype gays and lesbians, or (3) frame multiple sexualities as deviant, for example, based on heteronormativity.

SITES OF STRUGGLE

As a form of critical rhetoric, feminist perspectives examine popular culture texts as sites of struggle much like neo-Marxist critiques do. Feminist perspectives, however, expose preferred or oppositional readings to patriarchy, masculine hegemony, and heteronormativity. Recall that a preferred reading reinforces taken-for-granted status quo beliefs and behaviors as normal, desirable, and common sense. And an oppositional reading challenges these taken-for-granted beliefs and behaviors in some way. Preferred readings can be blatant (overt) or occluded (couched in the subtext). For instance, a TV program that shows a mother happily caring for her children in the home and a father working productively outside the home might offer a blatant preferred reading. A program that shows a mother working outside the home but miserable because she actually longs to stay home and care for her children, or a father unhappily caring for his children at home because he lost his "real job" and performing poorly because these skills "don't come naturally to him" might be examples of occluded preferred readings.

Oppositional readings can be *inflected* (a bending of hegemony to suit one's own needs) or *subverted* (outright rejection of hegemony replaced with an alternative worldview). A TV program that shows white middle-class women successfully negotiating their roles as both working professionals and mothers, but shows no women of color in these roles, might be an example of an inflected oppositional reading. On the contrary, a TV program that shows women from a variety of races, ethnicities, abilities, sexual orientations, or ages happily and successfully negotiating these roles might be an example of a subverted oppositional reading.

APPLYING WHAT YOU'VE LEARNED . . .

Consider the popular TV sitcom *Modern Family*. How does the program depict each character in terms of patriarchy? Masculine hegemony? Heteronormativity? Would you consider the program's messages to be preferred or oppositional in each regard? Why?

WAVES OF FEMINISM

The variety of feminist perspectives that exist today can best be understood as they reflect one of three *waves* (or time periods) of the feminist movement in the United States. Each time period reflects an identifiable set of goals feminists were (and are) attempting to achieve. Understanding the goal of each wave helps situate why each of the various feminist perspectives emerged.

First-Wave Feminism

The primary goal of first-wave feminism (which was lead by suffragettes such as Susan B. Anthony, Margaret Sanger, Anna Howard Shaw, and Elizabeth Cady Stanton) was to secure for women the right to vote. Many argue that first-wave feminism ended with the passage of the 19th amendment in 1920.

Second-Wave Feminism

Second-wave feminism focuses on the goals of equal rights and opportunities for women and men. Betty Friedan (1963) is often credited with defining second-wave feminism in her book *The Feminine Mystique.* Some scholars argue that second-wave feminism ended in the 1980s. They note that Title IX now promotes equal opportunities in high school and collegiate sports; that both women and men now can be firefighters, police officers, soldiers, doctors, and lawyers; and that both women and men now can be flight attendants, nurses, and stay-at-home parents. Others contend, however, that many of the goals of second-wave feminism have yet to be fully realized and, thus, continue to pursue them today. For example, on average, women today still earn 77 cents to every dollar earned by their male counterparts (Goodnight & Owens, 2012). And, women in business continue to experience the glass ceiling—a situation where they are not promoted when they are qualified just because they are women. Hence, it may be more accurate to acknowledge that second-wave feminism still exists but now exists along with third-wave feminism, which began roughly in the 1980s.

Third-Wave Feminism

Third-wave feminism emerged primarily out of the experiences of Americans born after 1960 who grew up enjoying many of the advantages second-wave feminists fought to achieve. Naomi Wolfe's (1991, 2002) *The Beauty Myth: How Images of Beauty Are Used Against Women* and Susan Faludi's (1991, 2006) *Backlash: The Undeclared War Against Women* are attributed with setting the stage for third-wave feminism.

Third-wave feminism focuses not only on women's issues but also on a variety of *standpoints.* Standpoints are essentially our understanding of the world as shaped by where we are situated within it (our life experiences) based on class, gender, race, sexual identity, and so on. Moreover, the perspectives of the elite (empowered group) are more limited than those of any oppressed group because the elite often fail to see inequality and, thus, continue to perpetuate it. Political correctness, for example, came about as a result of third-wave feminism.

The perspective of the elite could not see (and some still do not) that words like *fireman* (rather than firefighter) and *mailman* (rather than mail carrier) excluded women.

Third-wave feminism also realizes a deeper level of oppression than that of equal rights and opportunities. Third-wave feminism focuses on issues of oppression surrounding, for example, bullying and sexual harassment in schools and in the workplace, date rape, psychiatric abuse, breaking the silence, and "grrrl" power. Finally, third-wave feminism challenges common definitions of gender and sexuality that are often limited to predominantly white, middle-class, able-bodied, heterosexual people (Heywood & Drake, 1997). In other words, third-wave feminists seek to eliminate oppression not just for white, middle-class women but for all oppressed people.

Thus, another development of feminist thought that emerged in the 1980s acknowledges male feminists and the gender and power relations not only between women and men and masculinity and femininity but also among men and multiple masculinities. As mentioned earlier, Australian scholar R.W. Connell (1987) coined the term *masculine hegemony* in his groundbreaking book *Gender and Power* as a result of this development. In the United States, Alice Jardine and Paul Smith (1987) also contributed to these developing thoughts about male feminists in their anthology, *Men in Feminism*. In it, they propose the term femmenism as a perspective that situates the study of masculinity within the framework of gender and power.

Finally, queer theory emerged during the 1990s and complements issues of third-wave feminism by examining sexual identities and activities that hegemony labels as *normal* and *deviant*. In terms of critical rhetoric, queer theory informs feminist critiques by exposing the ways in which texts privilege heteronormativity. The classic film *Boys Don't Cry,* for example, operates to expose oppressive forces and consequences of hegemony regarding transgendered people and relationships. More recently, in 2012, Jenna Talackova "made international news headlines as the first [known] transgender competitor in the Miss Universe Pageant" (McQuigge, 2012).

FEMINIST PERSPECTIVES

With an understanding of the goals of each wave of feminism, let's now turn to a description of several feminist perspectives for examining popular culture texts. We'll look specifically at a *liberal, radical, Marxist,* and *cultural feminist perspectives.*

A Liberal Feminist Perspective

A liberal feminist perspective focuses primarily on providing opportunities for the inclusion of women in traditionally male-dominated areas. As such, it is situated within the goals of second-wave feminism. When I was growing up in the 1960s and 1970s, for example, Title IX did not exist. Hence, girls who wanted to do sports at my school were limited to cheerleading, synchronized swimming, and gymnastics. Until Title IX was passed, many high school sports programs in smaller schools like mine did not offer basketball, volleyball, track, competitive swimming, diving, and hockey for girls. This change is an example of what a liberal feminist perspective focuses on.

● ● ● **QUESTIONING YOUR ETHICS . . .** ● ● ● ● ● ● ● ● ● ● ● ● ● ● ● ●

Some high school and college sports programs have eliminated some teams for boys and men in recent years. They argue further that they had to because Title IX forced them to offer equal opportunities to female athletes. Some argue that this practice is sexist against males. Others say it is the only way to maintain equity. Do you think this practice is ethical? Fair? Why or why not?

When TV programs and movies show women in traditionally male-dominated fields as normal, successful, and happy, a liberal feminist perspective would suggest they are operating as a site of struggle by sending a message that is oppositional to or challenges the status quo. When shows depict women in these roles but also portray them as odd, unsuccessful, or unhappy, however, a liberal feminist perspective would argue they are actually operating as an occluded, preferred reading because the ultimate message is that women are not suited for these positions.

In the 1980s television program *Murphy Brown,* for example, Murphy Brown was portrayed as a woman "at the top of her profession but . . . paying the price for it" (Candice Bergen, 1989, p. 62). To clarify, this powerful feminist professional was often portrayed as unhappy and unfulfilled in her private life. When she became involved in a romantic relationship and when she gave birth to her baby, however, she was portrayed as blissfully happy (Dow, 1996). So, although the program seemed to be sending a pro-feminist message, it really served to reinforce patriarchy by presenting Murphy as unhappy in her professional role because, as a woman, she could only be truly fulfilled when she was in a romantic relationship and as a mother in her private life. More recently, *New Girls* has been criticized when it focused on Jess's desire to get pregnant because her "biological clock was ticking and 90% of a woman's eggs are gone by the time she is 30 years old" (Penn, 2012).

APPLYING WHAT YOU'VE LEARNED . . .

What do each of these popular TV programs argue from a liberal feminist perspective about "appropriate" roles for women and men in society?

- Game of Thrones
- Newsroom
- Modern Family
- Parks and Recreation
- Girls

A Radical Feminist Perspective

A radical feminist perspective assumes that inequities and oppression stem from how the system creates men and women differently (subject and object gender identities) and the value (or lack of value) associated with them. This perspective arose within second-wave feminism but is also a focus of third-wave feminists. From early childhood, girls are taught to be caring, supportive, and cooperative, and boys are taught to be independent, assertive, and competitive. Girls are told, for example, to look like a lady and are reprimanded when they don't act ladylike. Similarly, boys are told they don't cry and to take it like a man. Women who are assertive, independent, or competitive are often labeled negatively as a *bitch*, a *lesbian*, or even a *femme-Nazi*. Men who are caring and supportive are often labeled negatively as a *wimp* or *prissy*. Both boys and girls learn that boys are supposed to be subjects in their worlds and girls are supposed to be objects who should look pretty and act only as supporters of male agents and male agendas.

Feminist film theorist Laura Mulvey (1975) is credited with coining the term male gaze to describe this phenomenon wherein both males and females view women as objects. Research by queer theorists illustrates how gay men are also objectified and othered in society and how this perception is often reinforced and sometimes challenged in popular culture texts.

The goal in a radical feminist critique of popular culture texts is to reveal how objectifying hegemonic beliefs and behaviors based on sex, gender, or sexual orientation are reinforced or challenged in some way. They might point out, for example, how texts reinforce hegemony because men are depicted as subjects and women as objects. Numerous feminist critiques illustrate how media ranging from TV to movies to advertisements to

■ **FIGURE 7.1** Editorial Cartoon

Source: Used with permission.

video games to music videos objectify women (e.g., Berberick, 2010; Gervais, Vescio, Maass, & Suitner, 2012; Jhally, n.d.; Swami et al., 2010). Conversely, critics might illustrate how texts challenge hegemony. The 2012 blockbuster film based on a book of the same name *The Hunger Games,* for instance, posits an oppositional radical feminist reading through its main character, Katniss, who is not only portrayed as a subject but also, ultimately, the hero.

QUESTIONING YOUR ETHICS . . .

What messages might video games such as Bioshock (where gamers are rewarded for killing little girls) and Grand Theft Auto (where gamers in some versions can only "be" male protagonists and are rewarded for having sex with and then killing women) be sending from a radical feminist perspective? Do you think scoring points for these kinds of actions is ethical? Why or why not?

Radical feminist rhetoricians also might point out how texts reinforce hegemony because women are portrayed as subjects but are ultimately punished in some way for breaking the rules of hegemony by stepping outside the object role. The classic film *Thelma and Louise* (1991) is a good example. Thelma and Louise were the subjects of their world when they chose to leave their husbands and throughout their road trip. They were ultimately punished, however, and actually punished themselves by driving off a cliff. As such, the message from a radical feminist perspective is preferred and occluded. More recently, the popular TV sitcom *Cougar Town* appears at the surface to oppose hegemony by depicting 40-something divorcee, Jules Cobb (played by Courtney Cox), as a subject in charge of her life choices. Ultimately, however, Cobb is objectified as a "hot" divorcee who is punished as unhappy in her life as a "cougar" compared to her happily married best friend, Ellie Torres, a former corporate attorney turned stay-at-home mom.

Radical feminist critics might also focus on how gay, lesbian, bisexual, and transgendered people are portrayed in popular culture. They might highlight how texts reinforce hegemony, for example, by portraying gay men as objectified others or as subjects who are punished or mocked for behaviors that challenge the status quo for men. Conversely, they might highlight how a text challenges hegemony by portraying gay men as subjects and not punished for it. Marc Ambinder (2012) offers such a critique in his column, "The Golden Age of Gay TV?" In it, he compares depictions of gay characters on *Modern Family, The New Normal, Partners, Happy Endings, One Girl, Five Guys, Teen Wolf, Grey's Anatomy, Here Comes Honey Boo Boo!,* and *Glee.*

APPLYING WHAT YOU'VE LEARNED . . .

Identify a movie that seems, at the surface, to be sending a pro-radical feminist message. How does the movie end? Which characters are successful? Happy? Punished in some way? Do you believe the message ultimately conveyed is opposing the dominant ideology or actually reinforcing it in an occluded way? Why?

Let's consider the advertisement for a Vassarette bra in Figure 7.2 from a radical feminist perspective. At first glance, viewers are likely to dismiss it as just another example of using sex to sell a product. Without doubt, this is true. A radical feminist perspective would look deeper for messages it sends about patriarchy, masculine hegemony, or heteronormativity in terms of subject and object relationships for women and men in society.

■ **FIGURE 7.2** Vassarette Ad

First, consider how the model is dressed. She is presented as a beautiful object for viewers to enjoy. At the center of the page are her shapely breasts, her full red lips, and her curvaceous midsection. Viewers only notice the iron after gazing at this beautiful sex object. If one does not perceive her as a sex object at first, the multiple-choice questions eventually lead us to do so. She is a beautiful object who is ready to please her husband sexually even while she is supposedly getting ready for work and doing woman's work in terms of ironing. Notice also that she is ironing with her left hand so viewers can see the ring on her third finger.

These underlying messages offer a preferred reading, reinforcing patriarchy. Beautiful women (particularly married women) should look like this and act like this even while getting dressed for work. The fact that this advertisement comes from a women's magazine also demonstrates that women participate in perpetuating hegemony in terms of women as sex objects who act to please others, particularly men.

Important to note at this juncture is that rhetoricians who focus on a radical feminist perspective do not necessarily claim there is no place for advertisements like this one but, rather, that this is too often the only way women are portrayed in advertisements. Let's consider, for example, an advertisement for the Vassarette bra that showed a fully clothed woman engaged in some professional activity like arguing a case in court or managing a company. Or perhaps she is portrayed enjoying some recreational activity like sailing or skateboarding or trap shooting. Let's say the advertisement still noted that the bra she was wearing was comfortable, flexible, and priced under $10, and simply superimposed the bra somewhere on the page. Then it could be argued that the advertisement was sending an oppositional message from a radical feminist perspective. If an advertisement like this second one seems unusual, then you understand what radical feminists are saying about depicting women as objects.

APPLYING WHAT YOU'VE LEARNED . . .

Browse through a popular women's magazine, and count how many advertisements show women as sex objects. Consider what this is telling readers (women) about how they should look and act. Advertisements like these not only serve to reinforce patriarchy but also encourage women to participate in their own oppression if they believe these images represent how women ought to look and act to be normal and desirable.

A Marxist Feminist Perspective

A Marxist feminist perspective (which arose from within second-wave feminism) seeks to ensure economic equality for women, that is, equal pay for equal work. Critical rhetoricians examine texts as they reinforce or challenge hegemonic assumptions about these issues. Although the Equal Pay Act—prohibiting sex discrimination regarding the payment of wages by employers—was passed in 1963, the gender wage gap persists. In fact, census data collected by the U.S. Census Bureau in 2011 reveals that the gap has actually been widening since 1995, and women today earn, on average, 77 cents for every dollar men earn (Goodnight & Owens, 2012). Moreover, 2003 marks the first year of a steady decline in women's real earnings since 1995 (Longely, 2004). Scholars who study popular culture texts from a Marxist feminist perspective strive to reveal how texts perpetuate myths about this gap in order to help eliminate it.

Consider professional sports, for example. The discussion rationalizing the fact that professional male athletes are paid so much more than female athletes often comes up on sports radio and TV talk shows and in sports journalism. Commentators sometimes contend that male sports (other than figure skating) draw more spectators. The discussion rarely, if ever, points to the fact that spectatorship of male sports has been encouraged to the point of being institutionalized in ways that female sports has not. Even in a pro-feminist sport such as tennis, many tournaments pay male winners more than female winners. These are the types of economic inequities a Marxist feminist critic would reveal.

Sometimes episodes of entertainment TV perpetuate myths that are often used to justify the wage gap, such as the number of years women spend working part time, or the time women take off to have and raise children, or the idea that women have less education or fewer years of work experience than men. Consider, for instance, the classic 1990s TV program *Home Improvement*. Wife and mother of three boys, Jill Taylor, goes back to college as a nontraditional student once her boys are no longer little children. Although the program portrays her as empowered and independent in doing so (a seemingly pro-feminist message), she also perpetuates one myth as to why women earn less than men who work in similar professions. That is, women take time off to raise children before earning their degrees or focusing on their careers.

These kinds of myths continue to appear in TV sitcoms today. For example, the premise of the TV series *2 Broke Girls* is based on economic hardship issues. Caroline, one of the program's main characters, is a former high-society rich girl who never had to work or go to college. When her father goes to jail for his involvement in a Ponzi scheme, however, she is forced to get a job. Her lack of educational and work experience forces her to take the only job she can get, which is a low-paying job as a waitress.

A Marxist feminist perspective would expose these kinds of myths about females being less educated and having less work experience than males. For example, census statistics report that, although some women choose to attend college and begin careers after several years of childrearing, doing so has not been the norm for decades. In fact, the number of females attending college has outnumbered males since the 1970s, and the female-to-male ratio has been steadily increasing ever since. Today, about 60 percent of college students are female, and 40 percent are male (Borzelleca, 2012). Not only that, according to the U.S. Bureau of Labor Statistics (2012), nearly 61 percent of women with children under age 3 and 56 percent of women with children under age 1 worked full time in 2011, and most working mothers returned to work within a year of having a child.

A Marxist feminist critique might also expose economics-related hegemonic claims suggesting the wage gap itself is a myth. For example, consider the news report, "The $200,000-a-Year-Nanny," which tells the stories of a few nannies who earn more than $200,000 per year. Such stories told out of context may perpetuate misconceptions not only about what women earn generally but also what nannys typically earn, which ranges,

> **APPLYING WHAT YOU'VE LEARNED . . .**
>
> Identify a television program where a woman work(s) outside the home. Identify her marital status, whether or not she has children, whether she works full time or part time and in what profession. Did she ever take time off to have children? Did she enter her career later in life? Is she portrayed as happy? Based on your answers, what does this program teach viewers from a Marxist feminist perspective?

on average, from $25,000 to $30,000 annually (Davidson, 2012). A Marxist feminist critique might suggest such stories perpetuate a myth that any nanny could earn $200,000 if she or he was really good at the job.

A Cultural Feminist Perspective

A cultural feminist perspective seeks to promote as valuable the socialized skills, activities, behaviors, and viewpoints that have traditionally been defined as feminine and, thus, trivialized. This perspective emerged during second-wave feminism but is also aligned with third-wave feminism. Examples range from activities such as cooking, cleaning, sewing, and child rearing as unimportant "women's work" to being cooperative, nurturing, and emotional as "weak." Betty Friedan (1963) argued that women should be afforded equal opportunity to work outside the home, in part, because the work that women were doing inside the home was not only not compensated for economically but also was trivialized as unimportant and not valuable. Most sitcoms of the 1950s and 1960s, such as *Father Knows Best, Leave It to Beaver, I Love Lucy,* and *The Dick Van Dyke Show* perpetuated this very perception. These programs portrayed women in the home as normal and common sense. There is nothing inherently wrong in doing so. However, a cultural feminist analysis of *I Love Lucy Show* (the most watched show in the United States four of its six seasons) would point out that Lucy (1) often begged for money from her husband Ricky because she didn't have a job, (2) was given an allowance like a parent gives to a child, and (3) was often chastised by Ricky for spending his hard-earned money frivolously.

Cultural feminists argue that stereotypically feminine skills, activities, behaviors, and characteristics (e.g., cooking, cleaning, child rearing, nurturing) are valuable and should be embraced by both women and men. Messages in songs like Meredith Brooks' "Bitch" offer an oppositional message from a cultural feminist perspective. Brooks sings: "I do not feel ashamed" about showing a variety of emotions and, in fact, "you wouldn't want it any other way" so "take me as I am," and "this might mean you'll have to be a stronger man," and "don't try to change me" (Brooks, 1997). Similarly, Martina McBride's (2003) "This One's for the Girls" celebrates women's experiences from age "one to ninety-nine" and Jamie O'Neal's (2005) "Somebody's Hero" argues that these stereotypically feminine skills, activities, and behaviors are far from trivial. They are, in fact, heroic.

Cultural feminists might also examine movies like *Kindergarten Cop* (with Arnold Schwarzenegger as an elementary schoolteacher), *Daddy Day Care* (with Eddie Murphy as a day-care provider), and *What to Expect When You're Expecting* (with dads caring for their babies) that appear to argue that it is appropriate for men to engage in these stereotypically feminine activities too. Similarly, TV programs such as *Modern Family, Parenthood,* and *The Stay at Home Dad* feature males as cooking, cleaning, and child rearing and might be examined as they reinforce or challenge hegemony from a cultural feminist perspective. Thus, the cultural feminist perspective argues that the trivialized activities and characteristics gender socialized as feminine are, in many cases, activities and characteristics all human beings should value, embrace, and enact.

APPLYING WHAT YOU'VE LEARNED . . .

Consider a television program or popular movie where a man is engaged in a stereotypically feminine activity, skill, or behavior or embodying a stereotypically feminine characteristic. Are viewers led to identify with him as a role model for men or as something else, such as a wimp, clown, fool, or chump. As such, does the message conveyed reinforce or oppose masculine hegemony from a cultural feminist perspective?

In summary, feminist perspectives focus on discovering what and how popular culture texts communicate about appropriate and inappropriate roles and rules for women and men as they are linked to inequities and oppression. Subsequently, the critic's goal is to challenge these taken-for-granted beliefs and behaviors as a means by which to rise above them in our daily lives and encounters with others.

CONDUCTING A FEMINIST ANALYSIS

Feminist perspectives are useful because they call attention to the ways in which arguments that reinforce or challenge patriarchy, masculine hegemony, and heteronormativity are embedded in popular culture texts. The following paragraphs explain how to conduct a feminist criticism of mediated popular culture texts by first selecting an appropriate artifact to analyze as a text and then examining it using the tools of a feminist perspective.

Step 1: Selecting an Appropriate Text

In addition to considering the rhetorical situation, you'll typically select a text for one of two additional reasons. You might select a text because it seems to reinforce taken-for-granted hegemonic beliefs or behaviors for women and men in society. Here your goal is to make clear that such beliefs or behaviors are not necessarily normal, appropriate, or desirable. That is, your analysis will expose the ways in which the text perpetuates patriarchy, masculine hegemony, or heteronormativity. On the other hand, you might select the popular culture text because it seems to be functioning as a site of struggle by challenging taken-for-granted hegemonic beliefs or behaviors for men and women in society.

Step 2: Examining the Text (Describe and Interpret)

As with any popular culture analysis, you examine the artifact though description, interpretation, and evaluation. When conducting a feminist analysis, however, you focus only on the roles and rules being proposed as normal or abnormal, appropriate or inappropriate, and desirable or undesirable for women and men, and their potential implications in terms of how hegemony is reinforced or challenged. You do so by drawing from one or more of the feminist perspectives discussed in this chapter.

Begin by describing the characters and interpreting subject positions as models and anti-models. For example, you might see that women are typically portrayed as caregivers and men as career professionals. You might see that women are portrayed as objects of male interest, such as sexual objects or sex kittens. Perhaps women or men are absent altogether. Perhaps some women are trivialized or missing altogether.

As you describe the characters, consider which ones are presented as models that receivers might be encouraged want to be like and anti-models that viewers might be encouraged to not want to be like. Which male characters might male viewers be encouraged to identify, with and which are not? Why? Which female characters might female viewers be encouraged to identify, and which are not? Why? Are certain characters portrayed as more and less desirable than others? If so, what are their characteristics and behaviors? Characters are portrayed explicitly in TV programs and movies. In some advertisements and in music, however, the critic must conceptualize implicitly who the model and anti-model are.

Once you have identified the subject positions as model and anti-model characters, interpret the text according to what messages it perpetuates about patriarchy, masculine hegemony, or heteronormativity. Who is empowered and disempowered as a result? In other words, determine (1) each character and the roles and rules they enact, (2) the actions of and interactions between and among characters, and (3) whether the model and anti-model subject positions tend to support or challenge patriarchy, masculine hegemony, or heteronormativity.

Step 3: Evaluating Potential Implications of the Text

Finally, evaluate the text by determining what potential implications its messages about women and men in society might have on various audiences. If you discover that men are the subjects and women the objects, you might point out how that ideology is detrimental not only to women but to all of society. If you find that men are always portrayed in traditionally male roles and women in traditionally female roles, you can discuss those implications for individuals and society. Likewise, if you find that feminine characteristics are trivialized and masculine characteristics privileged, but only when enacted by heteronormative male characters, you can point out the potential consequences of accepting this as normal or desirable in society. If, on the other hand, you discover that the text challenges the taken-for-granted beliefs or behaviors for women and men in society, then you can discuss how the text actually serves to reveal an alternative way of knowing and being that, if embraced, can make the world a better place for all.

SAMPLE ANALYSIS

To help clarify how this works, let's consider the classic comic strip *Dennis the Menace*. From a feminist perspective, the series conveys a blatant preferred reading, reinforcing masculine hegemony. In the follow paragraphs, we'll examine it from feminist perspective by describing the main characters, subject positions, what is valued and trivialized, and the potential implications its messages might have on society.

Consider the primary characters in the series and the corresponding subject positions. What characteristics are being portrayed as normal or abnormal and desirable or undesirable for males and females and what degree of value or lack thereof is attributed to what they do and the characteristics they exhibit?

The comic strip portrays four primary female characters (Mrs. Mitchell, Mrs. Wilson, Margaret, and Gina) and four primary male characters (Mr. Mitchell, Mr. Wilson, Dennis, and Joey). Dennis's mom, Mrs. Mitchell, is portrayed as a happily married stay-at-home mom and Dennis's primary caregiver (see Figure 7.3). All other caregivers are also female including Mrs. Wilson, who seems to have a never-ending supply of cookies and milk for Dennis, as well as the numerous babysitters who give Mrs. Mitchell a welcome break from her role as Dennis's mom. Readers see both Mrs. Mitchell and Mrs. Wilson as desirable women in that they enact "appropriate" feminine characteristics, such as being nurturing caregivers who support their husbands and love Dennis.

Two female children also appear in the comic strip from time to time. One is Margaret, an independent, assertive, intelligent, and also plain-looking girl who is supposed to represent a young feminist. She is ultimately punished for being a subject in her world. That is, Dennis and Joey don't like her because she is, in their opinion, a know-it-all. Readers are not led to identify with Margaret. The other female friend is Gina. Gina is portrayed as pretty and ladylike and, thus, likeable. Gina, the "ideal female" who perpetuates the hegemonic ideal of a perfect girl is also the childhood crush of Dennis and Joey. Just as Margaret is not someone viewers are lead to identify with, Gina is that very person, at least when it comes to girls.

As for male characters, Dennis's dad, Mr. Mitchell, is rarely portrayed in a nurturing caregiver role. Although readers don't know what he does for a living, the fact that he wears

■ **FIGURE 7.3**   Dennis the Menace Cartoon

"I GUESS I WASN'T INVITED TO YOUR WEDDING, 'CAUSE I DON'T REMEMBER IT."

Source: Dennis the Menace © North America Syndicate.

a suit and carries a briefcase leads us to believe he works as a professional outside the home. When he is portrayed at home, he is usually reading the newspaper, eating dinner, mowing or watering the lawn, or fixing things like Dennis's bike. As such, his character further perpetuates a blatant preferred reading in terms of "normal" roles and rules for men in society. Mr. Wilson is portrayed as a grumpy old man who orders Mrs. Wilson around and doesn't like kids, particularly Dennis. With regard to subject positions, readers are not led to identify with him. However, he does still perpetuate the notion that normal men embody masculine characteristics.

As for Dennis and his best friend, Joey, they are both portrayed as "typical" boys who get into mischief at every turn but who are excused for doing so because they didn't know any better. After all, the strip suggests, boys will be boys. Readers find the comic strip funny because it reflects what the dominant ideology suggests to be normal in the real world. As such, it perpetuates patriarchy and masculine hegemony.

Now consider the strip in Figure 7.4. At first, it catches our attention because it seems to value women when Dennis salutes "our founding mothers." Upon closer analysis, however, Mr. Wilson's retort is what makes the strip believable, as it supports the dominant ideology, and is also why the strip still reinforces masculine hegemony. Mr. Wilson describes Dennis as a "born politician" because he can already lie well enough to get what he wants. The assumption, then, is that our mothers (whether Susan B. Anthony or Mrs. Wilson) aren't necessarily "another bunch of amazin' people" as Dennis describes them. Rather, Dennis knows just what to say to keep getting cookies from and being coddled by Mrs. Wilson. Unfortunately, this episode perpetuates masculine hegemony in an occluded way.

■ **FIGURE 7.4** Dennis the Menace Cartoon

Source: **Dennis the Menace** © North America Syndicate.

Ultimately, the potential implications include devaluing women and what women have to offer both by female readers and male readers who accept the argument of the comic strip as valid in the real world. Comic strips can be powerful persuasive forces to maintain the status quo because much of their humor is ascribed to making light of the way things are. Unfortunately, claiming that these taken-for-granted beliefs and behaviors are normal serves to simultaneously reinforce them as the way things ought to be. Analyses of them, however, can prove valuable by revealing the underlying assumptions presented in them for what they are.

APPLYING WHAT YOU'VE LEARNED . . .

Identify a popular TV program (an episode or the entire series). Analyze it according to one or more of the feminist perspectives discussed in this chapter. Does it reinforce or oppose hegemony? In what ways do you think the messages it sends about roles and rules for women and men contribute to its success?

SAMPLE PUBLISHED ESSAYS

(1) Read the article titled, "Hegemony, Feminist Criticism and *The Mary Tyler Moore Show*" written by Bonnie Dow (1990) and published in volume 9 of *Critical Studies in Mass Communication*. *The Mary Tyler Moore Show* is interesting because it was touted as a 1970s program embracing Mary Richards (played by Mary Tyler Moore) as an independent, self-sufficient woman—a feminist if you will. Dow's analysis reveals, however, how Mary Richards and her colleagues in the newsroom actually enacted traditional masculine and feminine behaviors that undermined any feminist goals the writers may have intended. The essay is an excellent example of conducting a feminist criticism to reveal how the underlying messages of a seemingly pro-feminist program continue to reinforce masculine hegemony.

(2) Read the article titled, "Gay Characters in Conventional Spaces: *Will and Grace* and the Situation Comedy Genre," coauthored by Kathleen Battles and Wendy Hilton-Morrow and published in *Critical Studies in Media Communication* (2002). Ultimately, the authors argue that, although the program appeared to challenge hegemony in terms of its representations of gay men, it essentially reinforced hegemony by "equating gayness with a lack of masculinity" and by infantilizing the "most potentially subversive characters," among other things. Consider the following questions as you read: Which characters were viewers encouraged to want to be like" (models) and not be like (anti-models)? What are their characteristics? What is their status? How do they interact with others? Ultimately, do you think the messages about heteronormativity that producers envisioned actually reached viewers? Why or why not?

SAMPLE STUDENT ESSAY

Read the student paper written by Elizabeth Petrun for a class project. In it, she examines how Katniss is portrayed in *The Hunger Games* as the model subject position viewers are encouraged to be like in terms of her heroic leadership role and her caregiving actions and attitude. In these ways, *The Hunger Games* posits an oppositional reading that challenges hegemony and serves as an exemplar alternative worldview. As you read, consider what you've read about a liberal, radical, Marxist, and cultural feminist perspective. Do you agree with Elizabeth's conclusions and implications? Why or why not?

The Hunger Games: A Feminist Perspective

Elizabeth L. Petrun

Television and film are powerful vehicles that often reify hegemonic constructions of women as domestic, soft-spoken, and dependent on men for survival and fulfillment. Tuning in to MTV, Bravo, or Lifetime television channels quickly illustrate this point (see: *Sixteen and Pregnant*, *Teen Mom*, *Keeping Up With the Kardashians*, any of the six *Real Housewives* shows, *Dance Moms*, *Army Wives*, etc.). Even movies across genres like 2012's *The Vow* (romantic drama), *This Is Forty* (comedy), and *The Bourne Legacy* (action) exemplify this point. Many of these texts perpetuate stereotypes of women acting petty, cat fighting, getting worked up about trivial matters, and most notably as being unable to care for themselves. What's more, the arguments proposed in these programs and films reinforce the notion that women must rely on men (e.g., fathers, husbands, brothers) for safety, security, and survival.

Such depictions perpetuate masculine hegemony as both normal and appropriate. When we accept hegemonic social structures that foster and maintain inequality between the sexes, it becomes exceedingly easy to participate in reproducing oppressive practices. Those who seek to unmask and challenge hegemonic masculinity subscribe to a feminist ideology. Thus, feminists include "anyone (male or female) whose beliefs and actions counter the hegemony in that they respect and value women and a feminine perspective" (Sellnow, 2010, p. 89).

Shugart, Waggoner, and Hallstein (2001) discovered a subset of entertainment media produced during the 1990s that portrayed women who embrace "having the power to make choices, regardless of what those choices are" (p. 195). Decades later, we still see TV like *Keeping Up With the Kardashians* and *Real Housewives*, as well as any number of "chick flicks" that earn millions of dollars each year as they continue to perpetuate masculine hegemony. *The Hunger Games,* one

(Continued)

(Continued)

of 2012's top-grossing American films, how-ever, is a subversive text that offers an oppo-sitional account of a young woman who is not only independent and able to care for herself but also cares for those around her, rejects fascination with material goods, and ultimately, rises

Television and film are powerful vehicles that often reify hegemonic constructions of women as domestic, soft-spoken, and dependent on men for survival and fulfillment. Tuning in to MTV, Bravo, or Lifetime television channels quickly illustrate this point (see: *Sixteen and Pregnant, Teen Mom, Keeping Up With the Kardashians*, any of the six *Real Housewives* shows, *Dance Moms, Army Wives*, etc.). Even movies across genres like 2012's *The Vow* (romantic drama), *This Is Forty* (comedy), and *The Bourne Legacy* (action) exemplify this point. Many of these texts perpetuate stereotypes of women acting petty, cat fighting, getting worked up about trivial matters, and most notably as being unable to care for themselves. What's more, the arguments proposed in these programs and films reinforce the notion that women must rely on men (e.g., fathers, husbands, brothers) for safety, security, and survival.

Such depictions perpetuate masculine hegemony as both normal and appropriate. When we accept hegemonic social structures that foster and maintain inequality between the sexes, it becomes exceedingly easy to par-ticipate in reproducing oppressive practices. Those who seek to unmask and challenge hegemonic masculinity subscribe to a feminist ideology. Thus, feminists include "anyone (male or female) whose beliefs and actions

counter the hegemony in that they respect and value women and a feminine perspective" (Sellnow, 2010, p. 89).

Shugart, Waggoner, and Hallstein (2001) discovered a subset of entertainment media produced during the 1990s that portrayed women who embrace "having the power to make choices, regardless of what those choices are" (p. 195). Decades later, we still see TV like *Keeping Up With the Kardashians* and *Real Housewives*, as well as any number of "chick flicks" that earn millions of dollars each year as they continue to perpetuate masculine hege-mony. *The Hunger Games*, one of 2012's top-grossing American films, however, is a subver-sive text that offers an oppositional account of a young woman who is not only independent and able to care for herself but also cares for those around her, rejects fascination with mate-rial goods, and ultimately, rises to become the hero when she wins a tournament she is forced to compete in. In the process, she earns the admiration of those around her both in the film itself and in theatres as movie viewers.

This analysis employs a feminist perspective to examine *The Hunger Games* movie and, more specifically, how main character Katniss Everdeen is portrayed in the film. *The Hunger Games* is an appropriate choice because of its critical acclaim and popularity.

The Hunger Games book on which the movie is based is a *USA Today, New York Times*, and *Wall Street Journal* (among others) #1 Bestseller. All three books in the trilogy, book two being *Catching Fire* and the conclusion titled *Mockingjay*, topped both Amazon Kindle's top 20 e-book list while simultaneously capturing the fourth, seventh, and eighth most popular positions on Amazon's top 20 print list (Habash, 2013). In July of 2012, Scholastic announced that book sales reached 50 million copies.

The first film in the trilogy was released on March 23, 2012. In 2012, the film earned $408,010,692 million in the United States and over $686,533,290 million when international sales are accounted for (Box Office Mojo, 2013). *The Hunger Games* movie ranks 13th in overall gross domestic earning films in the United States, only behind considerable giants like *Avatar* (number one), *Titanic* (number two), the original *Star Wars* (number six) and *E.T.: The Extra-Terrestrial* (number nine) (Box Office Mojo, 2013). Further, Collins' trilogy is hardly losing momentum. The second episode is on target for release in 2013, and all signs point to even larger earnings for both the book and the film. Thus, it seems prudent to discover what this story proposes to audiences about appropriate roles and rules for women and men.

RHETORICAL PERSPECTIVE AND METHOD

This essay uses a feminist perspective to examine *The Hunger Games* film. Three assumptions of feminist theory are that (1) gender is socially constructed in ways that oppress women and heteronormativity, (2) patriarchy fashions these constructions, and (3) "women's experiential knowledge best helps" to envision a future nonsexist society (Humm, 1997, p. 5). Further, these tenets serve to meet the purpose of both

refuting gender stereotypes and constructing new models (Humm, 1997).

Feminist rhetorical analyses serve to illuminate the "taken for granted" as "normal roles" that are prescribed for men and women in society (Sellnow, 2010, p. 89). Feminist perspectives reveal dominate ideologies and how they form structures that slowly seem to become "common sense" (p. 89). Ironically, both men and women perpetuate these structures. Those who seek to reveal and challenge these structures of inequality subscribe to a feminist ideology. Entertainment media complicate the unbinding of hegemonic systems because they typically play and replay depictions of men and women that fortify existing hegemonic social structures (hooks, 2000). Critiquing such texts from a feminist perspective may draw attention to how they do so and, thus, set the stage for positive change.

Feminist critiques may focus more specifically on a liberal, radical, Marxist, or cultural feminist perspective. Liberal feminism contends that women ought to be afforded "equal opportunity to earn and be trained and have [their] own voice in the big decisions of [their] destiny" (Friedan, 1963, p. 19). Radical feminism unmasks subject–object structural constraints that oppress women by objectifying them and denying them agency (except as sexual objects of male affection) (Madsen, 2000). Marxist feminism advocates for equality in women's pay and access to resources. Marxist theory suggests that those in power perpetuate wealth and social capital. Marxist feminism contends that hegemonic structures unfairly place women in a lower class than men and, thus, must depend on men

(Continued)

(Continued)

for survival. Finally, cultural feminism promotes the value of stereotypically feminine-gendered tasks (e.g., cooking, cleaning, nurturing, family-care giving). By redefining these tasks as meaningful, cultural feminists argue that they become acknowledged as valuable tasks that "should be embraced by both men and women" (Sellnow, 2010, p. 97). Cultural feminists argue that "women's work" as it has been traditionally defined in dominant American culture (both in and outside the home) is important and honorable work for both men and women.

The analysis begins with a description of *The Hunger Games* plotline followed by an examination of the hegemonic arguments proposed via the main characters via these feminist perspectives. More specifically, subject positions as models and anti-models are explained and supported with specific examples. Based on the analysis, several conclusions and possible implications are suggested regarding the messages it sends about hegemonic roles and rules for women and men.

THE HUNGER GAMES PLOTLINE

The Hunger Games movie (2012), which is based on Suzanne Collins's (2008) book of the same name, takes place in the ambiguous future in a place "once known" as North America. A post-apocalyptic society operates with one capital city, known as Panem, which is surrounded by twelve outlying working districts. Each submissive district has a distinct function (e.g., farming, mining, producing clothing), yet all produce and export goods to the wealthy ruling class of Panem. The story's main character and narrator, Katniss Everdeen, lives in District 12. District 12 is one of the poorest districts and is responsible for mining coal. Katniss lives with her mother and younger sister (Primrose Everdeen) in a small, nearly unbearable house that boasts few luxuries. Food is scare throughout the nation of Panem but is especially scare for the very poor like the Everdeens. Katniss regularly ventures outside District 12's borders to hunt game with her close friend Gale Hawthorne. She uses the game to feed her family or to barter for other goods the family needs.

The capital city of Panem imposes what is known as the "Hunger Games" on the 12 districts each year. The games were created after the districts once sought to overthrow the capital city. Thus, the games serve to remind the districts each year of their egregious error in attempting to do so. The Hunger Games mandate that each district send two "tributes" (one male and one female aged 12 to 18) as representatives to participate in this fight-to-the-death survival match. The games are televised throughout the districts for all to see. This year, young Primrose Everdeen's name was drawn to serve as the female tribute for District 12 (even though it was her first year of eligibility, which is rare). Without hesitation, Katniss immediately volunteers to go in her sister's place. This decision sends Katniss into the deadly competition with fellow tribute from District 12, Peeta Mellark, who was selected next. Katniss and Peeta ascend into the games, and much of the movie portrays what they do to prepare for and then survive in the games.

The Hunger Games Character Analysis

The main characters in *The Hunger Games* examined for this analysis are Katniss Everdeen, Primrose Everdeen, Peeta Mellark, Gale Hawthorne, Effie Trinket, Rue, Haymitch Abernathy, and Coriolanus Snow. Each is described in terms their role, their relationship to Katniss, and their subject position as a model or anti-model with regard to masculine hegemony from a liberal, radical, Marxist, and feminist perspective.

- Katniss Everdeen—Katniss is not only the protagonist in *The Hunger Games* but also the story's hero. She is portrayed as strong, resourceful, capable, and cunning, as well as compassionate and caring. Viewers are invited to agree that this female hero is worthy of the role. What follows are several representative examples that serve as evidence to support this position.

When the name of Katniss's 12-year-old sister, Primrose, is drawn to be District 12's female tribute, Katniss quickly volunteers to take her place. Never before had anyone from District 12 volunteered for the games. As one of the poorest districts, even the most experienced tribute was likely to fail. Knowing this, Katniss volunteered to save her sister, who would surely die if she were forced to participate.

After volunteering, Katniss gives her mother instructions on how to care for Primrose while she is away competing. This scene is important because it illustrates the fact that Katniss had stepped up to be the family's main provider, caregiver, and head of household after her father died. Her mother is portrayed as physically and emotionally ill equipped for the task.

Although Katniss and her family are poor, Katniss does not appear to care about material things. Her clothes are simple, functional, and unimportant to her. What is more important to her is that they are functional as she hunts for food to feed her family. In fact, she is ambivalent about her appearance until Panem officials dress Katniss for her games debut. Thus, she doesn't mind dressing up and looking "pretty;" however, doing so is not important to her in the "big picture" of life.

Katniss's character is truly solidified, however, when she enters the arena to fight in the games. She is self-sufficient, calm, and creative with the few resources available to her. She kills her opponents without hesitation when necessary but does not do so when she sees another option.

Katniss is the model character in *The Hunger Games* because she is the cunning hero who demonstrates leadership and resourcefulness in ways that still maintain her humanity. She not only saves herself but also finds a way to save her male counterpart Peeta from dying several times. She again demonstrates good character by being both resourceful and humane when she manages to finagle a way for both of them to get out of the games alive in the end, something that was unheard of in the history of the games.

(Continued)

(Continued)

- Primrose Everdeen—Primrose is Katniss's younger sister. Early in the film, Katniss is depicted as providing for Primrose. In doing so, Katniss is portrayed as a competent provider, a role traditional hegemony suggests belongs to men. She also cares for and nurtures Primrose, a culturally feminine characteristic. And Katniss volunteers for the games to save Primrose from certain death, demonstrating altruistic leadership, love, and agency from a radical feminist perspective.

- Peeta Mellark—Peeta is the male tribute selected from District 12 for the games. Peeta professes his love for Katniss during an interview prior to the start of the games. However, he later leaves her to fend for herself during the games when he thinks he will stand a better chance by aligning himself with members of another team. Katniss does not give up on him, however, and even bargains to save his life in the end when the "rules" were to kill him because only one person was supposed to be left standing (alive) in the end.

Peeta is portrayed as timid and unsure of himself at the point of the reaping and throughout the games. While Katniss asserts that her mission is to win the games and to return home to her district, Peeta articulates a more fatalistic mentality and sets as his goal making a statement to the capital before he is killed. After entering the game arena, Peeta teams up with a pack of aggressive tributes because he cannot fend for himself. Eventually, they turn on him, and he is seriously injured and left for dead.

When the game master announces that tributes from the same district can team up and work together to win, Katniss seeks out the injured Peeta, who is hiding near the river. Katniss saves Peeta's life by caring for him to heal his injuries and by protecting him from attacks by other tributes. Eventually, she even risks her life to retrieve medicine needed to save Peeta's life. In these ways, Peeta is actually portrayed as needing Katniss for survival and Katniss as the savior who does so, which challenges stereotypically gendered hegemonic roles and rules for women and men.

- Gale Hawthorne—Gale is Katniss's best friend from District 12. She hunts regularly with him and has an on-and-off-again crush on him. Katniss's genuine confidence in Gale is illustrated when she entrusts him with caring for Primrose while she fights in the games. (Recall that Katniss's mother has already been depicted as not up to the task.) In accepting the responsibility to do so, Gale displays both gendered masculine characteristics of provider and gendered feminine characteristics of nurturer.

Sellnow (2010) also discusses a phenomenon know as "male gaze," which in part describes the pleasurable looking by viewers of women (p. 99). During the early scenes in this film, viewers are invited to look pleasurably at Gale. He is a tall and handsome fellow, an attractive trophy who will wait for Katniss to return. Unlike Katniss, Gale does not display agency in terms of trying to improve his own condition. Rather, he appears resolved to operate within the boundaries set for him by the ruling class as an inhabitant of District 12. Hence, in this regard, Gale seems to enact more characteristics and behaviors typically ascribed to women within hegemonic structures than men.

- **Rue**—Rue is a young female tribute from District 11. She appears to be about the age of Katniss's sister, Primrose. Rue elicits sympathy from Hunger Games viewers for her perceived youth and innocence. She is also portrayed as a model for her courage and knowledge in spite of her age. Katniss and Rue form an alliance and work together to destroy the resources of an aggressive group of top-ranked tributes, which demonstrates the benefits of collaboration (a stereotypically feminine-gendered behavior within hegemonic structures).

Rue befriends Katniss during the games when she helps her heal from an injury. Eventually, Rue is killed by another tribute. After killing Rue's attacker, Katniss violates game tradition by attending to Rue's body in a type of funeral before resuming the hunt. Again Katniss displays both competence as a shrewd hunter in the games (stereotypically masculine-gendered characteristic) and compassion as a human being in caring for Rue as she lay dying (stereotypically feminine-gendered characteristic).

- **Effie Trinket**—Effie Trinket is the official sent from the capital city (Panem) to oversee the District 12 reaping ceremony to select tributes for the games and then to serve as their manager as they prepare for and participate in them. Her attire at the reaping is extremely flamboyant, which stands in stark contrast to the citizens of District 12. Throughout the film, she is portrayed as a self-centered, shallow, and uncompassionate anti-model.

Whether as a demand of her job or a moral failing, Effie shows little compassion for her tributes (Katniss and Peeta). Rather, she sees their involvement in the tournament as a privilege rather than human sacrifice. Effie is ostentatious like all capital residents and not only dresses in brightly colored, elaborate ensembles but also touts an extravagant hairdo and makeup. She offers little advice or meaningful insight and often remarks on inconsequential matters.

For example, when Katniss grows frustrated with Haymitch's (to be discussed next) refusal to divulge helpful information about preparing for the games, Katniss slams a kitchen knife into the table. Effie does not respond about the issue but instead retorts, "Hey, that [referring to the table] is mahogany." Effie's self-centered and shallow narcissism stands in drastic contrast to Katniss's rational and thoughtful character.

- **Haymitch Abernathy**—Haymitch is a former victor of the games and the only tribute from District 12 ever to win. Thus, Haymitch is selected to serve as mentor to Peeta and Katniss as they prepare for and participate in the games. It appears, however, that he did not handle very well the wealth and status that winning the games

(Continued)

(Continued)

afforded him. He is initially portrayed as a self-centered, spoiled, arrogant, and callous alcoholic. As such, Katniss quickly decides he is no role model for her and proceeds to prepare herself using others means. Peeta, on the other hand, does try to be mentored by Haymitch, something that does not prove very helpful at all. Haymitch's anti-model status does shift during the games, however, when even he begins to admire and root for Katniss, our competent and compassionate hero.

- Coriolanus Snow—Coriolanus Snow is president of Panem. Snow is portrayed as a ruthless tyrant who seeks to maintain order among the districts. Ultimately, his goal is to maintain status by doing whatever he can to maintain the existing power structure. The characteristics and behaviors he embodies as an anti-model serve to reinforce Katniss along with her characteristics and behaviors as the model subject position viewers are encouraged to want to be like.

President Snow is presented as a heartless proprietor of fear to be overcome. Not only must Katniss figure out how to win the games without help from her appointed mentor, Haymitch, but also how to overcome the structural constraints that Snow's regime maintains and propagates. This challenge serves as a catalyst for Katniss to begin a revolution—an uprising that will eventually overturn decades of tradition and oppression.

Obviously, there are more characters in *The Hunger Games* than described here. However,

these main characters encompass the story's core models and anti-models. Moreover, they clearly set Katniss apart as the hero and, in the process, challenge many taken-for-granted as normal roles and rules for women and men in terms of hegemony.

CONCLUSIONS AND IMPLICATIONS

Based on this examination of several of the main characters, *The Hunger Games* seems to clearly challenge masculine hegemony regarding taken-for-granted as normal roles and rules for women and men. Katniss—a female—is the movie's hero, reversing the stereotypical hegemonic subject position of male heroes and female victims. As such, space is opened for viewers to see female (as well as male) heroes as legitimate. After watching Katniss both care for and protect other characters including her mother, her sister, Peeta, and Rue, viewers are invited to acknowledge the benefits that both males and females derive from empowered females. *The Hunger Games* does not in any way argue, however, that all females are inherently superior to males. By depicting Katniss's mother as a frail and incompetent caregiver and provider, as well as Effie as a self-centered, materialistic, and uncompassionate manager, the argument that Katniss's characteristics and actions are what set her apart as the hero rather than the fact that she is female.

More specifically, from a liberal feminist perspective, women in the post-apocalyptic world portrayed in *The Hunger Games* are not excluded from participating in the games.

Rather, one female and one male are chosen from each district to fight in the games. Both women and men can take on roles as heroes, hunters, gathers, and more.

During the movie, audiences also come to discover that both Gale and Peeta have romantic feelings for Katniss. Rather than focus on Katniss's struggle to decide which suitor to date, which would reinforce hegemony, she remains focused on the issue at hand—winning the games and returning home. This is not to say Katniss is incapable of love but, rather, that romance is not her sole ambition or purpose as a woman (radical feminist perspective).

The class systems and hierarchies are established by the "haves" and "have nots" based on where people are born. In this sense, hegemony is clearly reinforced in terms of economic inequality. But the class-based inequality is rooted in which district one was born into rather than biological sex or gender.

Finally, from a cultural feminist perspective, *The Hunger Games* illustrates the need for and value of both feminine- and masculine-gendered tasks and traits for men and women. Katniss demonstrates intelligence, skill, strength, competitiveness, sensitivity, collaboration, and cooperation during her journey to victory. Peeta acknowledges that the skills he learned as a baker helped him become a master of camouflage. And after Katniss volunteers for the games, Gale is shown caring for her family.

The Hunger Games provides an alternative reality by challenging hegemony. It portrays Katniss not as being oppressed but as in control of her destiny even during the games. She is also portrayed as the responsible provider and caregiver for her family (mother and sister) and the protector and defender of herself and others (Rue and Peeta), while enacting stereotypically feminine-gendered characteristics and traits (caregiving, nurturing, compassionate, collaborative). As such, Katniss may serve as a positive role model for girls and women. For example:

1. Women can control their own destinies;

2. Women do not necessarily need to be in a romantic relationship with a man above all else to be happy or fulfilled;

3. Women are capable of providing for themselves (and others); and

4. Stereotypically feminine-gendered characteristics are valuable.

Frankly, these lessons are equally positive for boys and men. The freedom from oppression women achieve also frees men (1) from feeling the burden of being the sole provider in a hegemonic system and (2) to engage in fulfilling activities hegemonically ascribed to women (cooking, baking, caregiving, nurturing, and even conveying emotions). These kinds of messages unfortunately remain uncommon in most blockbuster U.S. films that garner large viewerships. Thus, *The Hunger Games* is a refreshing alternative to those portraying women as helpless victims needing a male hero to save them in order to "live happily ever after."

Since *The Hunger Games* accumulated a record $152.5 million dollars during its opening weekend at the box office, its popularity and reach have only continued to grow (Kaufman, 2012). *Forbes* predicts that *Catching Fire* will be even more successful than its predecessor in 2013 (Pomerantz, 2013). Katniss Everdeen

(Continued)

wii continue her reign as hero. Viewers (both male and female) of all ages need more role models like the fearless, competent, and compassionate Katniss Everdeen.

In conclusion, this rhetorical analysis explored the arguments conveyed through the main characters in *The Hunger Games* from a feminist perspective. In doing so, this essay illustrates how Katniss as hero serves as a positive prototype rejecting hegemony. *The Hunger Games* stands in contrast to other entertainment media that reinforce hegemonic structures that perpetuate the oppression of women. Films that represent women as capable and worthy role models and heroes are important for mass audiences to see. Unlike many films that propose arguments that oppose hegemony, *The Hunger Games* did earn broad viewer appeal. Our hero Katniss is one of few female heroes that succeed in appealing to mass audiences comprised of both males and females as a champion for women and humanity in her post-apocalyptic Earth.

References

Box Office Mojo. (2013). *The Hunger Games*. Retrieved from http://www.boxofficemojo.com/movies/?id=hungergames.htm

Collins, S. (2008). *The hunger games*. New York: Scholastic.

Friedan, B. (1963). *The feminine mystique*. New York, NY: W.W. Norton & Company, Inc.

Habash, G. (2013, January 4). The best selling books of 2012. *Publisher's Weekly*. Retrieved from http://www.publishersweekly.com/pw/by-topic/industry-news/bookselling/article/55383-the-bestselling-books-of-2012.html

hooks, b. (2000). *Feminism for everyone: Passionate politics*. Cambridge, MA: South End Press.

Humm, M. (1997). *Feminism and film*. Scotland: Edinburgh University Press.

Kaufman, A. (2012, March 29). Movie projector: "The Hunger Games" to dominate box office—again. *Los Angeles Times*. Retrieved from http://latimesblogs.latimes.com/entertainmentnewsbuzz/2012/03/box-office-hunger-games-dominate-again.html

Madsen, D. L. (2000). *Feminist theory and literary practice*. Sterling, VA: Pluto Press.

Pomerantz, D. (2013, January 3). "The Hunger Games: Catching Fire" is the most anticipated movie of 2013. *Forbes*. Retrieved from http://www.forbes.com/sites/dorothypomerantz/2013/01/03/the-hunger-games-catching-fire-is-the-most-anticipated-movie-of-2013/

Scholastic. (2012, July 19). Scholastic announces updated U.S. figures for Suzanne Collins' best-selling The Hunger Games trilogy. *Scholastic*. Retrieved from http://mediaroom.scholastic.com/press-release/scholastic-announces-updated-us-figures-suzanne-collinss-bestselling-hunger-games-tril

Sellnow, D. D. (2010). *The rhetorical power of popular culture: Considering mediated texts*. Thousand Oaks, CA: Sage.

Shugart, H. A., Waggoner, C. E., & Hallstein, D. L. O. (2001). Mediating third-wave feminism: Appropriation as postmodern media practice. *Critical Studies in Media Communication, 18*(2), 194–210. DOI: 10.1080/07393180128079

Summary

This chapter outlined guidelines by which to conduct a critical rhetorical analysis from a feminist perspective. We began by discussing the nature of hegemony, patriarchy, masculine hegemony, and heteronormativity and the three waves of feminism as they influenced the development of various feminist perspectives. Then, we detailed the steps involved in conducting a feminist analysis of popular culture texts. Finally, we presented examples of feminist rhetorical criticisms to highlight the utility of conducting this type of scholarship. Feminist rhetorical critiques help to expose the potential consequences of privileging patriarchy, masculine hegemony, and heteronormativity and illustrate how and why empowering multiple world views can make the world a better place for all.

Challenge

Watch the 1959 Rock Hudson and Doris Day movie *Pillow Talk* followed by the 2003 Renee Zellweger and Ewan McGregor film *Down With Love*. Both are romantic comedies, but the second is a spoof on the 1960s story line, girl who thinks she doesn't want a man and eventually realizes she needs and wants a man and who finally settles down to be a happily married wife. Watch each film, and identify what each one presents as normal or abnormal and desirable or undesirable roles and rules for women and men in society. Use the following questions to guide your viewing of each one.

1. Before examining the program, do you think it is likely to reinforce or oppose hegemony and why?

2. Identify the main characters and primary subject positions, in other words, which characters are portrayed as models and anti-models. Who are viewers led to want to be like and not be like and why?

3. What roles, skills, and characteristics do the models and anti-models embody?

4. Does the ultimate message reinforce or oppose hegemony and why?

5. What are some potential implications of these kinds of messages on the various target audiences who watch the program? On society as a whole?

References

Ambinder, M. (2012, September 27). The golden age of gay TV? *The Week*. Retrieved March 28, 2013, from http://theweek.com/article/index/233952/the-golden-age-of-gay-tv

Battles, K. & Hilton-Morrow, W. (2002). Gay characters in conventional spaces: *Will and Grace* and the situation comedy genre. *Critical Studies in Media Communication, 19*(1), 87–105.

Berberick, S. N. (2010). The objectification of women in mass media: Female self-image in misogynist culture. *The New York Sociologist, 5,* 1–15.

Borzelleca, D. (2012, February 16). The male-female ratio in college. *Forbes*. Retrieved March 28, 2013, from http://www.forbes.com/sites/ccap/2012/02/16/the-male-female-ratio-in-college/

Brooks, M. (1997). *Blurring the edges*. [CD]. Nashville, TN: Capitol Records.

Candice Bergen. (1989, December). *Playboy*, 61–81.

Connell, R. W. (1987). *Gender and power*. Sydney, Australia: Allen and Unwin.

Davidson, A. (2012, March 29). The $200,000-a-year-nanny. National Public Radio. Retrieved March 28, 2013, from http://www.npr.org/blogs/money/2012/03/29/149525587/the-200-000-a-year-nanny

De Beauvoir, S. (1949). *The second sex* (H. M. Parshley, Trans.). New York: Penguin.

Dow, B. (1990). Hegemony, feminist criticism and *The Mary Tyler Moore Show*. *Critical Studies in Mass Communication, 7*, 261–274.

Dow, B. (1996). *Prime time feminism*. Philadelphia: University of Pennsylvania Press.

Faludi, S. (1991, 2006). *Backlash: The undeclared war against women*. New York: Random House.

Friedan, B. (1963). *The feminine mystique*. New York, NY: W.W. Norton & Company, Inc.

Gervais, T. K., Vescio, J. F., Maass, A., & Suitner, C. (2012). Seeing women as objects: The sexual body part recognition bias. *European Journal of Social Psychology, 42*(6), 743–753.

Goodnight, L., & Owens, E. (2012). Pay gap still at 77 cents, should be a wake up call. *American Assocation of University Women*. Retrieved March 28, 2013, from http://www.aauw.org/media/pressreleases/Gender_Wage_Gap_091212.cfm

Heywood, L., & Drake, J. (Eds.). (1997). *Third wave agenda: Being feminist, doing feminism*. Minneapolis: University of Minnesota Press.

Jardine, A., & Smith, P. (Eds.). (1987). *Men in feminism*. New York: Routledge.

Jhally, S. (n.d.). Advertising, gender and sex: What's wrong with a little objectification? [Blog post]. Retrieved March 28, 2013, from http://www.sutjhally.com/articles/whatswrongwithalit/

Lindsey, C., Lindsey, H., & Mayo, A. (2003). *This One's for the Girls*. [CD]. Nashville, TN: BMG Music.

Longely, R. (2004, September 1). Gender wage gap widening, census data shows: First decline in women's real earnings since 1995. Retrieved July 25, 2005, from http://usgovinfo.about.com/od/censusandstatistics/a/paygapgrows.htm

Lovaas, K. E., & Jenkins, M. M. (Eds.). (2007). *Sexualities and communication in everyday life: A reader*. Thousand Oaks, CA: Sage.

McQuigge, M. (2012, December 31). Jenna Talackova TV show: Transgender beauty says she's made a reality show. *The Canadian Press*. Retrieved March 28, 2013, from http://www.huffingtonpost.ca/2012/12/31/jenna-talackova-tv-show_n_2388197.html

Mulvey, L. (1975). Visual pleasure and narrative cinema. *Screen, 16*(3), 6–18.

O'Neal, J., Smith, S., & Hill, E. (2005). *Somebody's hero*. [CD]. Nashville, TN: Capitol Records.

Penn, V. (2012, November 27). *New Girl*: Jess and Cece and their biological clocks. *MSN Entertainment*. Retrieved March 28, 2013, from http://social.entertainment.msn.com/tv/blogs/recaps-blogpost.aspx?post=c913bd98-0735-41e6-ba47-3cda31d24388

Rubin, G. S. (1993). Thinking sex: Notes for a radical theory of the politics of sexuality. In Henry Abelove, Micháele Aina Barale, & David M. Halperin (Eds.), *The lesbian and gay studies reader* (pp. 3–44). New York: Routledge.

Swami, V., Coles, R., Wilson, E., Salem, N., Wyrozumska, K., & Furnham, A. (2010). Oppressive beliefs at play: Associations among beauty ideals and practices and individual differences in sexism, objectification of others, and media exposure. *Psychology of Women Quarterly, 34*(3), 365–379.

U.S. Bureau of Labor Statistics. (2012, April 26). *Economic news release*. Washington, DC: United States Department of Labor. Retrieved March 28, 2013, from http://www.bls.gov/news.release/famee.t06.htm

Warner, M. (Ed.). (1993). *Fear of a queer planet: Queer politics and social theory*. Minneapolis: University of Minnesota Press.

Wolfe, N. (1991, 2002). *The beauty myth: How images of beauty are used against women*. New York: Harper-Collins.

Student Study Site

Visit the Student Study Site at www.sagepub.com/sellnow2e to read interesting SAGE journal articles, view mobile-friendly key term flashcards, take chapter-specific online web quizzes to test your knowledge, and more!

Chapter 8

A Music Perspective

The Illusion of Life

T he perspectives we've discussed so far were each originally created to examine arguments communicated primarily via discursive symbols. Discursive symbols are essentially units (e.g., words and numbers) with fixed associations. For the rhetorical critic, they are words that represent things. For example, *d-o-g* represents a four-legged mammal domesticated as a household pet in the dominant American culture. Rhetorical critics examine these discursive verbal texts to understand the arguments in them that reinforce or challenge taken-for-granted beliefs or behaviors.

Rhetorical critics may also examine nondiscursive nonverbal texts as rhetoric either in conjunction with verbal symbols or as texts that stand entirely on their own. In fact, many of the perspectives we have already discussed have been used to examine both verbal and nonverbal texts. This chapter and the two that follow focus on some rhetorical perspectives that were intentionally created to investigate the nondiscursive messages unique to music, to visual images, and to electronic and new media.

American philosopher Susanne Langer is among those credited with conceptualizing nondiscursive symbolism in her books *Feeling and Form* (1953) and *Philosophy in a New Key* (1957). Nondiscursive symbols are all symbols beyond the realm of words and numbers that humans use to create meaning. For rhetoricians, these symbols range from nonverbal body language and tone of voice cues accompanying words in a speech to musical sounds and visual images. Whereas discursive symbols tend to represent thoughts, nondiscursive symbols tend to represent emotions. Nondiscursive rhetoric, then, is the study of how these symbol systems function as persuasion regarding taken-for-granted beliefs and behaviors. Because this chapter focuses specifically on how musical sounds function rhetorically,

I encourage you to read the chapter when and where you can access technology that will allow you to actually listen to the examples offered to illustrate concepts.

MUSIC AS RHETORIC

Few would argue with the notion that music (with or without lyrics) communicates. If it didn't, we wouldn't choose to listen to upbeat music when we're excited and mellow music when we're relaxing. Moreover, music pervades our lives. Whether driving to work or school, grocery shopping, exercising, or riding in an elevator, music fills the air. The reasons we have for listening to or performing music may vary for different individuals based on purpose and occasion. For example, some people listen to background music to stay energized while exercising or to stay focused while reading or writing. For others, however, listening to music while exercising or reading might actually be a distraction. Moreover, some of us choose to listen to music performed by a certain entertainer or group because we enjoy their style. And some of us might listen to a specific musical work over and over because it's a favorite. For example, I like to attend a live performance of Handel's "Messiah" every December. I never tire of hearing it performed. Doing so has become a tradition I look forward to each year. All of these reasons are valid, but not all would fall within the definition of music as *rhetoric*. Thus, before exploring how we might go about examining music as rhetoric, we must first be able to distinguish music as rhetoric from music as aesthetic expression and music as communication.

Music as aesthetic expression, or musical aesthetics, is essentially the appreciation and evaluation of musical form or design. Some argue that music appreciation is achieved if one simply enjoys listening to the music. Others contend that one must be able to evaluate what they hear not only for its beauty but also for its authenticity based on well-defined aesthetic criteria for music of a given era (e.g., Baroque, Classical, Romantic, Impressionistic) (Kivy, 1995). Stravinsky (1962) went so far as to claim that "form is everything," and those misguided listeners who look for meanings miss out on the purely musical experience (p. 115). For our purposes, both are valid examples of musical aesthetics, and neither is a valid example of musical rhetoric.

Music as communication refers to the individual and unique meanings each of us might attach to a musical work. In other words, music as communication functions for us individually as signs but not for groups collectively as symbolic artifacts. Certainly, music as communication has meaning, but that meaning is not socially grounded because it is not widely shared by some identifiable community or group.

At this juncture, I want to explain my rationale for selecting certain examples as illustrative supporting material. I have learned through years of teaching this perspective that students often find it difficult to set aside music as communication meanings of current songs they still listen to regularly. Their struggle to do so serves as a constraint to understanding and employing music as rhetoric. Thus, I intentionally use examples that are less current, examples most students can examine without having to first lay aside personal music as communication meanings.

Music as rhetoric, or musical rhetoric, refers to persuasive arguments conveyed through music that reinforce or challenge a taken-for-granted belief or behavior. To be an artifact, the meaning (whether intended by the creator or not) must be widely shared by an identifiable group. For example, when I hear the song "Pleasant Valley Sunday" by The Monkees, it has meaning for me as communication when I associate it with my childhood and happy times. But that's not what the song is arguing rhetorically as an artifact. In fact, its rhetorical message is actually bleak:

> Another pleasant valley Sunday;
>
> Charcoal burning everywhere;
>
> Rows of houses that are all the same;
>
> And no one seems to care. (Goffin & King, 1967)

When we consider music as rhetoric, we examine the unified arguments it communicates to identifiable audiences rather than the various individual meanings you and I might attach to it. Moreover, we do so because when messages are "couched in music . . . listeners do not ordinarily anticipate persuasion and, as a result, [may not be] aware of its complete implications" (Irvine & Kirkpatrick, 1972, p. 273).

APPLYING WHAT YOU'VE LEARNED . . .

What song(s) do you play when you're getting ready to go out with friends? What song(s) do you play when you're relaxing for the evening? Are they the same? Why or why not?

Rhetorical analyses of music might examine arguments conveyed in the lyrics using any number of perspectives including those we've discussed in the previous chapters. In fact, a good number of communication scholars have studied music as rhetoric using a variety of rhetorical perspectives (e.g., Aldridge & Carlin, 1993; Balaji, 2012; Bloodworth, 1975; Booth, 1976; Chesebro, Davis, Nachman, & Yanelli, 1975; Francesconi, 1986; Gonzalez & Makay, 1983; Grossberg, 1986; Hess, 2006; Holmberg, 1985; Irvine & Kirkpatrick, 1972; Jones & Schumaker, 1992; Knupp, 1981; LeCoat, 1976; Lewis, 1976; Morris, 2011; Phillipov, 2012; Rasmussen, 1994; Rein & Springer, 1986; Rohlfing, 1996; Root, 1986; Roth, 1981; Sellnow & Sellnow, 2001; Smith, 1980; van Dick, 2006; Weisman, 1985). Hence, the perspective we explore in this chapter—the illusion of life—is by no means the only approach for examining music as rhetoric.

The illusion of life perspective is particularly useful for several reasons. First, it is one of only a few perspectives designed to examine both lyrics and music as they work together to function rhetorically. Second, it provides a means by which to understand how music conveys both conceptual and emotional content. And it can be employed on its own or in conjunction with another perspective to examine the rhetorical arguments conveyed in music.

THE ILLUSION OF LIFE _____

The name—the illusion of life—comes from Susanne Langer's explanation of nondiscursive symbolism in *Feeling and Form* (1953) and *Philosophy in a New Key* (1957). She uses this phrase to account for what occurs when human beings symbolize life experiences through music. Music itself is not actual life. Rather, music represents human experiences and emotions. Thus, Langer explains that music offers itself as an *illusion*—or symbolic representation—of life. Just as *discursive symbols*—words—are not the actual things they represent, *nondiscursive symbols*—music—are not the actual emotions they represent. Moreover, music does not cause or cure feelings. Rather, music represents them. Essentially, music offers itself as an illusion of life by sounding the way feelings feel (Davies, 1980).

Music communicates emotions by symbolizing the *intensity and release patterns*—or rhythms—we experience regularly as part of daily human living (Langer, 1953, pp. 126–127). In actual life, intensity patterns are feelings of tension and release patterns are feelings of relief from them (Dewey, 1934). When we experience feelings of tension, our hearts tend to beat faster than normal and then return to normal when we experience subsequent feelings of relief (McLaughlin, 1970). For instance, let's say you are driving down a slippery road in the pouring rain and momentarily lose control of your vehicle. At that moment, you experience an intensity pattern as your heart pounds faster and your muscles tighten up. When you regain control, you experience a release pattern as your heartbeat settles back down and your muscles relax.

Intensity patterns are symbolized in music, for example, when the rate is faster than a resting heartbeat (e.g., allegro), by speeding up the rate (accelerando), and by increasing the volume (crescendo). Release patterns are symbolized in music, for example, when the rate is slower than a resting heartbeat (e.g., largo), by slowing the rate (ritardando) or reducing the volume (decrescendo). Thus, by symbolizing intensity and release patterns, music helps us make sense of "stresses involved in living that defy linear, discursive expression" (Rasmussen, 1994, p. 151).

Finally, emotion is progressively articulated in music and ascertained holistically much like it is in speech. To clarify, paralanguage refers to the nonverbal vocal cues that accompany words (e.g., pitch, volume, rate, pauses) to convey the emotional tone of a message. However, the same vocal cue (e.g., increased volume) can be used to communicate any number of different emotions. For example, if you speed up your rate as you speak (intensity pattern), you might be conveying "rage, anger, excitement, or fear" (Sellnow & Sellnow, 2001, p. 398). We can only determine which emotion is communicated by considering all of the paralinguistic cues holistically in conjunction with one another and with the words.

Similarly, emotional content is progressively articulated and ultimately determined holistically in music. In other words, intensity and release patterns are symbolized in music via rhythm, harmony, melody, phrasing, articulation, and instrumentation. However, the rhetorical critic's goal differs from that of a music theorist who might dissect each of these elements in order to evaluate a musical work for authenticity from a musical aesthetics perspective. As when listening to a speech, rhetorical critics listen to music holistically to come to a conclusion about the emotions they are representing.

Music functions rhetorically by representing actual life experiences and emotions as an illusion of life based on the artist's perspective. In this way, music conveys an argument about how we ought to or ought not to believe or behave. As this illusion of life merely symbolizes a perspective about how to understand actual life, we explain how it does so via virtual experience (lyrics) and virtual time (music). We use the *virtual* adjective to distinguish that each is a symbolic representation of actual life experiences and emotions. The rhetorical critic examines (1) what the music is communicating and (2) what the lyrics are suggesting. Ultimately, the critic determines the argument proposed based on the congruent or incongruent interaction between lyrics and music.

Virtual Time

Actual time is a one-dimensional succession of moments (e.g., minutes, hours, days, weeks). Music functions as virtual time by suspending actual time and then substituting for it. Music represents time through patterns of intensity and release communicated via rhythm, harmony, melody, phrasing, and instrumentation (see Table 8.1). Remember, however, that music is a nondiscursive symbol system. Thus, none of these musical elements can be reduced to an absolute fixed definition that operates in isolation of the others.

Recall that the rhetorical critic's goal is to determine holistically whether the music represents primarily intensity or release patterns. Thus, a hard rock song that employs a fast, driving tempo, loud dynamics, and full instrumentation (e.g., amplified guitars, keyboards, drums) might represent intensity even if the melody (considered in isolation) seems to represent release. A ballad, on the other hand, that employs a slower tempo, softer dynamics, mellow harmonies, and lots of long-held as opposed to short-held tones is likely to represent release even if it is performed by a symphony (many instruments).

Holistic consideration of intensity and release patterns requires critics to go beyond the general analysis just described to also consider genre and artist. For our purposes, a musical genre is a generally recognized category of music (e.g., blues, classical, country, jazz, hip-hop, pop, rap, rock). What constitutes an intensity or release pattern might differ somewhat based on the conventions of a particular genre. Let's reconsider the hard rock example. The conventions of the genre call for as typical the things we just described as representing intensity patterns (e.g., fast, driving tempo, loud dynamics, full instrumentation). Based on the conventions of the genre, however, a rock ballad that contradicts some (though maybe not all) of the genre's conventions might actually symbolize release. Similarly, an artist or group known for performing hard-driving rock songs that performs a song that contradicts the pattern represents release in that song for that artist or group. Thus, when classic heavy metal band Metallica performs songs like "One," "To Live Is to Die," "Bleeding Me," or "The Unforgiven," these songs are more representative of release than of intensity.

APPLYING WHAT YOU'VE LEARNED . . .

Identify two or three songs you hear a lot on the radio. Identify whether each seems to symbolize predominantly intensity or release patterns. Why?

■ **TABLE 8.1** Representative Intensity and Release Patterns in the Musical Elements

	Intensity	*Release*
(1) Rhythmic Structure:	Fast, driving tempo	Slow tempo
	Changing meter	Consistent meter
	Syncopated, unpredictable	Predictable
(2) Harmonic Structure:	Dissonant, harsh	Consonant, mellow
	Avoids tonic (home) tone	Frequent tonic tone
(3) Melodic Structure:	Ascending	Descending
	Disjunct (sporadic)	Conjunct (smooth)
	Short-held tones	Long-held tones
(4) Phrasing:	Staccato (separated)	Legato (connected)
	Accented (punched)	Legato (smooth)
	Crescendos (gets louder)	Decrescendos (softer)
	Loud	Soft
	Ritardando (gradually slower)	Accelerando (get faster)
(5) Instrumentation:	Many	Few
	Amplified	Acoustic

Virtual Experience

Virtual experience differs from actual experience by representing it as influenced by an artist's perspective. Langer (1953, 1957) explains that virtual experience is represented as primarily comic or tragic.

Comic as it is used here is not defined as funny, humorous, or related to comedy. Rather, comic lyrics focus on the protagonist's determination to beat the odds. Failing is not an option. Hence, comic lyrics tend to represent intensity patterns. Take, for example, the classic song made popular by Gloria Gaynor, "I Will Survive" (Perren & Fekaris, 1978). The lyrics are not funny. They do, however, argue that the protagonist is determined to beat the odds:

At first I was afraid. I was petrified.

Kept thinking I could never live without you by my side

But then I spent so many nights thinking how you did me wrong.

And I grew strong and I learned how to get along.

And so you're back from outer space.

I just walked in to find you here with that sad look upon your face.

I should have changed that stupid lock.

I should have made you leave your key.

If I'd have known for just one minute you'd be back to bother me . . .

Go on now go. Walk out the door.

Just turn around now, 'cause you're not welcome anymore.

Weren't you the one who tried to hurt me with good-bye?

Did you think I'd crumble?

Did you think I'd lay down and die?

Oh no, not I.

I will survive.

Oh, as long as I know how to love, I know I'll stay alive.

I've got all my life to live.

I've got all my love to give.

And I'll survive.

I will survive.

Interestingly, this song has been performed by a variety of artists since its first release in 1978 and today is considered an anthem of hope and determination for many oppressed groups, as well as one of *Rolling Stone's* top 500 songs of all time.

Tragic lyrics focus on the protagonist's self-consummation, sense of hopelessness, and attempt to cope with fate. Hence, tragic lyrics tend to represent release patterns. Beck's (1993) "Loser" is an extremely poignant example:

Yo cut it. Soy un perdedor, I'm a loser baby, so why don't you kill me,

Double-barrel buckshot

Soy un perdedor, I'm a loser baby, so why don't you kill me.

The meaning conveyed in the comic or tragic lyrics sometimes may be augmented when situated within a poetic illusion (backward-looking reflection on the resolved virtual past) or dramatic illusion (forward-looking into the unresolved virtual future). Because one cannot typically change the past, lyrics set in a poetic illusion tend to reinforce a release pattern. Lyrics set in a dramatic illusion offer a sense of suspense, seeking resolution that tends to reinforce an intensity pattern. In "I Will Survive," for example, the lyrics shift from poetic illusion ("I was petrified. Kept thinking I could never live without you by my side.") to dramatic illusion ("I've got all my life to live, and I've got all my love to give. I will survive."). In doing so, the emotional intensity of the comic lyrics about determination and ultimate success at beating the odds is augmented.

Congruity and Incongruity

Ultimately, the critic's goal is to determine whether the lyrical and musical meanings are congruent or incongruent. A congruent interaction is one where the emotional meanings of music and lyrics reinforce one another, making the argument abundantly clear and poignant. For example, most school fight songs offer comic lyrics of determination to beat the opponent (i.e., we will go, fight, and win). At the same time, the music symbolizes predominantly intensity patterns, making the argument that "we will prevail" more poignant. Similarly, most lullabies convey congruent lyrical and musical emotional meanings about being calm and going to sleep. An incongruent interaction is one where the emotional meanings of the music and lyrics contradict one another, which tends to alter the meaning that would have been conveyed via either lyrics or music alone. If the comic lyrics of the school fight song were combined with release musical patterns as in a lullaby, the result would be incongruity.

Congruity

Congruity transpires when comic lyrics are combined with intensity musical patterns or tragic lyrics are combined with release musical patterns. Moreover, (1) comic lyrics set in the forward-looking dramatic illusion combined with intensity musical patterns (e.g., "I Will Survive" and (2) tragic lyrics set in the backward-looking poetic illusion combined with release musical patterns ("Loser") make for the most clear and poignant arguments.

 Classic rock anthems such as "Rock-n-Roll All Nite" (KISS; Stanley & Simmons, 1975), "Born to Run" (Bruce Springsteen), "Welcome to the Jungle" (Guns N' Roses), "We Will Rock You" (Queen), "I Love Rock 'n' Roll" (Joan Jett and the Blackhearts), and "Bitch" (Meredith Brooks) are good examples of congruent interactions between comic lyrics and intensity musical patterns. Congruity makes the emotionally charged argument very clear.

 Examples of congruent interactions between tragic lyrics and release musical patterns include "Tears in Heaven" (Eric Clapton), "The Freshmen" (The Verve Pipe), "Goodbye to Love" (The Carpenters), "Hurt" (Nine Inch Nails), "Tha Crossroads" (Bone Thugs-n-Harmony), "Swim Good," (Frank Ocean), and "Streets of Philadelphia," which is Bruce Springsteen's (1994) academy award-winning song about coping with certain fate of death from HIV/AIDS:

> I walked the avenue 'til my legs felt like stone
>
> I heard the voices of friends vanished and gone
>
> At night I could hear the blood in my veins
>
> Black and whispering in the rain
>
> On the streets of Philadelphia.
>
> Ain't no angel gonna greet me
>
> It's just you and I my friend
>
> My clothes don't fit me no more
>
> I walked a thousand miles
>
> Just to slip into this skin . . .
>
> On the streets of Philadelphia. (Springsteen, 1994)

APPLYING WHAT YOU'VE LEARNED . . .

Consider the two or three songs you identified earlier. Identify whether each offers primarily comic or tragic lyrics as well as whether each is set primarily in a poetic or dramatic illusion. Are the lyrics and music congruent or incongruent? Why?

The critic's goal is to offer potential conclusions and possible implications about the rhetorical effect of congruity on particular audiences.

Congruent tragic release pattern songs may be successful in terms of conveying a clear and emotionally poignant argument and even win awards as "Streets of Philadelphia" did; however, when the message is too depressing, its appeal may be short-lived if at all (Sellnow & Sellnow, 1990). In addition, although music does not cause or cure feelings, such songs do represent emotions and, thus, may point to a covert plea for help. That is, people who listen to congruent tragic release pattern songs regularly might be doing so because these songs represent inner feelings of despair and a desire to be heard and valued by others (Manson, 2002).

Congruent comic intensity pattern songs may function effectively, for example, as teaching tools within children's music. Award-winning singer–songwriter Red Grammer's song "Say Hi" is a good example of convincing kids to overcome shyness:

So when someone is sayin' hi!

And it's your turn for feeling shy.

You might want to run and hide, but don't turn your head away.

You've gotta stand up tall,

Gather up a smile,

Take a big breath.

Look 'em in the eye and say "Hi!" (Grammer & Grammer, 1986)

Congruent comic intensity pattern songs may also function effectively as what Stewart, Smith, and Denton (2001) call "in-group" messages, or anthems to rally people around a cause or mission. "Do They Know It's Christmas?" (Geldof & Ure, 1984), first performed by the Band Aid charity supergroup comprised of British and Irish musicians as a Feed the World anthem in 1984, and the U.S. song it inspired the next year, "We Are the World" (Jackson & Ritchie, 1985), as a Live Aid anthem, serve as examples. Both inspired people to feed the people starving in Africa at the time. Moreover, both have been remade and remixed numerous times since then and continue to serve as rallying cries inspiring people to do our part to help those in need around the world.

Sometimes when the cause or mission challenges the ideology of the status quo, however, its persuasive appeal for potentially drawing in new members will suffer. Some have argued this about Meredith Brooks's song "Bitch." The song essentially recasts the negative connotation of the word *bitch* into a positive connotative one as she sings, "I'm a bitch, I'm a lover, I'm a child, I'm a mother, I'm a sinner, I'm a saint," and "I do not feel ashamed" (Brooks &

Peiken,1997, track 2). Although the song did serve as an anthem for women, it may have failed to appeal to males at least at the time to also accept the connotative shift. The rhetorical critic might claim, then, that controversial messages conveyed using congruent intensity patterns may have limited appeal only to those who already accept the cause as legitimate rather than to grow the movement's membership. Interestingly, today the song does enjoy broad appeal. Hence, perhaps controversial messages that challenge dominant ideology couched in music serve as seeds for incremental persuasion over time.

When the cause or mission challenges the dominant ideology and seems potentially harmful to people, groups, or society, implications of its success as a rallying cry for members and for drawing in new members might also be questioned. For example, some argue that neo-Nazi skinhead music functions in this way (Sellnow, 1994).

Sometimes congruent tragic release patterns are couched in a dramatic illusion (forward looking), thereby providing a glimmer of hope amidst the despair. Eric Clapton's (1992) "Tears in Heaven" is an example. He sings about the tragic death of his young son but places it in the uncertain future when he sings "Would you know my name if I saw you in heaven? Would it be the same if I saw you in heaven . . . There'll be no more tears in heaven" (track 4). Likewise, congruent comic intensity pattern songs may be couched within a poetic illusion (reflective resolve, not forward looking). Doing so can make the message more palatable to broad audiences; however, it might also lose its ability to incite action.

Incongruity

Incongruity transforms the argument from what a listener would get by listening to the lyrics or music alone. When (1) comic lyrics interact with release musical patterns or (2) tragic lyrics interact with intensity musical patterns, a number of things can occur. Listener appeal can be broadened, meaning can be misinterpreted, persuasive appeal can be strengthened, and meaning can be altered.

A couple of examples of songs that used incongruity to successfully broaden listener appeal at the price of misinterpretation include Bruce Springsteen's "Born in the USA" (tragic lyrics about the plight of Vietnam veterans with intensity musical patterns) and "Dancing in the Dark" (tragic lyrics about being stuck in a rut with intensity musical patterns). Both suffered misinterpretation among many listeners. "Born in the USA" was actually used as an anthem for the Reagan presidential campaign as a result of misinterpretation. Similarly, Janet Jackson's song, "Together Again," which is essentially a lament about loved ones she lost to HIV/AIDS, made it to the top of the Billboard charts, so it definitely had broad listener appeal. Yet, many listeners misinterpreted it as merely a catchy little love song rather than as a lament about the friends she lost to HIV/AIDS smiling down on her from the heavens.

Sometimes incongruity can successfully persuade listeners to accept a controversial message as legitimate. Collin Raye's "I Think About You," (Schlitz & Seskin, 1995) is an example. The intensity musical patterns draw in listeners to listen to a tragic message about women's oppression. Hence, incongruity can serve to make a potentially controversial message more palatable, drawing in larger audiences and serving to persuade them gradually to accept the validity of an argument.

Incongruent messages can also alter the original meaning of a song. Toad the Wet Sprocket, for example, did a cover of KISS's "Rock and Roll All Nite." They did it slowly, with acoustic instruments, hovering melodically and harmonically around the tonic chord. The

APPLYING **WHAT YOU'VE LEARNED** . . .

Consider a cover you've heard done where the musical style of the cover differed from the original version. How did that affect the meaning of the message?

result transformed the message from one about going out to party all night to one about merely reflecting on the thought of doing so.

Ambiguity and Ascription

Two additional rhetorical strategies that may be used to overcome potential communication barriers in both congruent and incongruent songs are strategic ambiguity and rhetorical ascription. Strategic ambiguity is essentially making a claim using language that avoids specifics. Strategic ambiguity can be used to gradually lead listeners to accept a claim they may, at first, have opposed. Jewel's 1998 song, "Hands," is a good example of strategic ambiguity in a comic congruent interaction. She uses ambiguity to thread in a message that her hands are essentially God's hands:

My hands are small I know;

But they're not yours, they are my own.

But they're not yours, they are my own.

And I am never broken.

We are never broken.

We are God's eyes.

God's hands.

God's mind.

We are God's eyes.

God's hands.

God's heart.

We are God's eyes.

God's hands.

God's eyes.

We are God's hands.

We are God's hands. (Kilcher & Leonard, 1998, track 3)

Similarly, Collin Raye's "I Think About You" is a good example of strategic ambiguity in an incongruent message. His use of strategic ambiguity helps listeners gradually come to realize and accept that his argument challenges hegemony from a radical feminist perspective. He eventually reveals that every "woman on a billboard sign . . . saying 'drink this beer and you'll be mine'" and every "pretty woman walking down the street" who gets ogled by men "like she's some kind of treat," as well as "battered and abused" was and still is "somebody's little girl" and doesn't deserve to be treated in these ways (Schlitz & Seskin, 1995, track 1).

Rhetorical ascription is a term coined by communication scholars Alberto Gonzalez and John Makay (1983) in their article "Rhetorical Ascription and the Gospel According to Dylan." Essentially, music draws in listeners by using lyrical ascription (integrating examples and stories from popular culture to which members of a target audience will likely relate) and musical ascription (imitating a musical sound that appeals to a particular target audience). "Breakfast" by the Newsboys uses both lyrical and musical ascription to draw in its audience (teenagers) of unbelievers while also serving as an anthem for Christian believers. Evangelism is a controversial topic for popular music listeners of any age; however, the inherent rebellious nature of adolescents trying to discover themselves makes it particularly so. Musically, "Breakfast" sounds like any rock anthem one might hear on pop radio. Lyrically, the examples about Cheerios and Captain Crunch, serve to draw in the target audience as they identify with them:

> Hold the milk, put back the sugar.
> They are powerless to console.
> We've gathered here to sprinkle ashes from our late friend's cereal bowl.
> Breakfast clubbers say the motto that he taught us to repeat:
> "You will lose it in your gym class if you wait 'til noon to eat."
> Back when the chess club said our eggs were soft.
> Every Monday he'd say grace and hold our juice aloft.
> Oh, none of us knew his check-out time would come so soon.
> But before his brain stopped waving, he composed this tune:
> WHEN THE TOAST IS BURNED AND ALL THE MILK HAS CHURNED
> AND CAPTAIN CRUNCH IS WAVING FAREWELL,
> WHEN THE BIG ONE FINDS YOU, MAY THIS SONG REMIND YOU
> THAT THEY DON'T SERVE BREAKFAST IN HELL . . .
> Oh, rise up Fruit Loop lovers—sing out sweet and low.
> With spoons held high, we bid our brother, "Cheerio." (Taylor & Fuller,
> 1996, track 5)

So, music can be examined using the illusion of life perspective to understand how music and lyrics interact to convey an argument comprised of both conceptual and emotional content. The critic begins by determining (1) the intensity and release patterns conveyed in the music and (2) the comic and tragic meanings in the lyrics. From there, the critic interprets how they function rhetorically in terms of congruity and incongruity—often embellished by strategic ambiguity or rhetorical ascription. Ultimately, the goal is not to claim music causes feelings but rather to determine what and how such music may be communicating to and for particular audiences.

CONDUCTING AN ILLUSION OF LIFE ANALYSIS

The illusion of life perspective can be used to analyze a song, a series of songs, or even a genre. The following paragraphs detail how to conduct an illusion of life criticism first by selecting a text and examining it and then by offering some sample essays that use it.

Step 1: Selecting an Appropriate Text

In addition to considering the rhetorical situation, your goal in selecting a text ought to be guided by your hunch that more is being said about how or what we ought to believe or behave than a casual listener might realize. You might select one song by an artist or group or an entire album or series of recordings by an artist or group. Or, you might look at a genre of music (e.g., rap, punk, hip-hop) as the genre communicates for a particular group. When selecting your text, it is important to identify its target audience or audiences. Doing so will ultimately help you evaluate its potential implications in your analysis.

APPLYING WHAT YOU'VE LEARNED . . .

Consider a song or musical group that was popular among you and your friends in high school. Did that song or group also appeal to your parents? To your grandparents? Why or why not?

Step 2: Examining the Text (Describe and Interpret)

You should recall that every rhetorical criticism is examined via description, interpretation, and evaluation. When conducting an analysis of music using the illusion of life perspective, begin by describing the predominant intensity and release patterns conveyed in the music and the predominant comic and tragic meanings offered in the lyrics. You might also note whether the comic or tragic lyrics are situated more in the forward-looking and unresolved dramatic illusion or backward-looking and resolved poetic illusion. Your analysis of the lyrics might also be informed by another perspective (e.g., neo-Aristotelian, narrative, dramatistic, symbolic convergence or fantasy theme, neo-Marxist, feminist). Then, interpret whether the interaction between music and lyrics is congruent or incongruent. Finally, evaluate the potential implications of the message ultimately communicated to various audiences.

Begin by describing the lyrics (virtual experience) and the music (virtual time) in isolation. With regard to music, consider whether the musical elements that predominant (e.g., rhythm, phrasing, melody, harmony, instrumentation) represent primarily intensity or release patterns. Does the music seem to represent a fast heart rate (intensity) or slow heart rate (release)? Do the intensity and release patterns shift from intensity to release or vice versa during the song? Do the patterns represent what is typical for a particular artist or genre?

With regard to lyrics, in addition to examining conceptual content, consider emotional stance by discovering whether they are primarily comic (the protagonist determined to beat the odds) or tragic (the protagonist attempting to cope with fate). Then, explore whether the lyrics seem to be set in the forward-looking and unresolved dramatic illusion or backward-looking and resolved poetic illusion. Perhaps this will impact congruity or incongruity. Finally, investigate whether the lyrics employ strategies of strategic ambiguity and/or rhetorical ascription.

Next, interpret whether the interaction is primarily congruent (comic/intensity; tragic/release) or incongruent (comic/release; tragic/intensity) as well as any points at which congruity and incongruity shifts if, in fact, it does. If the interaction is congruent, how might that poignancy affect the message? If the interaction is incongruent, how might that affect the message, particularly on different target populations?

Step 3: Evaluating the Potential Implications of the Text

Ultimately, your goal when conducting an analysis of music as communication is to determine what and how it might be communicating to and for various target audiences. It may serve effectively or ineffectively, for example, as an in-group anthem as a means by which to persuade listeners to accept an argument as legitimate or as a means by which to appeal to broad audiences. What might be some possible implications of these arguments to and for various audiences?

SAMPLE PUBLISHED ESSAYS

(1) Read the article titled, "Music as Persuasion: Refuting Hegemonic Masculinity in 'He Thinks He'll Keep Her,'" which is published in *Women's Studies in Communication* (Sellnow, 1999). The article suggests that the intensity patterns of the music serve to draw in broad audiences as a catchy, foot-tapping tune. The use of strategic ambiguity in the repeated chorus also tames the story in the verses so as not to lose listeners along the way. By the time the song concludes, all listeners hear the point that "she" is better off in the "typing pool at minimum wage" as a subject in her world than at home, underappreciated and treated as an object (feminist perspective). The song was actually based on a Geritol commercial where a man decides to "keep her" because his wife takes Geritol every day. Likening his wife to a fishing trophy must have bothered Mary Chapin Carpenter. The result was a song that successfully drew listeners in to ultimately accept her argument as legitimate.

(2) Read the article titled, "A Rhetorical Analysis of Oppositional Youth Music of the New Millennium," written by Sellnow and Brown and published in the 2004 issue of *The North*

Dakota Journal of Speech and Theatre. The article focuses on the arguments made in Eminem's first two CDs. The article considers how the dynamic interaction between lyrics and music augments arguments about justifiable reasons (motives) for breaking society's rules for living (dramatistic perspective). As you read, consider what casual listeners (regardless of whether they like or dislike Eminem's music) miss when they focus only on the acts performed in each song. As you can see, digging beneath the surface messages to reveal underlying motives can be quite telling. If Eminem's music does speak to and for youth, what do we learn and how might we respond? Do you think these themes pervade modern music still today (e.g., hip-hop, punk, heavy metal)? Why or why not?

SAMPLE STUDENT ESSAY

Wyl McCully uses the illusion of life perspective in his essay "Rhetorical Strategies in Music as a Voice for Social Movements: Creed as a case study." Essentially, he argues that Creed's musical messages about faith and spirituality competed successfully in the mainstream market, in part, through the use of strategic ambiguity in the lyrics and musical ascription in the music. He goes on to illustrate what those messages are, that is, starting with lyrics that typify what the target audience listens to (backward-looking, tragic messages without hope). Then, song after song and album after album, the message shifts to that of faith and hope through spirituality. Whether or not doing so was Creed's intent, Wyl makes a compelling case that the music does, in fact, pervasively purport them.

Rhetorical Strategies in Music as a Voice for Social Movements: Creed as a Case Study

Wyl McCully

In the halls of a drug rehabilitation clinic, a recovering addict relaxes while the sounds of minor chords fill his ears with musical distortions and deafening volumes. Just a few miles away at the city arena, thousands of screaming teenagers throw themselves together in a sort of mosh pit at the front of the stage. The lead singer stands before them dressed in dark clothes, making vaguely religious motions and barking lyrics into the microphone. This is a typical scene that can be found in thousands of cities across the country.

There is an allure to music. It is one of the largest industries in our nation as well as in the world. One thing that makes music interesting to rhetorical scholars is its use of both lyrics and music to communicate and persuade. Chesebro Davis, Nachman, and Yanelli (1985) describe music as a form that is essential in communicating our human experiences. Since the 1980s, Christian musicians have been making a concerted effort to find a market for themselves. Some Christian contemporary music (CCM) artists have claimed their music to be a form of ministry, where lyrics

(Continued)

(Continued)

communicate evangelical ideas (Romanowski, 1992). Keith Green, for example, chose the CCM market because he believes he can best communicate his message when aligned with a Christian label (Dueck, 2000).

Unfortunately, music as persuasion often functions only as in-group messages within subcultures comprised of people who believe the same thing (Stewart, Smith, & Denton, 1994). Essentially, music functions primarily as a unifying force for those within the subculture (Chesebro et al., 1985). CCM is a perfect example. Reid (1993), for example, found that many teens use CCM instead of secular music to uplift themselves in times of trouble. Furthermore, Reid discovered eight main themes in CCM that relate directly to the Christian faith and concludes that many secular listeners are turned off as a result.

An interesting new trend seems to be occurring, however, in recent years. That is, contemporary Christian musicians are signing with secular labels. Contemporary Christian artist Toby McKeehan of DC Talk, for example, signed with Virgin records. He contends that Christian music is a joke if it doesn't reach people who are not Christians (Fiermann & Flynn, 1999).

Creed is a band that has earned much success in the secular popular music industry. For example, their first two albums sold more than 15 million copies and followed with a third album that sold more than 4 million copies in just over 2 months (Heath, 2002). They earned awards such as Billboard's Rock Artist of the Year (Jenkins, 1999). However, their success has been met with a significant amount of controversy from both Christian audiences and secular music critics. Heath (2002) quotes Stapp, Creed's lead singer, as saying, "There's just people who don't want anything positive to come out of this world" (p. 28). Stapp is referring to the use of positive lyrics in almost all of their songs. This strategy is ultimately the same one that contemporary Christian artists use (Reid, 1993). Hence, when Creed's music was released, Christian listeners claimed Creed to be a Christian band (i.e., Dueck, 2000; Romanowski, 1992). Members of Creed, however, replied that they are Christians, but they aren't attempting to force any Christian agenda on people (Gardner, 2001).

This analysis seeks to understand what messages Creed sends in their music and how. In other words, what messages about spirituality are conveyed in Creed's music? What rhetorical strategies are employed to communicate those messages to secular audiences?

THE ILLUSION OF LIFE

To investigate this, Sellnow and Sellnow's (2001) illusion of life rhetorical perspective was used to examine the songs on all three of Creed's albums. Essentially, Sellnow and Sellnow (2001) argue that music communicates through the dynamic interaction between virtual experience (lyrics) and virtual time (music). Although the critic begins by examining each aspect alone, it is only by determining congruity or incongruity between the two elements together that one ascertains rhetorical meaning.

More specifically, virtual experience may be set in the forward-looking dramatic illusion or backward-looking poetic illusion. Within either illusion, the content is likely to be either primarily comic (an optimistic message about the protagonist beating the odds) or tragic (a pessimistic message about the protagonist coping with fate). Virtual time represents patterns of intensity and release as they convey emotions of human living. These patterns can be examined according to rhythm, melody, harmony, phrasing, and instrumentation. Ultimately, lyrics and music that are congruent reinforce each other, making the holistic message poignant for listeners. Conversely, incongruent lyrics and music transform the message from what might be ascertained via an analysis of lyrics or music alone. Finally, ambiguity in either lyrics or music can make controversial messages more palatable to broad audiences, including listeners who may not ascribe to the ideology of the movement (Sellnow, 1999; Sellnow & Sellnow, 2001).

This analysis extends the work of Sellnow and Sellnow to include concepts of rhetorical ascription (musical and lyrical) as they function to further couch controversial messages for broad audiences (Gonzalez & Makay, 1983). That is, contemporary Christian messages can be couched in lyrical themes around which target audiences may identify. Likewise, they might be couched in musical styles and sounds that are likely to draw in listeners of particular target audiences.

ANALYSIS

To examine each song on the three Creed CDs, I begin with an explanation of the intensity and release patterns offered in the music as they function rhetorically to draw listeners in and to convey emotions. Then I articulate what themes are being conveyed lyrically and how they are conveyed in terms of the elements of virtual experience. Finally, I consider the dynamic interaction between lyrics and music as they work together to communicate via congruity or incongruity.

Virtual Time (Intensity and Release Patterns in Creed's Music)

The most obvious pattern associated with intensity and release patterns is that every album begins with an explosion of sound. The next few songs are very intense and do not seem to resolve the tension that they suggest. By the end of each album, however, the band makes a transition to a release pattern (see Table 1). The songs seems to be more rooted in major keys and use a lot less distorted guitar. However, there is also a pattern that arises. That is, from the first album to the last, there is a transition from very intense music to music that is much more representative of release.

■ **TABLE 1**   Intensity/Release

My Own Prison

	Intensity	Release	Both	Notes
"Torn"	X			
"Ode"	X			
"My Own Prison"	X			
"Pity for a Dime"		X		Becomes intense at end

(Continued)

(Continued)

	Intensity	Release	Both	Notes
"In America"	X			
"Illusion"	X			
"Unforgiven"	X			
"Sister"	X			
"What's This Life For"		X		
"One"		X		

Human Clay

	Intensity	Release	Both	Notes
"Are You Ready"	X			
"What If"	X			
"Beautiful"			X	Release in verse, intense chorus
"Say I"		X		Release until end, then explodes
"Wrong Way"			X	Soft verse, intense chorus
"Faceless Man"			X	Builds through to end
"Never Die"		X		Release until end, then explodes
"With Arms Wide Open"			X	
"Higher"			X	
"Wash Away Those Years"			X	
"Inside Us All"			X	

Weathered

	Intensity	Release	Both	Notes
"Bullets"	X			
"Freedom Fighter"	X			
"Who's Got My Back"		X		Builds at end only
"Signs"	X			
"One Last Breath"		X		
"My Sacrifice"		X		
"Stand Here With Me"		X		

	Intensity	Release	Both	Notes
"Weathered"	X			
"Hide"		X		
"Don't Stop Dancing"		X		Becomes intense at end
"Lullaby"		X		

My Own Prison begins with "Torn." This is an intense song rooted in a minor key and accented with highly distorted guitars. This is characteristic of most of the songs on this album. However, the last two songs make a complete departure from this and suggest their messages using major chords that seem to leave the album with a feeling of resolution.

Human Clay begins in the same intense, minor key with the same distortion on the guitar as *My Own Prison*. However, this album provides more examples of songs that lie on the border of intensity and release. For example, "Say I" seems to possess two distinct forms. In the chorus, the music is slow, relaxing, and in a major key. When the chorus arrives, the score builds into an intense, minor exclamation. However, there is a return to the calm, major key when the chorus is over. A second example is the song "Faceless Man." Here, the score begins with a release pattern but builds evenly through to the end when it erupts.

Weathered is the next step in this pattern. Whereas *My Own Prison* was primarily intensity and *Human Clay* seems to ride the middle, *Weathered* is made up of mostly release patterns. It does, however, begin with an explosion of intense sound. This is quickly brought under control to a much less uncomfortable feel. This album also provides an anomaly in Creed's music. However, the location makes it seem more

like a logical step. The song "Lullaby" is a calm, quiet song that is completely acoustic with no intense build at any point. This is the only song that Creed produced that has this sound.

Virtual Experience (Lyrical Messages in Creed's Music)

In contrast to the explosive, painful sounds that characterize the score on each of Creed's albums, the lyrics provide the listener with hope. Moreover, this hope is most frequently found in faith in a higher power. Each song tends to follow the same pattern of a hopeless beginning that quickly develops into an optimistic outlook that leads the main character toward a hopeful future. To investigate the virtual experience, the lyrics are analyzed for three things: first, the amount of ambiguity used by Creed in their lyrics; second, whether the rhythm is comic (optimistic) or tragic (pessimistic); and third, the lyrics are analyzed for poetic (backward-looking) or dramatic (forward-looking) illusions.

Spiritual Themes Conveyed

The most frequently conveyed theme throughout the three albums is a need for spirituality. Creed communicates that the world is without the light

(Continued)

(Continued)

of some sort of higher being. The themes also follow a pattern. In the first album, there is a lot of anger and hatred toward God. This anger cools off and becomes a much deeper desire for the love of a higher power by the last album. The second album provides a sort of segue into the desire by examining the world's situation and finding a deep need for a spiritual side. The lyrics that communicate these messages have two powerful meanings. First, they are, on the surface, simple lyrics that discuss concepts that most people are familiar with and allow the listener to make an interpretation based on their life experiences. The second meaning goes much deeper into the communication with the audience and presents distinctly Christian themes disguised in terms of Christian code. However, those not familiar with the code hear strangely ambiguous lyrics that do not seem to promote any one religion over another.

Ambiguity in Themes

This analysis provided the most obvious pattern results. There are three specific patterns that arise in analyzing the ambiguity employed in Creed's lyrics. First, the amount of ambiguity on each album increased from the first to the last. Second, the variety of themes addressed in the music decreased in each latter album. Third, the order in which the messages are communicated becomes much more organized. There is one concept that ties all the albums together. Throughout each one, the ambiguity in each of the songs is tied to a religious theme or message.

My Own Prison offers a sample of the spiritual ideas that Creed is willing to communicate to their audience. This album contains the most thematic variety out of the three of them. The themes are also more precise; for example,

"Sister" is a song blatantly about child neglect. This album also sets up the use of ambiguity to communicate religious themes. Most of the religious themes use biblical references that are not as well known by people who are outside of the Christian faith. "A lion roars in the darkness/Only he holds the key." This is a reference to a verse in Revelation suggesting Christ as "The Lion of the Tribe of Judah." The last song on this album begins a trend that is repeated throughout the rest of the albums. The last song deals with the subject of world peace and does it very blatantly.

Human Clay lessens the amount of blatant songs and adds to the ambiguity that Creed employs throughout their music. There is also a shift in the location of the ambiguity. That is, the album begins with ambiguous content that is collected at the beginning of the album. The first song, "Are You Ready," is a perfect example of the ambiguity that Stapp provides throughout the rest of the album. "Don't want to follow/Down roads been walked before," never making mention to exactly what the roads are or where they head. The end of the album is a collection of blatant themes, including the last song, "Inside Us All," about world peace, just like the first album.

The last album, *Weathered,* provides almost a complete removal from blatant themes. It becomes more evident that Creed is communicating about spirituality but does not advocate one specific belief system. "Signs" is an excellent example of this occurrence. Here, Stapp explains to the audience that his lyrics are not about a number of things. All he asks is "Can you see the signs?" It is difficult to comprehend his thoughts as he does not mention what signs we should be seeing. This album is not, however, without some blatant themes that resurrect themselves from the first two. "Don't Stop Dancing" is a powerful song that simply discusses the struggle that we all have to get through life. The final song follows the pattern of the previous two albums in that it is obviously about world peace.

■ **TABLE 2**   Themes and Ambiguity

My Own Prison

	Theme	*Ambiguous*	*Blatant*
"Torn"	Anger at God/struggling through life	X	
"Ode"	Need for spirituality	X	
"My Own Prison"	Anger toward organized religion	X	
"Pity for a Dime"	Apathy toward the world situation		X
"In America"	Questioning America's values		X
"Illusion"	Reality of life		X
"Unforgiven"	Anger toward organized religion	X	
"Sister"	Child neglect		X
"What's This Life For"	Suicide	X	
"One"	World peace		

Human Clay

	Theme	*Ambiguous*	*Blatant*
"Are You Ready"	Seeking knowledge	X	
"What If"	Spiritual ignorance	X	
"Beautiful"	Definition of beauty	X	
"Say I"	Lack of spirituality	X	
"Wrong Way"	Questioning truth	X	
"Faceless Man"	Lack of spirituality	X	
"Never Die"	Staying young		X
"With Arms Wide Open"	Bringing child into world	X	
"Higher"	World peace		X
"Wash Away Those Years"	Domestic violence		X
"Inside Us All"	Seeking inner peace		X

(Continued)

(Continued)

Weathered

	Theme	Release	Both
"Bullets"	Desire to be ignorant	X	
"Freedom Fighter"	Fighting for spirituality	X	
"Who's Got My Back"	Increase of ignorance	X	
"Signs"	Need for spirituality	X	
"One Last Breath"	Suicide	X	
"My Sacrifice"	Friendship	X	
"Stand Here With Me"	Friendship	X	
"Weathered"	Need for spirituality	X	
"Hide"	Friendship/staying young	X	
"Don't Stop Dancing"	Struggling through life		X
"Lullaby"	Living a loving life		X

Comic and Tragic Rhythms

There seems to be no change in pattern from album to album in regards to comic and tragic messages. However, each album does follow the same pattern within itself. That is, each album tends to begin with tragic themes and makes a movement into comic ideas. One interesting observation is that two of the three albums provide examples of songs that are both comic and tragic. What makes these two songs interesting is that, when they discuss the past, they carry a tragic tone. But when the eye turns toward the future, the voice turns optimistic and therefore comic in tone.

My Own Prison contains one of these examples. "Unforgiven" claims that the protagonist thinks he's "unforgiven to this world." However, at the end of the song, the protagonist has changed his opinion: "The gold was put to flame/To kill, to burn, to mold its purity." The other songs on this album seem to choose one form. But, like the other albums, *My Own Prison* begins with a pessimistic view: "The peace is dead in my soul." Near the end of the album, there is an obvious shift in opinion. At the end of the album, the band sends the message "[I] Want to ch ange the world. . . . Don't try to change my mind." Many of the songs in the middle of the album follow this pattern.

Human Clay is similar in pattern to *My Own Prison,* in that, overall, the messages begin pessimistic and change in tone to a positive feel at the end. It is interesting to note that the first song on this album begins comic: "If you keep seeking, you will find." The next song begins the pattern by proclaiming, "I know I can't hold the hate inside my mind." However, by the end of the album, the tone has changed to optimism. "There's a peace inside us all. . . . Oh, can't it be your friend."

Weathered continues this pattern by loudly exclaiming, "At least look at me when you shoot a bullet through my head." This album quickly changes in tone to an optimistic outlook. It is interesting to note that the song where the change in tone takes place deals with suicide. The message of the song claims that life is difficult, but there is someone who will "hold me now/I'm six feet from the edge . . ." This final album closes out with a lullaby and asks "just give love to all/Lets give love to all."

■ **TABLE 3** Comic/Tragic

My Own Prison

	Comic	Tragic	Both	Notes
"Torn"		X		
"Ode"		X		
"My Own Prison"		X		
"Pity for a Dime"		X		
"In America"	X			
"Illusion"	X			
"Unforgiven"			X	Negative, pain of past, positive end
"Sister"			X	Negative until end, opportunity to change
"What's This Life For"	X			
"One"	X			

Human Clay

	Comic	Tragic	Both	Notes
"Are You Ready"	X			
"What If"			X	More questioning, not an outlook
"Beautiful"		X		
"Say I"		X		
"Wrong Way"			X	Personal pessimist, others optimist
"Faceless Man"	X			

(Continued)

(Continued)

"Never Die"	X			
"With Arms Wide Open"	X			
"Higher"	X			
"Wash Away Those Years"		X		
"Inside Us All"	X			

Weathered

	Comic	Tragic	Both	Notes
"Bullets"		X		
"Freedom Fighter"		X		
"Who's Got My Back"			X	Negative past, hope for future
"Signs"		X		
"One Last Breath"	X			
"My Sacrifice"	X			
"Stand Here With Me"	X			
"Weathered"	X			
"Hide"	X			
"Don't Stop Dancing"	X			
"Lullaby"	X			

Poetic and Dramatic Illusions

Although there is no immediate pattern that appears throughout the three albums, there is a shift that occurs between the first and second albums. The third album does not continue this shift but rather echoes the style of the second. The first album is evenly distributed between forward- and backward-looking themes. The second album makes a shift to much more dramatic themes that look forward to the future. The third album is similar to the second in that it looks more toward the future.

My Own Prison opens by declaring "the peace is dead in my soul." It spends the first four songs wavering between poetic and dramatic. Then the shift happens. Two songs look back in an attempt to decide the future that the protagonist will choose. "In America" suggests that there is a problem with our American culture, but it concludes by suggesting that "No one's right and no one's wrong/In America." Then, "Illusion" grumbles about how depressing life currently is and ends by reminding the listener that "Life still goes on," looking forward. The album comes to a close by declaring that "the only way is one."

Human Clay exemplifies the shift that Creed underwent. They begin the album looking into the future: "Count down to the change in life that's soon to come." It's followed by a second dramatic song and then into songs not unlike the songs falling into both categories on *My Own Prison.* These songs seem to break into two parts. For example, "Human Clay," the title track, begins with a story: "The dust has finally settled on the field of human clay." When the song reaches the chorus, it looks forward: "We'll surely melt in the rain." The album then becomes, generally, dramatic and ends looking into the future: "There's a peace inside us all / . . . / It will help you carry on."

Weathered is similar in structure to *Human Clay.* It begins looking forward, "Hey, I want what's real." The album follows this dramatic outlook until the middle, where there are three songs that look backward. The first two songs seem to be about the loss of a friend. "My Sacrifice" states, "Hello, my friend, we meet again" but then goes on to remember what life has been. "We've seen our share of ups and downs." "Weathered" is a lamentation about the mistakes that the protagonist has made. After these songs, there is a return to dramatic themes. The album ends with two really powerful songs that are both uncharacteristic of Creed. "Children Don't Stop Dancing" tells the audience to do just that, keep dancing and "Believe you can fly away." The last song tells listeners that "everything will be all right."

■ **TABLE 4**   Poetic/Dramatic

My Own Prison

	Poetic	Dramatic	Both	Notes
"Torn"	X			
"Ode"		X		
"My Own Prison"	X			
"Pity for a Dime"		X		
"In America"			X	Looks back to decide future
"Illusion"			X	Looks back to decide future
"Unforgiven"	X			
"Sister"	X			
"What's This Life For"		X		
"One"		X		

(Continued)

(Continued)

Human Clay

	Poetic	Dramatic	Both	Notes
"Are You Ready"		X		
"What If"		X		
"Beautiful"			X	Current until end, then future
"Say I"			X	Verses back, chorus forward
"Wrong Way"			X	Personal back, others forward
"Faceless Man"	X			
"Never Die"		X		
"With Arms Wide Open"		X		
"Higher"		X		
"Wash Away Those Years"	X			
"Inside Us All"		X		

Weathered

	Poetic	Dramatic	Both	Notes
"Bullets"		X		
"Freedom Fighter"		X		
"Who's Got My Back"			X	Back in despair, forward in hope
"Signs"		X		
"One Last Breath"		X		
"My Sacrifice"	X			
"Stand Here With Me"	X			
"Weathered"	X			
"Hide"		X		
"Don't Stop Dancing"		X		
"Lullaby"		X		

Interaction

Creed offers us an unmistakable experience that is created through virtual experience and virtual time. A listener experiencing only the music (virtual time) notices only the intense tone of the music. The minor keys and forceful tempos and feelings seem to flood the audience with negativity. But this is not the complete picture. Creed provides the listener with an escape from the morbid, depressing emotions that flood the world. The virtual experience that is provided through the music seems to mimic every emotion that humans feel in their daily lives. The listener is provided with conflicting emotions. The music screams an angry tone into the ears but is met with an optimistic message that claims to free the listener from the pain felt through the score. This pattern is almost identical throughout all three albums. The biggest difference between the three is that the music becomes progressively more mellow. Less distortion is used, and the open fifths and minor keys are replaced by complete triads of major chords.

CONCLUSIONS

There is one main message that Creed employs throughout all of their music: They are trying to communicate that the world needs some sort of spirituality. They do not offer any sort of advocacy about which religion is the most correct they instead leave that up to ambiguity. Or, as Stapp explains on his website, there is no agenda; the music is left up to the listeners to be interpreted the way that they want. This message is further narrowed down to the idea that the world is in trouble, that things are not so great right now, but there is hope. Stapp seems to claim that the first message of spirituality is the cure for the problems of the world.

The former seems like a way to avoid the dilemma of the stigma placed on CCM artists. It is a way for the members of Creed to continue their artistry and not be censored like the bands in the CCM market are (Dueck, 2000). In this case, the songs that discuss spirituality tend to be much more ambiguous in their messages; they leave out who the "higher power" is and leave that up to the listener. What's more, the theme of spirituality bleeds into this thought that there is hope for a world in trouble. Even the songs that communicate the pain of life end with some sort of uplifting lyric, even if it is only the last line, like in the song "Sister," where Stapp delivers a painful story of a daughter who was abandoned by the family. In this case, he ends by telling the main character to "change."

The music of Creed is very much founded on the angry sounds of popular hard rock bands like Stone Temple Pilots. The vocals mimic those of teen angst bands like Pearl Jam and Nirvana. All of these bands have been very successful, even to the point of beginning a new trend in music. It seems that Creed has been able to take this well-accepted musical sound and hide the message of hope in it. The messages Creed employs are actually similar to those used by most popular hard rock bands, but their message takes one step further; they claim that there is a way to change the world. This supports the study done in Sellnow (1999) with the music written by Mary Chapin Carpenter. However, the research here goes one step forward. That is, while the message is couched in a format that is easy for popular audiences to swallow, there is another strategy employed by Creed to communicate to a larger audience.

By examining the amount of ambiguity in the lyrics, the data support the idea that audiences are more willing to accept a controversial message if it is not presented as the only option. Furthermore, it is important to note that, while the music does not immediately follow the

(Continued)

(Continued)

same concept of CCM, that "uplifts respondents in times of trouble" (Reid, 1993), it does seem to provide an uplifting tone at the end of many of its songs. This pattern is not only evident within the songs themselves but throughout the entire album. All of them begin with some sort of negative emotion and intense feelings but soon develop, as if telling a story, into a positive outlook on the world's situation. This is the second strategy that Creed employs to communicate the messages of spirituality.

The data from this project seem to support the theory that music exists in both virtual experience and virtual time and that it is the real experience of both of these working together where music communicates. In the case of Creed, the music is very depressing but is redeemed by the use of positive lyrics. This is also another example of a message that can be difficult for mainstream masses to accept, but it is couched in a style of music that is very easy to hear because it is similar in style to many popular bands. However, this study adds the element of ambiguity. It is suggested that lyrics cannot simply be hidden in acceptable music. There must also be some sort of ambiguity that communicates at two different levels. First of all, there must be some blatant communication to the subgroup or the "preaching to the choir" idea, but these messages must be in the subculture's code to appeal to a broader audience.

There are two specific areas where research could be done to continue this investigation. First, the music previously examined by the illusion of life perspective can be revisited while applying this table of ambiguity and themes to find any use of ambiguity that may make the message easier to swallow. Second, the religious implications of this could be further investigated—that is,

using this theory and applying it to other bands that have either claimed to be Christian or have been claimed by audiences as Christian. For example, POD has released a number of popular songs in the mainstream that have messages that border on blatant religious themes. Other bands like this could be investigated for ambiguity and the style of the music.

References

Chesebro, J. W., Davis, F. A., Nachman, J. E., & Yanelli, A. (1985). Popular music as a mode of communication. *Critical Studies in Mass Communication, 2,* 115–135.

Dueck, J. (2000). Crossing the street: Velour 100 and Christian rock. *Popular Music and Society, 24,* 127–149.

Fierman, D., & Flynn, G. (1999, December 3). Christian entertainment: The greatest story ever told. *Entertainment Weekly,* 54–60.

Gardner, E. (2001, November 27). Creed stays the course. *USA Today,* p. 1D.

Gonzalez, A., & Makay, J. (1983). Rhetorical ascription and the gospel according to Dylan. *The Quarterly Journal of Speech, 69,* 1–14.

Heath, C. (2002, February 28). Creed's "Stairway to Heaven." *Rolling Stone,* 35–40, 70.

Jenkins, M. (1999, September 28). Creed's true calling; Band says it's not about rock, not religion. *The New York Post,* p. C01.

Reid, J. E. (1993). The use of Christian music by youth group members. *Popular Music and Society, 17,* 33–46.

Romanowski, W. D. (1992). Roll over Beethoven, tell Martin Luther the news: American evangelicals and rock music. *Journal of American Culture, 15,* 79–89.

Sellnow, D. (1999). Music as persuasion: Refuting hegemonic masculinity in "He Thinks He'll Keep Her." *Women's Studies in Communication, 22,* 66–81.

Sellnow, D., & Sellnow, T. (2001). The illusion of life rhetorical perspective: An integrated approach to the study of music as communication. *Critical Studies in Media Communication, 18,* 395–415.

Stewart, C. J., Smith, C. A., & Denton, R. E., Jr. (1994). *Persuasion and social movements.* Prospect Heights, IL: Waveland Press.

Summary

This chapter outlined the guidelines by which to conduct an analysis of music using the illusion of life rhetorical perspective. We began by articulating how music functions as communication for individuals and for groups. Then, we discussed the illusion of life perspective as a means by which to examine how music and lyrics function together to communicate and persuade. Then we laid out the steps for examining musical texts using the illusion of life perspective. Finally, we shared sample essays that use the illusion of life to examine music as rhetoric.

Challenge

Examine the song, "Last Resort" by Papa Roach using the illusion of life method.

1. What does the song say about justifiable reasons for cutting one's self or even for suicide? Use the tools of the dramatistic perspective from Chapter 4 to help you examine conceptual content.

2. Does the music convey primarily intensity or release patterns, and how does this influence the argument?

3. Are the lyrics comic or tragic? Are they set in a poetic or dramatic illusion? How does this impact the argument?

4. How might this song speak to and for listeners?

5. How can examining such music help one understand those who identify with it and why they do so?

References

Aldridge, H., & Carlin, D. (1993). The rap on violence: A rhetorical analysis of rapper KRS-One. *Communication Studies, 44,* 102–116.

Balaji, M. (2012). The construction of "street credibility" in Atlanta's hip-hop music scene: Analyzing the role of cultural gatekeepers. *Critical Studies in Media Communication, 29*(4), 313–330.

Beck, C. S. (1993). Loser. [Single]. Los Angeles, CA: Bong Load Custom Records.

Bloodworth, J. (1975). Communication in the youth counter culture: Music as expression. *Central States Speech Journal, 26,* 304–309.

Booth, M. (1976). The art of words in songs. *Quarterly Journal of Speech, 62,* 243–249.

Brooks, M., & Peiken, S. (1997). Bitch. [Recorded by Meredith Brooks]. *Blurring the Edges.* [CD]. Hollywood, CA: Capitol Records.

Chesebro, J. W., Davis, F. A., Nachman, J. E., & Yanelli, A. (1985). Popular music as a mode of communication. *Critical Studies in Mass Communication, 2,* 115–135.

Clapton, E. (1992). Tears in heaven. [Recorded by Eric Clapton]. *Eric Clapton Unplugged.*. New York: Reprise Records.

Davies, S. (1980). The expression of emotion in music. *Mind, 89,* 67–86.

Dewey, J. (1934). *Art as experience.* New York: Minton, Balch, & Company.

Francesconi, R. (1986). Free jazz and black nationalism: A rhetoric of musical style. *Critical Studies in Mass Communication, 3,* 36–49.

Geldof, B., & Ure, M. (1984). "Do they know it's Christmas?" [Single]. London: Phonogram.

Goffin, G., & King, C. (1967). Pleasant valley Sunday. [Recorded by The Monkees]. *Pleasant Valley Sunday.* [Single record version]. Hollywood, CA: RCA Victor Studios.

Gonzalez, A., & Makay, J. (1983). Rhetorical ascription and the gospel according to Dylan. *Quarterly Journal of Speech, 69,* 1–14.

Grammer, R., & Grammer, K. (1986). Say hi. [Recorded by Red Grammer]. *Teaching Peace.* Nashville, TN: Rednote Records.

Grossberg, L. (1986). Is there rock after punk? *Critical Studies in Mass Communication, 3,* 50–74.

Hess, M. (2006). Hip-hop realness and the white performer. *Critical Studies in Media Communication, 22*(5), 372–389.

Holmberg, C. B. (1985). Toward the rhetoric of music: Dixie. *Southern Communication Journal, 51*(1), 71–82.

Irvine, J., & Kirkpatrick, W. (1972). The musical form in rhetorical exchange: Theoretical considerations. *Quarterly Journal of Speech, 58,* 272–284.

Jackson, M., & Ritchie, L. (1985). "Feed the World." [Single]. Los Angeles, CA: Columbia.

Jones, S. C., & Schumacher, T. G. (1992). Muzak: On functional music and power. *Critical Studies in Media Communication, 9*(2), 156–169.

Kilcher, J., & Leonard, P. (1998). Hands. [Recorded by Jewel Kilcher]. *Spirit.* [CD]. Atlantic City, NJ: Atlantic Recording.

Kivy, P. (1995). *Authenticities: Philosophical reflections of musical performance.* Ithaca, NY: Cornell University Press.

Knupp, R. (1981). A time for every purpose under heaven: Rhetorical dimensions of protest music. *Southern Speech Communication Journal, 46,* 377–389.

Langer, S. (1953). *Feeling and form.* New York: Charles Scribner's Sons.

Langer, S. (1957). *Philosophy in a new key* (3rd ed.). Cambridge, MA: Harvard University Press.

LeCoat, G. (1976). Music and the three appeals of classical rhetoric. *Quarterly Journal of Speech, 62,* 157–166.

Lewis, G. (1976). Country music lyrics. *Journal of Communication, 26,* 37–40.

Manson, M. (2002). Interview. In M. Moore. [Director]. *Bowling for Columbine.* United States: United Artists.

McLaughlin, T. (1970). *Music and communication.* London: Faber.

Morris, D. (2011). Hick-hop hooray? "Honky Tonk Badankadonk," musical genre, and the misrecognitions of hybridity. *Critical Studies in Media Communication, 28*(5), 466–488.

Perren, F., & Fekaris, D. (1978). I will survive. [Recorded by Gloria Gaynor]. [Single]. Studio City, CA: Mom and Pops Records.

Phillipov, M. (2012). In defense of textual analysis: Resisting methodological hegemony in media and cultural studies. *Critical Studies in Media Communication, 29,* 1–15.

Rasmussen, K. (1994). Transcendence in Leonard Bernstein's kaddish symphony. *Quarterly Journal of Speech, 80,* 150–173.

Rein, I. J., & Springer, C. M. (1986). Where's the music? The problems of lyric analysis. *Critical Studies in Media Communication, 3*(2), 252–256.

Rohlfing, M. E. (1996). "Don't say nothin' bad about my baby": A re-evaluation of women's roles in the Brill building era of early rock 'n' roll. *Critical Studies in Media Communication, 13*(2), 93–114.

Root, R., Jr. (1986). A listener's guide to the rhetoric of popular music. *Journal of Popular Culture,* 15–26.

Roth, L. (1981). Folk song lyrics as communication in John Ford's films. *Southern Speech Communication Journal, 46,* 390–396.

Schlitz, D., & Seskin, S. (1995). I think about you. [Recorded by Collin Raye]. *I Think About You.* [CD]. New York: Sony Music Entertainment.

Sellnow, D. (1994). Music as a unifying social force for neo-Nazi skinheads: Skrewdriver's *White Ryder* as a case study. Paper presented at the annual conference of the Speech Communication Association, New Orleans, LA, November 19–22, 1994.

Sellnow, D. (1999). Music as persuasion: Refuting hegemonic masculinity in "He Thinks He'll Keep Her." *Women's Studies in Communication, 22,* 66–81.

Sellnow, D., & Brown, A. (2004). A rhetorical analysis of oppositional youth music in the new millennium. *North Dakota Journal of Speech and Theatre, 17,* 19–36.

Sellnow, T. L., & Sellnow, D. D. (1990). The appeal of the tragic rhythm: Bruce Springsteen as a case study. *Speaker and Gavel, 27,* 38–49.

Sellnow, D., & Sellnow, T. (2001). The illusion of life rhetorical perspective: An integrated approach to the study of music as communication. *Critical Studies in Media Communication, 18,* 395–415.

Smith, S. (1980). Sounds of the south: The rhetorical saga of country music lyrics. *Southern Speech Communication Journal, 45,* 164–172.

Springsteen, B. (1994). Streets of Philadelphia. [Recorded by Bruce Springsteen]. *Streets of Philadelphia.* [CD]. New York: Columbia Records.

Stanley, P., & Simmons, G. (1975). Rock and roll all nite. [Recorded by KISS]. *Alive.* [Album]. Casablanca Records.

Stewart, C., Smith, C., & Denton, R., Jr. (2001). *Persuasion and social movements* (4th ed.). Prospect Heights, IL: Waveland Press.

Stravinsky, I. (1962). *Expositions and developments.* New York: Doubleday.

Taylor, S., & Furler, P. (1996) Breakfast. [Recorded by the Newsboys]. *Take Me to Your Leader.* Brentwood, TN: Star Song Communications.

van Dick, J. (2006). Record and hold: Popular music between personal and collective memory. *Critical Studies in Media Communication, 23*(5), 357–374.

Weisman, E. (1985). The good man singing well: Stevie Wonder as noble lover. *Critical Studies in Mass Communication, 2,* 136–151.

Student Study Site

Visit the Student Study Site at **www.sagepub.com/sellnow2e** to read interesting SAGE journal articles, view mobile-friendly key term flashcards, take chapter-specific online web quizzes to test your knowledge, and more!

Chapter 9

Visual Perspectives

Just as music pervades our daily lives so, too, do visual images and objects. And just as musical arguments are conveyed via nondiscursive symbols so, too, do visual arguments influence our "thinking and behavior through the strategic use of [nondiscursive] symbols" (Ehninger, 1972, p. 3). And again, as with music, developing the ability to critically examine arguments embedded in visuals is vital because "they are an important means through which social life happens" (Rose, 2007, p. xiii).

Any number of rhetorical perspectives including those we have already discussed in this book (e.g., neo-Aristotelian, narrative, dramatistic, symbolic convergence, neo-Marxist, feminist) can be employed to understand the arguments communicated in visuals. Thus, as with music, many scholars have published analyses of visual texts using any number of viable rhetorical perspectives (e.g., Barnhurst, Vari, & Rodriguez, 2004; Berger, 1989; Blair, 1996; Calafell & Delgado, 2004; Demo, 2007; Finnegan, 2001, 2003; Foss, 1988; Goodings, 2012; Hariman & Lucaites, 2002; Kimble & Olson, 2006; Olson, 2007; O'Neil, 1991; Shugart, 2003; Walker & Chaplin, 1997). Finally, entire academic journals, books, courses, and degree programs exist that focus solely on visual rhetoric. So this chapter addresses only the tip of the iceberg, so to speak.

As we did with musical rhetoric, we must first distinguish visual communication and rhetoric from visual art aesthetics. **Visual art aesthetics** is devoted to the creation and appreciation of art. Within this paradigm, visual images and objects are judged for beauty based on taste and genre conventions. **Visual communication,** on the other hand, focuses on how images and objects convey meaning. And **visual rhetoric** focuses even more specifically on how visuals communicate meanings that reinforce or challenge taken-for-granted ideological beliefs and behaviors. Thus, although visual art critics and visual rhetorical critics might examine the same image or object (e.g., painting, sculpture, photograph), their reasons for and goals in doing so may be quite different.

With these distinctions in mind, let us turn to a brief discussion of the history and nature of visual communication followed by an explanation of three theoretical perspectives that ground our understanding of it. Then, we focus specifically on one perspective—visual pleasure theory—as it can be used to examine visual arguments conveyed in mediated popular culture texts. Finally, we provide some sample published and student essays.

HISTORY AND NATURE OF VISUAL COMMUNICATION

Historians have traced the human use of visuals to around 9000 BC when ancient civilizations around the world used pictograms—pictures that resemble what they signify—and ideograms—pictures that resemble ideas—as a primary means of communication (e.g., Haring & Kaper, 2009). Given its long history as communication, however, the formal academic study of visual communication and rhetoric is fairly new. Some early pioneers include, among others, Charles Sanders Peirce (1839–1914), Ferdinand de Saussure (1857–1913), Charles Morris (1901–1979), and Roland Barthes (1915–1980).

In recent years, the central role visuals play in both reflecting and shaping beliefs and behaviors has grown exponentially. Scholars have coined the term visual culture to denote the countless ways in which visuals are inextricably embedded in social life. As a result of this ever-increasing saturation of visual images in day-to-day life, visual rhetoric is quickly becoming a primary means by which we make sense of the world around us (e.g., Debord, 1977; Hall, 1997; Jay, 1993; Jenks, 1995; Olson, 2007; Mirzoeff, 1999; Virilio, 1994). Consequently, visual literacy—the set of skills required to "effectively find, interpret, evaluate, use, and create images and visual media"—is now even a core competency standard in higher education (Hattwig, Burgess, Bussert, & Medaille, 2011).

Visual images and objects operate using a visual language, which consists of form-related usage rules related to things such as color, layout, texture, sequencing, imagery, style, as well as in some cases animation and sound. As our focus is on mediated popular culture texts, we frame our discussion on visual language elements represented in static media, motion media, and interactive media.

Static media visuals include, for example, paintings, photographs, drawings, charts, graphs, and maps that may be displayed in newspapers, newsletters, and magazines, as well as on billboards, posters, websites, or computerized slide shows. Chalk drawings on the sidewalk, graffiti on the side of a building, and a tattoo prominently displayed on a person's body are also examples of static media visuals. Motion media generally use video or animation technology to create an illusion of motion. Thus, visuals on TV programs and advertisements, films, and YouTube videos are examples of motion media visuals. Interactive media allow viewers to participate and edit content. Examples include interactive video games, social media websites, blogs, and TV programs that invite viewers to vote for their favorite.

VISUAL THEORY PERSPECTIVES

Visuals communicate and persuade based on what we tend to notice and not notice in them and then how we interpret or assign meaning to what we see (Berger, 1972). Three sets of theories that help explain these processes are gestalt, semiotics, and cognitive theory.

Gestalt Theory

Gestalt theory originated among a group of German psychologists in the early part of the 20th century. The German word for *whole* is *gestalt.* Of these psychologists, Max Wertheimer is credited with coining the phrase *the whole is different from the sum of its parts* to capture the essence of gestalt theory (Lester, 2011, p. 46). According to gestalt theory, our brains group individual items based on what seems to go together and what does not. Some of the principles that guide us in doing so are similarity, proximity, continuity, closure, and common fate.

Similarity has to do with our tendency to group together things that look similar (e.g., color, shape, size). Our interest is piqued when something in a visual image or object is dissimilar. You might recall a game played on the children's TV program *Sesame Street,* called "One of These Things Is Not Like the Other." If you are not familiar with it, you can easily find a clip on YouTube. The goal is to pick the dissimilar item from a group of images or objects (Figure 9.1).

■ **FIGURE 9.1**   Similarity (http://muppet.wikia.com/wiki/One_of_These_Things)

Proximity comes in two forms. We tend to associate objects that are or appear to be close to each other, and we tend to notice things that are or appear to be close to us. If, for example, you see two people sitting next to each other in a movie theater with an open seat on either or both sides, you are likely to think they go together (e.g., friends, partners). And the photograph in Figure 9.2 illustrates the other proximity tendency. Viewers are likely to notice and focus on the gun because it appears to be closer than the person holding it.

■ **FIGURE 9.2**   Proximity

Continuity is our tendency to desire a smooth continuation of perceived movement. In other words, we follow lines and curves that are arranged in an orderly fashion over those that change direction abruptly. Closure has to do with "seeing" an object or image as complete even when it is not (Figure 9.3). And common fate is our tendency to mentally

■ **FIGURE 9.3**   Closure

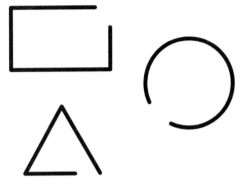

group objects that appear to be going in the same direction. A vehicle going in the wrong direction on a one-way street, for instance, would be likely to get a viewer's attention based on this principle.

APPLYING WHAT YOU'VE LEARNED . . .

Examine an issue of *The Wall Street Journal* and *USA Today*. Based on the principles of gestalt theory we've discussed, which is more likely to engage the reader and why?

Semiotics

Semiotics is the study of signs. Recall from Chapter 1 that a *sign* is anything that stands for something else. *Semeion* is actually the Greek word for sign, which is where the founder of the theory, Augustine of Hippo (354–430 AD), lived (Bonner, 1986). More recently, Ferdinand de Saussure, a Swiss linguist, and Charles Sanders Peirce, an American scientist and philosopher, among others, contributed greatly to our understanding of how signs and symbols communicate (Parmentier, 1985). More specifically, **semiosis** is the relationship between a sign, which represents an object (*referent*), and a meaning (*interpretation*) attached to it. In their influential book *The Meaning of Meaning: A Study of the Influence of Language Upon Thought and the Science of Symbolism,* C. K. Ogden and I. A. Richards (1923) conceptualized the semantic triangle to clarify this tripartite relationship (see Figure 9.4). And French literary critic, Roland Barthes (1973, 1977), further refined the theory by delineating the denotative and connotative meanings signs carry with them.

Semiotic analyses go beyond gestalt principles designed to explain "ways of seeing" (Berger, 1972) to examine the social meanings of visual images or objects for a particular culture or group and the potential effects such meanings may have regarding ideological beliefs and behaviors. They do so by analyzing the signs embedded in them.

■ **FIGURE 9.4**   The Semantic Triangle

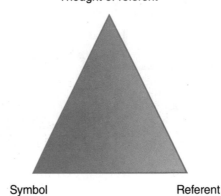

Thought of referent

Symbol   Referent

Recall our discussion in Chapter 1 about three kinds of signs. Iconic signs stand for something else because they resemble the thing they represent. Indexical signs have a logical connection to the thing they represent rather than a straightforward resemblance. And symbolic signs stand for something based on the meanings attached to them rooted in the cultural norms of a particular group.

Two additional kinds of signs used to examine visual texts are syntagmatic and paradigmatic. Syntagmatic signs gain their meaning from the signs that surround them in a static image (e.g., painting, photograph, magazine advertisement) or by signs that come before and after them sequentially in a moving visual (e.g., TV program, commercial, film). Paradigmatic signs gain meaning as they fit with or in contrast to other signs. Look at the visual in Figure 9.5. In what ways is it functioning syntagmatically or paradigmatically?

Visuals convey both denotative and connotative meanings (Barthes, 1977). Denotative meanings are fairly easy to decode. These meanings are typically what we notice first as overt and at-the-surface meanings. Connotative meanings are the underlying messages related to social norms and practices. Two types of connotative signs are metonymic and synecdochal. Metonymic signs are associated with something else and, thus, serve to represent that something else. Synecdochal signs are a part or piece of something that serves to stand in for the whole. The American flag, for example, represents (1) the United States of America (the country) as a synecdochal sign and (2) freedom and democracy as a metonymic sign. Consider the visual in Figure 9.5 again. What are some metonymic and synecdochal signs in it, and what meanings might one derive from them?

Semiotics has been and is still used across disciplines to examine the meanings conveyed in visual images and objects. Scholars study what the signs mean as they reinforce or challenge the ideology and social norms of a cultural group.

Cognitive Theory

Cognitive theory focuses on what is going on in our minds when we view an image or object and how that affects our perception. All of the rhetorical perspectives we discuss in

■ **FIGURE 9.5**   Syntagmatic and Paradigmatic Signs (images.wildammo.com)

this book are rooted in cognitive theory. For example, when we bring preconceived notions about what we expect to see, we may fail to notice other things. Similarly, when we focus only on the most obvious signs in a visual, we might fail to realize underlying ideological messages in it. Consider the advertisement in Figure 9.6. How might preconceived expectations and selectivity of a viewer influence what is taken-for-granted as "normal" in dominant American culture?

■ **FIGURE 9.6**   Cognitive Theory

A visual might also trigger memories about something we've experienced before. The positive or negative valence we attach to those memories may influence our perception of it. For example, if you see a visual image of a group of people dressed in army fatigues and you or someone close to you had served in the military, your memories might influence your perception and interpretation. Similarly, if you grew up in a certain place and then see a photograph of it or a movie filmed on location there, the photo or film may have more salience for you.

Dissonance can also influence perception. When multiple things compete for our attention, we might have difficulty interpreting the meaning. The visual in Figure 9.5 as compared to Figure 9.6 might cause dissonance for some viewers. Similarly, our cultural identity and ideology can influence how we see and interpret visuals.

One branch of visual cognitive theory that may be used to examine mediated popular culture texts is psychoanalysis. Psychoanalytic theories focus primarily on how the mind, psyche, "human subjectivity, sexuality, and the unconscious" are constructed in rhetorical texts (Rose, 2007, p. 107). These theories actually stem from Sigmund Freud's (1905) psychoanalysis methods for treating mental illness. Today, however, they are only vaguely related to Freud's original ideas. Psychoanalytic rhetorical criticism assumes that all popular culture texts have deeper meanings about how we interpret subjectivity and sexuality. Visual pleasure theory is one such psychoanalytic theory.

VISUAL PLEASURE THEORY

British film theorist Laura Mulvey first published articles describing and applying visual pleasure theory to films in the 1970s. It wasn't until the 1980s, however, that it became widely known in a variety of disciplines, including rhetorical studies. As with any theory, visual pleasure theory has its critics. Some of these criticisms stem from the fact that early works tended to privilege white heterosexuality (e.g., de Lauretis, 1994; Gaines, 1988; White, 1995). Today, however, some applications have extended it in ways that make room for understanding arguments about multiple sexualities (e.g., Dyer, 1990; Modleski, 1988; Silverman, 1988; Thornham, 1997) and race (e.g., Doane, 1991; Fanon, 1986; Young, 1996). With these potential limitations in mind, the theory still provides a useful means by which to understand one way in which visual images function rhetorically in mediated popular culture texts.

Visual pleasure theory argues that visual images in media encourage viewers to look pleasurably at images via a male gaze (Mulvey, 1989, 1996). A male gaze describes the way in which viewers (both male and female) look at the people presented and represented in visual images by identifying with the male actor(s). In other words, viewers don't simply watch the images, but gaze upon them in ways that influence our subconscious beliefs about our own psyches.

Psychoanalytic Theory, Scopophelia, and Narcissism

The essence of visual pleasure theory is grounded in psychoanalytic theory. French psychoanalytical theorist Jacques Lacan (1977) first proposed the *mirror stage* as a permanent structure of human experience throughout life (as opposed to something we experience only during infancy and early childhood). The **mirror stage** symbolizes an ongoing sexual relationship we have with body image. We experience the mirror stage throughout our lives as we identify with and desire to be like various images we encounter. Our **self-image** (mental picture of one's self) is formed from these mirror stage experiences.

Two key principles of visual pleasure theory are *scopophelia* and *narcissism*. **Scopophelia** can be defined as the love of or pleasurable (i.e., sexually arousing) looking. Popular culture critics use this notion to suggest that viewers are drawn to gaze at an image as beautiful, erotic, or fantastic. Beautiful women, for instance, are often used in advertisements to help sell products. Moreover, these beautiful wo*men* are typically portrayed as sexy and dressed scantily. Beautiful men are also used more in advertisements today than in the past. Consider, for example, the male image in the Old Spice advertisement in Figure 9.7. Male and female viewers alike are encouraged to view the image pleasurably as beautiful and sexy.

■ **FIGURE 9.7** Scopophelia

The other important psychoanalytic construct grounding visual pleasure theory is *narcissism*. Viewers of popular culture images experience the mirror stage when we are led to identify with certain characters, models, or body images. **Narcissism** is the label used to describe excessive self-love based on one's self-image as a result of our mirror stage experiences. What makes visual pleasure theory particularly interesting to rhetorical critics is the notion that viewers are led to do so at a subconscious level. Thus, visual pleasure theory helps critics discern what those subconscious messages about beauty and desirability are, as well as how those messages influence our day-to-day, taken-for-granted beliefs and behaviors.

Fetishism, Voyeurism, and Narcissism in Visual Pleasure Theory

The three constructs of visual pleasure theory are *fetishism, voyeurism,* and *narcissism.* Fetishism can be described as getting pleasure from openly looking at an object that is "satisfying in itself" (Mulvey, 1975, p. 14). When women or men are portrayed in advertisements wearing scanty undergarments to sell any product other than underclothes, for instance, they are being portrayed as fetishes, that is, spectacles to be gazed at as beautiful objects. Although women are most often portrayed in this way, examples of men as beautiful objects also exist. In the original *Rocky* film, for instance, Sylvester Stallone is ultimately portrayed in this way after training for his big boxing match with Apollo Creed. In fact, images of men as fetishes have becoming increasingly prevalent in movies and advertisements in recent years. When images of people are reduced to certain body parts, those body parts essentially replace the person as a synecdochal sign or object of pleasurable looking. Ripped abdominal muscles on men and large breasts or full lips on women are some examples. The key here is the person is being portrayed openly as an object to be gazed at. In the advertisement for GUESS footwear illustrated in Figure 9.8, viewers are drawn to look pleasurably at the slinky legs. As such, the legs are functioning as fetishes.

■ **FIGURE 9.8**   A Fetish

> **APPLYING WHAT YOU'VE LEARNED . . .**
>
> Consider a television commercial or magazine advertisement where a person or a body part of a person is portrayed as an object in this way. Describe the image, what product is being advertised, and what the fetish might be communicating to viewers about what is desirable or undesirable in terms of appearance?

Voyeurism can be described as instances where people engaged in sexual, sordid, or scandalous acts are being watched without them knowing it. The viewer is something like a peeping Tom, watching illicitly without being invited to look or noticed. An obvious example of voyeurism occurs when viewers watch actors and actresses engaging in sexual intercourse. When actors, actresses, or models engage in activities that are not typically considered appropriate for public display, the behaviors are considered voyeurism. The key to remember with voyeurism is the models do not consent to being watched. Viewers seem to be watching them in secret.

Recall from our earlier discussion that *narcissism* is when the image draws the viewer to want to be like him or her. The viewer is led to identify with the image and to mirror what the image looks like or acts like. Narcissism occurs when viewers recognize their own likenesses in the images or imagine they can mirror those images somehow. Advertisements for exercise equipment, diet programs, cosmetic surgery, and beauty products often use narcissism as a visual pleasure marketing strategy. The advertisement for Pond's eye therapy in Figure 9.9, for example, is targeted to women over age 40. The goal is to lead the 40-something-year-old viewer to believe she can have smooth skin and wrinkle-free eyes like the air-brushed model if she uses the product. The Body By Jake advertisements make similar claims about physical fitness and their products for men and women.

Visual pleasure theory is so compelling from a rhetorical perspective because of the potential implications it might have for viewers who strive to achieve the ideals portrayed in visual images. Women who are bombarded with unattainable propositions about how they ought to look might lead to depression, eating disorders, and obsessive plastic surgery. Men who are similarly inundated with messages about physique could experience similar implications. A plethora of images of bedroom scenes with multiple partners in soap operas, TV dramas, and films could lead to increases in sexually transmitted diseases, unwanted pregnancies, and so forth. Rhetoricians would never go so far as to claim a causal link between any of these images and implications; however, the theory does give rise to the possibilities and does afford us a means to be more educated and critical consumers.

CONDUCTING A VISUAL PLEASURE ANALYSIS

You conduct a rhetorical analysis using visual pleasure theory as you would any rhetorical analysis of a popular culture text. That is, in addition to considering the

■ **FIGURE 9.9** Narcissism

flirtier at 40

Banish circles.
Deflate puffs. Forget lines.
age defEYE
with soy, vitamin k and
anti-oxidants. For smoother,
brighter eyes. So you can flirt
in a way that separates the
girls from the women.

POND'S
age defEYE
anti-circle, anti-puff
eye therapy
with vitamin k and anti-oxidants

ponds.com   POND'S® age defEYE

QUESTIONING YOUR ETHICS . . .

Do you think any constraints ought to be honored in how the human body and body parts are portrayed in advertisements and entertainment media? Why or why not?

rhetorical situation, you select an artifact based on a hunch that it is saying something beyond the surface message, something about our taken-for-granted beliefs or behaviors. You then examine the text by describing, interpreting, and evaluating it. In this case, you do so using the constructs of fetishism, voyeurism, and narcissism. Visual pleasure analyses are usually also grounded in a feminist perspective. Focusing on the visual images via this psychoanalytic perspective tends to reveal richer implications tied to how our minds, personalities, and psyches may be influenced by them regarding subjectivity and sexuality.

Step 1: Selecting an Appropriate Text

Text selection is guided by what the visual images seem to be saying regardless of the verbal messages being told. If you are considering a television program or advertisement or a movie, you might turn off the sound as you view it. Doing so helps determine whether the visual images themselves seem to be saying something important about our taken-for-granted beliefs and behaviors.

APPLYING WHAT YOU'VE LEARNED . . .

Watch a TV program or commercial with the sound turned off. What messages of fetishism, voyeurism, and narcissism do the visual images seem to communicate regarding ideal beauty and self-image?

Because photographs and print advertisements are not confounded with the use of sound, many student critics start by searching magazines for advertisements whose pictures seem to be telling a story other than one about the product being marketed in them. Consider, for example, the GUESS footwear advertisement we looked at earlier. Certainly, its overt intent is to advertise shoes; however, other messages are also being conveyed about acceptable beliefs and behaviors as normal or desirable. To further clarify, let's focus on a set of pictures of several Hollywood celebrity couples (Jennifer Aniston and Justin Theroux, John Krazinski and Emily Blunt, Jimmy Kimmel and Molly McNearney) printed in a popular celebrity gossip magazine (Figure 9.10) ("Aniston's," p. 23). We'll examine these photographs via the constructs of fetishism, voyeurism, and narcissism regarding "appropriate" and "desirable" roles and rules for women and men.

Step 2: Examining the Text (Describe and Interpret)

Begin by describing the messages in the images via fetishism, voyeurism, and narcissism. Both Aniston and Theroux are clearly portrayed as fetishes, that is, as beautiful objects to be gazed at. Aniston is scantily clad in a string bikini top, and Theroux is

■ **FIGURE 9.10** "Aniston's Sexy Mexican Escape"

Hard-Bodied Couple!

"She snacked on apple slices," a source tells *Us* of Aniston (with Theroux Dec. 27).

Aniston's Sexy Mexican Escape

THE MORE, THE MERRIER! BEFORE CHRISTMAS, **Jennifer Aniston** and fiancé **Justin Theroux** jetted to a $12,000-a-night abode in Puerto Los Cabos, Mexico. Their daily routine: yoga in the morning, afternoon tanning and moonlight margaritas. On December 27, they held a fiesta for the foursome of **John Krasinski**, wife **Emily Blunt** (*inset*), **Jimmy Kimmel** and fiancée **Molly McNearney** (*right*). Shares a source, "They laughed until sunset!"

topless in several photos and wearing a muscle shirt with visibly ripped muscles in the other. One photo is a synecdochal sign—his tattooed back—represented as a fetish. Viewers are led to gaze at their bodies and body parts as beautiful objects. Even when their faces are shown, they are wearing sunglasses, so viewers are not led to "interact" with them as human beings but to view their beautiful body parts as fetishes. Viewers are drawn to look at their bodies as objects rather than at them as people. In one photo, we see only their backs and voyeuristically observe Theroux grabbing Aniston's bottom, an intimate scene not necessarily meant for public display. Let's also consider the other celebrity images taking part on the rendezvous. The photo insert of Krasinski and Blunt invites viewers to narcissistically identify with them as happily in love. And Kimmel and McNearney, each dressed in non-revealing shorts and shirts, seem to be portrayed as onlookers as opposed to participating in the "fun." In relation to the others, they seem to be the anti-model subject positions viewers of *Us Weekly* do not want to look like (fetishism) or act like (voyeurism and narcissism).

Once you have described the images via fetishism, voyeurism, and narcissism, you can interpret what those messages mean in terms of taken-for-granted beliefs and behaviors about the roles and rules for women and men. With regard to fetishism, these photographs suggest that it is normal and even desirable for women and men to be gazed at as objects. Moreover, what is proposed in the photographs as normal and beautiful is thin and scantily clad women and ripped and scantily clad men, even for people in their 40s like Aniston and Theroux. Finally, the fact that all are white and all are portrayed as couples suggests that white heterosexual romantic relationships are also both normal and desirable.

Step 3: Evaluating Potential Implications of the Text

In evaluating the images, consider the target audience of a magazine such as *Us Weekly.* The celebrity magazine is devoted to sharing stories, photographs, and breaking news about the most popular celebrities of the day. Its primary target audience, made up of 18- to 49-year-old women, learn how they ought to and ought not to look and act if they want to be like these celebrities they aspire to be like (*Us Weekly,* 2012). If viewers are persuaded by the underlying messages of photographs like these three, then they could suffer emotional and physical consequences when they realize the body images portrayed by Aniston and Theroux are unrealistic for them. And they could be influenced to believe that heterosexuality is normal and other sexualities are deviant and bad.

Obviously, not all viewers are likely to be swayed by one series of pictures like these. Still, these are the visual pleasure-based arguments communicated in them. And, if these are the only kinds of pictures being portrayed consistently to viewers, alternative models of normalcy and desirability are being ignored. Images that are not included also send clear messages reinforcing a certain ideological perspective as right or as better than others. Remember, the role of the rhetorical critic is not to determine cause and effect but to reveal what the underlying messages are and then suggest possible implications. As such, readers can become more critical consumers of such messages portrayed in visual images.

SAMPLE PUBLISHED ESSAYS

(1) Read the article titled, "Rhetorical Strategies of Visual Pleasure in Situation Comedies: *Friends* and Female Body Image," published in the *Communication and Theater Association of Minnesota Journal* (Sellnow & Ziniel, 2007). Essentially, the article argues that the visual messages conveyed by and about the female characters reinforce hegemonic ideals of femininity and an ideal female body image that is excessively thin. Messages of narcissism draw adolescent female viewers to identify with Rachel and Monica and to distance themselves from Phoebe and "Fat Monica." Messages of voyeurism deepen impressions that the illicit behaviors enacted by Rachel and Monica that support hegemony are appropriate, whereas illicit behaviors enacted by any of the female characters that challenge hegemony are inappropriate. Messages of fetishism advocate that the ideal female body image is a sex object, and the most desirable sex objects are excessively thin. What are some potential implications for women and men based on this analysis? Consider the definition of *female beauty* sent in the program and how that might impact women's self-perceptions regarding happiness, health, and success.

(2) Read the article titled "Do You Want to Watch? A Study of the Visual Rhetoric of the Postmodern Horror Film," published in *Women's Studies* (Keisner, 2008). Essentially, the article explores the psychological and social effects of slasher movies today by focusing on the 2003 thriller, *feardotcom*. The article ultimately argues that postmodern horror films empower men and disempower women. The author argues that the "Final Girls" of *Scream, I Know What You Did Last Summer,* and *feardotcom* are regressing to depict them as "cowering their way through scenes" (p. 426) and surviving only thanks to intervention by strong male characters. As such, females are encouraged to see themselves as victims. As you read, ponder these questions. How do postmodern slasher films encourage all viewers to watch according to a male gaze? What are some potential implications for both women and men based on this analysis? Do you agree with the author's conclusions? Why or why not? Can you think of some examples of postmodern horror films today that do propose agency for women?

SAMPLE STUDENT ESSAY

Jonathan Foland wrote the following essay as a final class paper. His paper, "From Seeing to Looking to Participating: Embracing Multiple Sexualities by Fixing the Gaze on Brandon Teena," illustrates how visual pleasure theory can be used to exemplify issues related to sexuality by examining the film *Boys Don't Cry*. His analysis reveals how viewers are invited to recognize Brandon Teena not as an abnormal object, if you will, but as a human being, a subject worthy of acceptance, respect, and love. As you read, consider how the subject positions of Brandon Teena, Lana Tisdel, and others help viewers come to accept the argument as valid. Sometimes looking back on what popular culture texts argued in the past can reveal how ideological perspectives may or may not have changed. How do you think the story of the film would be received if released for the first time today? Do you know of other films or TV programs that propose similar arguments? If so, what sort of viewership and acclaim have they earned?

From Seeing to Looking to Participating: Embracing Multiple Sexualities by Fixing the Gaze on Brandon Teena

Jonathan Foland

In 1993, Brandon Teena, a queer youth living in Falls City, Nebraska, was beaten and raped by John Lotter and Tom Nissen. Because Brandon reported the rape to authorities, Lotter and Nissen then shot and stabbed Brandon to death and executed the friends with whom he was staying ("Triple Murder," 1994; "Woman Who Posed," 1994; Worthing, 1994). Brandon Teena was born genitally female and raised as Teena Brandon. However, his move to Falls City as a young adult afforded Brandon an opportunity to live "in a community where he had no history as a woman," and thus to leave Teena behind (Sloop, 2000, p. 165). Brandon dated local women and became friends with Lotter and Nissen. However, when the two discovered Brandon's female genitalia, they exposed him to friends, raped him, and eventually killed him ("Triple Murder," 1994; Worthing, 1994).

Events from the final weeks of Brandon Teena's life inform the story of Kimberly Pierce's 1999 film *Boys Don't Cry* (Sharp, Hart, Kolodner, Vachon, & Pierce, 1999). Though not a box office blockbuster, *Boys Don't Cry* earned favorable reception from critics, and in early 2000, Hilary Swank received both a Golden Globe and an Oscar for her performance as Brandon Teena. *Boys Don't Cry* is "a surprisingly sympathetic telling of a story about a transgendered individual" (Sloop, 2004, p. 50). By comparison, news reports of the real Brandon Teena story frequently depicted Brandon as a deceiver, a lesbian, and "really" a woman (thus reiterating sex and gender norms) (Sloop, 2000, 2004).

Moreover, media representations of transgender or transsexual individuals are often framed as shocking, repulsive, and deserving of ridicule. For example, Halberstam (2005) describes the importance of the twist ending to *The Crying Game*, in which the character Dil is initially perceived as "'properly' gendered" only to be "revealed" (for shock value) as male, prompting the audience "to rewind the film [and] reorganize [its] narrative logic" (p. 78). *Boys Don't Cry*, however, attempts "to give the viewer access to the transgender gaze" (Halberstam, 2005, p. 78). As Halberstam (2005) suggests, perhaps the film's success with mainstream audiences rests not only on the emotional weight of the story but also on the depiction of Brandon as likeable, appealing, and attractive. Both Hird (2001) and Cooper (2002) consider *Boys Don't Cry* an interventionist film capable of influencing viewers' perceptions of and attitudes toward transgender individuals in these ways.

Brandon Teena was killed more than 20 years ago and *Boys Don't Cry* released more than a decade ago, yet contemporary news stories illustrate continued struggles against what remains normative gender expression and identity. Angie Zapata, a transgender woman in Colorado, for example, was beaten to death in 2008 by a man she had dated because he learned that Zapata still had male genitalia (Frosch, 2008). Zapata's family and friends, in the wake of her death, maintain a website, *Light a Candle for Angie Zapata*, that both remembers Zapata and educates the site's visitors on transgender matters

(Continued)

(Continued)

(see http://www.angiezapata.com/). In 2009, a jury found Dwight DeLee guilty of manslaughter in the death of Lateisha Green, an African-American trans woman living in New York (Kailey, 2009). The conviction of DeLee is significant as a hate crimes verdict, but his conviction "was based on anti-gay bias," suggesting that "DeLee saw Green as a gay man," thereby reducing Green's identity to her genitals (Kailey, 2009). Nevertheless, the recent deaths of Zapata and Green are evidence of continued violence against individuals whose gender is perceived as deviant. Clearly, the continued news reports of violence against transgender people serve as evidence that the story told in *Boys Don't Cry* remains relevant today.

This analysis contributes to existing research by focusing specifically on the visual arguments posited in the portrayals of Brandon Teena, his positioning in relation to other characters, and the significance of character points of view in the film as key rhetorical components (Cooper, 2002; Halberstam, 2005; Hird, 2001; Holbrook, 2000; Sloop, 2000, 2004). More specifically, this analysis explores answers to the following questions. In what ways does Pierce's film invite viewers to relate to Brandon and, in turn, critically engage the narrative? In what ways do the images of a cinematically embodied Brandon Teena have an impact on the viewer's experience of *Boys Don't Cry*? How does the film direct viewers to identify or empathize with Brandon's story? What role does Lana Tisdel play as a point of access for viewers to engage the narrative and, ultimately, both see and relate to Brandon? How does the film reject other points of view, thereby discouraging viewers from accepting the attitudes of Lotter or Nissen? Ultimately, this analysis may provide insight into arguments that serve to draw heterosexual viewers to realize transgender as normal rather than deviant.

GENDER AND SEX—OR, IT'S BRANDON, NOT TEENA

Many reviews of *Boys Don't Cry* and news stories of the 1993 murder of Brandon Teena often reduce Brandon to his biological sex (Sloop, 2004). In other words, Brandon becomes "really" Teena, deceiving her friends into thinking that she is a he. Conversely, the present analysis acknowledges that Brandon is Brandon (not Teena) regardless of his anatomical sex.

To clarify, sex and gender are often wrongly conflated. Sex relates to one's biology and bodily capability for reproduction, whereas gender is influenced by environmental factors such as cultural and social values and practices (Bornstein, 1995). To signify one's gender, one performs gender roles, the culturally and socially accepted gender behaviors expected of one based on her or his genital sex (Bornstein, 1995; Peate, 2008). As Butler (1990) explains, gender "is not a noun [but] always a doing" (p. 33).

Transgender individuals establish gender identities that may not correspond with their genital sex or with conventional sex and gender norms (Bornstein, 1995; Califia, 1997; Halberstam, 1998, 2005). Transgressing sex-based gender norms is often interpreted as aberrant, abnormal, and deviant behavior. *Gender variance* and *gender dysphoria* are examples of terminology that refer to the "incongruence" between one's gendered self and one's biological sex (Califia, 1997; Peate, 2008). Bornstein (1995) and Califia (1997), for example, discuss how gender cross-identification is constructed as an illness or sickness—diagnosable and (possibly) curable through modern psychology and medicine (e.g., sex reassignment).

In addition to having their gender expressions labeled as afflictive medical conditions, transgender individuals may encounter other forms of discrimination. For example, Feinberg (1998) recalls personal struggles with doctors and nurses who were prejudiced toward Feinberg's gender expression. More recently, a transgender woman living in Maine was forbidden from using a women's restroom (Curtis, 2009a), while a transgender child living in Maine faced restricted access to school restrooms (Curtis, 2009b). A teenage boy from Seattle was accused of attacking a transgender woman in June 2009 ("Transgender," 2009). And in Illinois, two women sued the state for refusing to change their birth certificates after they underwent sex reassignment outside the United States (Schmadeke, 2009).

Gender and sex, clearly, are not as simple as giving birth to a healthy baby girl or boy and watching him or her grow into a woman or a man. Furthermore, much is at stake for the people who do not seem to "fit" the gender and sex norms. To describe Brandon as really Teena is to deny him the right to express himself authentically.

RHETORICAL PERSPECTIVES: LOOKING, SEEING, PARTICIPATING

This analysis employs Mulvey's (1975, in Mulvey, 2009) theory of visual pleasure. Visual pleasure is a feminist perspective for examining how "film reflects, reveals and even plays on the straight, socially established interpretation of sexual difference" (Mulvey, 2009, p. 14). Mulvey describes the elements of visual pleasure theory via narcissism, fetishism, and voyeurism.

Visual pleasure theory assumes that the act of gazing upon an object or an image is pleasurable (Mulvey, 2009). Freud (1905) associated the "pleasure in looking" with the curiosity of completing "the sexual object by revealing its hidden parts" (p. 22). Thus, pleasurable looking satisfies one's curiosity to see what is usually concealed. According to Mulvey (2009), the viewer assumes the role of voyeur, and the characters become fetishes (objects) to gaze upon pleasurably.

Narcissism refers to perceiving and treating one's own body as an object of desire (Freud, 1914). With regard to narcissistic identification, visual pleasure draws from Lacan's (1949) concept of the mirror stage, in which an infant recognizes its mirror image and, subsequently, misrecognizes the reflection as more complete, thus perceiving an *ideal-I*. The viewer experiences narcissism and recognition or misrecognition in the "identification of [one's] ego with the object on the screen through the [viewer's] fascination with and recognition of" an ego ideal (Mulvey, 2009, p. 19).

Mulvey (2009) contends that a male gaze frames the visuals of cinema and shapes the roles of the male and female characters. The male gaze also represents the perspective of a film's male protagonist, to whom other characters are related as objects and with whom the viewer is likely to identify (Mulvey, 2009).

(Continued)

(Continued)

Identification with the male protagonist suggests that the viewer adopts the protagonist's traditionally male gaze. Extending Mulvey's (2009) conceptualizations of the male gaze, Halberstam (2005) suggests "more flexible conceptions of looking and imaging" (p. 83). Halberstam (2005) proposes a transgender look that "confronts powerfully the way that transgenderism is constituted as a paradox made in equal parts of visibility and temporality" (p. 77). Moreover, Halberstam (2005) maintains that more than one gendered way of looking (gaze) allows the viewer "to look *with* the transgender character instead of *at* him" (p. 78). In a film employing the transgender look, the transgender character inhabits a subject (rather than object) position with whom the viewer (regardless of sex, gender, or sexual orientation) can identify.

Because the viewer is gendered, the viewing experience may involve cross-gender identifications with the transgender subject (Halberstam, 1998). Mulvey (1981, in Mulvey, 2009) argues that the male gaze is accessible to both men and women. For women, adopting the male gaze involves a "trans-sex" or cross-gender identification with the male protagonist (Mulvey, 2009). Similarly, Halberstam (1998) suggests that a transgender subject position queers the gaze by "call[ing] for many different identificatory strategies from viewers" (p. 176). In other words, the viewer can identify with the transgender protagonist based on the viewer's perceived similarities with the transgender character.

Viewers function as voyeurs who experience pleasure from looking at images on screen and seeing what is usually concealed. The viewer

may identify the protagonist of the film as an ego ideal-type—a standard to which the viewer compares other characters or him or herself—and assume the protagonist's gaze, or way of looking. Halberstam (2005) raises the possibility that the gaze need not be exclusively male, nor must a transgender character function as a spectacle. Although Halberstam (2005) acknowledges that the transgender gaze allows a viewer to identify with the transgender subject, absent from Halberstam is a consideration of the viewer as voyeur. If part of the pleasure in looking is to satisfy one's curiosity to see what is typically hidden, perhaps the viewer is drawn to a queer film out of a curiosity to see a queer (e.g., transgender) character in detail (Cooper, 2002). What might be the impact on the viewer upon discovering that the object of curiosity (the transgender character) is the subject position with whom the viewer must identify?

Finally, Mulvey's (2009) visual pleasure theory assumes that stories on screen are "indifferent to the presence of the audience, producing for them a sense of separation" (p. 17). Mulvey (2009) contends that films deny the viewer's look "an intrinsic force" (p. 26). The viewer, though active in looking, is passive with regard to unfolding events. However, some films rely on the awareness of the audience, such as when a film breaks the "fourth wall" to remind the audience of its "sense of self as an audience" (Recchia, p. 259). Characters may address the audience (an explicit reflexive technique), or the audience's awareness may be reinforced by subtle, implicit means. Film reflexivity requires the viewer to play the role of audience member, so that he or she will "actually become [one of the] actors in the drama" (Recchia, 1991, p. 259). Recognizing its role as viewers of unfolding events, the audience reflects on the film's broader implications (Recchia, 1991). What role might reflexivity as a rhetorical strategy play for viewers encouraged to identify with Brandon Teena in *Boys Don't Cry?*

ANALYSIS

To examine *Boys Don't Cry*, I begin by analyzing key scenes with regard to the viewer as a voyeur permitted to witness aspects of Brandon that are generally hidden from the other characters (who represent heteronormativity) as well as hidden from heterosexual members of society. Second, Halberstam's (2005) transgender look grounds the discussion of gendered ways of looking offered in the film. In addition to arguing that viewers identify with Brandon as a subject position, I propose that Lana plays an important second subject position role. Third, the film's reflexivity, or its dependence on a cognizant viewing audience, is examined as it encourages the viewer to play a role in completing Brandon's story once the film ends, a story that was essentially unfinished at the time of his death.

Seeing the Transgender Subject

Certainly, a viewer might be drawn initially to *Boys Don't Cry* out of a curiosity to see a transgender film character or because of the real-life events that inspired the story. As Bornstein (1995), Cooper (2002), and Halberstam (1998, 2005) observe, representations of transgender individuals often reduce the character to a spectacle, an oddity, or an object of ridicule. Scenes depicting Brandon intimately dealing with his female body might reduce him to a spectacle, as well. As Cooper (2002) argues, though, the film's willingness to show Brandon's masculine gender expression and his female body challenges the conflation of gender with physiological sex. Brandon, as Halberstam (2005) proposes, "surprises audiences with his ... ability to remain attractive, appealing and gendered" despite the audience's awareness of his biology (p. 76).

The opening scenes of *Boys Don't Cry* reveal aspects of Brandon that many of the other characters do not know—that Brandon uses physical and behavioral cues to project a masculine gender identity. In the very first scene, for instance, Brandon is dressed in a men's style shirt and jeans. Visually, Brandon conforms to conventional expectations for men's appearance. He even stuffs a rolled sock down the front of his pants to simulate a bulge. After giving Brandon a "man's" haircut, his cousin Lonny remarks, "So, you're a boy. Now what?"

With his new look complete, Brandon soon meets a young woman at a skating rink. Her interaction with Brandon confirms for him (and the viewer) the successful expression of his masculine identity. The film cuts to Brandon and the girl kissing outside her house. Visually, the scene shows a young man and woman kissing (seemingly reiterating heteronormativity); however, having witnessed Brandon create his look, the viewer remains aware of an incongruence between Brandon's gender and sex. Nevertheless, Brandon's ability to "pass" as a "man" is confirmed for the viewer by the end of the evening.

(Continued)

(Continued)

Throughout the film, viewers observe Brandon's private moments spent alone addressing his biologically female body. As such viewers witness Brandon confronting his female body in order to downplay his gender and sex incongruence. In one series of scenes, for example, viewers watch as Brandon awakens in the night at Candace's house to realize that his body is menstruating. The scene shifts to Brandon in the bathroom where viewers see him frantically cleaning the blood from his jeans while on guard should Candace awaken and discover him. This series of scenes culminates as viewers follow Brandon into an all-night gas station and watch him steal tampons.

In another scene, viewers watch Brandon after taking a shower. Brandon glances in the mirror and quickly looks away in disgust before getting dressed. Viewers watch Brandon use a bandage to bind and flatten his chest, stuff a sock down his pants to simulate a bulge, and then dress and comb his hair. Visually, the scene leads the viewer to understand the extent of Brandon's investment in his gender by showing the lengths he goes to in order to conceal and transform his female body and physical appearance to match his gender identity. After dressing, Brandon again looks in the mirror. This time he admires his reflection, a stark contrast to what viewers observed before the transformation. Brandon only admires his reflection when fully dressed as Brandon. As such, viewers are "encouraged to share that image" and perceive Brandon as an ideal image of the man that he is (Cooper, 2002, p. 54).

Viewers also see Brandon perform his masculine gender socially. Though Brandon imitates some of the behaviors modeled by John and Tom, Brandon's masculinity is clearly distinct from their hyper-masculinity. Brandon's form of masculinity affords him more intimate interactions with women generally and with Lana in particular. Both Lana and her mother perceive Brandon to be "polite, responsible, attentive, considerate" and nonviolent, unlike John or Tom (Hird, 2001, p. 436). The interactions depicted between Brandon and Lana convey her preference for his form of masculinity. Brandon makes Lana laugh. Viewers also watch them kiss passionately and engage in physical sex (both before and after Lana becomes aware of Brandon's female body). In contrast, viewers see that Lana does not find John's form of masculinity appealing. One compelling scene shows John and Lana in her bedroom as she wraps a birthday gift for Brandon. In the scene, John's stance is formidable and aggressive—markedly different from Brandon's stance. Viewers do not see a playful or intimate relationship like they do with Lana and Brandon.

The rhetorical strategies employed in depicting Brandon's visual gender presentation attempts to lead viewers to understand that Brandon, as a transgender person, knows his gender identity. Viewers see that Brandon's masculine gender expression is his authentic expression even though his body is biologically female. Even more compelling, however, is how visual presentations show that Brandon's actions and appearance allow him to "pass." Ultimately, showing that Lana prefers Brandon's masculinity to John and Tom's masculinity, Brandon is portrayed as a masculine ideal, thus encouraging viewers to identify with him.

Subject Positions and Gendered Ways of Looking

Halberstam (2005) explains that the transgender look is not a gaze, per se, because the transgender look "involves embedding several ways of looking" (p. 78). Brandon's role as the protagonist provides viewers with one of several ways of looking that populate the film. These ways of looking are attached to specific characters and thereby are gendered accordingly. As the clearly preferred performer of masculinity in the film, viewers are granted access to his more desirable masculine way of looking.

By looking with Brandon, rather than only at Brandon, viewers encounter and make sense of Brandon, the other characters, and their relationships (Halberstam, 2005). Brandon's adoption and implementation of a masculine gender performance and decision to test his ability to "pass" in public initiate the events leading to his tragic end. To clarify, while "passing," Brandon meets Candace, who not only finds Brandon attractive but also introduces him to John and Tom. Successfully passing in his interactions with John and Tom, Brandon is allowed to accompany the three to Falls City where he meets (and dates) Lana. Thus, the other characters and the unfolding journey come to exist cinematically for the viewer because of Brandon's ability to interact convincingly with others as Brandon. Also, the characters' initial acceptance of Brandon's masculinity not only grants him access to their social circle but also encourages viewers to embrace Brandon's gender expression as valid.

Identifying with Brandon encourages viewers to adopt his way of looking. It is with Brandon that viewers first meet (and gaze at) Lana in a bar. Because Lana is the person to whom Brandon is emotionally and sexually attracted (his sexual object choice), the argument could be made that Brandon frames Lana through a traditional male gaze that is in keeping with the way

of looking described by Mulvey (2009). Brandon certainly eroticizes Lana, but it is important to recognize that *Boys Don't Cry* develops Lana's character into another subject position whose gendered way of looking further encourages viewers to accept the authenticity of Brandon's gender.

Lana's character gradually becomes an integral figure as the film unfolds. Lana represents a heterosexual, woman-identified, and female way of looking that compels viewers to embrace Brandon's masculine identity. While Brandon's commitment to his gender expression is conveyed through the steps he takes to conceal his body, Brandon's "passing" depends on his friends' interpretation of his gender cues (Bornstein, 1995; Hird, 2001). Just as Candace, John, and Tom did early in the film, Lana interprets Brandon's gender expression as authentic masculinity. That this heterosexual (presumably) female continues to see Brandon as a man even after learning that his body is biologically female further compels viewers to recognize Brandon's masculine gender.

As a second subject position, Lana grants viewers access to her way of looking, thus becoming the gaze that "keeps the viewer trained on the seriousness of Brandon's masculinity" (Halberstam, 2005, p. 89). Lana also functions as a conventionally gendered subject position, meaning her gender seems to correspond with her sex. Thus, Lana represents a subject through whom viewers access and understand her intimate relationship with Brandon. Through Lana's perspective, viewers are permitted to see the first sexual encounter between her and Brandon. Through Lana's flashbacks, viewers realize that Lana perceived an incongruity between Brandon's gender and

(Continued)

(Continued)

sex. To assuage her suspicions, Lana gropes Brandon for "proof" of his male sexuality. Lana does not vocalize her suspicions, instead reconstructing the experience for Candace and Kate as what could be called a normative heterosexual encounter. Rather than voice suspicions, Lana adheres to her perception of Brandon's masculinity (Cooper, 2002).

A third significant gendered way of looking in *Boys Don't Cry* is associated with the perspectives of John and Tom. As previously mentioned, the women exhibit a preference for Brandon's expression of masculinity over John's or Tom's. As the men grow suspicious of Brandon's gender and sex, they begin investigating Brandon's background. Brandon's attempts to conceal his female body are not foolproof because his past as Teena Brandon survives in the form of public (legal) records. Likewise, Brandon's attempts to hide evidence of his menstrual cycle fail when Candace discovers discarded tampons. Visibly unnerved, Candace succumbs to John's and Tom's intrusive questioning. Upon locating newspaper accounts of Teena Brandon, John and Tom attempt to hijack the film's narrative with their hyper-masculine perspective by systematically confronting each of Brandon's and Lana's friends.

John's and Tom's way of looking is in stark contrast to Brandon's and Lana's ways of looking. Without choice, viewers must follow John and Tom into Lana's bedroom as the men search for evidence to confirm Brandon's legal identity and genital sex. Their way of looking attempts to destabilize Brandon's masculinity and (especially) Lana's acceptance of Brandon's gender as authentic. The men's subsequent seizure of Brandon and exposure of his body is a forced invasion (foreshadowing the rape to come). John and Tom want Lana to "look" and "see" for herself Brandon's female sex—which, to John and Tom, proves Brandon is not a real man, that his masculinity is not authentic.

Lana's refusal to comply and her insistence that the men "leave him alone" reaffirms her way of looking that perceives Brandon's masculinity as authentic (Cooper, 2002; Halberstam, 2005). Immediately following Lana's assertion of Brandon's masculinity, the film breaks from the loud, confusing, frenetic action in the bathroom to a silent depiction of two Brandons, one exposed in the midst of mayhem, the other a passive viewer. The scene juxtaposes the Brandon defined by gender from the Brandon defined by genitals.

The connection between the two Brandons is obstructed by the shocked faces and shouting voices of Brandon's (former) friends. Brandon's self is split, foreshadowing the destabilization of his identity that will occur in the buildup to his death. Important to note is the fact that amidst the chaos of onlookers, Lana keeps her eyes shut, refusing to look when commanded by John and Tom. Lana's refusal to comply and look at Brandon's body during the violence invites viewers to identify with Lana and refuse to concede power to John and Tom to define Brandon's identity.

Following the scene in the bathroom, identifying solely with Brandon's way of looking and sustaining confidence in his masculine gender expression are complicated by further assaults against his identity. John and Tom's raping and beating of Brandon is illustrated through flashbacks while a sheriff interrogates Brandon. The rape and assault are John and Tom's methods for asserting power over and dehumanizing Brandon, but the sheriff approaches Brandon as a freak. The sheriff's questions force Brandon to explain how he was raped (in the vagina), admit to having female genitalia, and confirm that he is "really a woman"—all of which attempt to destabilize Brandon's masculine gender identity.

Lana remains concerned for and protective of Brandon even as other characters increase their distance from him. During Lana's visit to Brandon as he seeks refuge in Candace's shed, Lana asks about his life, his existence, and what he was like "before." Lana's questions, by comparison to the sheriff's, are a genuine attempt to intimately understand Brandon as a complicated gendered being. The sex that follows, revealed (like the earlier encounter) through Lana's flashbacks, has sparked debate about how to interpret Brandon's identity. While Cooper (2002) reads the sexual encounter as evidence that Lana embraces Brandon's masculinity and female sex, Halberstam (2005) argues that the scene depicts Brandon and Lana as lesbians (conventionalizing Brandon's identity). When packing her bags to leave Falls City with Brandon, Lana appears to experience cognitive dissonance while remembering the encounter. The doubt conveyed through Lana's facial expressions suggests Lana is conflicted over her attraction to a person of the same sex (despite Brandon's gender expression). Nevertheless, Lana's cognitive dissonance does not prevent her from attempting to stop the violence that ends Brandon's life, nor does her emotional attachment to him ever wane.

Lana represents a vital point of identification for viewers as the film draws to a close.

Brandon's presence as a physically visible subject in the film ends dramatically as John and Tom execute him and Candace. In the wake of Brandon's death, Lana serves as the only character with whom the audience can actively identify. Lana's narrative developed as a part of Brandon's story, but it is Lana's narrative that continues. By identifying with Lana, viewers experience vicariously her grief over losing Brandon. Figuratively speaking, viewers can retain a "live" identification with Lana and, in turn, follow her as she attempts to move beyond the tragedy.

The Role of the Viewer

Boys Don't Cry invites viewers to participate in Brandon's story, extending their role beyond only seeing Brandon and identifying with either him or Lana. Film reflexivity relies on an "interrelationship" between the film as spectacle and the viewer as spectator, an interrelationship in which the viewer understands his or her role as a member of an audience that watches and accepts the unfolding story (Recchia, 1991). Through reflexivity, viewers play a participatory role but realize, too late, that they have been implicated by the film in a "larger, three-dimensional drama" that extends the drama of the visual story to include "what is happening in [the viewers'] minds and hearts" (Recchia, 1991, p. 259). Thus, the reflexive film calls on the viewer to consider and reflect on the story as it relates to a bigger picture.

Boys Don't Cry offers brief, subtle moments in which the viewer's spectatorship is acknowledged. Prior to Brandon's beginnings in Lonny's house, the film opens with a car chase—the very

(Continued)

(Continued)

one repeated later in the film—down a dusty road. The viewer sees Brandon's eyes reflected in the rearview mirror. Brandon looks into the mirror and meets the viewer's gaze, and in that moment, Brandon seemingly invites the viewer to join him on his fateful journey.

In taking a ride with Brandon, the viewer witnesses the story unfold, accepts the events, and chooses to remain with the film through the end. As Brandon's ride continues, flashes from Brandon's past serve as tantalizing pieces of the Brandon puzzle: legal documents bearing the name "Teena Brandon" fill the screen; mug shots of Teena stare in the viewer's direction; and a news clipping of Brandon's (or Teena's) arrest confronts both Brandon and the viewer. The specter of Teena is never removed from the story. Brandon's private moments, his interactions, and his way of looking encourage the viewer to identify Brandon as the protagonist. In maintaining the viewer's fascination and curiosity, the movie jars the viewer with John and Tom's violent exposure of and physical assault on Brandon to prove that "he is really a she." The violence breaks the viewer's concern for defining Brandon and identifying through him, thus cuing the character's impending doom. Once John and Tom track down and kill Brandon, the viewer is not spared a graphic and horrific display that ends Brandon's life.

In the execution's aftermath, the viewer watches helplessly as Lana mourns Brandon. The camera hovers over Brandon to ensure that the viewer sees his body. As morning comes, the viewer (through the camera's movement) takes a disembodied survey of the crime. Once again, the camera captures Brandon's body (Lana clutching him in her sleep) and reveals the pool of blood under his head. The viewer must stare at Brandon, who had so fascinated and excited the viewer's curiosity, and acknowledge the brutal violence. Lana's mother comes to take her daughter away, leaving the viewer to take one last look. The screen fades to white, and the viewer rejoins Lana who, driving away from Falls City, stares in the direction of the viewer, returning Brandon's gaze from the beginning of the film. The voice-over during Lana's final drive is Brandon, his voice narrating the letter he had written for Lana. The final memory for Lana and the viewer are Brandon's words in the letter, ending with his name—*Brandon*.

CONCLUSIONS, IMPLICATIONS, AND SUGGESTIONS

Viewers of *Boys Don't Cry* may have approached the film to satisfy a curiosity about Brandon's transgender body or the details of his well-publicized death. To this end, the movie satisfies curiosity by showing Brandon in his biologically female body and reinforcing his masculinity through his "passing" in his circle of friends. However, the film also invites viewers to identify with Brandon as an ideal of masculine identity by comparing Brandon's gender expression to two decidedly unappealing forms of hyper-masculinity in John and Tom. Moreover, *Boys Don't Cry* positions Lana so that viewers see Brandon as she sees him, creating access to more than one gendered way of looking. Finally, the viewer's role in the unfolding drama stems from wanting to see the transgender subject of Brandon Teena, wanting to join Brandon on a ride through the film's story, and wanting to understand Brandon's complicated story. Thus, viewers do not function merely as spectator of *Boys Don't Cry*. Instead, viewers participate in the narrative throughout and, thereby, come to understand the implications of Brandon Teena's story within a larger context.

Cooper (2002), Hird (2001), and Holbrook (2000) claim that *Boys Don't Cry* has the potential to generate audience reactions that interrogate the rigidity of heteronormative gender and sex norms. Cooper (2002), Hird (2001), and Holbrook's (2000) assertions of *Boys Don't Cry* as an interventionist text rest on the assumption that viewers may experience changes in attitudes toward the treatment of transgender individuals. As an interventionist text, the film encourages the viewer to reflect on what he or she sees in the movie, from the incongruence of Brandon's gender expression and genitalia, to the influence of Teena on Brandon's life, to the interrelated events culminating in his death. Perhaps, as a result of self-reflection, the viewer may determine that it is too late to save Brandon, but it is not too late to fight transphobia and end the mistreatment of transgender individuals (Cooper, 2002). Clearly, the recent news stories cited earlier reveal the persistence of discrimination against transgender individuals, making it imperative to continue to push against transphobia and the violence facing many transgender individuals.

Although *Boys Don't Cry* was first released more than a decade ago, the argument posited in it remains relevant and potentially useful in understanding and combating transphobia and discrimination based on gender and sexuality.

Along with other mainstream films released since then (e.g., *Philadelphia, Brokeback Mountain, Transamerica*) that propose subversive hegemonic messages, maybe heteronormative transphobic ideals will eventually erode and be replaced with egalitarian norms for multiple gender identities.

The purpose of this analysis of *Boys Don't Cry* was to expand Mulvey's (2009) visual pleasure theory in ways that integrate Halberstam's (2005) transgender look and reflexivity (Recchia, 1991) to identify and unpack multiple gendered ways of looking. Because viewers may identify with more than one gendered subject position, that is, both Brandon's transgender subject position and Lana's heterosexual subject position, the gaze framing the story of *Boys Don't Cry* is queered. By combining aspects of visual pleasure, the transgender look, and reflexivity, critics are encouraged to interrogate texts not only for queer subject positions but also for strategies in them regarding the viewer's role–relationship with queer texts as they make the arguments both more accessible and persuasive to broader audiences.

References

Bornstein, K. (1995). *Gender outlaw: On men, women, and the rest of us.* New York: Vintage Press.

Butler, J. (1990). *Gender trouble: Feminism and the subversion of identity* (1999 ed.). New York: Routledge.

Califia, P. (1997). *Sex changes: The politics of transgenderism.* San Francisco, CA: Cleis Press.

Cooper, B. (2002). *Boys Don't Cry* and female masculinity: Reclaiming a life & dismantling the politics of normative heterosexuality. *Critical Studies in Media Communication, 19*(1), 44–63.

(Continued)

(Continued)

Curtis, A. (2009a, May 20). Panel backs transgender woman in restroom case. *Bangor Daily News.* Retrieved July 21, 2009, from http://www .bangordailynews.com

Curtis, A. (2009b, July 1). State rules in favor of young transgender. *Bangor Daily News.* Retrieved July 21, 2009, from http://www .bangordailynews.com

Feinberg, L. (1998). *Trans liberation: Beyond pink or blue.* Boston: Beacon Press.

Freud, S. (1905). *Three essays on the theory of sexuality* (J. Strachey, Trans.). New York: Basic Books. (Reprinted 1962)

Freud, S. (1914). On narcissism. In S. Freud, *General psychological theory* (pp. 41–69). New York: Simon & Schuster. (Reprinted 1963)

Frosch, D. (2008, August 2). Death of a transgender woman is called a hate crime. *New York Times.* Retrieved July 26, 2009, from http://www .nytimes.com

Halberstam, J. (1998). *Female masculinity.* Durham, NC: Duke University Press.

Halberstam, J. (2005). *In a queer time & place: Transgender bodies, subcultural lives.* New York: New York University Press.

Hird, M. (2001). Appropriating identity: Viewing *Boys Don't Cry. International Feminist Journal of Politics, 3*(3), 435–442.

Holbrook, N. M. (2000). Media review: *Boys Don't Cry. Educational Studies, 31*(4), 480–484.

Kailey, M. (2009, July 18). Hate crimes verdict in Lateisha Green's murder. *Examiner.* Retrieved July 26, 2009, from http://www.examiner .com

Lacan, J. (1949). The mirror stage as formative of the *I* function as revealed in psychoanalytic experience. In B. Fink (Trans.), *Écrits* (pp. 75–81). New York: W. W. Norton.

Mulvey, L. (2009). *Visual and other pleasures* (2nd ed.). London: Palgrave Macmillan.

Peate, I. (2008). Understanding key issues in gender-variant children and young people. *British Journal of Nursing, 17*(17), 1114–1118.

Recchia, E. (1991). Through a shower curtain darkly: Reflexivity as a dramatic component of *psycho. Literature Film Quarterly, 19*(4), 258–266.

Schmadeke, S. (2009, January 28). 2 transsexuals sue state to switch the gender on their birth certificates. *Chicago Tribune.* Retrieved July 21, 2009, from http://archives.chicagotribune.com

Sharp, J., Hart, J., Kolodner, E., & Vachon, C. (Producers), & Pierce, K. (Writer/Director). (1999). *Boys don't cry.* [Motion picture]. United States: Fox Searchlight.

Sloop, J. M. (2000). Disciplining the transgendered: Brandon Teena, public representation, and normativity. *Western Journal of Communication, 64*(2), 165–189.

Sloop, J. M. (2004). *Disciplining gender: Rhetorics of sex identity in contemporary U.S. culture.* Boston: University of Massachusetts Press.

Transgender woman victim of hate crime. (2009, June 11). *United Press International.* Retrieved July 21, 2009, from http://www.upi.com

Triple murder has unusual twist—one female slaying victim had been living as a man. (1994, January 4). *Chicago Tribune.* Retrieved July 23, 2009, from NewsBank online database (Access World News), http://infoweb.newsbank.com

Woman who posed as a man is found slain with 2 others. (1994, January 4). *New York Times.* Retrieved July 23, 2009, from ProQuest Historical Newspapers The New York Times (1851–2006). (Document ID: 116550762).

Worthing, R. (1994, January 17). Deadly deception—Brandon Teena's double life may have led to triple murder. *Chicago Tribune.* Retrieved July 23, 2009, from NewsBank online database (Access World News), http://infoweb .newsbank.com

Summary

This chapter focused on visual perspectives that inform rhetorical analyses of visuals in mediated popular culture texts. We explained the nature of visual communication and some fundamental theories and principles grounding it. Then we explored one psychoanalytic visual perspective—visual pleasure theory—as a means by which to examine underlying messages about subjectivity and sexuality in visual artifacts through the constructs of fetishism, voyeurism, and narcissism. Ultimately, the critic's role is not to reveal causal links between rhetorical arguments proposed in visual texts and viewer perceptions or behaviors but, rather, to reveal what those underlying messages might be and suggest potential implications of them on various audiences.

Challenge

Select a popular TV program, one that enjoys high viewership. Watch an entire episode with the sound turned off. As you do so, answer the following questions:

1. Consider those characters that are portrayed as fetishes, that is, as objects to be gazed at. Describe how they are portrayed as objects. Why do you suppose they are? What messages might this be communicating to viewers?

2. Consider any scenes that might be considered inappropriate for public display in everyday life but that are being shown as "normal" on the program? What messages might this be communicating to viewers?

3. Which characters might viewers be led to identify with, and how are those characters portrayed? That is, how do they look and act? What messages might this be communicating to viewers?

4. Which characters might viewers be led to disassociate with, and how do those characters look and act? What messages might this be communicating to viewers?

5. Considering your answers to the previous questions, what might be some potential implications of the messages sent via visual pleasure theory on various audiences (positive or negative)?

References

Aniston's sexy Mexican escape. (2013, January 14). *Us Weekly,* p. 23.

Barnhurst, K. G., Vari, M., & Rodriguez, I. (2004). Mapping visual studies in communication. *Journal of Communication, 54,* 616–644.

Barthes, R. (1973). *Mythologies* (A. Lavers, Trans.). London: Paladin.

Barthes, R. (1977). *Image-music-text* (S. Heath, Ed. and Trans.). London: Fontana.

Berger, J. (1972). *Ways of seeing.* London: British Broadcasting Association.

Berger, A. A. (1989). *Seeing is believing: An introduction to visual communication.* Mountain View, CA: Mayfield.

Blair, J. A. (1996). The possibility and actuality of visual arguments. *Argumentation and Advocacy, 33,* 1–10.

Bonner, G. (1986). *Augustine of Hippo: Life and controversies.* London: Canterbury Press.

Calafell, B. M., & Delgado, F. P. (2004). Reading Latina/o images: Interrogating *Americanos. Critical Studies in Media Communication. 21,* 1–21.

Debord, G. (1977). *Society of the spectacle.* Detroit, IL: Black and Red.

De Lauretis, T. (1994). *The practice of love: Lesbian sexuality and perverse desire.* Bloomington: Indiana University Press.

Demo, A. T. (2007). The afterimage: Immigration policy after Elian. *Rhetoric and Public Affairs, 10*(1), 27–50.

Doane, M. A. (1991). *Femmes fatales: Feminism, film theory, psychoanalysis.* London: Routledge.

Dyer, R. (1990). *Now you see it: Historical studies on lesbian and gay film.* London: Routledge.

Ehninger, D. (1972). *Contemporary rhetoric: A reader's coursebook.* Glenview, IL: Scott Foresman.

Fanon, F. (1986). *Black skin, white masks.* New York: Grover Press.

Finnegan, C. A. (2001). The naturalistic enthymeme and visual argument: Photographic representation in the "skull controversy." *Argumentation and Advocacy, 37,* 133–149.

Finnegan, C. A. (2003). *Picturing poverty: Print culture and FSA photographs.* Washington, DC: Smithsonian.

Foss, S. (1988). Judy Chicago's *The Dinner Party:* Empowering of women's voice in visual art. In Barbara Bate & Anita Taylor (Eds.), *Women communicating: Studies of women's talk* (pp. 9–26). Norwood, NJ: Ablex.

Freud, S. (1905). *Three essays on the theory of sexuality* (J. Strachey, Trans.). New York: Basic Books. (Reprinted 1962)

Gaines, J. (1988). White privilege and looking relations: Race and gender in feminist film theory, *Screen, 29,* 12–27.

Goodings, L. (2012). Understanding social networks: Lessons from MySpace. *Visual Communication, 11*(4), 485–510.

Hall, S. (Ed.). (1997). *Representation: Cultural representations and signifying practices.* London: Sage.

Hariman, R., & Lucaites, J. L. (2002). Performing civic identity: The iconic photograph of the flag raising on Iwo Jima. *Quarterly Journal of Speech, 88,* 363–392.

Haring, B. J. J., & Kaper, O. E. (Eds.). (2009). *Pictograms or pseudo-script? Non-textual identity marks in practical use in ancient Egypt and elsewhere.* Leuven, Belgium: Peeters.

Hattwig, D., Burgess, J., Bussert, K., & Medaille, A. (2011). *ACRL visual literacy competency standards for higher education.* Retrieved April 13, 2013, from www.ala.org/acrl/standards/visualliteracy

Jay, M. (1993). *Downcast eyes: The denigration of vision in twentieth-century French thought.* Berkeley: California University Press.

Jenks, C. (1995). *Visual culture.* London: Routledge.

Keisner. J. (2008). Do you want to watch? A study of the visual rhetoric of the postmodern horror film. *Women's Studies, 37,* 411–427.

Lacan, J. (1977). *Ecrits* (A. Sheridan, Trans.). New York: Basic Books.

Lester, P. M. (2011). *Visual communication: Images with messages* (5th ed.). Boston: Wadsworth Cengage.

Kimble, J. J., & Olson, L. C. (2006). Visual rhetoric representing Rosie the Riveter: Myth and misconception in J. Howard Miller's "We Can Do It!" poster. *Rhetoric and Public Affairs, 9*(4), 533–569.

Mirzoeff, N. (1999). *An introduction to visual culture.* London: Routledge.

Modleski, T. (1988). *The women who knew too much: Hitchcock and feminist theory.* London: Medhurst.

Mulvey, L. (1975). Visual pleasure and narrative cinema. *Screen, 16,* 6–18.

Mulvey, L. (1989). *Visual and other pleasures.* Bloomington: Indiana University Press.

Mulvey, L. (1996). *Fetishism and curiosity.* Bloomington: Indiana University Press.

Ogden, C. K., & Richards, I. A. (1923). *The meaning of meaning: A study of the influence of language upon thought and of the science of symbolism.* United States: Harvest/HBJ.

Olson, L. (2007). Intellectual and conceptual resources for visual rhetoric: A re-examination of scholarship since 1950. *Review of Communication, 7*(1), 1–19.

O'Neil, J. (1991). *Plato's cave: Desire, power, and the specular functions of the media.* Norwood, NJ: Ablex.

Parmentier, R. J. (1985). Signs' place in *Medias Res:* Peirce's concept of semiotic mediation. In Elizabeth Mertz & Richard J. Parmentier (Eds.), *Semiotic mediation: Sociocultural and psychological perspectives* (pp. 23–48). Orlando, FL: Academic.

Rose, G. (2007). *Visual methodologies* (2nd ed.). Thousand Oaks, CA: Sage.

Sellnow, D., & Ziniel, J. (2007). Rhetorical strategies of visual pleasure in situation comedies: *Friends* and female body image. *Communication and Theater Association of Minnesota Journal, 34,* 62–77.

Shugart, H. A. (2003). She shoots, she scores: Mediated constructions of contemporary female athletes in coverage of the 1999 US women's soccer team. *Western Journal of Communication, 67,* 1–31.

Silverman, K. (1988). *The acoustic mirror: The female voice in psychoanalysis and cinema.* Bloomington: Indiana University Press.

Thornham, S. (1997). *Passionate detachments: An introduction to feminist film theory.* London: Arnold.

Us Weekly. (Fall 2012). Audience profile. *MRI.* Retrieved April 13, 2013, from http://srds.com/mediakits/UsWeekly-print/Demographics.html

Virilio, P. (1994). *The vision machine.* London: British Film Institute.

Walker, J. A., & Chaplin, S. (1997). *Visual culture: An introduction.* Manchester, UK: Manchester University Press.

White, P. (1995). Governing lesbian desire: *Nocturne's* Oedipal fantasy. In L. Pietropaulo & A. Testaferri (Eds.), *Feminisms in the cinema* (pp. 86–105). Bloomington: Indiana University Press.

Young, L. (1996). *Fear of the dark: "Race," gender and sexuality in the cinema.* New York: Routledge.

Student Study Site

Visit the Student Study Site at www.sagepub.com/sellnow2e to read interesting SAGE journal articles, view mobile-friendly key term flashcards, take chapter-specific online web quizzes to test your knowledge, and more!

Chapter 10

Media-Centered Perspectives

We talked about the pervasive nature of music in Chapter 8 and of visuals in Chapter 9. Perhaps even more dramatic, however, is the far-reaching way in which old and new media technology seems to permeate our very existence today. Although one could argue that media have been doing so since the 1960s, it has become increasingly true with the birth of each newly conceived and modified technology tool and application (e.g., Dresner, 2006; Finnemann, 2011; Logan, 2010; Meyrowitz, 1985, 2005; Postman, 1985, 1992). Thus, what I offer as "new" media technologies in this chapter may well be considered "old" or perhaps even obsolete by the time the book is published. Consequently, this chapter will instead focus more on methods by which to examine the role of media in influencing people and society. In doing so, I hope these ideas will translate in meaningful ways to how media technologies function rhetorically even as they continue to be transformed in the years to come.

As with the perspectives for examining music and visuals, a number of media-centered perspectives have been developed to demonstrate the unique ways in which the medium itself influences people and society. Researchers who study media effects commonly employ these perspectives. Media effects research uses social science methods to examine audience responses to media messages. Popular culture critics, however, may also draw upon many of these theories to examine the rhetorical arguments proposed in them.

In this chapter, we focus on several media-centered perspectives that propose how both old and new media function uniquely to influence how we believe and behave. To begin, we discuss what Marshall McLuhan (1964) and McLuhan and Fiore (1967) first conceptualized and then Neil Postman later labeled *media ecology theory* (Postman &

Weingartner, 1969). Then we consider *media logic* as first described by David Altheide and Robert Snow in 1979 followed by *social learning theory* as originally developed by Albert Bandura in 1977. Then we introduce *parasocial relationship theory* as first described by Donald Horton and Richard Wohl in 1956 and *cultivation theory* as initially conceived by George Gerbner and Larry Gross in 1976. As with each chapter, we close with some published and student sample analyses.

MEDIA ECOLOGY THEORY

Media ecology theory focuses expressly on how media and communication processes affect human perception, understanding, beliefs, and behaviors. Although media theory pioneer Marshall McLuhan (1964) is perhaps best known for coining the phrase *the medium is the message* (a.k.a. massage), his ideas about the ways in which media and society interact and influence each other are far more significant than what the catchphrase might imply. Essentially, the theory suggests that media (1) infuse every act and action in society, (2) fix our perceptions and organize our experiences, and (3) tie the world together into a *global village* (McLuhan, 1962).

McLuhan's ideas garnered a good deal of criticism among academics during the 1970s and 1980s. Much of this criticism was actually based on their misinterpretation of the catchphrase to mean he dismissed the importance of message content altogether. What McLuhan, in fact, argued was that message content affects our conscious state and the medium affects our unconscious state. The medium is the message because "the medium's effects remain the same, no matter what the content" (Morrison, 2006, p. 178). The essence of media ecology theory can be explained according to several historical turning points.

Media History

First, during the *preliterate* [tribal] *era,* people communicated in face-to-face settings through storytelling and the spoken word. Then, the introduction of the phonetic alphabet "shattered those bonds of tribal man [sic]" (McLuhan, 1964, p. 173). During this *literate* [print] *era,* writing replaced speaking as the primary mode of communication. People no longer had to be physically present with others and, consequently, people became more individualistic. The invention of the printing press (a.k.a. *Gutenberg era*) intensified these effects of individualism, fragmentation, and isolation. Mass production also made it possible to deliver the same content over and over again. Thus, another effect of the medium was the production of citizens that were similar to one another.

The *electronic era* emerged with the invention of the telegraph, telephone, typewriter, radio, and TV. Since then, electronic and new media have become increasingly dominant forces pervading our lives and allowing us to be connected with others across time and space. In the 1960s, for example, TV allowed us to "see" the Vietnam War as if we were there while sitting in our living rooms. Today, computers, smartphones, the Internet, and wireless technology make doing so even more accessible 24/7. Similarly, telephones made it possible to talk synchronistically with far away others even though we were not physically present with them. Today, we can do so nearly anytime and anyplace by talking, texting, Facebook chatting, or videoconferencing on smartphones and iPads as well as on laptop and desktop computers. And, records and phonographs made it possible to choose the music we wanted to hear without attending a live performance. Then we could purchase and play albums and CDs comprised of a set of musical numbers performed by a musical artist or group. Today, we often download only certain songs rather than entire albums. Neil Postman (1992) coined the term technopoly to describe the endless ways in which technology dominates our thinking and behaviors today. Essentially, we are living examples of McLuhan's predictions regarding the role and effects of electronic and new media on individuals and societies.

QUESTIONING YOUR ETHICS . . .

Today, groups of people with similar interests often join web forums or groups where they can share stories and support one another. Participants of *pro-ana* web forums support one another in claiming that anorexia is a "lifestyle choice" that should be respected by doctors and family. Considering the conflicting issues between freedom of speech and health and safety, do you think such forums are ethical? Explain.

Media Laws

After McLuhan died in 1980, his son published their notion of the tetrad as an organizing concept for understanding the impact of technology on society (McLuhan & McLuhan, 1988):

(1) What does the medium enhance or amplify in society? For example, the telephone enhanced the face-to-face spoken word, and the cell phone further enhanced its effect. Similarly, checks made it possible to pay for goods without actually having cash in hand. Credit cards, ATM machines, and the Internet amplified these effects.

(2) What does the medium make obsolete? Some argue, for example, that the Internet is gradually making the traditional postal service obsolete, mobile phones are making landlines obsolete, and e-books and newspapers are making libraries and print journalism (i.e., printed copies of newspapers) obsolete. Similarly, computers have rendered typewriters pretty much obsolete.

(3) What does the medium retrieve from the past? Today, the Internet allows us to retrieve TV programs and commercials that aired in the 1950s and 1960s. We can also retrieve information on websites that have been retired via programs like the Way Back Machine (http://web.archive.org).

(4) What does the medium flip into when pushed to its limits? Many argue the Internet has immeasurably transformed how we think and behave. Many board games, for example,

morphed into video arcade games, then into computer games, and now into multiplayer online games. Writing and sending letters and greeting cards has morphed into e-mail, e-cards, Tweets, and Facebook posts.

APPLYING WHAT YOU'VE LEARNED . . .

How do you feel when your mobile phone battery is dead, you have no bars, or you can't get Internet access? If you feel anxious, then you understand something of what McLuhan meant by "the medium is the message."

MEDIA LOGIC

Media logic focuses on the degree to which users tend to take the medium and its social uses for granted and, thus, fail to realize how it influences us to believe and behave about what is normal, good, desirable, and so forth. In their book *Media Logic*, David Altheide and Robert Snow (1979) argued that TV was the dominant medium in our culture. Since the publication of their book, however, new media technology has exploded far beyond TV. Some scholars have introduced the term mediatization to account for the "logic" of this new media and these new areas of application. As we mentioned earlier, many people today own personal computers, laptops, mobile and smartphones, iPads, iPods, and GPS navigation devices or apps. We own high-definition flat screen digital TVs with access to multiple network, cable, and satellite stations. We own digital recording and streaming devices that allow us to record and watch programs at our convenience. And many of us are regular users of any number of social networks such as Facebook, Twitter, LinkedIn, and YouTube. Thus, media logic is probably even more prominent in shaping our beliefs and behaviors today than it was when Altheide and Snow first conceptualized the theory.

APPLYING WHAT YOU'VE LEARNED . . .

How often do you do a quick Google search to find an answer to a question? Where and when? Do you consciously think about doing so, or is it second nature? The latter is an example of media logic.

Closely related to media ecology, media logic focuses specifically on the ways in which the medium and its social uses influence us about how to live. Last weekend, for example, I watched the Golden Globe Awards. I was doing laundry at the time, so I paused the program whenever I went to fold another load of clothes. If I missed something, I hit the reverse button so I could catch it again. I ended up going to bed before the program was over, so I hit the record button and watched the rest the next morning. It didn't take long, however, because I fast-forwarded through all the commercials. I didn't think twice about doing any of these things. This is an example of media logic.

I also become frustrated when I attempt to Google something or someone and fail to get the information I want quickly or when I want to get a quick overview of a concept on Wikipedia and the entry is underdeveloped. While watching the Golden Globes last weekend, for example, I wondered how old actress Helen Hunt was. A quick Google search provided the answer while I watched. Similarly, the other day my spouse and I were driving to pick up some groceries, and he asked me what the actual meaning of fondue was. A quick search online via my iPhone again provided the answer before we even got to the store. I expect instant access to information from the Internet and don't think twice about it unless my attempts to do so fail me in some way. This is also an example of media logic.

Each person in my family has a smartphone. I've become accustomed to having instant access to them 24/7. Even if I'm in a meeting, they can text me, and I can step out of the room to see what's up. When I was growing up, my parents didn't have the luxury of instant access to me as I do with my own children. My smartphone is also synched to both my e-mail and appointment calendar. It also synchs to my car so I can play music and answer calls without taking my hands off the steering wheel. I don't own a camera or iPod anymore because I use the apps on my phone to take pictures and listen to music. I take my smartphone for granted in these ways. Media logic is interesting to the rhetorical critic because various media and their social uses shape our perceptions of what is normal or abnormal, right or wrong, desirable or undesirable, and so on.

Media logic manifests itself in our taken-for-granted social uses of media, but it also does so in the actual programs we watch. Consider a TV program or film from the 1970s, 1980s, or 1990s. Do you notice the outdated computers, telephones, radios, and televisions touted in them as state-of-the-art? The fact that such outdated media are so noticeable is also a reflection of media logic. Now consider a current TV program or film set in the present day. Do you notice the technology being used in them? The fact that we don't notice them because they are normal also reflects media logic. Moreover, when someone in a contemporary TV program or film uses what we consider to be outdated media, we usually interpret it as odd or even comical. One funny scene in *A Night at the Roxbury,* for example, occurs when Steve's (played by Will Ferrell) and Doug's (played by Chris Kattan) mother (played by Loni Anderson) provides them with enormous, out-of-date cell phones so they can contact her if necessary.

Commodification

Two particularly compelling aspects of media logic are commodification and amplification and reduction. Commodification has to do with advertisements blending with programming. Initially, commodification had to do with commercials certain products aired intermittently throughout a program. While such advertisements do still occur, our ability to channel surf during commercials or fast-forward through them on our DVRs has led to more advertising of products during the actual programs themselves. To clarify, TV programs in the 1950s and 1960s could not show a brand name of a soda pop or beer. The first film to show a brand name of a product was *ET: The Extraterrestrial* in the 1980s, where the characters ate Reese's Pieces. Today, doing so is a common practice. It is so common, in fact, that the fictional Duff beer Homer drinks on *The Simpsons* is used for comic effect. You may recall the 1990s film *The Truman Show,* which was filled with commodification. Truman's wife would often stop while in mid-conversation with Truman to advertise the coffee beans or some other product she was using.

Another interesting shift in terms of TV commercials is the time allotted for each one. Again, in the 1950s and 1960s, a commercial often ran for a full minute. Today, commercials are usually no more than 10 to 15 seconds long and interrupt the program more frequently. Moreover, a program might show the same commercial several times during the 30-minute or 60-minute time slot. Why? Because media logic suggests viewers will likely only catch it once if at all.

Finally, TV commercials are sometimes more compelling than the programs they are aired with. Interestingly, sometimes the commercials are compelling, but viewers fail to even realize what product they're selling. At any rate, this notion of ads blending with programming has become practically seamless on TV today. Consequently, viewers may be led to believe certain apparel, products, and even hairstyles are normal and desirable based on what they see worn and used by the characters on their favorite programs.

Commodification occurs on the Internet as well. I like to show YouTube clips as examples when I teach. Unfortunately, sometimes I have to allow an advertisement to play (or at least a part of it) in order to get to the clip I'm trying to show. Remixes are another form of commodification that occurs on the Internet. Advertisers will remix a popular song, program, film, or image to sell their product. The "He Went to Jared" visual of Gollum from *The Lord of the Rings* trilogy in Chapter 9 is an example.

QUESTIONING YOUR ETHICS . . .

How does commodification differ from subliminal advertising? Why might commodification be deemed appropriate by producers when subliminal advertising is deemed unethical? Where do you stand on the issue and why?

Amplification and Reduction

Amplification and reduction has to do with what is shown and not shown on a TV program, film, Internet website, or video game. For example, TV news programs are market driven, and as such, program directors must make choices about what to air partly based on ratings. Hence, what is shown on TV news may not be a complete story at all. What is not being told may be as important to the rhetorical critic as what is being told. Viewers of TV news in April 2003, for instance, watched as President Bush "declared victory in Iraq." Not until months later did the news programs begin to air stories that revealed the fighting was far from over. The rhetorical critic seeks to deconstruct what is and is not being told as normal, right, and good on TV news as well as on other programs.

TV's influential power with regard to amplification and reduction has decreased somewhat thanks to our easy access to the Internet today. When we question something we see on TV news, for example, we are likely to conduct some personal fact-checking by going to multiple online news websites or to social network posts for clarification. Sometimes, however, breaking news stories that appear first on Internet websites are based on incomplete or even incorrect information. Following the December 2012 massacre at Sandy Hook elementary school, for example, officials actually warned that, if caught, people posting misinformation on Twitter could be prosecuted.

SOCIAL LEARNING THEORY

Albert Bandura (b. 1925), a cognitive psychologist at Stanford University, is credited with conceptualizing *social learning theory*. Social learning theory focuses on how we learn to believe and behave based on observation, imitation, and modeling. Essentially, Bandura (1977) argues that most human behavior is not learned from the effects of our own actions but by observing others who model certain behaviors and the consequences they experience as a result. Then, we imitate behaviors based on the consequences we observe. In other words, the actions and consequences we observe lead us to imitate the behavior of those we aspire to be like and to avoid enacting the behaviors of those we do not want to be like.

We learn how we ought to and ought not to believe and behave from live models (actual people demonstrating a behavior) and symbolic models (people demonstrating a behavior through a medium such as TV, film, video games, and so forth). Bandura (1977) suggests that social learning occurs when four conditions are met. First, we must pay attention to the model demonstrating the behavior. In other words, if a TV program happens to be on, but no one is actually watching it, social learning cannot occur from it. We must be able to remember the behavior we observed. To continue with the TV example, if several of the programs I watch portray people drinking alcohol and having fun without negative consequences (e.g., vomiting, driving drunk, having a hangover, destroying relationships), I'm likely to remember it's fun to drink alcohol. We must be able to replicate the behavior. If I am a recovering alcoholic or a minor, I probably should not replicate the behavior, however, I might be influenced to try to do so because of my memory of observing others having fun. Finally, we must be motivated to imitate the behavior we observed. We are motivated to learn to imitate behaviors based on how we interpret the consequences of others who enact them. If the TV programs I watch show people drinking alcohol followed by negative consequences, I might not be motivated to imitate the behavior.

> **APPLYING WHAT YOU'VE LEARNED . . .**
>
> Consider a favorite TV program. Can you identify the good guys and the bad guys in terms of whose behaviors viewers are likely to imitate. Why? Explain what actions and consequences occur to lead you to this conclusion.

PARASOCIAL RELATIONSHIP THEORY

Parasocial relationship theory describes one-sided relationships where one party knows a great deal about the other party, but not vice versa. Parasocial relationships often occur between celebrities and fans as well as between TV characters and viewers (Brooks, 1997). For example, I sometimes say "I grew up with Jodie Foster." She and I are the same age, and I've watched many of her movies and interviews over the years while both of us were kids, teens, and adults. So I will admit I cheered for her when she won the Cecil B. DeMille Golden Globe award for lifetime achievement in 2013. Obviously, my "friend" Jodie and I didn't actually grow up together, and she certainly doesn't know me. But I have followed her career for decades, and I know quite a bit about her as a result.

Parasocial relationships emerge by establishing a bond of intimacy. A bond of intimacy is created when a viewer begins to feel he or she really knows the celebrity or character even though the celebrity or character does not know the viewer. For example, while the popular TV program *Friends* was in production, viewers often referred to Rachel, Monica, Phoebe, Chandler, Ross, and Joey as though they were real people rather than as characters being portrayed on a sitcom. And I would argue that my mom has established a bond of intimacy with Matt Lauer from NBC's *Today* show. She often talks to me about Mr. Lauer as though she knows him personally. She will say things like, "Oh, that Matt is so 'dishy'" and "I just love Matt." Of course, my mom never met Matt Lauer. Yet, she talks of him as though they are on a first-name basis. Two factors that contribute to the bond of intimacy are realism and privacy.

Realism refers to how believable the characters and their encounters are perceived to be. Again, the characters and their encounters on *Friends* seemed believable to viewers. They experienced the kinds of fun, arguments, setbacks, and so forth viewers thought to be normal for 20-somethings trying to make it in the city. Today, *Modern Family* attempts to create a similar sense of realism. Also, programs like *Justified* seem believable because the action takes place in real cities and counties in Kentucky and the plots are about real-life issues currently in the Kentucky news. And programs like *Newsroom* seem real because the action takes place in what looks very much like a real newsroom and the plots and stories are based on contemporary stories and issues. Some people argue that films and video games go too far in depicting realism. This objection usually focuses on graphic violence in films like *Django Unchained* or *Zero Dark Thirty* and video games like MadWorld, Grand Theft Auto, and Postal 2. We often hear from proponents of this position after mass shootings like the ones at Columbine, Aurora, Virginia Tech, and Sandy Hook.

Privacy refers to how viewers often get to know characters personally as they watch them privately in the comfort of their own homes. Showing small, personal encounters and experiences of characters may make the characters seem more like friends and enemies than actors. The TV series *Downton Abbey* is good example of showing personal encounters and experiences that encourage viewers to believe they "know" the characters.

Strategies that enhance privacy include seeing things through the eyes (perspective) of the characters and hearing their inner thoughts. The TV series *How I Met Your Mother* uses voice-over techniques as a way to hear Ted's thoughts as he recounts the past to his kids. As the TV and film industries become more sophisticated in their ability to depict realism and intimacy, so will the potential implications of parasocial relationships increase.

A good deal of ongoing debate has emerged surrounding how and where to draw the line on privacy sharing on social networking sites like Facebook and Twitter. Some of it focuses on making choices about what we share about ourselves, and some of it focuses on how to manage the phenomenon of others posting information and images about us without our consent. For example, Alec Baldwin and Charlie Sheen both seemed to cross a line regarding what they posted in ways that hurt their public images. Thus, many celebrities, public figures, and corporations today actually hire people to maintain their online presence in ways that share private details that will not damage their image.

APPLYING WHAT YOU'VE LEARNED . . .

Consider a TV series about a family that has been on air for at least three years. To what extent does watching the children as they grow up and experience the rituals of growing up make the program seem like an example of everyday real life? To what extent do the characters take on lives of their own in terms of perceiving them as real people and *a real family?*

CULTIVATION THEORY

Former Communication professor, George Gerbner (1919–2005) and American screenwriter and producer Larry Gross are credited with conceptualizing *cultivation theory*. Cultivation theory (Gerbner & Gross, 1976) suggests that cumulative exposure to violent behaviors on TV, the Internet, and video games leads to significant long-term effects regarding what the everyday real world is like. In other words, continual exposure to a consistent message about what the real world is like can shape a user's attitude about the world. Their original work focuses on how repeated showings of violence on TV influence viewers to believe the world is a mean and scary place. Of course, media don't create or cause beliefs or behaviors but merely maintain and propagate them. Moreover, TV typically serves to reinforce rather than counter conventional beliefs and behaviors. Thus, people who watch a lot of TV are more likely to be influenced via cultivation effects than people who don't.

An argument about cultivation effects is often made about TV, film, and video game violence. Conclusions of numerous studies have been contradictory. Still it remains a fervent field of study. The concept of cultivation theory has been extended to consider repeated and consistent exposure to other types of messages as well. For example, some have argued that the thinning of Hollywood phenomenon (where the most popular female characters are noticeably thin) serves to cultivate a perception that women ought to be pencil thin. A similar correlation has been drawn regarding soap operas where casual sexual relationships with multiple partners are depicted as normal and perhaps even desirable. What these extensions of cultivation theory suggest is that repetition of a similar argument conveyed over and over again eventually leads users to believe the message to be in some way true in the real world.

Ultimately, electronic and new media function uniquely to shape viewers' beliefs and behaviors. Media ecology, media logic, social learning, and cultivation theory help reveal how they do so.

CONDUCTING AN ANALYSIS USING A MEDIA-CENTERED PERSPECTIVE

Although you can conduct an analysis relying on any one of these media-centered perspectives, rhetorical critics typically combine one or more of them with another rhetorical perspective (e.g., neo-Aristotelian, narrative, dramatistic, symbolic convergence, neo-Marxist, feminist, illusion of life, visual pleasure theory). As with the other approaches, once you've selected an artifact to examine as a text and considered the rhetorical situation, you follow the processes of description, interpretation, and evaluation.

Step 1: Selecting an Appropriate Text

Two general considerations guide you in selecting an artifact to examine as a text. First, you might consider the verbal and nonverbal messages (i.e., talk and visual images) as interesting in terms of what they say about how we ought to or ought not to believe or behave. Oftentimes, this is guided by one of the traditional rhetorical perspectives. For example, if you wanted to examine the HBO comedy–drama *Girls* according to the roles and rules it conveys for men and women in society, your analysis would be grounded in a feminist perspective. You might decide to focus on one episode, one season, or several seasons. However, your focus would be on what those episodes are saying from a feminist perspective. Second, if you want to focus on how the TV medium itself works to send those messages via commodification, amplification and reduction, intimacy, realism, or cultivation effects, then your feminist analysis would be framed around those media-centered constructs. In other words, what messages of commodification are being sent that relate to the roles and rules for men and women in society? What messages are being amplified and reduced with regard to the roles and rules for women and men in society? And so on.

Step 2: Examining the Text (Describe and Interpret)

Let's continue with the *Girls* example. You begin by describing the text. You might explain the overt story line as well as the major characters. The primary story line follows the lives of a close group of 20-something young adults living in New York City. The main characters are Hannah (an aspiring writer whose parents cut her off financially), Jessa (world-traveling Bohemian cousin of Shoshanna), Marnie (Hannah's serious and responsible best friend), Shoshanna (bubbly and innocent American cousin of Jessa who loves *Sex and the City*), and Adam (Hannah's aloof lover as well as part-time carpenter and actor). The overt humor stems from what they learn from the mistakes they make trying to navigate their lives in the big city each day.

Once you've described the overt story, you proceed to interpret the text according to media-centered constructs. Your goal, however, remains grounded in what is being said via these constructs related to a feminist perspective. In terms of commodification, you might argue that tattoos like Hannah's and vintage attire are appropriate and normal for 20-something young women. You might mention that women are amplified as subjects with agency. The only male main character is Adam. His story line revolves mostly around being Hannah's lover. You might discuss when characters text and sext rather than communicate in other ways (media logic). These young adults are portrayed as making mistakes while working in low-end jobs but still aspiring to make it in their dream careers (realism and intimacy). You would again cite some examples. You might ultimately talk about social learning theory (What is the viewer led to model?) and cultivation effects (What is the consistent message sent over time about normal and desirable behaviors for young women and men in society?).

Step 3: Evaluate Potential Implications of the Text

As in any analysis, you end with an answer to the so-what question. What are the potential implications of this argument on viewers? You might talk about positive implications for young adults and perseverance to navigate adulthood successfully or young women as subjects rather than objects. Or you might discuss potentially negative implications of its messages about casual sex. What are the potential implications of doing a media-centered analysis of a television program like this? You might talk about social learning theory in that viewers might decide it's normal to engage in casual sex. Granted, your analysis of the program would be more detailed than what I've described here. I merely offer these suggestions as the kinds of things your media-centered criticism might bring out.

SAMPLE PUBLISHED ESSAYS

(1) Read the article "Critiquing Reality-Based Televisual Black Fatherhood: A Critical Analysis of *Run's House* and *Snoop Dogg's Father Hood*," by Debra Smith (2008) and published in *Critical Studies in Media Communication*. The analysis compares images of black fatherhood portrayed in these two programs with that of the *The Cosby Show* of the 1980s. As you read, consider how she integrates media-centered constructs of realism and privacy for establishing a bond of intimacy with viewers. What conclusions and implications does she propose regarding these arguments and the audiences who watch the programs? Do you think other reality TV programs develop similar bonds of intimacy? Explain.

(2) Read the article "Examining the Effects of Hegemonic Depictions of Female Bodies on Television: A Call for Theory and Programmatic Research," by Alexandra Hendriks (2002) and published in *Critical Studies in Media Communication*. The article provides a nice example of an analysis rooted in a feminist perspective but doing so through the media-centered perspectives of cultivation theory and social learning theory. As you read, consider contemporary televised examples of her claims. Do you think television has changed much since her article was published? Explain.

(3) Read the article "What Good Is the 'You' in YouTube? Cyberspectacle and Subjectivity" by Elizabeth Clark (2008) and published in *Gnovis*. Although not a textual analysis of one artifact, she proposes interesting food for thought regarding the "pseudo-reality" we live in today as we interact with new media like YouTube. She argues that YouTube is a powerful example of new media functioning to distract and entertain passive viewers. Moreover, although the platform does allow space for marginalized voices to be heard, it also has

limitations. In her words, is it "liberatory or repressive, spectacle or subversion?" (Clark, 2008). Given the ways you interact with YouTube, do you agree with Clark? Why or why not?

SAMPLE STUDENT ESSAY

Holly Strandberg wrote "*Harry Potter and the Chamber of Secrets:* Why It Works" for a final class project. As you read the essay, consider how realism and intimacy are used to make the story believable and compelling. Do you agree? Why or why not?

Harry Potter and the Chamber of Secrets: **Why It Works**

Holly Strandberg

Muggles, hippogriffs, floo powder, and an exciting game of Quidditch mean nothing to the few people in the world who have yet to become engulfed in the frenzy that is Harry Potter. To followers, however, these once-insignificant terms have taken on meaning all their own. In J. K. Rowling's works, an entire world has been developed of wizards, witchcraft, mystery, and intrigue. The books, now enhanced by the cinema, have gained popularity that reaches beyond age and beyond literary maturity.

In the movie based on Rowling's second Potter book, *Harry Potter and the Chamber of Secrets,* the audience journeys with Harry and his friends. Harry, now in his second year at Hogwarts School of Witchcraft and Wizardry, finds himself—yet again—saving the day against his nemesis, Lord Voldemort (the most evil wizard who has ever been). When Harry was a baby, Lord Voldemort killed his parents and also tried to kill Harry. Unsuccessful in his attempts, Harry's triumph over this evil wizard grew legendary amongst the other wizards. Lord Voldemort's power was reduced to almost nothing, and he, on most counts, disappeared. Within the movies,

however, Harry and his friends see where Lord Voldemort's power still prevails and work toward ridding the world of his continued evil. While doing so, however, they find themselves in very precarious situations.

In *Harry Potter and the Chamber of Secrets,* Harry and his friends are faced with the struggle of discovering what the "chamber of secrets" really is and what powers lie within it. They face peril in the midst of a forest of spiders as well as fight a basilisk (a really big, ugly snake) to save the day. Within this text, even one of their own faces the terrible fate of being petrified while attempting to uncover Lord Voldemort's evil plot. Even our charmed Harry faces ridicule as he is suspected of being the heir who has opened the chamber and, in doing so, has unleashed the horror terrorizing Hogwarts.

In the end, however, through the strength of his friendship and the confidence he finds within himself, Harry is able to save the day and, one more time, stop Lord Voldemort's evil plan from being carried out. While doing so, he also clears a good friend's name (Hagrid) and helps the headmaster (Dumbledore) to regain control of the school. He also tricks another evil wizard, Lucius Malfoy, into freeing his house-elf (Dobby), and all of his good works are rewarded within the school setting when exams are cancelled for the entire student population. It's all in a day's work for Harry Potter.

The significance of studying the impact of the Harry Potter phenomenon is pretty obvious. Surveys suggest, for example, that almost 60 percent of U.S. children ages 6 to 17 have read at least one Harry Potter book (Race, 2001). Millions of children and adults have read the books, "making Harry Potter and his adventures a topic of household conversation" (Black & Eisenwine, 2001, p. 32).

In an article by Cole and Brooke Nelson, Cole (age 11) describes why he's crazy about Potter: "With the wand you could heal cuts without bandaids. The flying broom you could use so there would be no more pollution, and the Quidditch game is just so cool. It involves balls, goals, and players, but it's really neat because it's played 50 feet up in the air. It seems like it would be a little more challenging than our basketball. . . . If I could pick one to have of my own from the Harry Potter book, it would have to be a wand. My wand would be made of beech wood with a phoenix tail feather inside it, just like Harry's wand, but I don't know what size it would need to be. I guess I'd have to go get measured" (Nelson & Nelson, 2002, p. 20).

The Harry Potter phenomenon is not limited to youth. Consider, for instance, the testimony of New York City Board of Education Administrative Assistant Superintendent Winifred Radigan (2001): "The truth is, I love Harry Potter, and Hermione and Ron, and the world Rowling has

created. . . . What speaks to me is how the books console that inner child who still longs for her magic to be discovered and nurtured" (p. 694). The audience of the Potter frenzy is not limited to adolescents but to an entire world of Potter potentials. Some of the Harry Potter honors include "The British Book Awards Children's Book of the Year and the Smarties Prize," according to the Scholastic/Harry Potter website. In addition, book rights have been sold to England, France, Germany, Italy, Holland, Greece, Finland, Denmark, Spain, and Sweden. The books and, by association, the movies are as far-reaching as the literary world can take you. "The Potter series has already been translated into more than two dozen languages. In just two years, after being refused by at least two major publishers, J. K. Rowling is now the hottest property in children's literature and a serial prize-winner to boot" (Tucker, 1999, p. 221). Fandango, the nation's largest online ticketing company, claimed that, "'*Chamber of Secrets*' sold nearly twice the amount of advance tickets the first film had sold by this time last year" (Goodale, 2002, p. 2).

In short, there is a Potter mania sweeping the world. Who cares? Why does it matter that schools are changing their curriculum to include Harry and his friends? Why should it matter that people of all ages, races, and backgrounds are reading Rowling's books and standing in line to see the Potter movies? Do the movies "celebrate the notion of a different and exclusive form of education for a privileged few" (Tucker, 1999, p. 223), or do they help students "see themselves in [Harry]" (Gibbs, 2003, p. 61)? What secrets does the "chamber of secrets" really unlock about the reality of the world we're living in?

(Continued)

(Continued)

My overall purpose in this analysis is to demonstrate not that the Harry Potter phenomenon is a way in which to justify rebellion within adolescents today but that it in fact empowers a typically powerless group of individuals to make difficult choices. In the end of the movie, Albus Dumbledore (the headmaster of Hogwarts) tells Harry, "It is not our abilities that show who we really are. It is our choices" (Rowling, 1999). My amended version of this quote is that "it is not what we have that shows who we really are. It is the choices we make with what we've got."

Rhetorical Perspective and Method

In this essay, I use a media-centered approach to reveal messages that *Harry Potter and the Chamber of Secrets* sends about empowerment and disempowerment. As such, my analysis focuses on hegemony, which draws from a neo-Marxist perspective. Within this film (and, of course, the book as well), there is a constant and serious struggle over power, and the "powerful" and "powerless" characters are constantly changing.

By definition, neo-Marxist criticism is an "approach concerned with ideology, with class, and with the distribution of power in society" (Brummett, 1994, p. 111). The greatest overarching principle is that of power and, specifically, "the way material affects power" (p. 113). Moreover, "all forms of power have symbolic dimensions: Material and financial resources are associated not only with economics but with social status or domination. . . . That is where the ideology comes in" (Sillars & Gronbeck,

2001, p. 173). An ideology, according to Marx, is a false consciousness set forth by the ruling class and accepted by the lower classes even though accepting it also means accepting disempowerment. As such, the lower classes are "victims of the capitalistic ideology" (p. 261). By analyzing *Harry Potter and the Chamber of Secrets* from this perspective, we begin to see how the struggle between who ought to and ought not to have power is worked out in seemingly unimportant everyday actions and experiences.

Within a neo-Marxist perspective, we must consider whether the messages offered via economic metaphors (small signs and meanings associated with them) reinforce the status quo (a preferred reading) or whether they oppose it (oppositional). This analysis examines these issues of empowerment and disempowerment using several media-centered constructs. More specifically, what strategies of *commodification* (advertisements blending with programming) are offered as they relate to issues of power? Also, how is *realism* (what is seen and heard becomes "real" to viewers) employed? Finally, with regard to *intimacy,* in what ways are viewers encouraged to get to know the characters (including their thoughts and feelings) and essentially become "friends" with them?

REVIEW OF LITERATURE

The issue I focus on throughout this essay is that of children feeling empowered to be happy with who they are. Youth, particularly during adolescence, are faced with more problems today than ever before. Historically, youth have struggled to be accepted within their schools and amongst their friends. However, children today are trying to figure out how to be accepted even within their own families. They struggle with divorce, blended families, death of loved ones, not fitting in, not knowing where to fit in, peer pressure, and so on.

Many studies have been published regarding the development of youth and the impact of life experiences on them. With an ever-increasing divorce rate in the United States alone, children are no longer confident about the stability of their family units. Add to that chaos guns in schools, drug addiction, and peer pressure, and the youth of today need to be able to stand up with confidence in what they believe knowing that it will not always be the most preferred or accepted idea, particularly amidst their friends.

Within the reviews of *Harry Potter and the Chamber of Secrets,* there are a number of opinions as to the real message the film delivers. From devil worshipping to changing spirituality, from justifying rebellion to demonstrating how youth can depend on those around them, the film (and the series, for that matter) is a hotbed of conversion. Rowling herself answered these questions when she said, "I admire bravery above almost every other characteristic. . . . Bravery is a very glamorous virtue, but I'm talking about bravery in all sorts of places" (Gibbs, 2003, p. 62). In the same article, Gibbs writes how Rowling created an e-mail friendship with a young girl—Catie—who was battling cancer. Rowling explains how Catie's battle is one of the reasons she writes. "Hang on to hope, or surrender to fear. [Rowling] addresses children as though they know as much or more than she

does about the things that matter. Kids like the characters she has created, Harry above all, not because he is fantastic, but because he is familiar" (p. 63).

In an "adult" world, children are far too often disregarded as not having feelings, although they deal with the same grown-up issues without as many grown-up experiences. Battling a terminal illness, dealing with a financial difficulty, and trying to be accepted in a vicious world are only a few of the challenges many of them face on a daily basis.

ANALYSIS

In considering the issues of empowerment and disempowerment, many of the subject position relationships are visible in *Harry Potter and the Chamber of Secrets.* First, it's easily visible to the audience that Harry is helplessly disempowered in his aunt and uncle's home. He is treated horribly, and only in his escape to school is he saved from the reality of Privet Drive. In a similar fashion, the house-elf (Dobby) is a slave in his master's home. He punishes himself repeatedly for speaking ill of his housemaster, although he is treated worse than can be imagined. Both of these characters, however, commit their lives to trying to help other people around them and, in the end, find rewards by doing just that.

With regard to materialism, the audience easily recognizes that the Weasley family is poor. All of the children are dressed in worn-out wizard robes and use less than state-of-the-art supplies and books throughout school. Their red, tussled hair and dirty clothes are

(Continued)

(Continued)

the mark of a family not well-to-do in materialism but well-to-do in love. In contrast, the Malfoy family has everything, including the money to buy the rest of the members of the Slytherin Quidditch team the latest in flying brooms. Although they have money, however, they certainly do not have love. Viewers are led to dislike them as anti-models who should not be empowered.

Hermione, one of Harry's good friends, is not noticeably well-off or poor. However, Hermione is muggle-born and, therefore, not the "pure-blood" wizard some feel should be allowed into Hogwarts. Although brilliant and resourceful, Hermione finds herself battling the stereotypes of her non-pure wizard heritage.

Even with regard to the teachers at Hogwarts, there is a visible power struggle. Severus Snape, one of the nastiest teachers at Hogwarts, often displays his power over others (particularly Harry and his friends) to feel better about himself. However, even Snape is powerless over the great headmaster, Dumbledore, who seems to have everyone's best interests at heart.

Overall, *Harry Potter and the Chamber of Secrets* takes an oppositional inflected argument regarding issues of power. Although in contemporary society, most people—youth in particular—come to believe that having more is, in essence, being more, Harry and his friends demonstrate something different. Regardless of the relationships they encounter, even with the annoying bathroom ghost (Moaning Myrtle), Harry demonstrates that—above all else—humility, kindness, friendship, and loyalty are the traits most worthy of being exalted. In this way, the film empowers a group of adolescents who find themselves powerless in a constant world of upheaval, and it encourages them to make choices that will impact their lives in positive ways.

The obvious materialistic economic metaphors within this film are often defeated. For example, when Malfoy is playing against Harry during the Slytherin–Gryffindor Quidditch match, Malfoy is on a far superior broomstick. Harry is being chased by an out-of-control bludger (ball) and is also dealing with a severely broken arm. In the end, however, Malfoy loses control of his material superiority when he lands on his back in a pile of dirt on the Quidditch field. Harry, however, goes on to win the game. Again, the message reinforced is not that newer is better but that it's the type of person you are and the choices you make that make a difference.

In truth, the most influential rhetorical strategy of the Harry Potter film is how it draws the viewer in through realism and intimacy. As described earlier in this analysis, "Harry and his pals are old friends. I know them well" (Radigan, 2001, p. 694). Their lives and struggles become real for the viewers, as does the setting in which everything takes place. We, as an audience, see for ourselves what it's like to be a part of life at Hogwarts, and we do what we must to enter into the realm of that world for ourselves. In addition, viewers empathize with the problems Harry and his friends face. Although most youth have never likely gone into the Dark Forest to face an army of horrendous spiders, they still find themselves struggling with the monsters of life each day in their own ways, and Harry's experience becomes that much more real for them because of it.

We may not be able to purchase a Nimbus 2000 broom for ourselves, but we understand the societal message of owning "the best." The youth most influenced by this film, then, may understand what it's like to be left with hand-me-down clothing, used books, or—if nothing else—not being trendy in the latest styles. Even Hogwarts itself is an example of commodification. It is a private institution accepting only the "chosen" to attend. However, even within all of this materialism, the message of loyalty and friendship prevails.

CONCLUSIONS, IMPLICATIONS, SUGGESTIONS

We, as viewers, understand what it's like not to fit in because we've all experienced it at one time or another. Whatever the cause might be (and Harry and his friends cover pretty much everything—being an orphan, being singled out within the school, not being wealthy, being bullied, coming from a different background or race), Harry and his friends are each and every one of us. The reason it is so vital to analyze this film, then, is that it is defining us even as it develops the lives of Harry and his friends.

One of the greatest critic concerns of this film is that it may make us feel our own behaviors (or misbehaviors) are justified as long as they are for the greater good. Some suggest that Harry and his company are being rewarded because they broke the rules rather than in spite of their disobedience. However, this analysis suggests something different. Youth often disregard authority figures and, through the consequences reinforced in this film, know that it's possible and

sometimes necessary to step outside of the norm. Also, for youth struggling to find normalcy in an otherwise chaotic life—much like Harry and his friends—the "straight and narrow road" may not be nearby or easily traveled.

As stated by Dumbledore within the movie, our choices demonstrate who we are. Sometimes those choices are difficult, and sometimes the situations seems impossible, but coming through those trying times is what helps to define who we are and who we will become. Harry Potter simply helps youth understand that message a little earlier than most of us learned it.

References

Black, M. S., & Eisenwine, M. J. (2001). Education of young Harry Potter: Socialization and schooling for wizards. *Educational Forum, 66,* 32–37.

Brummett, B. (1994). *Rhetoric in popular culture.* New York: St. Martin's Press.

Gibbs, N. (2003, June 23). The real magic of Harry Potter. *Time,* 60–67.

Nelson, C., & Nelson, B. (2002). What is so magic about Harry? *ALAN Review, 28,* 20–21.

Race, T. (2001, April 9). Most wanted: Drilling down/ Harry Potter: Rowling's readers are ready for film. *New York Times,* Section 10.

Radigan, W. M. (2001). Connecting the generations: Memory, magic, and Harry Potter. *Journal of Adolescent & Adult Literacy, 44,* 694–695.

Rowling, J. K. (1999). *Harry Potter and the Chamber of Secrets.* New York: Scholastic.

Sillars, M. O., & Gronbeck, B. E. (2001). *Communication criticism: Rhetoric, social codes, cultural studies.* Prospect Heights, IL: Waveland Press.

Tucker, N. (1999). The rise and rise of Harry Potter. *Children's Literature in Education, 30,* 221–234.

Summary

This chapter outlined the guidelines by which to conduct an analysis of a mediated popular culture text in ways that consider the persuasive role of the medium through which it is being conveyed. We discussed media ecology and unpacked what is meant by "the medium is the message." We also discussed media logic as the taken-for-granted ways in which we use media without thinking about how they influence us to believe and behave. We talked about commodification (ads blending with programming) and amplification and reduction (what is and is not included) as they function rhetorically. Then, we talked specifically about social learning theory (observing models and imitating behaviors), parasocial relationship theory (developing one-sided relationships with celebrities or fictional characters), and cultivation theory (repeated messages over time) as each one functions rhetorically.

Challenge

Select a popular TV series. Consider what messages it might be sending in terms of the media-centered perspectives we've discussed in this chapter.

1. What program did you select and why?
2. Who are the major characters in the program? Describe each of them.
3. What are some attitudes and behaviors that seem to be rewarded? Punished? What might viewers "learn" about how to believe or behave as a result?
4. How does media logic play out in the stories?
5. What are some examples of commodification? What might these messages be communicating?
6. Who are the good guys we are supposed to imitate and why?
7. What are some examples of intimacy? Realism? How might they impact viewers?
8. Are there any recurring patterns that might lead listeners to experience a cultivation effect? What are they and what might they lead listeners to believe? Why?
9. What could you argue about the value of doing a media-centered criticism as a result of your analysis?

References

Altheide, D., & Snow, R. P. (1979). *Media logic.* Beverly Hills, CA: Sage.

Brooks, J. M. (1997). Beyond teaching and learning paradigms: Trekking into the virtual university. *Teaching Sociology, 25,* 1–14.

Bandura, A. (1977). *Social learning theory.* New York: General Learning Press.

Clark, E. (2008). What good is the 'you' in YouTube? Cyberspectacle and subjectivity. *Gnovis, 9*(1). Retrieved online on April 19, 2013, from http://gnovisjournal.org/2008/12/16/what-good-you-youtube-cyberspectacle-and-subjectivity/

Dresner, E. (2006). Middle region phenomena and globalization. *The International Communication Gazette, 68,* 363–378.

Finnemann, N. O. (2011). Mediatization theory and digital media. *Communications. European Journal of Communication Research 36*(1), 67–89.

Hendriks, A. (2002). Examining the effects of hegemonic depictions of female bodies on television: A call for theory and programmatic research. *Critical Studies in Media Communication, 19*(1), 106–123.

Horton, D., & Wohl, R. R. (1956). Mass communication and parasocial interaction: Observations on intimacy and disturbance. *Psychiatry, 19,* 215–229.

Gerbner, G., & Gross, L. (1976). Living with television: The violence profile. *The Journal of Communication, 26,* 172–199.

Logan, R. K. (2010). *Understanding new media: Extending Marshall McLuhan.* New York: Peter Lang.

McLuhan, M. (1962). *The Gutenberg galaxy: The making of typographic man.* Toronto, Canada: University of Toronto Press.

McLuhan, M. (1964). *Understanding media: The extensions of man.* New York: McGraw-Hill.

McLuhan, M., & Fiore, Q. (1967). *The medium is the massage: An inventory of effects.* New York: Bantam Books.

McLuhan, M., & McLuhan, E. (1988). *Laws of media: The new science.* Toronto, Canada: University of Toronto Press.

Meyrowitz, J. (1985). *No sense of place: The impact of electronic media on social behavior.* New York: Oxford University Press.

Meyrowitz, J. (2005). The rise of glocality: New senses of place in the global village. In K. Nyiri (Ed.), *A sense of place: The global and the local in mobile communication.* Vienna: Passagen.

Morrison, J. C. (2006). Marshall McLuhan: The modern Janus. In Casey Man Kong Lum (Ed.), *Perspectives on culture, technology, and communication: The media ecology tradition* (pp. 163–200). Cresskill, NJ: Hampton.

Postman, N. (1985). *Amusing ourselves to death: Public discourse in the age of show business.* New York: Penguin.

Postman, N. (1992). *Technopoly: The surrender of culture to technology.* New York: Knopf.

Postman, N., & Weingartner, C. (1969). *Teaching as a subversive activity.* New York: Delta.

Smith, D. (2008). Critiquing reality-based televisual black fatherhood: A critical analysis of *Run's House* and *Snoop Dogg's Father Hood. Critical Studies in Media Communication, 25*(4), 393–412.

Student Study Site

Visit the Student Study Site at www.sagepub.com/sellnow2e to read interesting SAGE journal articles, view mobile-friendly key term flashcards, take chapter-specific online web quizzes to test your knowledge, and more!

Appendix

Writing a Popular Culture Rhetorical Essay

One goal in writing this book has been to provide you with some tools to become a critical consumer of the messages sent through mediated popular culture texts. A second goal is to provide you with an organizational tool for sharing your discoveries with others. The primary means by which communication scholars do so is by writing critical essays we present at academic conferences and publish in academic journals. This appendix offers one step-by-step approach for researching and writing an essay that could be submitted to an academic journal and then describes guidelines for converting it into an academic presentation that could be shared at a professional conference.

COLLECTING RESEARCH AND EXAMINING YOUR TEXT

Although it probably goes without saying, before you can begin to write the essay, you must (1) select an artifact to examine as a text and formulate a research question, (2) identify a rhetorical perspective that will help answer the research question, and (3) analyze the artifact via the description, interpretation, and evaluation process we've talked about in the preceding chapters. Before writing the essay, you will also need to (4) review existing literature about the rhetorical situation (e.g., author, occasion, artifact, exigence, constraints) to build an argument for the artifact as a text worthy of analysis and for your analysis of it as extending what is already known. And you will need to (5) review existing literature about the rhetorical perspective and similar applications of it to build an argument for how your analysis might extend theory.

In each of the previous chapters, we discussed how to select a text and formulate a research question. Recall that you might start by finding an artifact to be examined as your text. That is, you find something intriguing about the artifact that leads you to believe something more is being communicated about how we ought to believe and behave than what is being told in the surface message. Or, you might start with the question. If you are particularly compelled by violence on TV, for instance, you might formulate your question about violence on TV and then apply it to a particular program or programs. Or, you might start with both the artifact and the question. When watching a particular program, commercial, or movie, for example, you might really notice something being said about the roles and rules for men and women in society as I did when I stumbled upon a particular episode of *Jerry Springer* showing three lesbian strippers pole dancing, kissing, and spreading whipped cream on each other, while the audience, comprised mostly of 18- to 26 year-old males, chanted and cheered them on.

Second, select a rhetorical perspective that seems appropriate for answering your research question. I saw the *Jerry Springer* episode while running on a treadmill at the gym. Because I had forgotten to bring my earbuds, I ended up keying in on the arguments being made visually. Thus, I might select a visual perspective (e.g., visual pleasure theory) for my analysis. When it comes to writing the essay, you will ultimately need to defend why you've chosen the perspective, the major tenets of it, and conclusions drawn in other analyses that examined similar artifacts. You should also review works by those who originated the perspective if possible. Essentially, you will need to make a compelling case for choosing the perspective you did to examine the artifact and answer your research question.

After examining your text by describing, interpreting, and evaluating it based on the rhetorical perspective you chose for doing so, you need to complete a review of literature. First, collect evidence to support your argument that both (1) the text and (2) the social issue or problem embedded in your research question are worthy of analysis. In other words, collect research about the rhetorical situation. Why is the text you've chosen worth examining? Perhaps it is widely listened to or viewed by a certain target audience. Perhaps it has received critical acclaim. Perhaps its creator is significant in some way. Also, what issue or problem does your analysis of the text address, and why is that issue or problem important? In the *Jerry Springer* analysis, I might look for evidence to support the value of the text in Nielsen ratings, viewership demographic characteristics, and Emmy award results. I might look for evidence to support the issue or problem in statistics related to degradation of women as objects ranging from self-esteem to violence and rape.

You will also review the literature to build a case for how your analysis will extend what is known about this particular text and similar artifacts as well as the rhetorical perspective itself. In my *Jerry Springer* analysis, I might look for existing publications that examine other entertainment media generally as well as similar TV talk shows, and the *Jerry Springer* show specifically, and the conclusions drawn in them. I would also want to find literature that examines the social issue or problem from a feminist perspective. Doing so helps make a case as to where and how the analysis will extend what is already known about mediated popular culture texts related to the issue or problem as well as the utility of the rhetorical perspective chosen to do so.

WRITING YOUR ESSAY

Like any essay, your popular culture rhetorical criticism consists of an introduction, a body, and a conclusion. Although many of the elements in each are similar across genres, there are some unique components in the rhetorical criticism genre. Moreover, while length can vary depending on the artifact(s) selected, most academic essays range from about 18 to 25 pages including references (typed and double-spaced).

The Introduction

Although there is no set rule for length, typically you should accomplish your introduction in about four to six pages. As with any good paper, the first thing to do is capture the interest of your audience by establishing relevance. You can achieve this by addressing the rhetorical situation. You might focus on the significance of the artifact; the significance of the social issue, belief, or behavior it addresses; and the significance of your particular study as it extends existing research.

One major means for establishing relevance has to do with making a case for the artifact. Perhaps your selected text has won awards, or smashed box office records, or garnered a great deal of public interest. Perhaps it introduced some new concept to the industry. Or perhaps it managed to address a taboo topic with integrity . . . or without integrity for that matter. One of my students, for example, examined the program *South Park,* establishing its significance in terms of the social commentary of each episode in addition to the Emmys its creators had won. Another student established significance for her analysis of *Harry Potter and the Chamber of Secrets* by noting that almost 60 percent of children ages 6 to 17 have read at least one book in the series. She also pointed to the success of the first Harry Potter movie, the predicted success of the one she chose to examine, and the awards the books had achieved.

Another aspect you must address to establish relevance is the social issue, problem, or taken-for-granted belief or behavior your analysis will address. This is typically linked to the rhetorical perspective you've chosen for analysis. In a student paper about the film *The Life and Death of David Gale,* for example, the writers focused on the controversial debate about whether capital punishment is justified. Their analysis was grounded in a dramatistic perspective, which would help address this issue. Another paper about the TV program *Cougar Town* focused on taken-for-granted roles and rules for women in terms of appearance and behavior. The author's analysis was grounded in a feminist perspective. Still another examined the Monopoly board game as it sends underlying messages regarding our taken-for-granted beliefs about wealth and power grounded in a neo-Marxist perspective.

Next, you need to ground your analysis as it extends existing research. Here is where you talk about similar studies that have been conducted so the reader can begin to see how your analysis will teach them something more than what has already been studied on the topic of, for instance, feminist messages in films, or messages of justification for breaking society's rules for living, or visual communication or music as rhetoric.

Finally, you conclude your introduction by stating your research question(s). If your introduction is organized in the way prescribed here, you will have built an argument for accepting your text and research question as worthy of study.

The Body

The body consists of (1) an explanation of your rhetorical perspective and the procedure you followed in your analysis as well as (2) the analysis itself. Again, although there exists no set-in-stone page limit here, typically the body will be approximately 10 to 12 pages long.

In terms of the rhetorical perspective, you need to explain what it is, who has helped shape it, and what it helps reveal as a method of analysis. You will likely draw on your literature review to develop this section. You also need to clarify why you've chosen it as a means by which to answer your specific research question. That is, why will this approach be useful for your analysis in particular? In this section, you also need to operationalize the rhetorical perspective. That is, you need to explain in detail the steps you followed in conducting your analysis. The explanation of procedures assures the reader that you did, in fact, conduct a systematic analysis grounded in rhetorical method and not just built a case for your opinion.

In the actual analysis portion of the body of your essay, you offer your description and interpretation of the text. In other words, who are the characters, what is going on, what is being said (verbally and nonverbally), and what does it mean? Interpret its meaning according to the rhetorical perspective you've chosen. In my *Jerry Springer* example, I would describe and interpret the visual images and behaviors of Springer, the strippers, and the audience members via the visual pleasure elements of the male gaze based on narcissism, fetishism, and voyeurism.

Conclusions

The conclusions section is typically about three to five pages long. Sometimes, this section is titled *Discussion;* however, rhetoricians commonly avoid that term, which is used extensively in quantitative studies. You will want to focus on conclusions, implications, and suggestions for future research.

In your conclusions, you essentially answer the research question or questions you've posed. Moreover, however, you must tie each conclusion to existing research. In other words, articulate how each conclusion teaches us something beyond what we already know from existing research. A conclusion might confirm, contradict, or further clarify the conclusions of some studies. If so, make that link for the reader. A conclusion might also take the field a step further in terms of understanding how a particular rhetorical perspective functions. This is often referred to as *extending theory.* The important point with your conclusions is to tie them to existing research so readers see how your study, in fact, offers something new to the field.

In your implications, answer the so-what question you identified in the evaluation portion of your analysis. How might these messages impact various target audiences related to the social issue or taken-for-granted belief or behavior you focus on? What should be done and by whom as a result of the conclusions you've discovered? Does the artifact call into question or offer a solution to an existing social issue or problem? If so, what ought to be done next and why? Or does the artifact perpetuate a taken-for-granted belief or behavior that is somehow problematic? If so, what ought to be done next and why? These implications are speculative, but the intent is to foster critical thinking about taken-for-granted beliefs and behaviors about everyday life in the minds of readers so as to help them, too, become critical consumers of such messages couched in mediated popular culture texts.

Finally, end with a paragraph or two that suggest future research questions emerging from your analysis. What else should be examined using this rhetorical perspective, why, and how? Should this artifact be examined using a different rhetorical perspective, why, and how? You want to leave the reader wanting more and, perhaps, even wanting to conduct some similar study him- or herself. Your goal is not to offer your essay as an end in and of itself. Rather, your goal is to stimulate critical thinking and future research ideas in the minds of readers.

PRESENTING YOUR ESSAY

One of the most common mistakes made by scholars when they present their essays at professional conferences is to merely read them or even just sections of them aloud in front of the audience. Although one would hope that scholars in the field of communication would not rely on this approach, all too often we do. This is unfortunate given the fact that our discipline is responsible for teaching effective public speaking skills and reading aloud in front of an audience is not touted as most effective. The one exception is when a speaker can make listeners believe he or she is not merely reading from a manuscript. That said, this section offers one approach for transforming your essay into a format appropriate for an effective conference presentation.

Typically, you are allotted about 12 minutes for your oral presentation. Sometimes you'll be allotted as many as 15 minutes, but 10 to 12 is the norm. This means you'll need to condense your 18- to 25-page paper into something that makes a compelling point succinctly. Remember, if some audience members want to read the paper, they certainly can. Your presentation should focus on highlighting key conclusions and, hopefully, fostering interest to pick up the paper at the end of the session. The following paragraphs provide guidelines for doing so in terms of your introduction, body, and conclusion.

The Introduction

The introduction should take only about one to three minutes. Hence, each of the elements in your introduction needs to be stated in only one or two sentences. Begin, as always, with an attention catcher. You might share a juicy quotation from the TV program or movie you've analyzed or a snippet from a song you've examined. The important point here, though, is to keep it short. Then, briefly mention the social issue, problem, or taken-for-granted belief or behavior you'll focus on and its significance in society. In a presentation a colleague and I did on the *Friends* essay, for instance, we talked about the prevalence of eating disorders among women in the United States today. We did so because the analysis focused on the thinning of Hollywood as role models for women. Be sure to cite sources. Then, mention the artifact and why it's worthy to study. You need to do so in only one or two sentences. Then, state the research question(s) and the rhetorical perspective you selected and why. This may take a few sentences; however, here is where so many young scholars make a big mistake. By that, I mean they share their entire literature review including their review of the rhetorical perspective and use up their allotted 10 to 12 minutes before they ever get to the conclusions. Ultimately, the moderator stops them before they ever share what listeners really want to hear. Finally, offer as a preview the main things you looked for to answer the research question. These are essentially derived from your conclusions.

The Body

Aim for eight to ten minutes in the body of your presentation. Begin by stating how many conclusions you found. Then, the main points for the body of your presentation are actually your conclusions. That is, for main point one, state what you found in conclusion number one. Then, to support the conclusion, tie it to the research question(s) and to the literature review so listeners can hear how it extends what we already know. Finally, share a snippet (audio, visual, or audiovisual) from the artifact to help listeners "see" or "hear" what you mean. Then, move on to main point two, which is conclusion number two and do the same thing. Although using your conclusions as main points might feel odd while you're preparing the presentation, listeners will be interested in what you have to say and, more importantly, won't get bored as they always do when someone reads the paper to them.

The Conclusion

The conclusion is very short, only one to two minutes. Begin by restating the answer to your research question in one sentence or two at the most. Then pose implications. Recall these are the answers to your so-what question. Tie the conclusions to the real-world issues, to taken-for-granted beliefs and behaviors, or to everyday problems. Remember that you are speculating here to foster critical thinking. You need not say much, just a couple of juicy ideas. For similar reasons, offer one or two suggestions for future research that arise from your study. Finally, offer a clincher that ties directly back to your attention catcher. Maybe you'll share another snippet from the television program, film, or song. Maybe you'll pose a new question related to the point made in the attention catcher. The key here is to tie the clincher back to the attention catcher. Doing so will make your presentation memorable in a positive way.

Summary

In this appendix, we focused on taking what you learn from your analyses of mediated popular culture texts to a larger audience. We offered a systematic plan for collecting appropriate research, for writing your essay, and for transforming it into an effective oral presentation at professional conferences. Certainly, becoming an educated critical consumer of the underlying popular culture messages in mediated texts is important. It can be even more rewarding, however, to share your findings effectively with others.

At this point, I challenge you to open the door to taking your analyses to broader audiences. Select one of the challenges or assignments you did during this course, and convert it into an essay worthy of review for possible publication in an academic journal or presentation at a professional conference. Once you start, I suspect you'll continue to pursue the journey. Good luck!

Glossary

absolute standards: confirm that the story is obviously well crafted compared to general societal expectations for quality

act: the rule-breaking behavior or action occurring in the drama; one of the five elements of human drama

active event: expresses an action of some sort; one of two items required for the mediated text to be a narrative

actual time: one-dimensional succession of moments (e.g., minutes, hours, days, weeks)

agency: tools, means, and techniques employed to accomplish the act

agent: character(s) engaged in rule-breaking behavior

agons: groups of associated symbols that reinforce opposites (points of conflict) or what versus what

amplification and reduction: what is shown and not shown on a TV program, film, Internet website, video game, and so forth

antagonist: villain in a drama

anti-models: character roles that receivers are led to disassociate with or not be like

arrangement: rhetorical canon focused on the organizational structure of a message

artifact: a sign or series of signs that is socially grounded, and its meaning is widely shared by some identifiable community or cultural group

artistic proofs: used internally by a speaker to create means of support via logos, or appeals to logical argument; ethos, or appeals to the speaker's character; and pathos, or appeals to emotion and their apparent effect on the audience

bond of intimacy: created when a viewer begins to feel he or she really knows the celebrity or character even though the celebrity or character does not know the viewer

canons: categories of rhetoric used to evaluate a text; the five canons are (1) invention, (2) arrangement, (3) style, (4) delivery, and (5) memory

causal relations: cause-and-effect relationship by human action, accident, or forces of nature

chaining out: dynamic process of circulating, revising, and elaborating on a theme or group of themes

closeness-of-fit standard: asks how well an individual theme works within the larger rhetorical vision

closure: "seeing" an object or image as complete even when it is not

clusters: groups of associated symbols that suggest what goes with what

cognitive theory: focuses on what is going on in our minds when we view an image or object and how that affects our perception

coherence: the degree to which the story hangs together

comic fool: when the guilty party is absolved of guilt because someone or something else is to blame and the error is portrayed as inevitable or as a common human failing

comic lyrics: focused on determination to beat the odds; failure is not an option

commodification: advertisements blending with programming

common fate: our tendency to mentally group objects that appear to be going in the same direction

comparative standard: looks at the quality of story compared to other stories competing for the same audience

congruent interaction: the emotional meanings of music and lyrics reinforce one another

congruity: transpires when comic lyrics are combined with intensity musical patterns or tragic lyrics are combined with release musical patterns

consciousness creating: the creation of a shared symbolic reality that did not previously exist

consciousness raising: where those who already share an existing vision attempt to attract and indoctrinate newcomers

consciousness sustaining: retelling the fantasy to keep everyone from losing sight of the shared story line

consubstantiality: identifying with other people and society

continuity: our tendency to desire a smooth continuation of perceived movement

critical rhetoric: orientation that encompasses a number of perspectives that examine how texts "create and sustain the social practices which control the dominated" (McKerrow, 1989, p. 92)

cultivation effect: cumulative persuasive effect on receivers caused by a bombardment of similar messages across texts targeted to a particular group

cultivation theory: suggests that cumulative exposure to violence (and other behaviors) on TV, the Internet, and video games has significant long-term effects regarding what the everyday real world is like

cultural feminist perspective: promotes as valuable the socialized skills, activities, behaviors, and viewpoints that have traditionally been defined as feminine and, thus, trivialized

decline: shared stories lose their power and dim in the face of better alternatives

delivery: rhetorical canon focused on the speaker's use of voice and body

deterrents: terministic screens preventing us from thinking or doing certain things

devil terms: terministic screens that cluster together around a theme that is regarded by the dominant social order as bad, wrong, or undesirable

discursive symbols: units (e.g., words and numbers) with fixed associations

dramatic illusion: forward-looking story into the unresolved virtual future dramatis personae: characters who populate a drama

dramatism: the study of human motivation by viewing events as dramas

dramatistic perspective: method of rhetorical criticism focused on how humans beings make sense of the world and act through dramas

economic metaphor: includes anything (e.g., images, language, objects, events, practices) that signifies (sheds light on) something about the culture's ideas, norms, values, and practices regarding wealth and empowerment

effect: the final phase of the analysis in which the critic must consider what happened or did not happen as a result of the speech

enablers: terministic screens that grant "permission" for thinking or doing certain things

ethics: principles about what is right and wrong, moral and immoral, fair and unfair

exigence: reason the speech needs to be given

fantasy theme: a basic unit of communication, like a joke, analogy, metaphor, wordplay, pun, double entendre, figure of speech, anecdote that, when shared with others, constitutes the base of social reality

fantasy theme analysis (FTA): the tool or methodology that rhetoricians use to identify, understand, and interpret converged symbols

fantasy theme artistry: the rhetorical skill and communication competence of the storyteller

fantasy type: "a stock scenario repeated again and again by the same characters or by similar characters" (Bormann, 1985, p. 7)

feminist: anyone (male or female) whose beliefs and actions challenge hegemony by respecting and valuing both men and women who embrace and enact multiple gender styles and sexualities

feminist perspective: analyzes what are conveyed as "appropriate" and "desirable" as well as "inappropriate" and "undesirable" roles and rules for men and women

femmenism: a perspective that situates the study of masculinity within the framework of gender and power

fetishism: pleasure derived from openly looking at an object that is in itself satisfying

fidelity: the degree to which the values offered in a story ring true with what we regard as truthful and humane

first-wave feminism: primary goal was to secure for women the right to vote

flat characters: predictable; not deviating from preconceived norms of the status quo

founding fantasy: a narrative tale about the inception of a group

frequency: how often clusters of terministic screens appear

gender: socioculturally constructed traits of masculinity and femininity

gestalt theory: focused on how our brains group individual items based on what seems to go together and what does not

glass ceiling: a situation where women are not promoted when they are qualified just because they are women

God terms: terministic screens that cluster together to reinforce a worldview embraced by the dominant social order

guilt: any feeling of tension or unease within a person

hegemony: privileging of a dominant group's ideology over that of other groups

heteronormativity: privileging of heterosexuality and an alignment among biological sex, sexuality, gender identity, and gender roles

hidden agenda: ulterior motive of alleged adherents within the vision

icon: when something or someone is a symbol of the thing it represents

iconically: when something or someone functions as an icon

ideograms: pictures that resemble ideas

ideology: a cultural group's perceptions about the way things are and assumptions about the way they ought to be

illusion of life perspective: focuses on how lyrics and music function together to persuade

inartistic proofs: external means of support such as facts, statistics, and personal examples found in books, journal articles, research reports, or interviews

incongruent interaction: the emotional meanings of the music and lyrics contradict one another

indexically: when a sign is associated with something else

inflected oppositional reading: a text whose messages merely bend hegemony rather than reject it outright

intensity: how forcefully the clusters of terministic screens are portrayed

intensity patterns: feelings of tension

interpellation: occurs when a text leads one to identify with certain roles

Internet Addiction Disorder (IAD): excessive computer use that interferes with daily life

intertextuality: the blending of texts in ways that make it difficult if not impossible to separate them from prior texts, context, and any other utterances that surround them (e.g., Barthes, 1981; Culler, 1981; Jasinski, 1997)

intimacy: characters are perceived as real people with real feelings, norms, and values

invention: rhetorical canon focused on the major ideas and lines of argument in the speech via artistic and inartistic proofs

liberal feminist perspective: focuses primarily on providing opportunities for the inclusion of women in traditionally male-dominated areas

live model: an actual person demonstrating a behavior

logos: logical arguments based on evidence and reasoning

lyrical ascription: integrating examples and stories from popular culture to which members of a target audience will likely relate

kairos: timing of the speech

male gaze: describes the way in which viewers (both male and female) look at the people presented and represented in visual images by identifying with the male actor(s)

Marxist feminist perspective: primary goal is to ensure economic equality for women

Neo-Marxist perspective: analyzes who is portrayed as empowered and disempowered in a popular culture text, often related to socioeconomic status

masculine hegemony: describes gender and power inequities that account for multiple masculinities and how hegemonic structures oppress all forms other than heterosexual masculinity

master analogues: three types of deep structure frameworks rhetorical visions tend to adhere to: righteous, social, or pragmatic

media ecology theory: focuses on how media and communication processes affect human perception, understanding, beliefs, and behaviors

media effects: causal and correlation effects of watching a particular TV program, viewing an advertisement or series of advertisements, and so on.

media effects research: uses social science methods to examine audience responses to media messages

media logic: focuses on the degree to which users tend to take the medium and its social uses for granted and, thus, fail to realize how it influences us to believe and behave

mediated popular culture: popular culture experienced through media channels (e.g., movies, TV, songs, comic strips, and advertisements) that may influence us to believe and behave in certain ways

mediated popular culture text: subset of the broad range of popular culture texts delivered through media channels

mediatization: extension of media logic that accounts for new media and new areas of application

memory: rhetorical canon focused on strategies that make the message positively memorable days, weeks, and even years later

metonymic signs: associated with something else and, thus, serve to represent that something else

mirror stage: symbolizes an ongoing sexual relationship we have with body image

mnemonic devices: strategies employed to translate information into a form that aids retention

models: roles receivers are led to identify with or be like

moral: value-laden ideological argument a story proposes directly or indirectly and intentionally or unintentionally about how we ought to or ought not to believe or behave

mortification: the actor confesses guilt and asks for forgiveness; actor is sometimes absolved of guilt

motive: offered as a justification for rule-breaking behavior that is generalizable to humankind

music as communication: refers to the individual, unique meanings each of us might attach to music

musical aesthetics: appreciation and evaluation of musical form or design

musical ascription: imitating a musical sound that appeals to a particular target audience

musical genre: generally recognized category of music

musical rhetoric: persuasive arguments conveyed through musical artifacts that reinforce or challenge a taken-for-granted belief or behavior

mystery: perceived difference or alienation from others

narcissism: excessive self-love based on one's self-image as a result of mirror stage experiences

narration: defined by Fisher (1987) as the "symbolic actions—words and/or deeds—that have sequence and meaning for those who live, create, or interpret them" (p. 58).

narrative paradigm: a conceptual framework that places narration and storytelling at the core of all human communication

narrative perspective: a rhetorical method for understanding the underlying moral of the story argued in a text

narrative rationality: our assessment of the value-laden ideological argument proposed in a story

narrator: mediates the events and, as such, offers an interpretation of the events and characters for the audience as the audience observes them

neo-Aristotelian approach: the first formal rhetorical criticism method for examining public speeches

neo-Aristotelian perspective: analyzes verbal messages by considering the context, audience, and the five classical canons of rhetoric

neo-Marxist materialism: posits that all ideas, rules, laws, norms, customs, and social practices of a given society come to be based on real, concrete, observable objects, conditions, and practices related to material possessions and wealth

neo-Marxist perspective: exposes that material conditions and economic practices shape the dominant ideology about who "ought to be" and "ought not to be" empowered

new media: all forms of digital media accessed from the Internet and satellite via computers and various handheld devices

nomophobia: fear of being out of mobile phone contact

nonartistic proofs: support appeals not invented by the speaker

nondiscursive rhetoric: the study of how nondiscursive symbol systems function as persuasion regarding taken-for-granted beliefs and behaviors

nondiscursive symbols: all symbols beyond the realm of words and numbers humans use to create meaning

occluded, preferred readings: status quo hegemony couched within a seemingly alternative worldview

old media: print media (e.g., newspapers, magazines) and traditional electronic media (e.g., television, radio)

oppositional readings: a text that challenges the dominant ideology with regard to taken-for-granted beliefs about empowerment

order: when people adhere to the expected norms of a social order

othering: devaluing consequence of hegemony that portrays those not in the empowered group as different from and as *them*

paradigm: a conceptual framework for understanding the world around us

paradigmatic signs: gain meaning as they fit with or in contrast to other signs

paralanguage: nonverbal vocal cues (including silence) that accompany words

parasocial relationship: a perception by a viewer of "knowing" a character as in a face-to-face relationship

parasocial relationship theory: describes one-sided relationships where one party knows a great deal about the other party, but not vice versa

pathos: emotions stirred in the audience by the speaker

patriarchy: the structuring of society around family units where the male is the authority figure and is responsible for the welfare of his family members and the community

Pentad: the five elements of human drama (act, actors, agency, scene, and purpose)

pictograms: pictures that resemble what they signify

plotline: provides the action of the narrative

poetic illusion: backward-looking or resolved story reflecting on the virtual past

pollution: when an individual rejects the hierarchy of the social order in some way

popular culture: the everyday objects, actions, and events that influence people to believe and behave in certain ways

popular culture text: comprised of an interrelated set of signs and artifacts that all contribute to the same rhetorical argument

pragmatic master analogue: values "expediency, utility, efficiency, parsimony, simplicity, practicality, cost effectiveness, and whatever it takes to get the job done" (Cragan & Shields, 1995, p. 42)

preferred reading: reinforces the status quo ideology about empowerment by promoting taken-for-granted assumptions as common sense

privacy: refers to how viewers often get to know the characters personally as they watch them privately in the comfort of their own homes

protagonist: hero in a drama

proximity: our tendency to associate objects that are or appear to be close to each other and the tendency to notice things that are or appear to be close to us

psychoanalytic theories: focus primarily on how the mind, psyche, human subjectivity, sexuality, and the unconscious are constructed in rhetorical texts

purification: absolution of guilt

purpose: explanation for why the agent(s) engaged in the rule-breaking behavior

queer theory: examines sexual identities and activities that hegemony labels as *normal* and *deviant*

radical feminist perspective: assumes that inequities and oppression stem from how the system creates men and women differently (subject and object gender identities) and the value placed on them

rational-world paradigm: a framework that assumes people are rational beings who make decisions based on logical arguments, evidence, and reasoning

ratios: pairings among Pentad elements

reading: ideological arguments about empowerment couched beneath the surface of texts

realism: refers to how believable the characters and their encounters are perceived to be

redemption: temporary rebirth into the social order of society

release patterns: feelings of relief from tensions

rhetoric: messages designed to influence people, a.k.a. persuasive communication

rhetorical argument: a message sent through text that either reinforces or challenges a taken-for-granted belief or behavior about what is "appropriate" or "inappropriate," "desirable" or "undesirable," "good" or "bad"

rhetorical criticism: the systematic analysis of an argument about the "way things are" or the "way things ought to be" conveyed in a text through signs as artifacts

rhetorical perspective: a lens through which you look to magnify the underlying messages that have to do with the question you are asking

rhetorical vision: shared ideology of a group

rhetorical vision life cycle: five stages within which rhetorical visions exist

rhetorical vision reality link: evidence of the senses that provide authentication for a vision

righteous master analogue: "stresses the correct way of doing things with its concerns about right and wrong, proper and improper, superior and inferior, moral and immoral, and just and unjust" (Cragan & Shields, 1995, p. 42)

round characters: unpredictable; deviate from the preconceived norms of the status quo

sanctioning agent: the legitimizing force that guides a narrative

scapegoating: an attempt to absolve guilt by blaming someone or something else

scene: location and situation where the act takes place

scopophelia: the love of or pleasurable (i.e., sexually arousing) looking

second-wave feminism: primary goal was and is equal rights and opportunities for women and men

self-image: mental picture of one's self based on mirror stage experiences

semiosis: the relationship among a sign, which represents an object (referent), and a meaning (interpretation) attached to it

semiotics: the study of signs

setting: where the action takes place

sex: biological traits of women and men

shared group consciousness: proof of a rhetorical community and audience buy-in

sign: something that makes you think of something else

similarity: our tendency to group together things that look similar (e.g., color, shape, size)

sin: not heeding the rules of the social order

site of struggle: occurs when the text reinforces or calls into question some taken-for-granted ideology about "the way things are" or "ought to be"

social learning theory: focuses on how we learn to believe and behave based on observation, imitation, and modeling

social master analogues: story lines focusing on friendship, trust, camaraderie, brotherhood or sisterhood, and being humane

standpoints: understanding of the world as shaped by where one is situated within it based on class, gender, race, sexual identity, and so on

stative event: an expression of a state or condition; one of two items required for the mediated text to be a narrative

strategic ambiguity: making a claim using language that avoids specifics

style: rhetorical canon focused on language choices

subject positions: economic metaphors embodied in roles of the characters in a text

subverted oppositional reading: a text whose messages reject hegemony outright

symbolic convergence theory (SCT): reveals a shared reality used by a particular community to make sense of the world around them

symbolic model: a person demonstrating a behavior through a medium such as TV, film, Internet, video games, and so forth

symbolic cue: "cryptic allusions to common symbolic ground" (Bormann, 1985, p. 6)

symbolically: when a sign leads us to think of something else merely by convention

synecdochal signs: a part or piece of something that serves to stand in for the whole

syntagmatic signs: gain their meaning from the signs that surround them in a static visual or by signs that come before and after them sequentially in a moving visual

target audience: the group of people whom the sender is attempting to persuade

technopoly: describes the endless ways in which technology dominates our thinking and behaviors today

teleology: the ways in which word clusters are ultimately completed

terministic screens: verbal and nonverbal symbols that represent a particular worldview

terminus: the end of the life-cycle process

tetrad: an organizing concept for understanding the impact of technology on society

text: any set of interrelated signs and artifacts that contribute to a unified message

third-wave feminism: primary goals are not only women's issues but also a variety of standpoints

tragic hero: when the rule-breaking action is portrayed as someone or something else's fault, but the rhetor still must be punished in order to reenter society

tragic lyrics: focused on self-consummation, hopelessness, and coping with fate

transcendence: justification based on following a higher calling

victimage: justification based on blaming someone or something else

virtual experience: emotional stance conveyed via lyrics

virtual time: emotional content conveyed via music

visual art aesthetics: devoted to the creation and appreciation of art

visual communication: focuses on how images and objects convey meaning

visual culture: denotes the countless ways in which visuals are inextricably embedded in social life

visual language: form-related usage rules-related things such as color, layout, texture, sequencing, imagery, style, as well as in some cases animation and sound

visual literacy: the set of skills required to "effectively find, interpret, evaluate, use, and create images and visual media" (Hattwig et al., 2011)

visual pleasure theory: focuses on how visual images in media encourage viewers to look pleasurably at female images via a male gaze

visual rhetoric: focuses expressly on how visuals communicate meanings that reinforce or challenge taken-for-granted ideological beliefs and behaviors

voyeurism: instances where people gain pleasure from looking at others engaged in sexual, sordid, or scandalous acts without them knowing it

Index

About the Author

Deanna Sellnow currently serves as the Gifford Blyton Endowed Professor of Oral Communication and Director of the Division of Instructional Communication and Research in the College of Communication and Information at the University of Kentucky. Her research interests include popular culture rhetoric and instructional communication. She has presented her work at state, regional, national, and international conferences and has published in a variety of journals. She also conducts faculty development workshops across the country. She and her husband, Tim, have two children: Debbie and Rick.

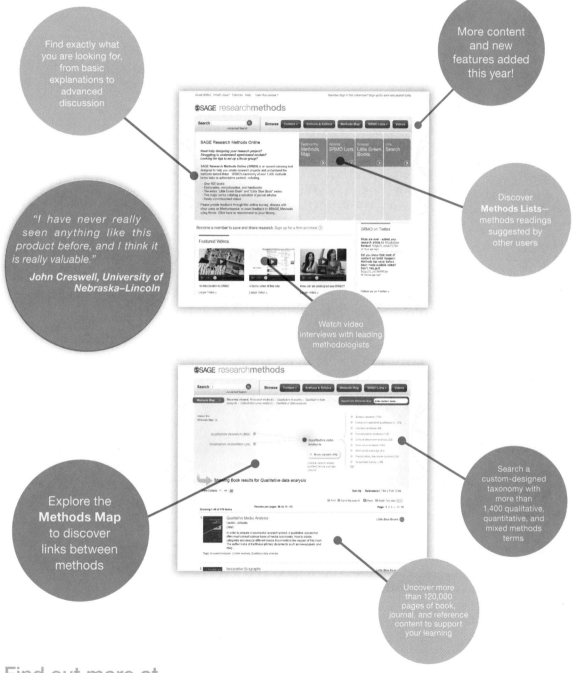